DATE DUE

Child Custody, Foster Care, and Adoptions

Child Custody, Foster Care, and Adoptions

Joseph R. Carrieri
Attorney-at-Law

LEXINGTON BOOKS
An Imprint of Macmillan, Inc.
NEW YORK

Maxwell Macmillan Canada
TORONTO

Maxwell Macmillan International
NEW YORK OXFORD SINGAPORE SYDNEY

Library of Congress Cataloging-in-Publication Data

Carrieri, Joseph R.
  Child custody, foster care, and adoptions / Joseph R. Carrieri.
      p.   cm.
  Includes index.
  ISBN 0-669-27638-3 (alk. paper)
  1. Foster children—Legal status, laws, etc.—New York (State)
2. Foster home care—Law and legislation—New York (State)
3. Adoption—Law and legislation—New York (State) 4. Custody of
children—New York (State) I. Title
KFN5603.5.C37   1991
346.74701'7—dc20
[347.470617]   91-9354
                        CIP

Lexington Books
An Imprint of Macmillan, Inc.
866 Third Avenue, New York, N. Y. 10022

Maxwell Macmillan Canada, Inc.
1200 Eglinton Avenue East
Suite 200
Don Mills, Ontario M3C 3NI

Macmillan, Inc. is part of the Maxwell Communication Group of Companies.

Printed in the United States of America

printing number
1 2 3 4 5 6 7 8 9 10

It is only fitting that this book be dedicated to the foster child. It is our hope that this book will in some way contribute to ameliorating the struggle of the foster child to be appropriately nurtured by the foster-care system through the waiting arms of foster parents when the child cannot be returned to a parent. It is with this thought that we here republish the foster children's bill of rights.

Bill of Rights for Foster Children

Ratified in Congress Hall, Philadelphia

Saturday, the Twenty-eighth of April,
Nineteen hundred and seventy three

EVEN more than for other children, society has a responsibility along with parents for the well-being of foster children. Citizens are responsible for acting to insure their welfare.

EVERY foster child is endowed with the rights inherently belonging to all children. In addition, because of the temporary or permanent separation from and loss of parents and other family members, the foster child requires special safeguards, resources, and care.

EVERY FOSTER CHILD HAS THE INHERENT RIGHT:

Article of the first: to be cherished by a family of his own, either his family helped by readily available services and supports to reassume his care, or an adoption family, or by plan a continuing foster family.

Article of the second: to be nurtured by foster parents who have been selected to meet his individual needs and who are provided services and supports, including specialized education, so that they can grow in their ability to enable the child to reach his potential.

Bill of Rights for Foster Children *(continued)*

Article of the third: to receive sensitive, continuing help in understanding and accepting the reasons for his own family's inability to take care of him, and in developing confidence in his own self-worth.

Article of the fourth: to receive continuing loving care and respect as a unique human being . . . a child growing in trust in himself and others.

Article of the fifth: to grow up in freedom and dignity in a neighborhood of people who accept him with understanding, respect, and friendship.

Article of the sixth: to receive help in overcoming deprivation or whatever distortion in his emotional, physical, intellectual, social, and spiritual growth may have resulted from his early experiences.

Article of the seventh: to receive education, training, and career guidance to prepare him for a useful and satisfying life.

Article of the eighth: to receive preparation for citizenship and parenthood through interaction with foster parents and other adults who are consistent role models.

Article of the ninth: to be represented by an attorney-at-law in administrative or judicial proceedings with access to fair hearings and court review of decisions, so that his best interests are safeguarded.

Article of the tenth: to receive a high quality of child welfare services, including involvement of the natural parents and his own involvement in major decisions that affect his life.

Contents

Acknowledgments

The practical aspects of the legal procedures outlined in the following pages were acquired over a twenty-year period of active participation in foster-care proceedings in the family courts. However, putting together this treatise of the many aspects of foster care could not be accomplished by any one individual without the help of many friends and associates. Thanks must therefore be given to my wife and six children. Their patience and understanding allowed me to devote many hours to my practice and the writing of this book. Acknowledgment must also go to my partner, John R. Lynch, Esq., for his understanding and encouragement. Special thanks to the administration and staff of St. Christopher-Ottilie and Little Flower Children's Services, two long-standing clients whose work involving foster children in the legal field has proved educational, challenging, and rewarding. Lastly, special thanks to my partner, Ralph R. Carrieri, Esq., and my associate, Jeffrey L. Blinkoff, Esq., for their contribution to the many aspects of this foster-care treatise.

Please note that the laws and practices referred to throughout the book are based on my experience and knowledge of such proceedings in the state of New York and do not necessarily reflect the policies adhered to in other states. However, the proceedings described in these pages should give the reader enough knowledge to obtain the legal information specific to his or her own state. Further information may also be obtained through your local social service organization.

Introduction

The Honorable Mario Cuomo, Governor of the State of New York, has declared the coming ten years to be the Decade of the Child. Presently, a greater amount of attention has been focused on the well-being of the child than in the past, and hopefully this trend will continue. The purpose of this book is to familiarize all those interested in children's rights with the legal aspects of child custody, from abandonment to adoption.

From time immemorial, our children have been used, abused, abandoned, neglected, battered, and bruised. This book is written on the premise that if those of us who care about these children take the time to educate ourselves about children's rights, the children would benefit. This book focuses on foster children.

Because of federal intervention and funding laws, many states have enacted foster-care review procedures that mandate that every child in foster-care have foster-care status reviewed by the family court or probate court every twenty-four months, or at shorter intervals if appropriate. Foster care review hearings were initiated in 1972, and family courts throughout the United States have been successful in placing many foster children in adoptive homes or, alternatively and where appropriate, in returning foster children to their natural parents.

This book, therefore, is written for practitioners who are involved in all aspects of custody proceedings, especially those involving foster children. Because of the author's experience, the book focuses primarily on the laws of New York State. It is not the intention of the author, however, to limit the scope of this book solely to attorneys in the field. It is hoped that this book will be useful to judges, social workers, educators, legislators, psychologists, psychiatrists, and all others interested in the welfare of these children.

This book is also intended as a practical guide and "how-to" book, replete with forms that would be helpful to attorneys involved in drafting the myriad forms connected with child custody proceedings, including but not limited to the summons, citation, petition, order of substituted service, order of commitment, order to show cause, writ of habeas corpus, notice of discovery and inspection, notice to produce, subpoena, voluntary commitment, surrender, ten-day removal notice, adoption forms, notice of appeal, and other related forms.

As the attorney for two of the largest authorized foster-care agencies in New York State, it is my intention to incorporate into this book every possible aspect of foster care and child custody in order to aid the legal practitioner and others concerned with the foster child.

List of Sidebars

Glossary of Key Terms

Abandoned Child A child is "abandoned" by his/her parent if such parent evinces an intent to forgo his/her parental rights and obligations as manifested by his/her failure to visit the child and communicate with the child or agency, although able to do so and not prevented or discouraged from doing so by the agency. In the absence of evidence to the contrary, such ability to visit and communicate shall be presumed (Section 384 B of the Social Services Law).

Abused Child A child less than eighteen years of age whose parent or other person legally responsible for his/her care:

1. inflicts, or allows to be inflicted, upon such child physical injury by other than accidental means that causes or creates a substantial risk of death, serious or protracted disfigurement, protracted impairment of physical or emotional health, or protracted loss or impairment of the function of any bodily organ,
2. creates or allows to be created a substantial risk of physical injury to such child by other than accidental means that would be likely to cause death, serious or protracted disfigurement or protracted impairment of physical or emotional health, or protracted loss or impairment of the function of any bodily organ, or
3. commits, or allows to be committed, an act of sexual abuse against such child as defined in the Penal Law (Section 371 of the Social Services Law).

Adoption Legal proceeding whereby an adult person takes another adult or minor person into the relation of child and thereby acquires the rights and incurs the responsibilities of parent with respect to said adult or minor (Section 110 of the Domestic Relations Law).

Agency Adoption The adoption of a person by an adult wherein an authorized agency is involved and is one of the parties consenting to the adoption.

Agency Boarding Home A family-type home for children and/or for minors operated by an authorized agency, in quarters or premises owned, leased, or otherwise under the control of such agency, for the purposes of providing care and maintenance therein for children or minors under the care of such agency (Section 371 of the Social Services Law).

Authorized Agency (1) Any agency, association, corporation, institution society, or other organization that is incorporated or organized under the laws of this state with corporate power or empowered by law to care for, to place out, or to board out children, that actually has its place of business or plant in this state and that is approved, visited, inspected, and supervised by the board or that shall submit and consent to the approval, visitation, inspection, and supervision of the board as to any and all acts in relation to the welfare of children performed or to be performed under this title; (2) any court or any public welfare official of this state authorized by law to place out or to board out children (Section 371 of the Social Services Law).

Board Out To arrange for the care of a child in a family, other than that of the child's parent, stepparent, or legal guardian, to whom payment is made for care and maintenance (Section 371 of the Social Services Law).

Burden of Proof The quantum of proof necessary in order to have a petition sustained. In the case of a termination-of-parental-rights proceeding, the burden of proof is by clear and convincing evidence, which is a more stringent burden than preponderance of the evidence.

Custody Having immediate physical charge of an infant or child, whether it be exercised by an agency, the natural parents, or foster parents.

Defective Child A child who is insance, epileptic, or feeble-minded (Section 371 of the Social Services Law).

Destitute Child A child who, through no neglect on the part of his/her parent, guardian, or custodian, is:

1. destitute or homeless, or
2. in a state of want or suffering due to lack of sufficient food, clothing, shelter, or medical or surgical care (Section 371 of the Social Services Law).

Diligent Efforts Reasonable attempts by an authorized agency to assist, develop, and encourage a meaningful relationship between the parent and the child, including but not limited to:

1. consultation and cooperation with the parents in developing a plan for appropriate services to the child and his/her family,
2. making suitable arrangements for the parents to visit the child,
3. provision of services and other assistance to the parents so that problems preventing the discharge of the child from care may be resolved or ameliorated, and
4. informing the parents at appropriate intervals of the child's progress, development and health (Section 384 B of the Social Services Law).

Disposition Hearing A hearing to determine what order of disposition should be made in accordance with the best interests of the child (Section 623 of the Family Court Act).

Fact-Finding Hearing In the case of a petition for the commitment of the guardianship and custody of a child, a hearing to determine whether the allegations required by paragraphs A, B, C, and D of Subdivision 1 of Section 614 of the Family Court Act are supported by clear and convincing evidence (Section 622 of the Family Court Act).

Fair Hearing A hearing conducted by a representative of the state to determine whether or not the decision of the agency to remove a foster child from one foster home to another is arbitrary, uncapricious, or unreasonable (Section 400 of the Social Services Law).

Foster Child Any person in the care, custody, or guardianship of an authorized agency, who is placed for temporary or long-term care.

Foster Parent Any person with whom a child, in the care, custody, or guardianship of an authorized agency, is placed for temporary or long-term care (Section 371 of the Social Services Law).

Group Home A facility for the care and maintenance of not fewer than seven, nor more than twelve, children, who are at least five years of age, operated by an authorized agency, except that such minimum age shall not be applicable to siblings placed in the same facility nor to children whose mother is placed in the same facility (Section 371 of the Social Services Law).

Guardian *Ad Litem* The person assigned by the court, not necessarily an attorney, to protect the interests of an infant, incompetent, or other incapacitated person.

Home Includes a family boarding home or a family free home (Section 371 of the Social Services Law).

Independent Review A review provided by the Commissioner of Social Services of the City of New York when a child who has been in one foster home for at least one year is removed and placed in another foster home. If the local official disagrees with the authorized agency, the child must remain with the original foster parents, and the decision is not appealable by the agency.

Jury Trial In a custody proceeding, the parties are not entitled to a jury trial, and all custody matters are heard by a judge or special referee without a jury.

Juvenile Delinquent A person over seven and under sixteen years of age who does any act that, if done by an adult, would constitute a crime (Section 371 of the Social Services Law).

Law Guardian An attorney assigned by the court to protect the interests of an infant.

Mental Illness An affliction with a mental disease or mental condition that is manifested by a disorder or disturbance in behavior, feeling, thinking, or judgment to such an extent that if such child were placed in or returned to the custody of the parent, the child would be in danger of becoming a neglected child as defined in the Family Court Act (Section 384 B of the Social Services Law).

Mental Retardation Subaverage intellectual functioning that originates during the developmental period and is associated with impairment in adaptive behavior to such an extent that if such child were placed in or returned to the custody of the parent, the child would be in danger of becoming a neglected child as defined in the Family Court Act (Section 384 B of the Social Services Law).

Natural Parent The biological parent of a child.

Neglected Child   A child of fewer than eighteen years of age:

1. whose physical, mental, or emotional condition has been impaired or is in imminent danger of becoming impaired as a result of the failure of the parent or other person legally responsible for the child's care to exercise a minimum degree of care,

    a. in supplying the child with adequate food, clothing, shelter, education, or medical or surgical care, though financially able to do so or offered financial or other reasonable means to do so; or

    b. in providing the child with proper supervision or guardianship, by unreasonably inflicting or allowing to be inflicted harm, or a substantial risk thereof, including the infliction of excessive corporal punishment, or by using a drug or drugs, or by using alcoholic beverages to the extent that he/she loses self-control of his/her actions, or by any other acts of a similarly serious nature requiring the aid of the court, or

2. who has been abandoned by his/her parents or other person legally responsible for his/her care (Section 371 of the Social Services Law).

Open Adoption   An adoption in which the natural parent(s) is permitted, by agreement with the adoptive parents, to visit the child(ren) subsequent to the adoption.

Permanently Neglected Child   A child who is in the care of an authorized agency and whose parent or custodian has failed for a period of more than one year following the date such child came into the care of an authorized agency substantially and continuously or repeatedly to maintain contact with or plan for the future of the child, although physically and financially able to do so, notwithstanding the agency's diligent efforts to encourage and strengthen the parental relationship when such efforts will not be detrimental to the best interests of the child. In the event that the parent defaults after due notice of a proceeding to determine such neglect, such physical and financial ability of such parent may be presumed by the court (Section 384 B of the Social Services Law).

Person in Need of Supervision   A male of fewer than sixteen years of age or a female of fewer than eighteen years of age who is habitually truant or who is incorrigible, ungovernable, or habitually disobedient and beyond the lawful control of the parent or other lawful authority (Section 371 of the Social Services Law).

Physically Handicapped Child   A child who, by reason of a physical defect or deformity, whether congenital or acquired by accident, injury, or disease, is or may be expected to be totally or partially incapacitated for education or for remunerative occupation, as provided in the Education Law, or is or may be expected to be handicapped, as provided in the Public Health Law (Section 371 of the Social Services Law).

Place or Commit   The act of a family court judge whereby a child is placed into foster care (Section 371 of the Social Services Law).

Place Out   To arrange for the free care of a child in a family other than that of the child's parent, stepparent, grandparent, brother, sister, uncle or aunt, or legal guardian, for the purpose of adoption or for the purpose of providing care (Section 371 of the Social Services Law).

Private Adoption An adoption, also called independent adoption, wherein an agency is not involved, and the natural parents contract directly with the adoptive parents to consummate the adoption.

Public Institution for Children An institution that is established and maintained by a public welfare district for the purpose of providing care and maintenance therein for children and minors for whose care such district is responsible and who require care away from their own homes (Section 371 of the Social Services Law).

Putative Father A child's biological father, who was not married to the child's natural mother at the time of the birth of the child.

Voluntary Commitment A method of placing a child in foster care when a written instrument is signed by a parent or legal guardian entrusting the care of the child to an authorized agency (Section 384 A of the Social Services Law).

Part I
Family Court Hearing

1
Jurisdiction

Jurisdiction is divided into two aspects: jurisdiction over the subject matter, and jurisdiction over the person.

Jurisdiction over the Subject Matter

With respect to child custody, most states have probate courts, juvenile courts, and family courts that deal with the custody of children. In New York State, all aspects of child custody relating to foster care are placed in the Family Court of the State of New York. The family court has jurisdiction over the following proceedings, among others:

1. Proceedings involving juvenile delinquents
2. Proceedings involving persons in need of supervision
3. Children who are alleged to be abused
4. Children who are alleged to be neglected
5. Children who are alleged to be abandoned
6. Destitute children
7. Visitation proceedings
8. Guardianship proceedings
9. Custody proceedings
10. Termination of parental rights proceedings involving terminations based upon
    a. abandonment
    b. permanent neglect
    c. mental illness
    d. mental retardation
    e. severe and repeated abuse
11. Foster-care review proceedings
12. Adoption proceedings.

It should be noted that in New York the state supreme court has all the powers of the family court and has jurisdiction over, and accepts, all writs of habeas corpus involving the illegal detention of infants. Although the supreme court has jurisdiction over all matter that may be entertained in the family court, as a matter of practice, the supreme court does not entertain any of these proceedings except the writ of habeas corpus and custody proceedings unrelated to foster care. With respect to the writ of habeas corpus, the supreme court and the family court have concurrent original jurisdiction. All of the proceedings mentioned above will be discussed in detail in later chapters.

Jurisdiction over the Person

Unlike some proceedings initiated in the Supreme Court of the State of New York, in all proceedings initiated in the family court involving child custody, parents or guardians must be served personally with a copy of a summons and petition unless a court order is first obtained to serve the parents or guardians by substituted service. The court will not order substituted service until it is satisfied that diligent efforts have been made to locate the parents or guardians. When the court is satisfied that diligent efforts have been made to first serve the parents or guardians personally and that, thereafter, diligent efforts have been made to locate the whereabouts of the parents or guardians, and their efforts have been unsuccessful, then, and only then, will the court permit either substituted service ("nail and mail"—the summons and petition is affixed to the respondent's door and then mailed to that address) or service by publication.

In New York State the courts, including the family court, are under the individual assignment system, whereby a judge is assigned to a case initially and remains with that case to its conclusion. When there is a motion within a particular case, the court clerk will see to it that the motion is referred to the assigned judge.

Unlike the supreme court, in civil cases, the attorney does not have the prerogative to initiate a proceeding by simply issuing a summons and petition. Before any action is commenced, the summons and petition must be filed with the petition clerk of the appropriate court. Sidebar 1-1 is a summons involving abandonment of a child whereby the authorized agency is seeking to terminate parental rights, thereby freeing the child for adoption.

The clerk will then review the petition and, if it is found to be acceptable, will have the chief clerk of the court sign the summons and include a return date in an intake part. The summons is usually returnable at least five to six weeks after the summons and petition are filed with the clerk's office. This allows the attorney sufficient time to obtain a conformed copy of the summons and then to personally serve the summons and petition upon the respondent parents at least twenty days prior to the return date (if served within the State

Sidebar 1-1. Summons to Terminate Parental Rights

FAMILY COURT OF THE STATE OF NEW YORK
COUNTY [county]

_____ x

In the Matter of

[child]   SUMMONS

A dependent child under the age of 14 years, to the custody of [agency], alleged to be an abandoned child pursuant to Section 384-b of the Social Services Law.

_____ x

IN THE NAME OF THE PEOPLE OF THE STATE OF NEW YORK

TO: [mother]
      [father]
      COMMISSIONER OF SOCIAL SERVICES OF THE CITY OF NEW YORK,

A verified Petition having been filed in this Court alleging that the above-named child in the care of [agency], the petitioner, is an abandoned child as defined by Section 384-b of the Social Services Law, a copy of said Petition being annexed hereto:

YOU ARE HEREBY SUMMONED to appear before the Family Court at 60 Lafayette Street, New York, New York, Part A, on the [calendar] day of [month], 19   at 9:00 o'clock in the forenoon of said day to show cause why the Court should not enter an Order depriving you of all the rights of custody of [child], awarding the custody of said child to the petitioning authorized agency as an abandoned child as provided by law.

PLEASE TAKE NOTICE that if said child is adjudged to be an abandoned child, and if custody is awarded to said authorized agency, said child may be adopted with the consent of said authorized agency without further notice to you and without your consent.

In the event of your failure to appear, said failure to appear will result in the termination of all your parental rights to the child.

PLEASE TAKE FURTHER NOTICE that your failure to appear shall constitute a denial of an interest in the child, which denial may result in the transfer or commitment of the child's care, custody, guardianship or adoption of the child, all without further notice to the parents of the child.

PLEASE TAKE FURTHER NOTICE that you are entitled to be represented by an attorney, and if you cannot afford to retain an attorney, one will be appointed to represent you by the Court free of charge to you.

Dated: By Order of the Court

                                                          _____
                                                          Clerk, Family Court

---

of New York. If the summons and petition are served personally upon the respondents outside the State of New York, service must be completed at least thirty days before the return date. If the respondents are served by publication, the publication must be advertised in the newspaper at least twenty-eight days before the return date. At least two days prior to the return date, the affidavit of personal service or affidavit of publication should be filed with the clerk. Many judges will accept the filing of proof of service on the return date.

On the return date, if the respondent parents appear and do not have sufficient financial resources to afford for an attorney, the judge presiding in Part A (Assignment Part) will assign an 18B attorney to represent the respondent parents free of charge. The judge will also appoint a law guardian, usually from the Legal Aid Society, to represent the interests of the infant, and a trial date is then scheduled.

If a foster child is involved in any of the proceedings, the commissioner of social services is also served with a copy of the summons and petition, and the commissioner will be represented by corporation counsel. Once it is established that all of the respondents have been properly served or have appeared, the case is ready for trial.

It should be noted that in the State of New York, the attorney for the authorized agency who commences a proceeding to terminate parental rights based upon abandonment has the choice of bringing the proceeding either in the family court or the surrogate's court. The surrogate's court has jurisdiction only over abandonment proceedings and not over the other four methods of terminating parental rights—namely, permanent neglect, mental illness, mental retardation, and severe and repeated abuse. In the surrogate's court, the initial process is not a summons but a citation. Sidebar 1-2 is a citation involving abandonment of a child by his/her parents whereby the authorized agency is seeking to terminate parental rights thereby freeing the child for adoption.

The citation and petition alleging abandonment must be served upon the respondent parents ten days prior to the return date, and thirty days prior to the return date if served outside the State of New York. Service by publication requires publication of the citation in a newspaper twenty-eight days before the return date of the citation pursuant to an order for service by publication. In

Sidebar 1-2. Citation to Terminate Parental Rights

By the Grace of God, Free and Independent:

TO: [mother, father] and the COMMISSIONER OF SOCIAL SERVICES OF THE CITY OF NEW YORK, the persons interested in the commitment of [child], a dependent child under the age of 14 years, to the custory of [agency] and the Commissioner of Social Services of the City of New York, under Section 384 B of the Social Services Law.

SEND GREETINGS:

WHEREAS, [agency], an authorized foster care agency, has applied lately to the Surrogate's Court of the County of Nassau for an Order committing the custody and guardianship of the person of [child], to said [agency] and the Commissioner of Social Services of the City of New York pursuant to Section 384 B of the Social Services Law.

THEREFORE, YOU ARE HEREBY CITED to show cause before the Surrogate's Court of the County of Nassau at the Nassau County Courthouse, 262 Old Country Road, Mineola, New York, on the day of   , 19   , at 9:30 o'clock in the forenoon of said day or as soon thereafter as counsel can be heard, why such an Order committing the custody and guardianship of the person of said dependent child to [agency] and the Commissioner of Social Services of the City of New York pursuant to Section 384 B of the Social Services Law, with the power of [agency] or the Commissioner of Social Services of the City of New York to place said child for adoption and to consent to her adoption, dispensing with the further notice to or consent of the parents based upon abandonment of the infant, should not be made.

PLEASE TAKE NOTICE that if said child is adjudged to be an abandoned child, and if custody is awarded to said authorized agency, said child may be adopted with the consent of said authorized agency, without further notice to you and without your consent.

In the event of your failure to appear, said failure to appear will result in the termination of your parental rights to the child.

PLEASE TAKE FURTHER NOTICE that your failure to appear shall constitute a denial of an interest in the child, which denial may result in the transfer of the commitment of the child's care, custody, guardianship or adoption of the child, all without further notice to the parents of the child.

PLEASE TAKE FURTHER NOTICE that you have a right to be represented by an attorney, and, if you cannot afford an attorney, the Court will appoint an attorney for you free of charge.

IN WITNESS WHEREOF, we have caused the seal of the Surrogate's Court, Nassau County, at the Nassau County Courthouse, 262 Old Country Road, Mineola, New York, in said County, on the [calendar] day of [month], 1991.

Clerk, Surrogate's Court

---

the surrogate's court, if the respondents default and have been served personally the court marks the calendar "submit for decision" and notes the default of the parents, who have been served personally. In the surrogate's court, when there is a default based upon personal service, the surrogate does not take any testimony and makes the decision based upon the allegations in the petition. On the other hand, in the family court, even if there is a default, the judge of the family court requires testimony from the caseworkers in order to sustain the petition.

2
Confidentiality

Traditionally, family court matters—especially those involving infants— have been confidential. Only parties and their attorneys who are necessary to the proceeding are allowed in the courtroom.

The trend has been away from complete confidentiality, and some judges upon proper application have permitted reporters to attend court proceedings. Others have allowed audiovisual coverage.

Audiovisual coverage is defined in Title 22 of the Uniform Rules, New York State Trial Courts, Chapter II, Section 131.2 B as follows:

> *Audio-visual coverage* or *coverage* shall mean the electronic broadcasting or other transmission to the public of radio or television signals from the courtroom, the recording of sound or light in the courtroom for later transmission or reproduction, or the taking of still or motion pictures in the courtroom by the news media.

Section 131.3 of Title 22 of the Uniform Rules sets forth the method of application for audiovisual coverage. Section 131.4 sets forth the criteria for determination of the application. Said section also states that:

> Where the proceedings of which coverage is sought involve *a child*, a victim, a prospective witness, or a party, any of whom object to such coverage, and in any other appropriate instance, the presiding trial judge may hold such conference and conduct. (emphasis added)

While consent of the parties (Section 131.4 B) is not required for approval of an application for such coverage, there are certain relevant factors that the presiding trial judge must consider. As set forth in Section 131.4 C of Title 22,

> In determining an application for coverage, the presiding trial judge shall consider all relevant factors, including but not limited to:
>
> 1. The type of case involved;
> 2. Whether the coverage would cause harm to any participant;

3. Whether the coverage would interfere with the fair administration of justice, the advancement of a fair trial, or the rights of the parties;

4. Whether the coverage would interfere with any law enforcement activity;

5. Whether the proceedings would involve lewd or scandalous matters;

6. The objections of any of the parties, prospective witnesses, victims or other participants in the proceeding of which coverage is sought;

7. The physical structure of the courtroom and the likelihood that any equipment required to conduct coverage of proceedings can be installed and operated without disturbance to those proceedings or any other proceedings in the courthouse; and

8. The extent to which the coverage would be barred by law in the judicial proceeding of which coverage is sought.

The presiding trial judge also shall consider and give great weight to the fact that any party, prospective witness, victim or other participant in the proceeding is a child.

The statutory authority for 22 N.Y.C.R.R., Section 131.1 *et seq.* is Section 218 of the Judicial Law.

Judicial Law Section 218 and 22 N.Y.C.R.R. Section 131.1 *et seq.* should be read together with Family Court Act Section 1043, which declares that hearings under Article 10 of the Family Court Act (child protective proceedings) are not open to the public. Said section states as follows:

The general public may be excluded from any hearing under this article and only such persons and the representatives of authorized agencies admitted thereto as have an interest in the case.

However, in one case, where the attorney for the infant requested that the courtroom be opened during the trial to spectators and the press, Judge Arthur J. Abrams of the Family Court, Suffolk County, granted such a request over the objections of the County attorney. See, for example, In re Baum [382 N.Y.S. 2d 672, 673 (Family Court, Suffolk County, 1976)].

In a recent case entitled Matter of Bruce [Docket No. Na-11846/87 (Family Court, Kings County)], the Honorable Joyce L. Sparrow was confronted with many applications by the news media to cover the dispositional hearing over a neglect proceeding, where four out of five infants had died in the custody of parents. The news media had made application, pursuant to Section 131.3 of the Rules of the Chief Administrative Judge, requesting permission to videotape and photograph the dispositional phase of the neglect proceeding, which was brought pursuant to Article 10 of the Family Court Act.

Judge Sparrow permitted the media the right to be present in the courtroom for written coverage but refused the media any audiovisual coverage.

Because the decision is unreported and because it is of precedential value to both the bench and the bar, the full decision is reprinted herein:

This court has pending before it a request for audio-visual coverage of the dispositional hearing in this matter. Conferences were held in which the positions of all parties were fully presented. With only one exception, essentially all participants oppose the coverage. The parents are vehemently opposed, citing the great harm they believe the publicity in this case has visited upon them.

Family Court Act Section 1043 specifically states "the general public may be excluded from any hearing under this article . . . ," and that only interested persons should be admitted. Family Court Rule Section 205.4 dealing with the privacy of Family Court proceedings further delineates the court's discretion. It is clear that under appropriate circumstances members of the media may be present, but that the court must be cognizant of anything that may disrupt or interfere with the orderly and sound administration of justice.

Part 131 of the rules of the Chief Administrative Judge of the Courts sets forth the standards for discretion relative to audio-visual coverage. Most important is that the public's understanding of the judicial system be enhanced, but that in weighing the appropriateness of such coverage many factors should be balanced.

Section 131.4 sub(c) lays out eight important factors. It is interesting that this extremely delicate child protective proceeding brings into play all eight factors, but amongst those factors several are most significant. These relevant factors are as follows: First, that this case involves a very young child who is the only survivor out of five siblings. This court made a finding of abuse based on the circumstances surrounding the deaths of the four siblings. Of primary concern is this young child's future. Second, extensive mental health studies of both the parents and grandparents have been prepared for the court. The material which will be presented in this hearing may well involve scandalous matters. Third, the physical structure of this courtroom (and all family court courtrooms) is not conducive to a non-intrusive camera because the room is too small for any participant to be unaware of the coverage. This could create a chilling effect on witnesses, etc., and interfere with the court's ability to hear all relevant evidence. Last, but not least, it is the court's interpretation that the legislature never intended to physically allow the general public to actually be present at this type of proceeding. (See FCA Section 1043). The ultimate effect of audio-visual coverage is to bring the public into the courtroom.

Accordingly, it is the court's determination that audio-visual coverage, in this matter, would be inappropriate and would interfere with the orderly and sound administration of justice and the search for the best interest of this child. The public's interest and right to know can adequately be met by this court's continuing permission granting the media the right to be present in the courtroom for written coverage.

In a more recent case, Matter of S Children [532 N.Y.S. 2d 192 (Family Court, Orange County, 1988)], the court again addressed the issue of whether a neglect proceeding under Article 10 of the Family Court Act should be opened to the press. The judge, in holding that the press would be allowed to cover the proceedings, weighed the traditional notion of confidentiality in the family court as created by Sections 1043 and 166 of the Family Court Act and 22 N.Y.C.R.R., Section 205.4 of the Uniform Rules of the Family Court against the salutory effect of the press.

The judge noted that while the respondent objected to the presence of the press "the underlying matter has already been widely publicised, the respondent has pled guilty to a manslaughter charge on the related matter in the County Court and the press has agreed not to identify the parties or the children." The judge set out the purpose of press as salutory because the press would inform the public and the state legislature about the crisis in the system presently in place to protect children in child abuse and neglect situations, and made specific note of the foster care system.

Finding that the respondent's objections were minimized by the regulations agreed to by the press while the presence of the press would maximize society's ability to comprehend and grapple with the inadequacies of child protective procedures, the court thus allowed the press to cover the proceeding and invited "the press to maintain a regular presence in her Court" [id at 200]. Specific guidelines of the press's presence were not defined with respect to future proceedings. Rather, the judge "invited the press to assist in drawing up workable guidelines" [Id at 200].

Part II
How a Child Comes Into Foster Care

3
Overview

A *foster child* is defined as any person in the care, custody, or guardianship of an authorized agency, who is placed for temporary or long-term care (see Section 371 of the Social Services Law). Custody in this context is physical custody, not legal custody. For example, if a natural parent voluntarily commits his/her child to an authorized agency, the agency has physical custody and the parent has sole legal custody. At this point only the parent can consent to an adoption; the agency cannot so consent because it does not have legal custody.

There are several ways that a child is placed in the foster-care system, as will be discussed in depth in the following chapters.

Death of Parent or Parents

Upon the death of both natural parents, and assuming there are no relatives willing to assume custody of the child, the child is taken into custody by the appropriate governmental agency. An order committing the guardianship and custody of a child may be granted upon the ground that both parents of the child are dead and no guardian of the person of such child has been lawfully appointed (Section 384 B [4][a] of the Social Services Law). In the City of New York, this governmental agency is the commissioner of social services. The commissioner in turn will usually place the child with an authorized agency, which is defined by Section 371 of the Social Services Law as any agency empowered by law to care for, to place out, or to board out children. Such an agency is inspected and supervised by the Board of Social Welfare. The authorized agency may then place the foster child in a foster home, institutional care, a group home, or an agency boarding home.

Voluntary Commitment

Parents may not be able to care for their children for a variety of reasons. Because of health reasons, a parent may wish to relinquish custody of a child to the commissioner for a temporary period, hoping to retain custody when the problem is ameliorated. Section 384 A of the Social Services Law provides that the care and custody of a child may be transferred by a parent to an authorized agency by a written instrument. The written instrument, called a *voluntary commitment*, shall be upon such terms, for such time, and subject to such conditions as may be agreed upon by the parties thereto. Pursuant to a voluntary commitment, the agency receives only physical custody and not legal custody. Parents sign voluntary commitments for numerous reasons: drinking problems, narcotic addiction problems, and financial, physical, and psychological problems.

Surrender

There are times when a parent may wish to relinquish all legal rights to his/her child. Section 383 C of the Social Services Law provides that the written surrender shall recite that the authorized agency shall have the right to consent to an adoption of the child in the place and instead of the parent. The written surrender gives not only physical custody but also legal custody of the child. The written surrender is recorded in the county clerk's office. Under present law a surrender may be executed before a judge of the family court or surrogate's court, or before two witnesses and notarized and within fifteen days court approved.

Need for Supervision

If a child between the ages of seven and sixteen is adjudged by a family court judge to be a habitual truant, incorrigibly ungovernable, or habitually disobedient and beyond the lawful control of his/her parent, the family court, upon finding this child in need of supervision, may place the child with an authorized agency for up to eighteen months, with court review permitting one-year extensions of placement (see Sections 711 and 783 of the Family Court Act). There shall be a fact-finding hearing and a dispositional hearing. The family court has exclusive original jurisdiction. The proceeding is brought in the county where the acts referred to in the petition occurred. If the child is ten years of age or over, the child may be detained in a certified secured detention facility but must be brought before a family court judge the next court date.

Juvenile Delinquency

The family court may find a child between seven and sixteen years, who does any act that if done by an adult would constitute a crime, to be a juvenile delinquent. Upon a finding by a family court judge that a child is a juvenile delinquent, the child may be placed with an authorized agency for up to eighteen months, with court review permitting extensions of placement for up to one year (see Sections 711 to 783 of the Family Court Act). The following persons may originate a proceeding to determine a child to be a juvenile delinquent:

1. parent;
2. peace officer;
3. victim or witness; or
4. agent of an authorized agency, association, society, or institution.

Destitution

A destitute child is a child under eighteen years of age who, through no neglect on the part of his or her parent, is destitute, homeless, or in a state of want or suffering due to lack of sufficient food, clothing, shelter, or medical or surgical care. The family court may remand the child to the care of an authorized agency (see Sections 371.3 and 398 of the Social Services Law).

Abandonment

An abandoned child is one under the age of eighteen years who is abandoned or deserted by his/her parent and is left in destitute circumstances without proper food, shelter, or clothing, without being visited or having payments made toward the child's support for more than six months. The family court may remand the child to an authorized agency (Section 398 of the Social Services Law) or grant the agency legal custody pursuant to Section 384 of the Social Services Law.

Neglect or Abuse

If a parent neglects or abuses his/her child, the law permits the appropriate authorities, such as protective services, to remove the child immediately from the parents' home and forthwith file a petition with the family court to have the issue adjudicated. See Article 10—Child Protective Proceedings—of the Family Court Act, which is designed to protect children from injury or mistreatment and to safeguard the well-being of children and provide for emergency removal of children from their homes without a court order. There shall be a fact-finding hearing and a dispositional hearing.

A child is *abused* when the child's parent inflicts, or allows to be inflicted, physical injury, or commits, or allows to be committed, a sex offense against the child. A child is *neglected* if the child's parent has failed to exercise a minimum degree of care (see Section 371 [4][a] of the Social Services Law, Family Court Act 1012, and Sections 411–428 of the Social Services Law).

If the parent is found guilty of neglect or abuse, the court may remand the child to the commissioner of social services, who in turn will usually place the child with an authorized agency. The agency will then place the child in its institution, a group home, or an agency boarding home, or with a foster parent.

It is estimated that 80 percent of all foster children in New York City are voluntarily placed and 20 percent are court placed because of findings of:

1. abuse;
2. neglect;
3. need for supervision; or
4. juvenile delinquency.

4

The Voluntary Commitment

The voluntary commitment is the most frequently utilized method for placing children in the foster-care system. Section 384 A of the Social Services Law of the State of New York provides the procedure and terms for the transfer of custody of children into the foster-care system.

Procedure

The care and custody of a child is transferred by a parent or guardian to an authorized agency by a written instrument executed in the presence of one or more witnesses. The written instrument must be kept in a file maintained by the agency accepting the care and custody of the child, and copies of the instrument must be given to the parent or guardian at the time of execution of the voluntary commitment.

The voluntary commitment instrument shall be upon such terms, for such time, and subject to such conditions as may be agreed upon by the parties to the agreement. It is, therefore, possible and preferable that the voluntary commitment be tailored to the particular needs of the parent and child rather than a printed document handed to the parent on a "take-it-or-leave-it" basis. Because the document is so important and because it may be tailored to the particular needs of the child and parent, it is also prefereable that an attorney represent the natural parent who is voluntarily committing the child to the Department of Social Services of the particular district or to the authorized agency.

The key provisions contained in Section 384 A of the Social Services Law are:

1. The child in foster care who is voluntarily committed by a parent, or guardian, must be returned to such parent or guardian upon request unless a court order is secured by the local social service district or by the authorized agency within a specified time.
2. Only parents and legal guardians may enter into voluntary placement agreements.

3. The voluntary placement agreement may contain provisions and conditions agreed to by the parent or the legal guardian and the social service district or authorized agency.

The method of return and the need for a court order will depend upon whether (1) the voluntary commitment instrument provided that the child was to be returned by the authorized agency on a specific date or upon the occurrence of a specific event, or (2) placement was for an indeterminate length of time.

Return by a Specific Date

If the placement agreement contains a specific date or event when the child shall be returned, placement, or the child's foster care status, ends on such date or upon the occurrence of such specific event, and the child must be returned to the parent unless the court order has been secured by the agency preventing the return of the child prior to said date. Such a court order can be secured pursuant to Section 384 B of the Social Services Law, Section 392 of the Social Services Law, Article 6 of the Family Court Act, or Article 10 of the Family Court Act.

If the agreement contains a specific date or event for return, but a parent requests the return of the child in writing prior to that date or event, the authorized agency or local social service district may either return the child or, within ten days after receipt of the written request, notify the parent that the request is being denied. In this event, the burden rests on the parent to obtain the return of the child by initiating a court proceeding.

Return by an Indeterminate Date

If the placement agreement does not include a specific date or event for the return of the child, the parent may request the return of the child at any time. Within twenty days of receipt of the request, the agency or local social service district must either return the child to the parent or guardian or secure a court order prior to the expiration of said twenty-day period, which court order may authorize the continuation of custody by the authorized agency. Such a court order may also be obtained pursuant either to Section 384 B or 392 of the Social Services Law or to Articles 6 and 10 of the Family Court Act.

Because a court order must be obtained within such a short period of time, it is imperative that the application to the court be made in the form of an order to show cause with a temporary stay of the return of the child pending the hearing and determination of the application by the judge of the family court. Sidebar 4–1 is a form of an order to show cause with the appropriate stay for the return of the child pending the hearing and determination of the application.

Sidebar 4–1. Order to Show Cause

At a Term of the Family Court of the State of New York, held in and for [county], on the [calendar] day of [month], 1991.

P R E S E N T:

Hon. [judge of the family court]

In the Matter of

[child],   ORDER TO SHOW CAUSE

A dependent child under the age of   Docket No. [   ]
14 years, to the custody of [agency],
alleged to be a permanently neglected
child pursuant to Section 384-b of the
Social Services Law.

Upon the Affidavit of [caseworker], sworn to on the [calendar] day of [month], 1991, and the exhibits annexed hereto:

Let the respondent, [mother or father], show cause at a Term of this Court to be held at 60 Lafayette Street, New York, New York, at Part A thereof on the [calendar] day of [month], 19   , at 9:30 o'clock in the forenoon thereof or as soon thereafter as counsel can be heard why an order should not be made pursuant to Section 384-a and Section 384-b of the Social Services Law preventing the return of the infant, [child], to the respondent, [mother or father], pending the determination of the permanent neglect proceeding pending in this Court and why petitioner should not have such other and further relief as the Court may determine; it is

ORDERED that pending the determination of this motion, the agency, [agency], need not transfer the physical custody of the infant, [child]; and it is further

ORDERED that personal service of this order, together with the papers upon which it was granted, upon respondent, [mother or father], and upon the Commissioner of Social Services of the City of New York, and upon the Legal Aid Society, Law Guardian for the infant, on or before the [calendar] day of [month], 1991, be deemed sufficient service.

E N T E R:

_____
Judge, Family Court

Sidebar 4–2 is a typical voluntary placement agreement between a parent or guardian and the Department of Social Services for the City of New York. Of course, this agreement may be adapted to the needs of any social service district or authorized agency and tailored to fit the needs of the parent and child involved. This voluntary placement agreement (Form W-864) by parent or guardian, revised September 1, 1990, reflects changes in the Social Services Law, Section 384 A(2)(c). While most of the language is similar to form W-864 dated September 1, 1978, certain of the information has been emphasized by being printed in very large type. There is also an additional section providing for the amount of a voluntary contribution by the parent for the care of the child if the parent is able to contribute to the support of the infant in foster care. Also attached to Form W-864, the voluntary placement agreement, is the designation of religious preference for the foster child, Form M-309 (sidebar 4–3), and the request for discharge of child from foster care, which is Form W-864(v) (sidebar 4–4).

Sidebar 4–2. Voluntary Placement Agreement by Parent or Guardian

Notice

- By signing this agreement, you will voluntarily transfer the care and custody of your child to the Commissioner of Social Services. You do not have to sign the Agreement and you will not be subject to any legal penalties if you do not sign it.

- You have the right to talk to a lawyer of your own choosing, prior to signing this Agreement or at any other time, about the consequences of signing this legal document. If you cannot afford a lawyer, there are several organizations which provide free legal services. The following are some of the organizations which provide free legal services:

Community Action for Legal Services
Legal Aid Society
MFY Legal Services

Name of Person Signing Agreement　　　Address

_____　　_____
Mother　　　　　　　　　　　　　　　　House No. and Street　　　Apt.

　　　　　　　　　　　　　　　　　　　_____
　　　　　　　　　　　　　　　　　　　Borough or PO　　　　　　ZIP

_____	_____
Father*	House No. and Street Apt.
	_____
	Borough or PO ZIP
_____	_____
Legal Guardian**	House No. and Street Apt.
	_____
	Borough or PO ZIP

Parent(s)/Legal Guardian of _____ born on _____, requests the Commissioner of Social Services to accept care and custody of my child.

Terms of Placement

I grant permission to the Commissioner of Social Services (Commissioner) to place my child in a foster care setting that is determined to be suitable for my child's care. I understand that I and the foster care agency with which my child is placed are expected to work cooperatively towards planning for the future of my child, and that the agency will offer whatever help is available to enable me to decide what is best for my child. I understand that it is both my right and responsibility to plan with the agency for my child's return home, or to actively participate in making alternate plans so that he or she can have the benefit of another home.

Indefinite Placement

I am placing my child with the Commissioner for an indefinite period of time. When I want my child discharged from foster care, I will give notice to the agency caring for my child. If possible, I will give such notice in writing using the "Request for Discharge of Child from Foster Care" form which is attached to this Agreement.

    The agency will return my child to me within twenty (20) days after receiving my request unless a court order exists that would

---

  * If child is born out-of-wedlock, attach acknowledgment of paternity form; or indicate the date and court where paternity was established: Date _____ Court _____
** If signing as legal guardian, specify the date and court where guardianship was obtained: Date _____ Court _____

not allow the return or a court order is obtained to prevent the return. A court order may be obtained by the Commissioner in any of the following court proceedings: (1) a custody proceeding; (2) a child protective proceeding; (3) a proceeding to terminate parental rights; or (4) a Section 392 Foster Care Review that directed continued care.

Limited Placement

I want my child to be placed with the Commissioner until [date] or until the following event takes place:

_____

My child will be returned by the above date or event specified unless a court order is obtained to prevent the return before the above date or event, or within ten (10) days after the date or event. If I am unable to receive my child, or I am unavailable or incapacitated, I consent to extend the time my child remains in care. I will notify the foster care agency when I am able to accept my child. My child must then be returned to me within ten (10) days after the receipt of my request unless a court order against the return is obtained within ten (10) days of my request.

I may request in writing to the foster care agency the return of my child before the above date or event. The agency must return my child or notify me within ten (10) days of my request if the request is denied. If the agency does not act upon my request, I have the right to seek the immediate return of my child in either Family Court or State Supreme Court.

Responsibilities of Parents

As the parent(s)/legal guardian of my child, I agree to:

(1) plan for the future of my child;
(2) cooperate with the representatives of the Commissioner of Social Services and the staff of the foster care agency where my child is placed in developing and carrying out the best plan for my child and me;
(3) keep appointments with my caseworker and answer the letters that the agency worker sends to me;
(4) follow-up on suggestions made by my agency worker in obtaining help for a problem;

(5) visit and otherwise communicate with my child, and have my child visit me; if I cannot visit, I will tell the caseworker why and make every effort to call my child or write regularly;

(6) keep the foster care agency informed of my address, telephone number, place of employment, income, living arrangements, and change of name, if it should occur; and

(7) contribute, if I am financially able, towards the cost of my child's foster care in the amount of $_____ for the period (week) (month) while my child remains in the care and custody of the Commissioner.

I understand that failure to meet my responsibilities could be a basis for court proceedings to terminate my parental rights and free my child for adoption. I understand that if my rights are terminated, my consent would no longer be needed for adoption.

Responsibilities of the Commissioner

I understand that the Commissioner of Social Services or the foster care agency where my child is placed, in accordance with the plan for supportive services and the extent that such facilities and services are available, agrees to:

(1) provide care, supervision, room, board, clothing, medical care, dental care, and education for my child;

(2) inform me of the name, address and telephone number of the foster care agency where my child is placed;

(3) clearly inform me of what is expected of me before my child will be returned home and to work with me to develop and carry out a service plan for my child and me, including those supportive services needed so that my child can return home;

(4) provide help, if needed, for any children who remain in my home;

(5) help me make arrangements to visit my child and to provide carfare if I am financially eligible; and

(6) hear and act upon any complaints I may have about care and services provided to my child and me. If my caseworker is unable to resolve my complaint, I may contact the Parents' Rights Unit at (212) 266-2500. A Parents' Rights Unit caseworker will mediate the problem between myself and the agency.

Visiting

I have been advised of my right to visit my child in foster care and I have been informed of the importance of visiting regularly. I have the right to determine, jointly with the agency, the terms and frequency of visitation. I agree to cooperate with the agency in establishing appropriate visiting periods. I understand that visiting schedules may not always be fixed and that at times it may be necessary to change them due to changes in my circumstances or because of circumstances where my child is placed.

No one from my child Welfare Administration or the foster care agency may stop or limit my visits without approval from a court proceeding. If they feel that my visits seriously hurt my child, they can refuse to allow me to visit but must obtain court approval within the next business day. I understand that I would be notified of such a proceeding and may appear at the proceeding. If I agree in writing with the decision to limit or stop the visits, court action may not be required.

Supportive Services

I have been advised of my right to have supportive services provided, including preventive and other supportive services, while my child remains in foster care. I understand that such supportive services should be provided so that my child can be returned to my home.

I further understand that it is my responsibility to plan for and to cooperate with the provision of such supportive services. Should I fail to cooperate and my child cannot be returned to my home in accordance with the plan for services, an action to terminate my parental rights might be brought.

I understand that the supportive services will not be discontinued while my child remains in placement unless I agree to this in writing. There are three exceptions to this rule: (1) if the continued provision of supportive services would be contrary to a court order entered in a proceeding of which I was notified; (2) if I do not keep the agency informed of my whereabouts; or (3) if I refuse to communicate with the agency or I refuse to accept the supportive services offered.

Health and Medical Care

As the parent(s)/legal guardian of my child:

(1) I understand that the Commissioner or his representative will keep me informed of my child's progress, development and health (other than routine health care);

(2) I agree to the administration of any medical immunizations, tests and treatments, including dental and surgical treatment, that are considered necessary for the well-being of my child. I understand that I will be consulted and my consent sought, if possible, whenever surgery is necessary.

(3) In the event that my child requires emergency surgery, I authorize the Commissioner of Social Services or his representatives to consent to such emergency surgery if I am unavailable or cannot be reached for consultation. Notification of the action will be given to me as soon as possible. I also agree that whenever an emergency arises requiring immediate medical and/or surgical care, and in the treating physician's judgment an emergency exists and that any delay caused by an attempt to secure consent for treatment would increase the risk to my child's life or health, necessary care may be provided immediately and notice to me will be given as soon as possible; and

(4) I understand that when my consent to a medical procedure is requested and if the Commissioner or his representatives believes that my failure to give such consent would endanger the life, health or safety of my child, a child protective proceeding may be initiated in order to obtain court authorization for the medical procedure.

Court Hearings

(1) According to the provisions of Section 358-a of the Social Services Law, if a child remains in care more than thirty (30) days, a proceeding will be filed in the Family Court to obtain a Court review of this Agreement. According to the provisions of Section 392 of the Social Services Law, a review of the foster care status of my child will be held before the end of the first eighteen (18) months and at least every two (2) years thereafter. The parent(s) or legal guardian will receive notice of these filings and have an opportunity to attend. At the hearing, the Court has the authority to order the Commissioner of Social Services to carry out a specific plan of action to exercise diligent efforts toward the discharge of my child from foster care, either to my child's own family or to an adoptive home. The court also retains continuing jurisdiction for certain purposes, and may review the case at the request of any of the parties involved, including the parent(s)/legal guardian.

(2) A parent's failure to maintain parental responsibilities may lead to action and termination of parental rights. Under the Social Services Law of the State of New York, the failure of the parent(s) to visit a child for six successive months, without good reasons, may be considered abandonment. Under the Social Services Law and the Family Court Act of the State of New York, the failure of the parent(s) to maintain regular contact with or plan for the future of my child, although physically and financially able to do so, for a period of more than one year following the date my child came into foster care, may be considered permanent neglect.

Right to a Fair Hearing

I understand that I have the right to request a State Fair Hearing if I disagree with any decision involving my child's placement. This request must be made within 60 days of such a decision. I may request a fair hearing for such decisions as:

- supportive services are denied, reduced, or discontinued
- supportive services arranged are not appropriate for my situation
- I disagree with any change in the placement conditions regarding my child
- I have been denied the right to visit with my child.

I may request a fair hearing by: (1) writing a letter stating my complaint to the New York State Department of Social Services, Fair Hearing Section, 40 North Pearl Street, Albany, NY 12243; or (2) calling (212) 488-6550.

The fair hearing will be held in New York City. I understand that I and the foster care agency representative must appear. I may be represented by a lawyer, relative or friend, or I may represent myself. Both I and the foster care agency must follow the decision made by the hearing officer unless I seek a court review and the court determines differently.

Signatures

I understand that I have the right to consult with an attorney prior to signing this Agreement or at any other time, as outlined in the Notice on the first page of this Agreement.

I understand that none of the above provisions may be changed without my consent or that of an individual acting in my behalf with my consent, and the consent of the Commissioner of Social Services or his designated representatives. If any such provision is to be changed, it shall be indicated in writing in a supplemental instrument which shall be acknowledged and signed in the same manner as this agreement, and shall be attached and become part of this original Agreement.

I have read and I understand this Agreement which will be in effect during the time that my child is in foster care placement. I have received a copy of this agreement.

_____

Signature of Parent or Legal Guardian

_____

Signature of Second Parent

Signed in the presence of:

_____

Title: _____   Date: _____

Note: A copy of the *Parent's Handbook* should be given to you when this Agreement is signed. If it is not available, you should ask the caseworker to mail it to you. It contains additional information about matters related to foster care. The caseworker can clarify and further explain any of the information in this publication at any time.

Sidebar 4–3. Designation of Religious Preference for Child(ren)

Case Name_____Case No._____Unit/Worker No._____

Notice to Parent(s)—Please Read Carefully

The Child Welfare Administration (CWA) contracts for foster care services from private non-profit foster care agencies associated with the Protestant, Jewish and Catholic religions, foster care agencies that provide care solely to children of specific religious groups, as well as foster care agencies not associated with any religion. CWA also provides foster care services through its own Office of Direct Child Care Services, which is not associated with any religion. Children are placed either with foster families or in group facilities depending on each child's service needs. Please use this form to inform CWA of your child(ren)'s religion and if you wish to have your child(ren) placed in a foster care agency associated with your child(ren)'s religion. Also, please ask your caseworker if there is a foster care agency that provides care solely to children of your child(ren)'s religion. Your decision will not affect the quality of care your child(ren) receives. The foster care agency in which your child(ren) is placed will allow your child(ren) to practice his/her religion. Your child(ren)'s religion will be taken into consideration in selecting an appropriate foster family if CWA determines that a foster family is best able to provide the services required by your child(ren), even if you do not express a wish for placement with a foster care agency associated with your child(ren)'s religion. If you do express a preference, CWA will honor your preference if an appropriate vacancy can be obtained in a timely manner and if such a placement is determined to be in your child(ren)'s best interests.

Children's Religion _____

Child's Name (Last, First)	Birth Date	Child's Name (Last, First)	Birth Date
_____	_____	_____	_____
_____	_____	_____	_____
_____	_____	_____	_____

Please choose one of the following options for the child(ren) listed above:

1. I/We prefer that the child(ren) be placed without regard to the religious association of the foster agency.

2. I/We prefer that the child(ren) be placed with a foster care agency associated with my/our child(ren)'s religion and if such placement is *not* available at this time:

   I/We wish the child(ren) to be placed without regard to the religious association of the foster care agency.

   I/We wish the child(ren) to be *temporarily* placed with a foster care agency not associated with my/our child(ren)'s religion until a placement with a foster care agency associated with my/our child(ren)'s religion is available.

My/Our child(ren) should then be placed with the foster care agency associated with my/our child(ren)'s religion.

(*FOR A VOLUNTARY PLACEMENT ONLY*) I/We wish my/our child(ren) to wait in his/her present location until such time as the child(ren) can be placed with a foster care agency associated with my/our child(ren)'s religion.

By signing below, you acknowledge receiving the information contained in this form and understanding the effects that your choice may have on the foster care placement that is provided to your child(ren).

Print Name(s) of parent(s) _____ _____

Signature(s) of parent(s) _____ _____

Witnessed by _____ Date _____

Case Name _____ Case No. _____ Unit/Worker No. _____

Child(ren)'s Religion _____

The information contained in this document pertains to the following child(ren):

Child's Name (Last, First)	Birth Date	Child's Name (Last, First)	Birth Date
_____	_____	_____	_____
_____	_____	_____	_____
_____	_____	_____	_____

Name of Parent(s): _____ _____

Name(s) of Guardian(s): _____ _____

	Deceased	Refuses to Sign	Unavailable	Other
The mother is:	[ ]	[ ]	[ ]	[ ]
The father is:	[ ]	[ ]	[ ]	[ ]

If the parent(s) is either "unavailable" or "refuses to sign" Form M-309 (Face) or other circumstances prevent completion of Form M-309 (Face), explain the situation briefly:

_____

_____

_____

Check the box located beside the source of information used to determine the child(ren)'s presumed religion and the presumed religious preference of parent(s)/guardian(s) and/or child(ren), and provide a brief description of the information:

[ ] Statement(s) made by the parent(s)/guardian(s): _____

_____

[ ] Statement(s) by one or more of the children (specify child):

_____

[ ] Statement(s) by relatives and/or neighbors: _____

_____

[ ] Presence of religious objects or insignia (describe): _____

_____

[ ] Information previously entered into the case record: _____

_____

[ ] Other (specify source): _____

_____

Based on the above, the religious preference of the parent(s), guardian(s) and/or child(ren) would be:

[ ] 1. The parent(s)/guardian(s) prefers that the child(ren) be placed without regard to the religious association of the foster care agency.

[ ] 2. The parent(s)/guardian(s) prefers that the child(ren) be placed with a foster care agency associated with the child(ren)'s religion, and if such a placement is *not* available at this time:

[ ] The child(ren) is to be placed without regard to the religious association of the foster care agency.

[ ] The child(ren) is to be *temporarily* placed with a foster care agency not associated with the child(ren)'s religion until an in-religion placement becomes available. The child(ren) should then be placed with the foster care agency associated with the child(ren)'s religion.

[ ] (*FOR A VOLUNTARY PLACEMENT ONLY*) The child(ren) is to wait at his/her present location until such time as the child(ren) can be placed with a foster care agency associated with the child(ren)'s religion.

Caseworker's Signature _____ Date _____

Sidebar 4–4. Request for Discharge of Child from Foster Care

My name _____

My current address _____

My current phone number _____

My child's name _____

My child's birthday _____

The name of the agency caring for my child _____

I want my child returned to me (fill in date) _____

Answer the questions below:

Will your child live with you after he or she comes home?

[ ] yes   [ ] no

If you answered no, tell us with whom your child will live.

_____
(Name of person and relationship to you)

_____
(Address)

Will you be caring for and supervising your child during the day?

[ ] yes   [ ] no

If you answered no, tell us who will care for and supervise your child during the day.

_____
(Name of person and relationship to you *or* name of agency)

How do you plan to support your child?
[ ] work [ ] public assistance [ ] Social Security or Supplemental Security Income (SSI)

[ ] Other (please specify _____)

Signed: _____ Dated: _____

PLEASE MAIL TO THE AGENCY CARING FOR YOUR CHILD.

5
The Need for Supervision

Another way a child comes into foster care is by court order after the child has been declared to be a person in need of supervision (more commonly known as a PINS). A person in need of supervision is defined as a child younger than sixteen years of age who has been adjudged by a judge of the family court to be habitually truant, incorrigibly ungoverned, or habitually disobedient and beyond the lawful control of his or her parent. Article 7 of the Family Court Act sets out the boundaries of PINS proceedings.

Jurisdiction, Venue, and Who May Originate Proceedings

The family court has exclusive original jurisdiction over a PINS proceeding.[1] The proceeding is brought in the county where the act referred to in the petition occurred.[2] Proceedings to adjudicate the need for supervision may be brought by:

1. a peace officer, acting pursuant to his or her special duties or a police officer;

2. a parent or other person legally responsible for the child's care;

3. any person who has suffered injury as a result of the alleged activity of a person alleged to be in need of supervision or has witnessed such activity;

4. a recognized agent of any duly authorized agency, association, society, or institution; or

5. the presentment agency that consented to substitute a petition alleging the person is in need of supervision for a petition alleging that the person is a juvenile delinquent pursuant to Section 311.4 of the Family Court Act.[3]

The Petition Originated a Proceeding to Adjudicate a Need for Supervision

The allegations that must be presented in a petition to originate a PINS proceeding closely follow the above definition of a person in need of supervision. The petition itself must allege that the respondent is an habitual truant or is incorrigible, ungovernable, or habitually disobedient and is beyond the lawful control of his/her parents, guardian, or lawful custodian. It must also specify the acts on which the allegations are based and the time and place they allegedly occurred. Further, the petition must allege that the child requires supervision or treatment. Finally, the petition must affirmatively allege the age of the child.[4] Notably, the age differential between boys and girls set out in definitional Article 7, Section 712 A, has been held unconstitutional on equal protection grounds. See Matter of Patricia A. [31 N.Y. 2d 83, 286 N.E. 2d 432, 335, N.Y.S. 2d 33 (1982)]; see also Matter of B. [68 Misc. 2d 95, 326, N.Y.S. 2d 702 (Family Court, Monroe County, 1971)]. The legislature has yet to settle on the revised age for both boys and girls. At the present time, however, courts limit the definition of persons in need of supervision to both boys and girls under sixteen. Sidebar 5–1 shows a sample petition to adjudge a respondent's need for supervision.

Importance of Documentation

The importance of making the petition specific and providing buttressing affidavits or depositions, or statements as to the petitioner's source of information, cannot be understated. Without this information, the petition is subject to a motion to dismiss.

In a recent case, Matter of J. [(Family Court, Suffolk County, 1982)] a boy under the age of sixteen years allegedly beat a thirty-one-year-old man with a stick and verbally abused him on several occasions. A PINS petition was brought against the boy by the victim's father. The victim's father had not witnessed the incidents, and the petition, while specific as to facts, was based entirely on information and belief and had no supporting affidavits.

The respondent moved to dismiss the petition based on the arguments that: (1) the father of the victim was not a witness to the incidents and thus was not a proper person to originate the action under Section 733; and (2) the respondent was denied due process of law as required under Section 711 in that the petitioner alleged facts upon information and belief within the petition without attaching a buttressing affidavit of any statement as to the petitioner's source of information.

The court held for the respondent on both points, relying on In re E. [327 N.Y.S. 2d 84 (Family Court, Suffolk County, 1971)]. It held that under either C.P.L.R. (civil procedure law and rules) or C.P.L. (criminal procedure law), a PINS petition based on information and belief is defective without some

Sidebar 5-1. Petition to Adjudge a Respondent in Need of Supervision*

FAMILY COURT OF THE STATE OF NEW YORK,
COUNTY OF [county]

_____ x

In the Matter of
[child]   PETITION

A Person alleged to be a Person   Docket No.
In Need of Supervision,   [assigned judge]

[child],   Respondent.

_____ x

TO THE FAMILY COURT:

The undersigned petitioner respectfully alleges that:

1. Petitioner, [petitioner], resides at [address].

2. Petitioner is a person authorized to institute a proceeding under Article 7 of the Family Court Act by reason of the fact that (s)he is [reason].

3. The respondent above-named is a (fe)male who was born on [calendar date of], 19   .

4. The following are the names and addresses of the parent(s) or other person(s) legally responsible for the care of respondent or with whom respondent is domiciled.

   NAME   RESIDENCE   RELATIONSHIP

   _____   _____   _____

   _____   _____   _____

5. (Upon information and belief,) (R) (r)espondent (does not attend school in accord with the provisions of part one of Article 65 of the Education Law) (and) (is incorrigible, ungovernable or habitually disobedient and beyond the lawful control of parent or other lawful authority) (and) (violates the provisions of Section 221.05 of the Penal Law) in that (s)he [set forth a concise statement of the acts on which the foregoing allegations are based and the time and place they allegedly occurred]:

   _____

   _____

6. Respondent was under sixteen years of age at the time of the foregoing acts and is now under eighteen years of age.

7. Respondent requires supervision or treatment.

8. As to the allegations herein made upon information and belief, the sources of petitioner's information and grounds of belief are (the statements and admissions of respondent). (the statements and depositions of witnesses now on file with this Court). [other].

WHEREFORE, petitioner prays that the respondent be adjudged a person in need of supervision and dealt with in accordance with the provisions of Article 7 of the Family Court Act.

Dated: [calendar date]   _____

Petitioner

West's, McKinney's Forms, Matrimonial and Family Law, 28:05, 437 (1986).

---

showing as to basis of the petitioner's allegations. In the matter of Howe (70 Misc. 2d 144, 332 N.Y. 2d 529), juvenile delinquency proceeding the respondent's motion to dismiss petitions as insufficient was granted when:

1. each petition was sworn to by an individual who had no personal knowledge of the facts contained within;

2. the petitions were not supported by other depositions or affidavits;

3. the petitioner would not be competent to testify in support of his allegations;

4. there were no supporting depositions of persons having personal knowledge of the facts; and

5. although the source of the petitioner's knowledge was identified, there was no indication as to what information was supplied by which of the petitioner's alleged sources.

The notice to dismiss appears in sidebar 5–2. The affidavit in support of motion appears in sidebar 5–3. The court order dismissing petition appears in sidebar 5–4.

Probation Intake

The probation intake procedure allows the probation service to confer with any person filing a petition, the respondent, and other interested persons with the purpose of either adjusting the case of referring it for formal court action.[5]

Sidebar 5-2. Notice to Dismiss Petition

FAMILY COURT OF THE STATE OF NEW YORK
COUNTY OF [county]

_____ x

In the Matter of

[child]

A Person alleged to be a Person
in need of Supervision,

[respondent], Respondent.

NOTICE TO
DISMISS PETITION

Docket No.

SIRS:

PLEASE TAKE NOTICE, that upon the annexed Affidavit of [attorney], sworn to on the [calendar] day of [month], 19 , and upon the Petition and Memorandum of Law, a Motion pursuant to Family Court Act Sections 711, 731, 733, and 751 will be made at Part V of this Court to be held at the Courthouse thereof, located at Veterans Memorial Highway, Hauppauge, New York, on the [calendar] day of [month], 19 at 9:30 o'clock in the forenoon of that day, or as soon thereafter as counsel can be heard, for an Order dismissing the Petition as insufficient and jurisdictionally defective, upon the grounds that (1) a proper person has not originated the within proceeding under Article 7 of the Family Court Act, and (2) the respondent has been denied due process of law in that the petitioner has alleged facts upon information and belief in the Petition without attaching thereto a buttressing Affidavit or any statement as to petitioner's source of information, and for such other and further relief as may be just, proper, and equitable.

PLEASE TAKE FURTHER NOTICE, that pursuant to CPLR 2214 (b) Answering Affidavits, if any, are required to be served upon the undersigned at least five (5) days before the return date of this Motion.

Yours, etc.,

Dated:

_____ , ESQS.

Attorneys for Respondents
[address]
[telephone number]

To: _____ , ESQ.

[county attorney]
Family Court
[address]

Sidebar 5–3. Affidavit in Support of Motion

FAMILY COURT OF THE STATE OF NEW YORK
COUNTY OF [county]

_____ x

In the Matter of

[child]

A Person Alleged to be a Person
in Need of Supervision,

[respondent], Respondent.

STATE OF NEW YORK

AFFIDAVIT IN
SUPPORT OF MOTION

Docket No.

[attorney], ESQ., being duly sworn, deposes and says:

1. I am associated with the law firm of [firm], ESQS., attorneys for the respondent, [respondent], with regard to the above entitled proceeding wherein it is alleged that the respondent, [child], is a person in need of supervision. The Affidavit is respectfully submitted in support of the respondent's Motion to dismiss the Petition as insufficient. A copy of the Notice and Petition, Docket Number [number], which is alleged to be insufficient, is annexed hereto and marked as Exhibit "A."

2. It is respondent's contention that the Petition is insufficient pursuant to Article 7 of the Family Court Act in that a proper person has not originated the within proceeding, and also because the respondent's right to due process of law has been violated since the Petition was not verified by a person having personal knowledge of the facts, and, in fact, is not an alleged injured party or a witness to the alleged incidents, and that there is no supporting Affidavit or Deposition attached to the Petition served upon the respondent which sets forth the basis and source of the petition's information and belief.

3. Submitted simultaneously herewith is a Memorandum of Law on behalf of the respondent and in support of the respondent's Motion to dismiss the Petition which is respectfully requested be considered upon this Motion.

4. This action was commenced by service of a Notice and Peti-

tion, copies of which are annexed hereto and marked as Exhibit "A," and no supporting deposition was served therewith.

5. The respondent appeared with the undersigned on [date], at [time], before the Hon. [judge], Judge of the Family Court, [county] County, Part [part], on the arraignment, at which the respondent denied the allegations stated in the Petition. The trial of this matter was scheduled by Judge [judge], for [date], 19 , Part , at [time].

6. No request for similar relief has been made.

WHEREFORE, your deponent respectfully requests an Order dismissing the Petition in the within proceeding.

Sworn to before me on this [calendar] day of [month], 19 ,

_____

Notary Public

Sidebar 5-4. Court Order Dismissing Petition

FAMILY COURT—STATE OF NEW YORK
SPECIAL TERM, PART , [county]

Present: Hon. [judge] MOTION DATE:

Docket No.

Petitioner's ATTY:

In the Matter of
[child],

A Person Alleged to be a Person Respondent's ATTY:
in Need of Supervision

Upon the following papers numbered 1 to   read on this Motion for an Order dismissing the instant Petition; it is,

ORDERED that this motion is decided as follows:

Respondent moves to dismiss the instant PINS petition upon the grounds the same is jurisdictionally defective due to its being filed by an improper party and due to its being based upon hearsay allegation without supporting deposition.

Respondent's contentions are both correct. See e.g. In re E., 327 N.Y.S. 2d 84; In re Howe, 332 N.Y.S. 2d 529. The within petitioner herein is also not a proper party pursuant to FCA, Sec. 733.

Accordingly, the within petition is dismissed.
So ordered.

ENTER

_____

[Judge of Family Court]

Dated: [date], New York

The power of the probation service to decide whether a case is suitable for adjustment is bound by the rules of the court implementing Section 734.

Right to Counsel

A juvenile has no right to appointed counsel free of charge in a probation intake. See, for example, In re David J. [70 A.D. 2d, 276, 421 N.Y.S. 2d appellate division, 187 (3rd Dept., 1979)]; In re Anthony S. [77 Misc. 2d 187, 341, N.Y.S. 2d 11 (Family Court, Richmond County, 1973)]; and In re Frank H [71 Misc. 2d 1042, 337 N.Y.S 2d 1818 (Family Court, Richmond County, 1972)]. See generally In re Luis R. [92 Misc. 2d 55, 399 N.Y.S. 2d 847 (Family Court, Kings County, 1977)]; and In re Charles C. [83 Misc. 2d 388, 371 N.Y.S. 2d 582 (Family Court, New York County, 1975)]. However, if desired, the respondent, as well as the complainants and potential petitioners, may obtain private counsel and have them present during the preliminary conference.

The respondent's statements at the adjustment conference are accorded confidentiality through the fact-finding phase of the PINS proceeding.[6] However, confidentiality does not extend to the dispositional hearing.[7]

Fact-Finding and Dispositional Hearings

As in all articles of the Family Court Act, there is a fact-finding and dispositional phase to a court proceeding under Article 7. It should be noted that the fact-finding and dispositional hearings have slightly different purposes in child protective proceedings under Article 10 than they do in supervision proceedings. See D. Besharov, _Practice Commentary to Family Court Act Section 716_ (McKinney 1983). In supervision proceedings the purpose of the fact-finding hearing is to determine whether the respondent did the act or acts alleged in the petition, and the purpose of the dispositional hearing is to determine whether the respondent requires supervision treatment or confinement. However, under Article 10, the focus of the fact-finding hearing is on the actions of the parent as they affect the child. Specifically, the adjudication of child abuse or neglect occurs at the fact-finding hearing. A dispositional hearing is then held to determine what order of disposition should be made.[8]

Fact Finding

The fact-finding hearing is held to determine whether the respondent did the acts, alleged in the petition, that would show the respondent to be in need of supervision. The attorney prosecuting the case is a public official such as a corporate counsel in the City of New York and the county attorney's office in the counties of New York.[9]

Evidence at Fact-Finding Hearings. Evidence at a fact-finding hearing must be competent, material, and relevant. The difference between these three forms of evidence is subtle. *Competent* evidence is evidence that goes to the very nature of what is to be proven; *material* evidence is evidence that is important and more or less necessary. *Relevant* evidence is that having any tendency to make the existence of any fact that is of consequence to the determination of the action more or less probable than it would be without the evidence.

The quantum or standard of proof in a fact-finding hearing is proof beyond a reasonable doubt.[10] An uncorroborated confession made out of court by the respondent is not sufficient proof. Rather, additional evidence must be provided to prove the allegations in the petition.[11] A sample determination on fact-finding form appears in sidebar 5–5.

Sidebar 5–5. Determination Made upon Fact-Finding Hearing on Need for Supervision*

At a Term of the Family Court of the State of New York, held in and for the County of [county], New York, on

Present: Hon. [judge], Judge

In the Matter of	DETERMINATION UPON
[child],	FACT-FINDING HEARING
A Person Alleged to be a Person in Need of Supervision,	Docket No. [assigned judge]
[respondent], Respondent.	

The petition of [respondent], under Article 7 of the Family Court Act, sworn to on [date] having been filed in this Court, alleging that the above-named respondent is a person in need of supervision; and

Notice having been duly given to respondent and [parent] or [custodian] pursuant to section 741 of the Family Court Act; and

Respondent (having appeared by counsel) (and   of respondent (not) having appeared) before this Court to answer the petition; and

[Strike out if inapplicable.] (Respondent having denied voluntarily, intelligently and knowingly admitted in open Court that (s)he [actions];)

[Strike out if inapplicable.] (Respondent having denied the allegations of the petition, and the matter having duly come on for a fact-finding hearing before this Court,) and the Court, after hearing the proof and testimony offered in relation to the case having found beyond a reasonable doubt that the respondent did the following act(s): [actions]

Now therefore, upon the findings made in the fact-finding and upon all papers and proceedings filed and had herein, it is

ORDERED AND ADJUDGED that the above-named respondent, while under sixteen years of age (does not attend school in accord with the provisions of part one of Article 65 of the Education Law) (and) (is incorrigible, ungovernable, or habitually disobedient and beyond the lawful control of parent or other lawful authority) (and) (violated the provisions of section 221.05 of the Penal Law); and it is

ORDERED

Dated: Enter,

_____
[Judge of Family Court]

*Based on *West's McKinney's Forms,* Matrimonial and Family Law, 28.06, 1986, p. 441.

Dispositional Hearing

Upon completion of the fact-finding hearing, the dispositional hearing may commence immediately. This, however, does not usually happen, and there are often adjournments between the fact-finding and dispositional phases.[12] The purpose of the dispositional hearing is to determine whether the respondent requires supervision in the form of treatment or confinement.

Evidence in Dispositional Hearings. Unlike the fact-finding hearing, evidence in the dispositional hearing is required to be only material and relevant. Also, the required quantum of proof in a dispositional hearing is a preponderance of the evidence rather than evidence beyond a reasonable doubt. [13]

Dispositional Alternatives

The court has four dispositional alternatives available to it upon the adjudication or appearance:

1. discharging a respondent with warning;
2. suspending judgment;
3. continuing the proceeding and placing the respondent; or
4. putting the respondent on probation. [14]

Discharging a Respondent without Warning

Because the family court is concerned with the welfare of children and not punishment, the court in an appropriate case may discharge warning. This warning provision would be appropriate if the court decided that the child was not in need of any treatment.

Suspended Judgment

The maximum duration or condition of a suspended judgment is one year, unless the court finds at the conclusion of the time period that exceptional circumstances require an additional period of one year. The court may order as a condition of suspended judgment restitution or services for public good. [15] See appendix 5A.

Continuing the Proceeding and Placing the Respondent

The court may place the child in his/her own home or in the custody of a suitable relative or other suitable private person or a commissioner of social services or the Division for Youth. Each of these placements is for up to eighteen months, with court review permitting one-year extensions. [16]

Probation

Like that of the suspended judgment, the maximum period of probation cannot exceed one year. However, if at the conclusion of one year exceptional circumstances require an additional period of probation, the court may continue the probation. Also as with suspended judgment, the court may order restitution or services for the public good. [17] See appendix 5B.

Sidebar 5–6 is a sample order of fact-finding and disposition.

Sidebar 5–6. Order of Fact-Finding and Disposition on Need for Supervision (FCA 750, 754 to 757)

At a term of the Family Court of the State of New York, held in and for the County of [county], New York, on [date].

Present: Hon. [judge], Judge

In the Matter of	ORDER OF FACT-FINDING
[child],	AND DISPOSITION
A Person Alleged to be a Person in Need of Supervision	Docket No.
[respondent], Respondent	[assigned judge]

The petition of [respondent] under Article 7 of the Family Court Act pursuant to section 741 of the Family Court Act; and

Respondent (having appeared by counsel) before this Court to answer said petition; and

[Strike out if inapplicable.] (Respondent having denied the allegations of the petition and the matter having duly come on for a fact-finding hearing before this Court; and)

The Court, after hearing the proof and testimony offered in relation to the case, finds beyond a reasonable doubt that the respondent did the following act(s): [actions]

;and

The matter having thereafter duly come on for a dispositional hearing before the Court, and the Court, after having made the examination and inquiry into the facts and circumstances of the case and into the surroundings, conditions and capacities of the persons involved and having made any reports available to counsel in accordance with section 750 of the Family Court Act, finds upon a preponderance of the evidence that respondent requires supervision or treatment; and the Court having fully considered the matter of a particular disposition pursuant to section 754 of the Family Court Act, finds that the respondent requires [disposition], for the following reasons: [reasons]

NOW, upon the findings made in the fact-finding and dispositional hearings herein and upon all papers and proceedings filed and had herein, it is hereby

ADJUDGED that the above-named respondent is a person in need of supervision who, while under sixteen years of age (does not attend school in accord with the provisions of part one of Article 65 of the Education Law) (and) (is incorrigible, ungovernable or habitually disobedient and beyond the lawful control of parent or other lawful authority) (and) (violates the provisions of section 221.05 of the Penal Law) and on the further ground that respondent requires supervision or treatment; and it is therefore

[Omit any inapplicable order.] (ORDERED, that respondent be and hereby is discharged with a warning.)

(ORDERED, that judgment herein be and the same hereby is suspended for a period of [ ] months upon the following terms and conditions: [See Appendix 5A].)

(ORDERED, that this proceeding be and the same hereby is continued and respondent be and hereby is placed for a period of [ ] in the custody of [custodian], subject to the further orders of this Court.)

ORDERED, that this proceeding be and the same hereby is continued and respondent be and hereby is placed for a period of [ ] in (the custody of the Commissioner of Social Services subject to the further orders of this Court) (the custody of the Commissioner of Social Services, for placement with [ ], subject to the further orders of this Court). In the event that the Commissioner of Social Services is unable to so place the child, (the Commissioner (shall) (need not) apply to the Court for an order to stay, modify, set aside or vacate such directive pursuant to Section 762 of the Family Court Act.) (the Commissioner (shall) (need not) return respondent to this Court for a new dispositional hearing and order.)

(ORDERED, that this proceeding be and the same hereby is continued and respondent be and hereby is placed for a period of [ ] in the custody of the New York State Division for Youth, subject to the further orders of this Court.)

(ORDERED, that respondent be and hereby is put on probation under the supervision of the Probation Department of the County of [county] for a period of [ ] upon the following terms and conditions of probation: [see Appendix 5B].) (and it is further

(ORDERED, that

.)

Dated: , 19   Enter,

_____

[Judge of Family Court]

Detention

If the child is ten years of age or over, he/she may be detained in a certified detention facility. However, the child must be brought before a family court judge on the next court date for a hearing.[18]

Substitution of Petition

On its own motion and at any time in the proceedings, the court can substitute a neglect petition under Article 10 for a petition to determine whether a person is in need of supervision.[19]

Appendix 5A
Permissible Terms and Conditons
of a Suspended Judgment
(22 N.Y.C.R.R. 205.66 [Subd. A])

An order suspending judgment pursuant to Section 754 of the Family Court Act shall be reasonably related to the adjudicated acts or omissions of the respondent and shall contain at least one of the following terms and conditions directing the respondent to:

1. attend school regularly and obey all rules and regulations of the school;
2. obey all reasonable commands of the parent or other person legally responsible for the respondent's care;
3. avoid injurious or vicious activities;
4. abstain from associating with named individual;
5. abstain from visiting designated places;
6. abstain from the use of alcoholic beverages, hallucinogenic drugs, habit-forming drugs not lawfully prescribed for the respondent's use, or any other harmful or dangerous substance;
7. cooperate with a mental health or other appropriate community facility to which the respondent is referred;
8. make restitution or require services for public good;
9. restore property taken from the petitioner, complainant, or victim, or replace property taken from the petitioner, complainant, or victim, the cost of such replacement not to exceed $1,500;
10. repair damage to, or defacement of, the property of the petitioner, complainant, or victim, the cost of said repair not to exceed $1,500;
11. abstain from disruptive behavior in the home and in the community;

12. cooperate in accepting medical or psychiatric diagnosis and treatment, alcoholism, or drug abuse treatment or counseling services; and permit an agency delivering that service to furnish the court with information concerning the diagnosis, treatment, or counseling;

13. with the consent of the Division of Youth, spend a specified portion of the probation period, not exceeding one year, in a facility provided by the Division for Youth, pursuant to Section 502 of the Executive Law;

14. comply with such other reasonable terms and conditions as the court shall determine to be necessary or appropriate to ameliorate the conduct which gave rise to the filing of the petition.

Appendix 5B
Permissible Terms and Conditions of Probation
(22 N.Y.C.R.R. 205.66 [Subd. B])

An order placing the respondent on probation in accordance with Section 757 of the Family Court Act shall contain at least one of the following terms and conditions in addition to any of the terms and conditions set forth in Subdivision A of Section 205.66 (see appendix 5A above), directing the respondent to:

1. meet with the assigned probation officer when directed to do so by that officer;

2. permit the assigned probation officer to visit the respondent at home or at school;

3. permit the assigned probation officer to obtain information from any person or agency from whom the respondent is receiving or was directed to receive diagnosis, treatment, or counseling;

4. permit the assigned probation officer to obtain information from the respondent's school;

5. cooperate with the assigned probation officer in seeking to obtain and in accepting employment and employment counseling services;

6. submit records and reports of earnings to the assigned probation officer when requested to do so by that officer;

7. obtain permission from the assigned probation officer for any absence from the county or residence in excess of two weeks;

8. do or refrain from doing any other specified act of omission or commission that, in the opinion of the court, is necessary and appropriate to implement or facilitate the order placing the respondent on probation.

Notes

1. Family Court Act, Section 713.
2. Family Court Act, Section 717.
3. Family Court Act, Section 733.
4. Family Court Act, Section 732.
5. Family Court Act, Section 734.
6. Family Court Act, Section 734 A, 735.
7. Family Court Act, Section 750.
8. Family Court Act, Section 712.
9. Family Court Act, Section 1045.
10. It is improper to distinguish among the different standards of proof. The *beyond-a-reasonable-doubt* standard is the strictest and requires that the evidence prove the acts alleged in the petition to a moral certitude. An intermediate standard applicable in child protective proceedings and termination-of-parental-rights proceedings (see chapter 21) is the *clear-and-convincing* standard. This requires that measure or degree of proof that will produce in the judge or jury a firm belief in the allegations sought to be established. Finally, the *preponderance-of-the-evidence* standard, the least strict of the three, requires the evidence to be of such weight as to produce a reasonable belief in the truth of the facts asserted. See, for example, Jarrett v. Madifari [67 A.D. 2d 396, 415 N.Y.S. 2d 644 (Appellate Division, 1st Dept., 1979)].
11. Family Court Act, Section 744.
12. Family Court Act, Section 746.
13. Family Court Act, Section 745.
14. Family Court Act, Section 754.
15. Family Court Act, Section 755, 758 A.
16. Family Court Act, Section 756.
16. Family Court Act, Section 757.
17. Family Court Act, Section 720.
18. Family Court Act, Section 716.
19. Family Court Act, Section 1045.

6
Juvenile Delinquency

Another way that a child comes into foster care is by court order declaring the child a juvenile delinquent. A *juvenile delinquent* is a person "over seven and less than sixteen years of age who, having committed an act that would constitute a crime if committed by an adult, (a) is not criminally responsible for such conduct by reason of infancy, or (b) is the defendant in an action ordered removed from a Criminal Court to the Family Court pursuant to Article 725 of the Criminal Procedure Law."[1]

Jurisdiction and Venue

The family court is granted exclusive original jurisdiction over any juvenile delinquency proceeding. However, as Section 114 of the Family Court Act notes, the act's provisions in no way impair the jurisdiction of the supreme court granted in the New York State Constitution, Article 6, Section 7 (a): "general jurisdiction in law and equity." The family court thus actually has jurisdiction concurrent with the supreme court over delinquency matters. Nonetheless, the supreme court so seldom exercises delinquency jurisdiction that the family court actually is the only court to hear and determine Article 3 cases.

The age of the person at the time the delinquent act was allegedly committed is controlling in determining jurisdiction.[2] The burden of alleging and proving the age of the respondent is upon the [presentment agency]. See Matter of Kalvin [99 Misc. 2d 996, 417 N.Y.S. 2d 826 (Family Court, Onondaga County, 1979)].

It should be noted that even if the respondent's age when the act was committed would grant the family court jurisdiction, the court may nonetheless dismiss the petition if the respondent's age at the time of the hearing precludes the dispositional alternatives allowed under Article 3. See Matter of Thomas [94 Misc. 2d 154, 404 N.Y.S. 2d 220 (Family Court, Bronx County, 1978)], and Matter of Coleman [117 Misc. 2d 1061, 459 N.Y.S. 2d 711 (Family Court, Erie County, 1983)].

The venue in juvenile delinquency proceedings is the county where the act or acts referred to in the petition allegedly occurred. Upon motion from the presentment agency or the respondent, the court may order, for good cause shown, that the proceedings be transferred to another county. In cases outside New York City, after entering a finding pursuant to Section 345.1 and before the dispositional hearing, the court may order in its discretion, and for good cause shown, that the case be transferred to the county in which the respondent resides.[3]

Application of Criminal Law to Juvenile Delinquency Proceedings

The provisions of the Criminal Procedure Law (CPL) do not apply to juvenile delinquency proceedings unless the Family Court Act specifically prescribes as such.[4] However, a court may consider traditional interpretations of appropriate provisions of the Criminal Procedure Law, to the extent such interpretations may assist the Court in interpreting similar provisions of Article 3.[5]

Provisions of CPL Expressly Applied to
Juvenile Delinquency Proceedings

The provisions of double jeopardy found in Article 40 of the Criminal Procedure Law apply in juvenile delinquency proceedings[6]: "The Double Jeopardy Clause protects against a second prosecution for the same offense after a conviction." See North Carolina v. Pearce [395 U.S. 711, 717]. A double jeopardy issue may be raised at any time during the appellate process." See In re James B. [92 A.D. 2d 937, 460 N.Y.S. 2d 361, citing People v. Michael, 48 N.Y. 2d 1,
6–7, 420 N.Y.S. 2d 371, 394 N.E. 2d 1134].

The provisions of Articles 25, 35, and 45 of Section 30.05 of the Penal Law are applicable to juvenile delinquency proceedings.[7]

Right to Counsel. Under Article 3, a child cannot be questioned unless both the child and the child's parent or person legally responsible for his/her care has been advised of the child's right to remain silent and the child's right to be represented by counsel. The child may choose his/her own counsel or, if indigent, may have a law guardian appointed by the court.[8]

Speedy Trial

After a petition has been filed, the respondent is entitled to a speedy fact-finding hearing.[9] The determination of whether there has been an unreasonable delay is determined on a case-by-case basis.[10]

Courts have looked to four factors in determining if the respondent's right to a speedy trial has been violated:

1. the length of the delay;
2. the reason for the delay;
3. the degree of actual prejudice to the juvenile; and
4. the seriousness of the offense. (In re Anthony P. [104 Misc. 2d 1024, 430 N.Y.S. 2d 479, citing, People v. Taranovich, 37 N.Y. 2d 442, 373 N.Y.S. 2d 79, 335 N.E. 2d 303]; People v. Staley [41 N.Y. 2d 789, 396 N.Y.S. 2d 339, 364 N.E. 2d 1111]; People v. Bryant [65 A.D. 2d 333, 411 N.Y.S. 2d 932]).

A lengthy and unjustified delay in instituting proceedings may result in dismissal even though no actual prejudice to the defendant is shown [Id at 481).

Suppression of Evidence

A respondent in a juvenile delinquency proceeding may make a motion to suppress evidence in accordance with Sections 710.20 and 710.60 of the CPL.[11]

Detention

No child detained under Article 3 may be kept in any prison, jail, lockup, or other place used for adults convicted of a crime or under arrest and charged for the crime without the approval of the Division for Youth in the case of each child and without a statement of its reasons.[12] Further, the detention of any child under ten years of age in a secure detention facility is prohibited.[13] Children under ten years of age may be detained in a nonsecure detention facility.

A detention facility that receives a child under Subdivision 4 of Section 305.2 (a child taken into custody by a police officer without a warrant) must immediately notify the child's parent or other person responsible for his/her case, or if such legally responsible person is unavailable the person with whom the child resides, that he or she has been placed in detention.[14]

Taking a Child under Sixteen into Custody

A private person can take a child into custody in cases where he/she could arrest an adult under Section 140.30 of the Criminal Procedure Law.[15] Similarly, a police officer or peace officer can take a child into custody without a warrant in cases where an adult could likewise be arrested under the CPL.[16]

Fingerprinting

Under Section 306.1, after the arrest of a child alleged to be a juvenile delinquent or the filing of a delinquency petition involving a child who has not been arrested, the arresting officer, other appropriate police officer, or agency must take fingerprints of the child if: (1) the child is eleven years of age or older and the crime that is the subject of the arrest or that is charged in the petition constitutes a Class C felony; or (2) the child is thirteen years of age or older and the crime that is the subject of the arrest or that is charged in the petition constitutes a Class C felony.[17]

Whenever fingerprints are required to be taken, the photographs and palmprints of the arrested child may also be taken. The taking of fingerprints, palmprints, photographs, and related information concerning the child and the facts and circumstances of the acts charged in the juvenile delinquency proceeding must be in accordance with standards established by the commissioner of the Division of Criminal Justice Services and by applicable provisions of Article 3.[18]

The officer or agency will then forward the fingerprints and other materials to the Division of Criminal Justice. A copy of the materials is not retained by the officer or agency. Copies of photographs and palmprints taken pursuant to Section 306.1, as described above, are kept confidential and in exclusive possession of such law enforcement agency, apart from the files of adults.

Retention and Destruction of Fingerprints of Persons
Alleged to be Juvenile Delinquents

The specific requirements regarding retention and destruction of fingerprints of persons alleged to be juvenile delinquents are found in Section 354.1. Basically, this section directs that the fingerprints, palmprints, or photographs taken pursuant to the guidelines discussed above must be destroyed unless (1) the respondent is eleven or twelve years old and was found to have committed an act that would constitute a Class A or B felony; or (2) the respondent is older than twelve and was found to have committed the felony.

It should be noted, however, that even in cases where the respondent is entitled to have records that are maintained by the Division of Criminal Justice Services and records maintained by the family court destroyed, the same privilege does not extend to records maintained by the Probation Department. See *Matter of Dennis B.* [104 Misc. 2d 166, 427 N.Y.S. 2d 716 (Family Court, Kings County, 1980)].

Family Court Appearance Tickets and Procedures

Family court appearance tickets and procedures are discussed in Sections 307.1 and 307.2 of Article 3. A *family court appearance ticket* is defined as a written notice issued and subscribed by a peace officer or a police officer, a probation service director or his designee, or the administrator responsible for operating a detention facility or his designee, directing a child and his parent, or other person legally responsible for his care, to appear without security at the designated probation service on a specified return date in connection with the child's alleged commission of the crime or crimes specified on such appearance ticket. Court rules prescribed by the chief administrator of the courts delineate the form of the appearance ticket.

The return date after the issuance of a family court appearance ticket varies, depending upon the crime alleged to have been committed. If the crime alleged to have been committed by the child is a designated felony as defined by Paragraph 8 of Section 301.2, then the return date must be no later than seventy-two hours, excluding Saturdays, Sundays, and public holidays, after the issuance of the family court appearance ticket. However, if the crime alleged to have been committed by the child is not a designated felony, the return date must be no later than fourteen days after the issuance of the appearance ticket. A copy of the family court appearance ticket must be forwarded by the issuing person or agency to the complainant respondent's parent and appropriate probation service within twenty-four hours after its issuance.

If a child fails to appear on the return date specified on the family court appearance ticket, the probation service is then given a choice. It may either refer the matter immediately to the appropriate presentment agency, or at its own discretion, it may attempt to secure the attendance of the child. The form that these efforts must take is not clearly defined in the statute. In any event, if the probation service decides to attempt to secure the attendance of the child, such efforts shall not extend beyond seven days subsequent to the return date, after which time the probation service must refer the matter to the appropriate presentment agency. Upon referral, the presentment agency is given the discretion to take whatever action it deems appropriate.

If a complainant fails to appear on the return date specified on the appearance ticket, the probation service may attempt to secure the complainant's voluntary attendance. As with the case of a child who fails to appear, the efforts to secure the voluntary attendance of a complainant are not to extend seven days subsequent to the return date, after which time the probation service must refer the matter to the appropriate presentment agency. Upon referral, the presentment agency may take whatever action it deems appropriate, including the issuance of a subpoena or the filing of a petition pursuant to Section 311.1.

Rules of Court Authorizing Release before Filing a Petition

If a police officer or peace officer exercises his/her authority to place a child in a detention facility, Section 307.3 authorizes the agency responsible for operating the detention facility to release the child in custody before the filing of a petition to either the child's parent, or person legally responsible for the child's care, or if neither is available, to a person with whom the child resides when the events which cause the child to be taken into custody do not appear to involve allegations that the child committed the delinquent act. Such release is also authorized when the events occasioning the child's being taken into custody do involve allegations that the child committed a delinquent act so long as there are no special circumstances which require the detention.

A basic guideline as to what these special circumstances might consist of can be found in the Uniform Rules for the Family Court, Section 205.21, which provide four sets of circumstances that can be deemed to require the detention of the child:

1. There is a substantial probability that the child will not appear or be produced at the appropriate probation service at a specified time or place; or

2. there is a serious risk that before the Petition is filed the child may commit an act which, if committed by an adult, would constitute a crime; or

3. the alleged conduct of the child involved the use or threatened use of violence; or

4. there is a reason to believe that a proceeding to determine whether the child is a juvenile delinquent or juvenile offender is currently pending.

If the child is released under Section 307.3, the child and the person legally responsible for the child's care must be issued a family court appearance ticket. However, if the agency chooses to detain the child, then the child must be brought before the appropriate family court within seventy-two hours or the next date that the court is in session, whichever is sooner. Thereafter, pursuant to the provisions of Section 307.4, a hearing must be held within seventy-two hours on the appropriateness of the detention. Under Section 307.4 the judge at the hearing must then order the release of the child to the custody of the parent or other person legally responsible for his/her care if:

1. the court does not appear to have jurisdiction and the matter is not to be transferred to a Criminal Court; or

2. the events occasioning the taking into custody do not appear to involve an allegation that the child committed the delinquent act; or

3. the events occasioning the taking into custody appear to involve acts which constitute juvenile delinquency, unless the Court finds and states facts and reasons which would support a detention order pursuant to Sec. 320.5.

Preliminary Adjustments

The requirements for preliminary adjustment are set out in Section 308.1, Article 3, and the Family Court Rules, Section 205.22. Initially, Section 308.1

provides that Rules of Court will determine the circumstances under which the probation service is granted the discretion to confer with any person seeking to file a juvenile delinquency petition, the potential respondent, and other interested persons concerning the advisability of requesting that the petition be filed. There are three limiting factors upon the probation services' ability to adjust the case.

First, under Section 308.1, Subparagraph 3, the probation service is prohibited from adjusting a case in which a child allegedly committed a designated felony act unless the probation services receive a written approval of a court.

Second, probation services are prohibited from adjusting a case in which the child allegedly committed a delinquent act that would be considered one of the following crimes: reckless endangerment in the second degree, manslaughter in the second degree, rape in the third degree, sodomy in the third degree, sexual abuse in the first degree, coercion in the first degree, burglary in the third degree, arson in the third degree, robbery in the third degree, criminal possession of a weapon in the third degree, criminal possession of a weapon in the second degree, criminal possession of a weapon in the first degree, if the child has previously had one or more adjustments of the case in which the child allegedly committed an act that would be a crime included above, unless the probation service has its records from the Court and from the appropriate presentment agency.

Any person who wishes to have access to the presentment agency for the purpose of requesting that a petition be filed under Article 3 of the Family Court Act cannot be prevented from doing so by the probation service.

Specific points with respect to preliminary adjustment, phase C, Section 308.1, note that adjustment is a voluntary and confidential process. However, the scope of confidentiality is limited to the fact-finding hearing. Statements made by respondents are admissible in the probable cause hearing and dispositional hearing.

Third, Family Court Section 205.22 lists the following circumstances as relevant to probation services' consideration of whether or not a case is appropriate for the adjustment process:

> In order to determine whether the case is suitable for the adjustment process, the probation service shall consider the following circumstances, among others:
>
> (1) the age of the potential respondent; and
> (2) whether the conduct of the potential respondent allegedly involved:
>> (i) an act or acts causing or threatening to cause death, substantial pain or serious physical injury to another;
>> (ii) the use or knowing possession of a dangerous instrument or deadly weapon;
>> (iii) the use or threatened use of violence to compel a person to engage in sexual intercourse, deviant sexual intercourse or sexual contact;

(iv) the use or threatened use of violence to obtain property;

(v) the use or threatened use of deadly physical force with the intent to restrain the liberty of another;

(vi) the intentional starting of a fire or the causing of an explosion which resulted in damage to a building;

(vii) a serious risk to the welfare and safety of the community;

(viii) an act which seriously endangered the safety of the potential respondent or another person;

(3) whether there is a substantial likelihood that a potential respondent will not appear at scheduled conferences with the probation service or with an agency to which he or she may be referred;

(4) whether there is a substantial likelihood that the potential respondent will not participate in or cooperate with the adjustment process;

(5) whether there is a substantial likelihood that in order to adjust the case successfully, the potential respondent would require services that could not be administered effectively in less than four months;

(6) whether there is a substantial likelihood that the potential respondent will, during the adjustment process:

(i) commit an act which if committed by an adult would be a crime; or

(ii) engage in conduct that endangers the physical or emotional health of the potential respondent or a member of the potential respondent's family or household; or

(iii) harass or menace the complainant, victim or person seeking to have a juvenile delinquency petition filed or a member of that person's family or household, where demonstrated by prior conduct or threats;

(7) whether there is pending another proceeding to determine whether the potential respondent is a person in need;

(8) whether there have been prior adjustments or adjournments in contemplation of dismissal in other juvenile delinquency proceedings;

(9) whether there has been a prior adjudication of the potential respondent as a juvenile delinquency or juvenile offender;

(10) whether there is a substantial likelihood that the adjustment process would not be successful unless the potential respondent is temporarily removed from his or her home and that such removal could not be accomplished without involving the court process;

(11) whether a proceeding has been or will be instituted against another person for acting jointly with the potential respondent.

(d) At the first appearance at a conference by each of the persons listed in subdivision (a) hereof, the probation service shall inform such person concerning the function and limitations of, and the alternatives to, the adjustment process, and that

(1) he or she has the right to participate in the adjustment process;

(2) the probation service is not authorized to and cannot compel any person to appear at any conference, produce any papers or visit any place;

(3) the person seeking to have a juvenile delinquency petition filed is entitled to have access to the appropriate presentment agency at any time for the purpose of requesting that a petition be filed under Article 3 of the Family Court Act;

(4) the adjustment process may continue for a period of two months and may be extended for an additional two months upon written application to the court and approval thereof;

(5) statements made to the probation service are subject to the confidentiality provisions contained in sections 308.1(6) and 308.1(7) of the Family Court Act; and

(6) if the adjustment process is commenced but is not successfully concluded, the persons participating therein may be notified orally or in writing of the fact that the case will be referred to the appropriate presentment agency; oral notification will be confirmed in writing;

(e) If the adjustment process is not commenced:

(1) the record of the probation service shall contain a statement of the grounds therefore; and

(2) the probation service shall give written notice to the persons listed in subdivision (a) hereof who have appeared that:

(i) the adjustment process will not be commenced;

(ii) the case will be referred to the appropriate presentment agency.

Preliminary adjustment, Section 308.1, provides that adjustment is a voluntary and confidential process. However, the scope of confidentiality is limited to the fact-finding hearing. As a result, information obtained in the adjustment process can be seen as otherwise admissible at any of the other hearings to occur later, for example, the probate cause hearing or dispositional hearing.

Origination of a Juvenile Delinquency Proceeding

The provisions concerning the origination of a juvenile delinquency proceeding are described in Section 310.1. The process is begun by the filing of a petition. Only a presentment agency may originate a juvenile delinquency proceeding, and if the appropriate presentment agency does not originate a proceeding within thirty days of receipt of notice from a probation service pursuant to Subdivision 10 of Section 308.1, the presentment agency is required to notify the complainant of that fact in writing. The question of which agencies are appropriate as the presentment agency is dealt with in Sections 254 and 254 A of the Family Court Act.

Generally, the appropriate presentment agency is corporation counsel. However, in cases of designated felony acts, corporation counsel can enter into an agreement whereby the district attorney will prosecute the case. The respondent, as already discussed, is entitled to a speedy trial. The provisions regarding speedy trial are specific to aspects of the overall process. For example, under Section 320.2, the general time period allowed from the time of filing until the initial appearance is ten days. However, from initial appearance to fact-finding, the general time period allotted under Section 340.1 is sixty days.

The Petition

Under Section 311.1, a petition must charge at least one crime and may in addition charge in separate counts, one or more other crimes provided that all such crimes are joinable under Section 311.6. Section 311.6 addresses the question of joinder severance and consolidation. Specifically, the petition must contain the following:

1. the name of the family court in which it is filed;
2. the title of the action;
3. the fact that the respondent is a person under sixteen years of age at the time of the alleged act or acts;
4. a separate accusation or count addressed to each crime charge if there be more than one;
5. the precise crime or crimes charged;
6. a statement in each count that the crime charged was committed in a designated county;
7. a statement in each count that the crime charged therein was committed on or about a designated date or during a designated period of time;
8. a plain and concise factual statement in each count, which without allegations of an evidentiary nature asserts facts supporting every element of the crime charged and the respondent's position thereof, with sufficient precision to clearly apprise the respondent of the conduct which is the subject of the accusation;
9. the name or names, if known, of other persons who are charged as co-respondents in the family court or as adults in a criminal court proceeding, in the commission of the crime or crimes charged;
10. a statement that the respondent requires supervision, treatment, or confinement; and
11. the signature of the appropriate presentment attorney.

The sufficiency of the petition is discussed in Section 311.2, which is straightforward. A petition may thereafter be dismissed, either because it is defective or in the furtherance of justice; see Sections 315.1 and 315.2. The court may also render, except in the case of a designated felony act and prior to the entering of a finding under Section 351.2, an order adjourning a matter in contemplation of dismissal. Such an adjournment cannot be made without the consent of the respondent.

The Initial Appearance and Probable Cause Hearing

The initial appearance, as might be inferred from its name, deals with the preliminary matters involved in juvenile delinquency proceeding. At the initial appearance the respondent is advised of his/her rights, the issue of a law guardian is dealt with, admissions or denials of allegations within the petition are heard by the court, and if necessary, a probable cause hearing is held. The court may also refer the case for adjustment to the probation service under Section 320.6 upon the consent of the victim or complainant and the respondent. The consent of the presentment agency is also required in the case of a designated felony petition.

Discovery in the Juvenile Delinquency Proceeding

Discovery in a juvenile delinquency proceeding is dealt with in Part 3 of Article 3 and includes Sections 330.1 through 335.2. One important note is that available to the respondent is a separate suppression hearing, because the juvenile delinquency proceeding as opposed to, for example, Article 10 proceedings, is much more akin to a criminal action rather than a civil action.

The Fact-Finding Hearing

Like other proceedings in the family court, a juvenile delinquency proceeding is bifurcated into a fact-finding hearing and dispositional hearing. The fact-finding hearing is discussed in Part 4 of Article 3 and Sections 340.1 through 346.1.

There are specific time limitations with respect to the fact-finding hearing. These are dealt with in Section 340.1. The general rule for having a fact-finding hearing in a nondetention case is that it must not commence more than sixty days after the conclusion of the initial appearance. If however, the respondent is in detention and the highest count in the petition alleges the commission of a class A, B, or C felony, then the fact-finding hearing must commence not more than fourteen days after the conclusion of the initial appearance. If the respondent is in detention and the highest count in the petition is less than a Class C felony, then the fact-finding hearing must commence no more than three days after the conclusion of the initial appearance. Provisions for adjournment are discussed in Subdivision 3 of Section 340.1. Additionally, under Section 340.2, general provisions are made to provide for continuity of the presiding judge, following either the commencement of the fact-finding hearing under Section 340.21 or the acceptance of an admission from a respondent by the judge under Section 321.3. Of course, there are certain circumstances under which a case may be transferred, and these are dealt with in Section 340.2.[19]

Exclusion of General Public

As in Article 10 proceedings, there is a provision in Article 3, Section 341.1, that leaves the decision of whether to exclude the general public from a fact-finding hearing to the discretion of the presiding judge. Also, as in Article 10, the actual result of this rule has been that "the public has routinely been excluded."[20]

Evidence in the Fact-Finding Hearing

The forms in evidence and the quantum of proof required in a fact-finding hearing in Article 3 are discussed in Section 342.2. Only competent, material, and relevant evidence may be admitted to a fact-finding hearing. The quantum of proof is proof beyond a reasonable doubt. This should be compared with the quantum of proof required in other sections of the Family Court Act. For example, in Article 10 proceedings, the applicable quantum of proof that must be shown before a finding of neglect or abuse will be made against a respondent's natural parent is a preponderance of the evidence.

Finally, proof beyond a reasonable doubt that a respondent did the act or acts specified within a petition will be presumed upon an order of removal pursuant to Sections 220.10, 310.85, and 330.25 of the Criminal Procedure Law. In other words, if a criminal finding of guilt is made or if the defendant pleads guilty in the criminal court and the matter is subsequently moved to family court, the criminal court finding will be deemed to establish the quantum of proof required in the family court. Specific rules of evidence are discussed in Sections 343.1 through 344.3.

Orders on Fact-Finding

Under Section 345.1, where crimes are established, the court must enter an order that specifies the count or counts upon which it is based and that refers to the section or sections of the Penal Law or other law that would make such action criminal if it was committed by an adult. The order must also state if the respondent is found to have committed a designated felony act. If the allegations of the petition are not established beyond a reasonable doubt, then the court must enter an order dismissing the petition or the counts therein.

The Dispositional Hearing

Part 5 of Article 3 deals with the procedures and practices involved in the dispositional hearing. It is structured much the same way as Part 4, beginning with the timing of a dispositional hearing in Section 350.1, moving on to the evidence admissible and required quantum of proof in Section 350.3, and to findings and possible orders of disposition.

Time of Dispositional Hearing

Like that of the fact-finding hearing, the time of the dispositional hearing varies, depending upon whether the respondent has been detained. If the respondent has been detained and has not been found to have committed a designated felony act, a dispositional hearing must begin not more than ten days after the entry of a fact-finding order. In all other cases, a dispositional hearing must begin not more than fifty days after the entry of a fact-finding order. Also, as in fact-finding proceedings, there are situations in which the court can adjourn a dispositional hearing; see Section 350.1, Paragraph 3. Finally, under Section 350.2, where the proceeding is commenced following an order of removal from criminal court, the date of filing in family court is deemed to be the equivalent of the entry of the fact-finding order for the purposes of Section 350.1. An appearance is then scheduled by the clerk of the court, within seven days from when the order of removal was filed. At that appearance the court must schedule a dispositional hearing in accordance with the timing provisions of Section 350.1.

Evidence in the Dispositional Hearing

The evidentiary and quantum of proof requirements in dispositional hearings are relaxed in comparison with those in fact-finding hearings. Unlike the fact-finding hearing, which requires that evidence be material, relevant, and competent, in a dispositional hearing the evidence is required only to be material and relevant. This, therefore, makes possible the admission of hearsay.

The required quantum of proof is by a preponderance of the evidence rather than beyond a reasonable doubt. The basic premise behind the differing standards between the fact-finding hearing and the dispositional hearing is that whereas a fact-finding hearing focuses on whether or not the respondent has committed a crime, in a dispositional hearing the purpose is to meet the needs of the respondent. For this reason, it is deemed imperative that the court hear as much evidence as possible regarding the needs of the respondent and that the court not be limited in its search. Finally, the presentment agency is also required to appear at the dispositional hearing.

Probation, Investigation, and Diagnostic Assessment Prior to the Dispositional Hearing

Prior to the dispositional hearing and after the determination that the respondent has committed a designated felony act, Section 351.1 mandates the Judge to order a probation investigation and diagnostic assessment of the respondent. If the respondent committed a felony, the court is mandated to order a probation investigation, but is given a choice as to whether to order a diagnostic assessment. Finally, if the respondent has committed any other delinquent act, the court is given discretion as to whether to order a probation investigation or a diagnostic assessement.

Findings and Orders upon the Conclusion of the Dispositional Hearing

At the end of the dispositional hearing, if the court determines that the respondent requires either supervision treatment or confinement, one of the following dispositions must be ordered, pursuant to Section 352.2:

1. conditional discharge of the respondent, in accordance with Section 353.1;
2. placement of the respondent on probation, in accordance with Section 353.2;
3. continuation of the proceeding and placement of the respondent, in accordance with Section 353.3;
4. placement of the respondent, in accordance with Section 353.4; or
5. continuation of the proceeding and placement of the respondent under a restrictive placement, in accordance with Section 353.5.

In determining an appropriate order, the court is to balance the needs of the community against the best interests of the respondent. In a case where the respondent has committed a designated felony act, the court is restricted to setting a disposition in accordance with Section 353.5. In other cases, the standard the court must apply in setting the appropriate disposition is to order the least restrictive available alternative that is consistent with the needs of both the community and the respondent. Provisions for extension of placement are discussed in Section 355.3.

Additionally, a motion may be made pursuant to Section 355.1 that, upon showing a substantial change of circumstances, will allow for a new fact-finding or dispositional hearing or allow for any order issued under Article 3 to be set aside, modified, terminated, or vacated. If a child has been placed under Section 353.3, then upon motion of the commissioner of social services or the Division of Youth with whom the respondent has been placed, such order can be set aside, modified, vacated, or terminated upon a showing of substantial change of circumstance. In any event, the issuance of an order of disposition is deemed to expire not later than the expiration date of the order. Finally, upon conclusion of the dispositional hearing, if the court determines that the respondent does not require supervision, treatment, or confinement, the petition must be dismissed.

Postdispositional Procedures Securing Testimony and Records and General Provisions

The topics of postdispositional procedures and securing testimony of records are dealt with in Parts 6 and 7 under Article 3. Part 6 begins with a discussion of jurisdiction of supervision upon the respondent placed on probation and provides that a respondent placed on probation remains under legal jurisdiction of the court pending the expiration or termination of the probation. The probation service supervises such probation.

Grants to Any Respondent to Appeal from Any Order of Disposition under Article 3

Presentment agencies are granted limited ability to appeal in the following situations:

1. from an order dismissing petition prior to commencement of fact-finding;
2. from an order of disposition, if the appeal is made on the grounds that the order of disposition was invalid as a matter of law; or
3. from an order suppressing evidence that was entered before the commencement of a fact-finding hearing under Section 330.2, so long as the presentment agency files statements concerning the suppression of evidence, as defined under Section 330.2, Subdivision 9.

Testimony and Records and General Provisions

Part 7 of Article 3 specifically pertains to methods of securing the attendance of witnesses and certain testimony. Part 7 also discusses the provisions of an order following the termination of the delinquency action in favor of a respondent. Finally, Sections 375.2 and 375.3 deal with a motion to seal records after a finding—other than a finding that the respondent committed a designated felony act—has been made, and the expungement of court records.

Part 8 mostly relates to the confidential aspect of delinquency proceedings and in Section 380.1 sets out the premise that no adjudication under Article 3 can be denominated a conviction and that no person adjudicated a juvenile delinquent may be denominated a criminal by reason of such adjudication. Specific issues involving the use of records in other courts, police records, reports, and the potential for consolidation of records within a city of a population of one million or more are dealt with in Sections 381.2 through 385.2.

Notes

1. Family Court Act, Section 301.2(1)
2. Family Court Act, Section 302.1(1)(2)
3. Family Court Act, Section 302.3
4. Family Court Act, Section 303.1(1)
5. Family Court Act, Section 303.1(2)
6. Family Court Act, Section 303.2
7. Family Court Act, Section 303.3
8. Family Court Act, Section 305.2, 320.3
9. Family Court Act, Section 310.2
10. ". . . Article 30 of the Criminal Procedure Law does not pertain to juvenile proceedings. Whether there has been an unreasonable delay in a particular case should be determined upon the facts therein and whether actual prejudice has, in fact, occurred." In re Walters [91 Misc. 2d 728, 398 N.Y.S. 2d 806 (Family Court, Suffolk County, 1977)].
11. Family Court Act, Section 330.2
12. Family Court Act, Section 304.1(2)
13. Family Court Act, Section 304.1(3)
14. Family Court Act, Section 304.1(4)
15. Family Court Act, Section 305.1(1)
16. Family Court Act, Section 305.2(2)
17. Family Court Act, Section 306.1(1)
18. Family Court Act, Section 306.1(2)(3)
19. Family Court Act, Section 340.2
20. Merril Sobie, commentary to McKinney's Section 341.1, 1983.

7
Neglect and Abuse

Many foster children come into foster care via court order pursuant to Article 10 of the Family Court Act, based on a finding of abuse or neglect against the natural parents.

Purpose of Child Protection Laws

Article 10 of the Family Court Act, entitled "Child Protective Proceedings," was enacted to establish procedures to protect children from injury or mistreatment by their parent or guardian. The purpose of Article 10 is to safeguard the physical, mental, and emotional well-being of children.

In our society it is well established that parental rights are accorded the greatest respect and that the state must weigh the delicate balance between the parental right to care for a child and the state's legitimate interest in appropriate intervention. Section 1011 provides that Article 10 is designed to provide a guideline for determining when the state, through the family court, may intervene against the wishes of a parent on behalf of a child so that the child's needs are properly met.

Duties of Child Protective Agencies

Section 1026 of the Family Court Act mandates that an appropriate person designated by the court or a child protective agency, when informed that there has been an emergency removal of a child from his/her home without a court order, shall make every reasonable effort to communicate immediately with the child's parent or custodian, informing the child's parent or custodian that the child has been removed, where the child is presently residing, and when court action may be taken. In cases involving neglect, said appropriate person or child protective agency may return the child to the parent if there is no imminent risk to the child's health.

In abuse cases, however, the appropriate person or child protective agency cannot return the child without a court order. If the child is not returned to the parent, the child protective agency must forthwith file a petition in family court alleging either abuse and neglect or abandonment.

Person Legally Responsible for Child's Care

A person legally responsible for a child's care appears to be limited to a parent, relative, guardian, or one standing *in loco parentis* and does not include entities; see In re Children [76 Misc. 2d 937, 352 N.Y.S. 2d 570]. Presumably pursuant to Article 10 of the Family Court Act, a child neglect or abuse proceeding may not be brought against a not-for-profit corporation, such as a state school or the Department of Health, or an authorized agency. See In re D. [70 Misc. 2953, 335 N.Y.S. 2d 638 (1972)].

Definitions and Indicators

Section 1012 defines the terms *abused child* and *neglected child*.

Abused Child

Basically, an *abused child* is a child less than eighteen years of age whose parent or other person legally responsible for his/her care inflicts or allows to be inflicted upon such child physical injury that creates a substantial risk of death, or serious or protracted disfigurement, or protracted impairment of physical or emotional health, or protracted loss or impairment of the function of any bodily organ; or that creates or allows to be created the above; or commits or allows to be committed a sex offense against such child. A single incident can constitute abuse; see Matter of Colleen [538 N.Y.S. 2d 361 (1989)].

Sexual Abuse.* The following are physical indicators of sexual abuse:

1. difficulty in walking or sitting;
2. torn, stained, or bloody underclothing;
3. pain or itching in genital areas;
4. bruises or bleeding in external genital, vaginal, or anal areas;
5. venereal disease.

Some of the behavioral indicators of sexual abuse are:

1. unwillingness to change clothes or participate in physical education class;
2. withdrawal;

3. bizarre, sophisticated, or unusual sexual behavioral knowledge;
4. poor peer relationships;
5. delinquency or running away from home.

Emotional Maltreatment.* The following may be physical indicators of emotional maltreatment:

1. speech disorder;
2. lack of physical development;
3. failure to thrive.

Some of the behavioral indicators of emotional maltreatment may be:

1. a habit disorder, such as sucking, biting, or rocking;
2. a conduct disorder, such as antisocial or destructive behavior;
3. a neurotic trait, such as a sleep disorder, or inhibition at play;
4. developmental deficiencies, both mental or emotional;
5. attempted suicide.

Physical Abuse. Some of the behavioral indicators for physical abuse may be:

1. wariness of adult contacts;
2. behavioral extremes, such as aggressiveness or withdrawal;
3. fear of parents;
4. fear of going home.

Neglected Child

Basically, a *neglected child* is defined as a child less than eighteen years of age whose physical, mental, or emotional condition has been impaired or is in imminent danger of becoming impaired as a result of the failure of his/her parent or other person legally responsible for his/her care to exercise a minimum degree of care; or by failure to supply the child with adequate food, clothing, shelter, or education, or medical, dental, optometrical, or surgical care, though financially able to do so; or by failure to provide the child with proper supervision or guardianship by unreasonably inflicting or allowing to be inflicted harm, or substantial risk of harm, including the infliction of excessive corporal punishment; or by misusing a drug or drugs; or by misusing alcoholic beverages to the extent that he/she loses self-control of his/her actions.

Physical Neglect.* Some of the behavioral indicators of physical neglect are:

1. begging or stealing food;
2. extended stays at school, such as early arrival and late departure;

3. constant fatigue;
4. alcohol or drug abuse;
5. delinquency.

Unreasonable Corporal Punishment. The following have been held to constitute unreasonable corporal punishment.

1. Twenty-six marks on the back of a seven-year-old boy with emotional difficulties, which marks were visible three days after the infliction of the marks. See In re C. [91 Misc. 2d 677, 398 N.Y.S. 2d 511].

2. An eleven-year-old boy, who was required to hold his ankles and keep his knees straight for variable lengths of time, which caused him to scream. In re C. [91 Misc. 2d 677, 398 N.Y.S. 2d 511].

3. A ten-year-old boy was forced to stay in a contorted position, which caused him to scream and to vomit. In re/supra.

---

*These physical and behavioral indicators of child abuse and neglect were adapted from the Nassau County Department of Social Services brochure entitled "When One Child Is Hurt . . . A Message on Child Abuse."

Jurisdiction

The family court has exclusive original jurisdiction over a proceeding where the child is alleged to have been abused or neglected. The family court also has concurrent jurisdiction and does not lose jurisdiction under Article 10 or the Family Court Act, notwithstanding the fact that a criminal court may also be exercising jurisdiction over the facts alleged in the petition or complaint. Section 1014 of the Family Court Act permits the family court to transfer, upon a hearing, any proceeding originating under Article 10 of the Family Court Act to an appropriate criminal court for criminal processing. Likewise, any criminal complaint charging facts amounting to abuse and neglect under Article 10 may be transferred by the criminal court in which the complaint was made, to the family court in the county in which the criminal court is located. Section 1014 provides that the family court and the criminal court may have concurrent jurisdiction and proceedings.

Under Section 1014 of the Family Court Act, the family court may grant the respondent or potential respondent testimonial immunity in any subsequent criminal court proceeding.

Person Who May Originate Proceedings

Pursuant to Section 1032 of the Family Court Act, only a child protective agency or a person appointed by the court may originate a proceeding alleging abuse and neglect.

The purpose of permitting only a child protective agency or persons designated by the court to originate abuse and neglect proceedings is to prevent malicious petitions from being filed and, further, to protect against intrusion into the family life by other persons who may disapprove of the life-style of the parent. See Humphry v. Humphry [103 Misc. 2d 175, 425 N.Y.S 2d 759]. In short, the legislature has mandated that child neglect and abuse proceedings may be brought only by a child protective agency, which may file such a petition wherever in its discretion it believes that said petition is warranted. All other persons and entities may file a petition for child abuse and neglect only if given permission by the family court; see Weber v. Stonybrook Hospital [60 N.Y. 2d 208, 469 N.Y.S. 2d 63].

Access to the Court for the Purpose of Filing a Petition

Any person seeking to file a petition alleging abuse, neglect, or abandonment, pursuant to Article 10 of the Family Court Act, at the court's direction, shall have access to the court for the purpose of making an *ex parte* application. The court has the discretion either to take testimony to determine whether sufficient evidence exists to warrant the filing of a petition, or to direct the appropriate child protective agency to conduct an investigation to determine whether sufficient evidence exists to initiate a petition under Article 10 of the Family Court Act.

The Neglect or Abuse Petition

A proceeding under Article 10 is originated by the filing of a petition in which facts sufficient to establish that a child is abused (see sidebar 7–1) or neglected (see sidebar 7–2) are alleged. Allegations of abuse and neglect may be contained in the same petition. If more than one child is alleged to be neglected or abused, only one petition need be drafted.

The court, on its own motion, may at any time substitute any petition for neglect for a petition alleging abuse where the facts are not sufficient to make a finding of abuse but would be sufficient to make a finding of neglect.

Even if the child is in the care and custody of a local social service agency, a child protective agency may still bring a petition for abuse and neglect if the petition alleges sufficient facts to establish that the return of the child to the care and custody of the parent would place the child in imminent danger of becoming an abused and neglected child.

Preliminary Orders after Filing of Petition

Section 1027 of the Family Court Act provides that in any case involving abuse or in any case where the child had been removed without court order, the fam-

Sidebar 7–1. Abuse Petition*
(FCA 1031)

FAMILY COURT OF THE STATE OF NEW YORK
COUNTY OF [county]

In the Matter of	PETITION
[child or children]	(Child Abuse Case)
(A) Child(ren) under the Age of	
Eighteen Years Alleged to be	
Abused by	Docket No.
[respondent(s)], Respondent(s).	[assigned judge]

To the Family Court:

The undersigned petitioner respectfully alleges that:

1. Petitioner [name] is (a duly authorized agency having its office and place of business at [address]) (a person directed by the court to originate this proceeding residing at [address]).
2. The child(ren) who (is) (are) the subject(s) of this proceeding (is) (are):

NAME	SEX	DATE OF BIRTH
_____	_____	_____
_____	_____	_____
_____	_____	_____

3. Said child(ren) reside(s) with [name] at [address], New York.
4. (Upon information and belief(s)) (t)(T)he father and mother of said child(ren) and their respective residences are:

NAMES OF CHILD(REN)	NAMES OF PARENTS		ADDRESS
_____	Father	_____	_____
_____	Mother	_____	_____
_____	Father	_____	_____
_____	Mother	_____	_____
_____	Father	_____	_____
_____	Mother	_____	_____

5. (Upon information and belief(s)) (s)(S)aid child(ren) (is) (are) a(n)

abused child(ren) in that: [Specify grounds of child abuse under Section 1012 of the Family Court Act.]

6. By reason of the facts alleged in paragraph (5) said child(ren) (is) (are) also (a) neglected child(ren).

7. (Upon information and belief) [name] (and) said child(ren), (is) (are) the person(s) who (is) (are) responsible for the abuse (and neglect) of said child(ren).

8. The (District Attorney of [county] County) (Corporation Counsel of the City of New York) is a party hereto pursuant to section 254(b) of the Family Court Act.

_____

[petitioner]

VERIFICATION

STATE OF NEW YORK

COUNTY OF [county]

[name] being duly sworn, deposes and says:

That (s)he is [ ] and is acquainted with the facts and cir-cumstances of the above-entitled proceeding; that (s)he has read the foregoing petition and knows the contents thereof; that the same is true to (his) (her) own knowledge except as to those matters therein stated to be alleged upon information and belief, and that as to those matters (s)he believes it to be true.

_____

Agency Title

Sworn to before me this day of [month], 19 .

_____

(Deputy) Clerk of the Court
Notary Public

_____

West's McKinney's Forms, vol. 10A, pp. 515–32.

Sidebar 7–2. Neglect Petition*
(FCA 1028)

FAMILY COURT OF THE STATE OF NEW YORK
COUNTY OF [county]

In the Matter of	PETITION
[child or children]	(Neglect)
(A) Child(ren) under the Age of Eighteen Years	
Alleged to be Neglected by	Docket No.
[respondent(s)], Respondent(s).	[assigned judge]

To the Family Court:

The undersigned petitioner respectfully alleges that:

1. Petitioner [name] is (a duly authorized agency having its office and place of business at [address]) (a person directed by the court to originate this proceeding residing at [address]).
2. The child(ren) who (is) (are) the subject(s) of this proceeding (is) (are):

NAME	SEX	DATE OF BIRTH
_____	_____	_____
_____	_____	_____
_____	_____	_____

3. Said child(ren) reside(s) with [name] at [address], New York.
4. (Upon information and belief) (t)(T)he father and mother of said child(ren) and their respective residence addresses are:

NAMES OF CHILD(REN)	NAMES OF PARENTS	ADDRESS
_____	Father _____	_____
_____	Mother _____	_____
_____	Father _____	_____
_____	Mother _____	_____
_____	Father _____	_____
_____	Mother _____	_____

The person(s) legally responsible for the care of said child(ren) (is) (are) [name] who reside(s) at [address], New York.

5.   (Upon information and belief) (s)(S)aid child(ren) is (are) neglected in that: [Specify grounds of neglect under Section 1012 of the Family Court Act]

6.   (Upon information and belief) (t)(T)he   of the said child(ren), (is) (are) the person(s) who (is) (are) responsible for the neglect of said child(ren).

WHEREFORE, petitioner prays that an order be made determining the said [child(ren)] to be (a) neglected child(ren) and otherwise dealing with said child(ren) in accordance with the provisions of Article 10 of the Family Court Act.

Dated: [petitioner]
                                         _____

STATE OF NEW YORK

COUNTY OF [county]

[name] being duly sworn, deposes and says:
     That (s)he is [ ] and is acquainted with the facts and circumstances of the above-entitled proceeding; that (s)he has read the foregoing petition and knows the contents thereof; that the same is true to (his) (her) own knowledge except as to those matters therein stated to be alleged upon information and belief, and that as to those matters (s)he believes it to be true.

                                         _____
                                         Agency Title
Sworn to before me this day of [month], 19 .

_____
(Deputy) Clerk of the Court ·
Notary Public

_____
*West's McKinney's Forms, vol. 10A, pp. 515–32.

ily court must hold a hearing as soon as practicable after the filing of a petition, pursuant to Article 10 of the Family Court Act, to determine whether the child's interest requires protection pending a final order of disposition. Upon such hearing, if the court finds that removal of the child from his/her home is necessary to avoid imminent risks to the child's life or health, the court shall order the removal of the child or the continuation of the removal of the child and remand the child to the commissioner of social services or place him/her in the custody of any suitable person other than the respondent. The 1988 amendment to Section 1027 requires the court to consider whether continuation of the child in the home would be contrary to the best interests of the child and whether reasonable efforts have been made to eliminate the need for removal of the child and whether such efforts are in fact necessary. The amendment authorizes the court to order administrative assistance to the child and family, pursuant to Section 1015 A or Section 1022 C.

While Section 1027 B authorizes the court to place a child with a suitable person, where a question arises as to the suitability of said person, the court must conduct at least a "minimal inquiry" before deciding to place the child with that person. See Matter of "Baby Girl" L. [133 A.D. 2d 458, 519 N.Y.S. 2d 673, 674 (Appellate Division, 2nd Dept., 1987)].

Application to Return a Child Temporarily Removed

A 1028 hearing is a hearing pursuant to Section 1028 of the Family Court Act, whereby upon the application of the parent or other person legally responsible for the care of a child temporarily removed or upon the application of the law guardian requesting an order returning the child, the court must hold a hearing to determine whether the child should be returned to the parent or guardian (see sidebar 7–3). Except for good cause shown, the hearing must be held within three court days of the application and may not be adjourned. Upon the completion of the hearing, the court must return the child to the parent or guardian, unless the court finds that the return of the child would present an imminent risk to the child's life or health.

A 1988 amendment to Section 1028 places a burden upon the local social service agency to use reasonable efforts to prevent or eliminate the need to remove the child from the child's home. If the court finds that appropriate and reasonable efforts were not made by the local social services agency to prevent or eliminate the removal or the child from his/her home, the court must order the child protective agency to provide or arrange for the provision of appropriate services or assistance to the child and the child's family. Further, the 1988 amendment to Section 1028 provides that the court may issue a temporary order of protection, pursuant to Section 1029 of Article 10, as an alternative to or in conjunction with any other order or disposition authorized under Section 1028.

Sidebar 7-3. Application for Return of Child
Temporarily Removed*
(FCA 1028)

FAMILY COURT OF THE STATE OF NEW YORK
COUNTY OF [county]

——————————————————— x

In the Matter of	APPLICATION FOR RETURN
[child or children]	OF CHILD TEMPORARILY
(A) Child(ren) under the Age of	REMOVED FROM HOME
Eighteen Years Alleged to be	
(Abused) (and) (Neglected) by	Docket No.
[respondent(s)], Respondent(s).	[assigned judge]

——————————————————— x

To The Family Court

The undersigned respectfully show(s) that:

1. [Respondent(s)], respondent(s) in the above-entitled proceeding (is) (are) the (parent(s)) (person(s) legally responsible for the care) of the above-named child(ren).

2. Said child(ren) (was) (were) temporarily removed from the place where the (child)ren resided under the provisions of Article 10 of the Family Court Act under Order of this Court dated   , 19 .

   [Omit inapplicable allegation.]

3. No petition has been filed under Section 1031 of the Family Court Act and the return of said child(ren) would not present an imminent risk to said child(ren)'s life or health.

4. A petition has been filed under Section 1031 of the Family Court Act and there is not a substantial probability that said child(ren) will be found to be (an) abused or neglected child(ren) under Article 10 of the Family Court Act, or that the final order of disposition will be an order of placement under Section 1055 of that Act, and temporary removal, pending entry of a final order of disposition, is not necessary to avoid an imminent risk to the child(ren)'s life or health.

5. No previous application has been made to any court or judge for the relief requested herein (except)

WHEREFORE, respondent(s) pray(s) that an order be granted returning said child(ren) to   .

Dated: , 19   .

_____

_____

Respondent(s)

_____

*West's McKinney's Forms, vol. 10a. pp. 515–32.

The new amendment to Section 1028 also permits the law guardian as well as the parent to make an application for an order to return a child who has been temporarily removed from his/her parents.

Temporary Order of Protection

Section 1029, which was amended in 1988, permits the Family Court judge, upon the application of any person who may originate a proceeding under Article 10 and for good cause shown, to issue a temporary order of protection, which may contain any of the provisions authorized pursuant to Section 1056. Under Section 1056 a person may be required to:

1. Stay away from the home, a spouse, or the child.
2. Permit a parent to visit with the child at stated periods.
3. Abstain from offensive conduct against the child or the other parent.
4. Give proper attention to the care of the home.
5. Refrain from acts of commission or omission that tend to make the home not a proper place for a child.
6. Provide, either directly or by means of medical and health insurance, for expenses incurred for medical care and treatment arising from the incident or incidents forming the basis for the issuance of the order.

A temporary order of protection is not a finding of wrongdoing, and the court may issue or extend a temporary order of protection *ex parte* or on notice simultaneously with the issuance of warrant directing that the parent be arrested and brought before the court pursuant to Section 1037. Violation of a valid order of protection can result in incarceration of up to six months. See Family Court Act, Section 1072 B.

Order of Visitation by a Respondent

Section 1030 of the Family Court Act is new, effective November 1, 1988, and provides that a respondent (parent) shall have the right to reasonable and regularly scheduled visitation with a child who is in temporary custody of the social services agency, unless such visitation is limited by an order of the family court.

This section presumes that visitation by a parent with the child is recognized and the burden is upon the agency to limit visitation only by court order. Section 1030 B of the Family Court Act provides that any parent who is not permitted to see or visit with the child may apply, upon notice, to the judge of the family court for visitation. Upon said application for visitation, the family court must grant reasonable and regularly scheduled visitation unless the court finds that the child's life or health would be in danger thereby; the court may order visitation under the supervision of an employee of a local services department upon a finding that such supervised visitation is in the best interest of the child.

Any order made by a judge of the family court permitting visitation may be modified by the court for good cause shown upon application by any party or by the law guardian, upon notice to all the other parties.

Power to Order Investigations

In any proceeding under Article 10, a family court judge may order a child protective service to conduct an investigation concerning the welfare of a child and report its finding to the court in order to determine whether a proceeding under this article should be initiated. Further, where there is probable cause to believe that an abused or neglected child may be found on any premises, on order under this section the court may authorize the child protective worker, accompanied by a police officer, to enter the premises to determine whether such a child is present.

The court may order such an investigation where, pursuant to Section 1033, a person seeks to file a petition at the court's direction.

The court may wish to avail itself of this type of investigation where the court believes that additional information is needed prior to conducting any fact-finding or dispositional hearing.

The court may also wish to avail itself of the services of a protective service investigator to determine whether an abused or neglected child is on any premises during a different type of proceeding, such as PINS or a juvenile delinquency proceeding.

Issuance of a Summons

Upon the filing of a petition alleging abuse under Article 10, the court shall cause a copy of the petition and summons to be issued forthwith, clearly marked on the face thereof "child abuse case," requiring the parent or other

Sidebar 7-4. Summons in a Child Abuse Case
(FCA 1035)

FAMILY COURT OF THE STATE OF NEW YORK
COUNTY OF [county]

In the Matter of	SUMMONS
[child or children]	(Child Abuse Case)
(A) Child(ren) under Eighteen Years of Age	
Alleged to be	Docket No.
Abused by	[assigned judge]
[respondent(s)]	

In the Name of the People of the State of New York to the Above-Named Respondent(s), (address) (A) (P)(p)etition(s) under Article 10 of the Family Court Act having been filed with this Court, and annexed hereto

You and Each of You are Hereby Summoned to appear before the Court on   , 19 , at   o'clock in the   noon of that day to answer the petition and to be dealt with in accordance with Article 10 of the Family Court Act.

On your failure to appear as herein indicated, a warrant may be issued for your arrest.

Dated: _____
                                               Clerk of the Court

Notice: This Proceeding Could Lead to a Proceeding Under the Social Services Law for the Commitment of Guardianship and Custody of the Above-Mentioned Child and Your Rights with Respect to this Child May be Terminated in Such Proceeding Under Such Law.

_____

West's McKinney's Forms, vol. 10A, pp. 515–32.

person legally responsible for the child's care to appear at the court within three days to answer the petition (see sidebar 7-4). The court shall also, unless dispensed with for good cause shown, require said person thus summoned to produce the child at the time and place named. In such a proceeding to determine abuse, the summons shall contain a statement clearly marked on the face thereof that the preceeding could lead to a proceeding under Section 384 B of the Social Services Law for the commitment of guardianship and custody of the child and that the rights of the parent with respect to said child may be terminated in such a proceeding.

Upon the filing of a petition in which neglect only is alleged, if the child has been temporarily removed, the court may cause a copy of the petition and a summons to be issued requiring the parent to appear at the court to answer the petition within three court days. Otherwise, the summons and petition will be issued requiring the parent to appear at the court to answer the petition within seven court days. The court may also require the person thus summoned to produce a child at the time and place named.

Where the summons is issued to a respondent who is not the child's parent, service of the summons and petition shall also be ordered on both the child's parents. When the respondent is only one of the parents, service of the summons and petition shall also be ordered on the child's other parent. This section permits relatives of the child to intervene for custody of the child, but only if the parent consents. If the parent does not consent to permit the relative to have intervenor status, then the extended family member may be requested to be evaluated as a resource, and of course the desires of the parent would be one of the many criteria determining whether to place the child with a relative. See In re Ricky P. [135 Misc. 2d 28, 513 N.Y.S. 2d 606 (Family Court, New York County, 1987)].

Section 1035 of the Family Court Act permits the child's nonrespondent parent to intervene and be heard on the limited question of temporary and permanent custody. The nonrespondent parent has the right to participate in all arguments and hearings during the fact-finding stage insofar as they affect temporary custody of the child. The nonrespondent parent has the right to participate in all phases of the dispositional proceedings. See In re Holmes [134 Misc. 2d 278, 510 N.Y. 2d 819 (Family Court, Kings County, 1986)].

Service of a Summons and Petition

In cases involving abuse, the summons and petition shall be served within two court days after their issuance. If the summons and petition cannot be served within two court days, then that fact shall be reported to the court with the reasons thereof within three court days after their issuance and the court shall thereafter issue a warrant. The court shall also, unless dispensed with for good cause shown, direct that the child be brought before the court.

Service of a summons and petition shall be made by delivery of a true copy thereof to the person summoned at least twenty-four hours before the time stated therein for appearance.

If, after reasonable effort, personal service is not made, the court may at any stage in a proceeding make an order providing for a substituted service in the matter provided for in civil process in courts of record. The court may, pursuant to Section 308 of the Civil Practice Law and Rules, issue substituted service either by mail, by publication, or by any other combination of recognized substituted service.

Issuance of Warrant and Reports to Court

The judge of the family court may issue a warrant (see sidebar 7–5) directing the parent to be brought before the court when a petition is filed with the court under Article 10 in six main situations:

1. when it appears that the summons cannot be served;
2. when the summoned person has refused to obey the summons;
3. when the parent is likely to leave the jurisdiction;
4. when the summons, in the court's opinion, would be ineffectual;
5. when the safety of the child is endangered;
6. when the safety of a parent, foster parent, or temporary custodian is endangered.

Records Involving Abuse and Neglect

Section 1038 of the Family Court Act provides that each hospital or public or private agency, having custody of any records, photographs, or other evidence relating to any abuse or neglect of a child, upon the subpoena of the court, or the corporation counsel, or county attorney, or district attorney, or counsel for the child, or counsel of one of the parties to the proceeding, shall be required to send such records, photographs, or other evidence to the court for use in any proceeding relating to abuse or neglect under Article 10. The section further provides that the court shall establish procedures for the receipt and safeguarding of such records.

It should be noted that the attorney who subpoenas the records does not receive them; rather, the records are required to go to the family court for safeguarding. In effect, this is a pretrial discovery tool, but when the attorneys for the parties actually get to see the records depends on the individual judge. Some judges permit attorneys to review the records and photographs prior to the fact-finding hearing, while other judges permit the attorneys to review the documents on the day of the fact-finding hearing. The better practice is for the judge to permit all the attorneys in the proceeding to have prior access to the documents so that the attorneys can be fully prepared at the time of the fact-finding hearing. Some judges permit the photocopying of the records, with the attorneys permitted to retain copies in order to be properly prepared for the hearing and to save court time.

The best way for attorneys representing respondents to ascertain what records are available is to review the foster-care agency's records. If the foster-

Sidebar 7-5. Warrant of Arrest in
Child Abuse Case*
(FCA 1037)

FAMILY COURT OF THE STATE OF NEW YORK
COUNTY OF [county]

In the Matter of	WARRANT OF ARREST
[child or children],	(Child Abuse Case)
(A) Child(ren) under Eighteen	
Years of Age Alleged to be	Docket No. [ ]
Abused by [respondent(s),]	[assigned judge]

In the Name of the People of the State of New York to Any Police Officer in the State of New York: A petition under Article 10 of the Family Court Act having been filed in this Court, a copy of which is annexed hereto, and it appearing that one of the grounds for issuance of a warrant as specified in the Family Court Act exists,

YOUR ARE THEREFORE COMMANDED forthwith to arrest [respondent] and bring said person(s) before this Court to be dealt with according to law.

Dated: _____

_____
_____
Family Court Judge

Bail in the sum of [amount] dollars is ordered.

_____
Family Court Judge

NOTICE: THIS PROCEEDING COULD LEAD TO A PROCEEDING UNDER THE SOCIAL SERVICES LAW FOR THE COMMITMENT OF GUARDIANSHIP AND CUSTODY OF THE ABOVE—MENTIONED CHILD AND YOUR RIGHTS WITH RESPECT TO THIS CHILD MAY BE TERMINATED IN SUCH PROCEEDING UNDER SUCH LAW.

_____
*West's McKinney's Forms, vol. 10A. pp. 515-32.

care agency will not permit the attorney to review its records prior to the hearing, then the attorney representing the respondent should obtain a court order to do so. Most judges permit this type of discovery.

In child abuse and neglect cases, pretrial discovery by examination before trial is not favored for at least two reasons. One, the examinations before trial of a child of tender years may not be appropriate and may be very frightening to the child; two, examinations before trial have a tendency to delay the actual hearings involved. Of course, the courts will decide questions of pretrial discovery on a case-by-case basis.

Discovery, Upon Court Order

Paragraph 1038 A of the Family Court Act is new, having been enacted and made effective in 1987. It provides that upon motion of a petitioner, the court may order a respondent to provide nontestimonial evidence only if the court finds probable cause that the evidence is reasonably related to establishing the allegations in a petition filed pursuant to Article 10 of the Family Court Act. Such order may include, but is not limited to, provision for the taking of samples of blood, urine, hair, or other material from the respondent's body in a manner not involving an unreasonable intrusion or risk of serious physical injury to the respondent.

Adjournment in Contemplation of Dismissal

Section 1039 of the Family Court Act provides that prior to or upon a fact-finding hearing involving neglect or abuse, the court may, upon motion by the petitioner with the consent of the respondent and the child's attorney or law guardian or upon its own motion and with the consent of the petitioner, the respondent, and the child's attorney or law guardian, order that the proceeding be adjourned in contemplation of dismissal. The provision goes on to state that under no circumstances can the court order any party to consent to an order under this section.

In many cases involving neglect or abuse, the attorney for the state may believe that the state has a weak case against the respondent parent and may offer the respondent parent a "deal." Instead of having a fact-finding hearing to determine whether abuse or neglect occurred, the entire proceeding is adjourned in contemplation of dismissal.

Section 1039 of the Family Court Act defines *an adjournment in contemplation of dismissal* as an adjournment of the proceeding for a period not to exceed one year with a view to ultimate dismissal of the petition in furtherance of justice. Such order of an adjournment in contemplation of dismissal (more commonly known as an ACD or ACOD) may include terms and conditions agreeable to the parties and to the court, provided that such terms and conditions shall include a requirement that that child and the respondent be under the supervision of a child protective agency during the adjournment period. Such agency shall report to the court in such manner and at such times as the court may direct.

An adjournment in contemplation of dismissal in a neglect proceeding is not a determination on the merits and is not the same as a finding of parental neglect, but actually leaves the question of neglect unanswered. See In re Marie B. [62 N.Y. 2d 352, 477 N.Y.S. 2d 87 (Court of Appeals, 1984)].

Further, the family court may not grant an adjournment in contemplation of dismissal over the objections of the law guardian of the child because such adjournment may not be made without consent of the petitioner, the respondent, and the child's attorney or law guardian. See In re Gary B [101 A.D. 2d 1026, 476 N.Y.S. 2d 695 (1984)].

Required Findings Concerning Notice

No fact-finding hearing concerning abuse or neglect may commence unless the court enters a finding pursuant to Section 1041:

1. That the parent or other person legally responsible for the child's care is present at the hearing and has been served with a copy of the petition; or
2. If the parent or other person legally responsible for the care of the child is not present, that every reasonable effort has been made to effect service under Section 1036 or 1037.

Basically, this section insures that a fact-finding hearing should not commence in the absence of a parent unless diligent efforts were made to locate and serve the parent with a copy of the charges, that is, the petition.

If the parent is served by substituted service and does not appear at the fact-finding hearing, the court will proceed without the parent, and an inquest is held; that is, the petitioner must present evidence of the abuse or neglect by a preponderance of the credible evidence.

Effect of Absence of Parent or Other Person Responsible for Care

If the parent is not present at the fact-finding or dispositional hearing, the court may proceed to hear a petition under this article only if the child is represented by counsel, a law guardian, or a guardian *ad litem*. If the parent or other person legally responsible for the child's care thereafter moves the court that a resulting disposition be vacated and asks for rehearing, the court shall grant the motion on an affidavit showing such relationship or responsibility, unless the court finds that the parent or other person willfully refused to appear at the hearing, in which case the court may deny the motion.

In the case of In re Yem [54 A.D. 2d 673, 388 N.Y.S. 2d 7 (Appellate Division, 1st Dept., 1976)], the Appellate Division reversed the judge of the family court and held that the mother's application to set aside her default should not have been denied unless and until the family court ascertained whether the mother's nonappearance was inadvertent or willful.

In the case of In re Baer [125 Misc. 2d 563, 480 N.Y.S. 2d 178 (Family Court, Suffolk County, 1984)], Judge Hurley held that the mother's default in appearing did not entitle her to a finding of neglect, but simply permitted the court to proceed in her absence and reach a determination based upon the facts presented.

Hearings Not Open to the Public

Section 1043 of the Family Court Act provides that the general public may be excluded from any hearing under this article and that only such persons and the representatives or authorized agencies admitted thereto as have an interest in the case.

The Fact-Finding Hearing

A fact-finding hearing is held to determine whether the child is an abused or neglected child, as defined by Section 1044, Article 10, of the Family Court Act (see sidebar 7–6). The actual adjudication of a child as an abused or neglected child occurs after the fact-finding hearing. If there is a finding of abuse or neglect against the respondent, then the court will hold a dispositional hearing to determine what order of disposition should be made. At the fact-finding hearing the state or one of the state's agents is the petitioner and is represented by corporation counsel, county attorney, or other public attorney. The respondents, usually the parents, are represented either by a law guardian or by assigned counsel, and if the parents are indigent, the attorney is provided free of charge.

The fact-finding hearing is held before a judge of the family court without a jury. The rules of evidence apply, and the respondent must be given a full opportunity to examine and cross-examine witnesses. The voluntary agency that may have the actual, physical custody of the child usually does not participate in the fact-finding phase of the abuse or neglect proceeding and is usually not represented by an attorney. In the City of New York Child Welfare Agency, personnel and caseworkers normally testify as to the abuse or neglect, along with any other eyewitnesses to the events and circumstances surrounding the abuse or neglect.

Dispositional Hearing

Section 1045 of the Family Court Act defines a dispositional hearing as a hearing to determine what order of disposition should be made with respect to the

Sidebar 7-6. Determination after Fact-Finding of Neglect or Abuse* (FCA 1044, 1046, 1051)

At a term of the Family Court of the State of New York, held in and for the County of [county],

Present: Hon. [judge]

In the Matter of	DETERMINATION UPON FACT-FINDING HEARING
[child or children], (A) Child(ren) under Eighteen Years of Age Alleged to be (Abused) (and) (Neglected) by	(Neglect-Child Abuse) Docket No. [ ] [assigned judge]

[respondent(s)]

The petition of [petitioner] dated [date], having been filed in this Court alleging that the above-named respondent(s) (neglected) (abused) the above-named child(ren); and

Notice having been duly given to the respondent(s) pursuant to section 1036 or 1037 of the Family Court Act; and

Respondent(s) and counsel for respondent(s), having appeared before this Court to answer the petition; and

[Omit if inapplicable.] (Respondent(s) having voluntarily, intelligently and knowingly admitted in open court that (s)(he) (they)

;)

[Omit if inapplicable.] (Respondent(s) having denied the allegations of the petition and the matter having duly come on for a fact-finding hearing before this Court); and

The (parent(s)) (person(s) legally responsible for the care) of the above-named child(ren) having been present at the hearing and (having been served with a copy of the petition) (every reasonable effort having been made to effect service of a copy of the petiton under sections 1036 or 1037 of the Family Court Act); and

The Court, after hearing the proofs and testimony offered in relation to the case, having found on a preponderance of the evidence that respondent(s) did [see Family Court Act Section 1051(d) and (e)]

Now therefore, upon the findings made in the fact-finding hearing and upon all the proceedings had herein, it is

(ADJUDGED that facts sufficient to sustain the petition herein have (not) been established, in that:

;

(and it is hereby)

(ADJUDGED that the above-named child(ren) (is) (are) (a) (neglected) (abused) child(ren) as defined in paragraph(s) (i) (ii) (iii) of Section 1012 Subdivision (e) of the Family Court Act)

(ORDERED, that the petition filed herein be dismissed); and it is further

(ORDERED

.)

Dated: Enter,

_____
Family Court Judge

_____
*West's McKinney's Forms, vol. 10A, pp. 512–32.

---

child. The dispositional hearing is held after the conclusion of the fact-finding hearing, and the family court judge will not commit the child to the care of the commissioner of social services without first holding a dispositional hearing. Stated differently, the actual finding of abuse or neglect is made in the fact-finding hearing, and the actual commitment or placement of the child is made after the dispositional hearing. A proper dispositional hearing must be held, and it is reversible error not to do so. See In re Marsha [488 N.Y.S. 2d 3 (Appellate Division, 1st Dept., 1985)], wherein the Appellate Division, in reversing the family court, held that it was in error not to hold an appropriate dispositional hearing. The Appellate Division wrote:

> Here, following the fact-finding hearing, a dispositional hearing was held, at which the Court received no evidence and no witnesses were called to testify. The failure to hold a proper dispositional hearing is dispositive and requires remand of the matter to the Family Court to conduct a full dispositional hearing, sufficient to permit the Court to make a reasoned decision as to the father's present capability to care for the children.

Evidence

In any hearing under Article 10 of the Family Court Act, the following rules of evidence apply:

1. Proof of the abuse or neglect of one child shall be admissible evidence on the issue of the abuse or neglect of any other child.

2. Proof of injuries sustained by a child as would ordinarily not be sustained except by reason of the acts or admissions of the parent shall be prima facie evidence of child abuse or neglect.

3. Proof that a person repeatedly misuses a drug or drugs or alcoholic beverages, which use would ordinarily have the effect of producing, in the user, either stupor, unconsciousness, intoxication, hallucination, disorientation or incompetence or substantial impairment of judgment shall be prima facie evidence that a child, who is the legal responsibility of such person, is a neglected child. The exception is where the person using said drug or alcohol is voluntarily and regularly participating in a recognized rehabilitative program.

4. Records, photographs, hospital records and other memoranda showing the condition, transaction, occurrence or event relating to a child in abuse or neglect proceeding of any hospital or other public or private agencies shall be admissible in evidence as proof of that condition, occurrence or event if the judge finds that the record, writing or memorandum was made in the regular course of the business of any hospital or other public or private agency and that it was in the regular course of such business to make it at the time of the occurrence or within a reasonable time thereafter.

5. Any report filed with the Statewide Central Register of Child Abuse and Maltreatment by a person or official required to do so pursuant to Section 413 of the Social Services Law shall be admissible in evidence.

6. Previous statements made by a child relating to any allegation of abuse or neglect shall be admissible in evidence, but, if uncorroborated, such statements shall not be sufficient to make a finding of abuse or neglect. Any other evidence tending to support the reliability of the previous statements, including, but not limited to the types of evidence defined in Section 1046 of the Family Court Act, shall be sufficient corroboration. For a recent decision illustrating the broad scope of this rule see *Matter of Christina F.*, N.Y. Court of Appeals, November 30, 1989. The testimony of a child shall not be necessary to make a finding of abuse or neglect.

7. The confidential communication privileges between husband and wife, physician and patient, psychologist and client, social worker and client, shall not be a ground for excluding evidence which otherwise would be admissible.

8. In a fact-finding hearing any determination that the child is an abused or neglected child must be based upon a preponderance of the evidence.

9. In a fact-finding hearing only competent, material and relevant evidence may be admitted.

10. In a dispositional hearing, only material and relevant evidence may be admitted. Hearsay testimony is thus admissible in a dispositional hearing.

Quantum of Proof

In all child protective proceedings and those under Article 10 of the Family Court Act, the quantum of proof is the fair preponderance of credible evidence. See Matter of Keith [123 Misc. 2d 617, 474 N.Y.S. 2d 254]. The quantum of proof in a termination of parental rights proceeding, pursuant to Section 384 B of the Social Services Law, is clear and convincing proof.

Proof of Abuse or Neglect on One Child Admissible with Respect to Others

Proof adduced as to abuse and neglect of a third daughter was admissible on issue of neglect of two other daughters in Matter of Victoria S.S. [108 A.D. 2d 989, 485 N.Y.S. 2d 384].

Prima Facie Evidence

Injuries of the child—including a bruised nose, black eyes, bruised buttocks, and infected finger—that would not ordinarily occur or exist except by reason of acts or admissions of the parent, constitute prima facie evidence of neglect for purposes of Section 1046 of the Family Court Act. See Matter of Marcelina F. [117 A.D. 2d 803, 499 N.Y.S. 2d 126].

Spontaneous Declarations

A child's statement to a paramedic within minutes of a fall from an apartment that "Mommy pushed me" is admissible in an abuse and neglect proceeding. Since by the time the dispositional hearing is held the child will have been in foster care for at least several months, therefore, the caseworker who has the most knowledge of the case is the caseworker employed by the voluntary agency where the child is placed rather than the direct care caseworker employed by the commissioner of social services.

In these situations, especially if the case is three or four months old, the caseworker employed by the agency having care of the child may give testimony as to the best interests of the child and as to the progress the child is making in foster care. Many times, the caseworkers for the voluntary agencies will therefore ask the attorney for the voluntary agency to accompany them at the dispositional hearing. However, unless the attorney for the voluntary agency makes a motion to intervene as a party and such application is granted, the attorney for the voluntary agency has no right to participate in the examination or cross-examination of the parties.

It is therefore important that the attorney for the agency make a motion to intervene with a supporting affidavit in writing so that the voluntary agency having the care and custody of the child, through its caseworkers, can fully participate in the dispositional hearing.

Special Consideration in Certain Cases

Section 1049 of the Family Court Act provides that in scheduled hearings and investigations, the judge of the Family Court shall give priority to proceedings under Article 10 that involve abuse or in which a child has been removed from his/her home before a final order of disposition. Any adjournments granted in the course of such a proceeding should be for as short a time as is practical.

Practitioners in the family court will recognize the priority given to cases involving child abuse, as well as to those where the parent requests a 1028 A hearing, seeking the return of a child removed from the parent's home without a court order. Many times, attorneys will be told by the court clerk that all the cases on the calendar will have to wait until the court hears the testimony in a 1028 A hearing. Many family courts provide for a child abuse part, where a judge is assigned to hear cases involving child abuse only.

Sustaining or Dismissing a Petition

Pursuant to Section 1051 of the Family Court Act, the family court judge, if the facts sufficient to sustain the petition are established, may enter an order finding that the child is an abused or neglected child (see sidebar 7-7). The order must state the grounds for the finding.

If the proof does not conform to the specific allegations of the petition, the court has the power to amend the allegations to conform to the proof. However, in such cases the respondent must be given a reasonable time to prepare an answer to the amended allegations.

If the facts sufficient to sustain the petition are not established or if the court concludes that the court's aid is not required on the record made before the court, the court shall dismiss the petition and state the grounds for the dismissal.

If the court makes a finding of abuse or neglect, the court may issue a preliminary order pursuant to Section 1027 of the Family Court Act if said order is required to protect the child's interest pending a final order of disposition.

**Sidebar 7–7. Order of Fact-Finding and Disposition
for Neglect or Abuse***
(FCA 1051, 1052, 1055, 1058)

At a term of the Family Court of the State of New York, held in and for the County of [county], New York on [date], 19 .

Present: Hon. [judge].

In the Matter of	ORDER OF FACT-FINDING

In the Matter of
[child or children],
(A) Child(ren) under Eighteen
Years of Age Alleged to be
(Abused) (and) (Neglected) by

[respondent(s)],

ORDER OF FACT-FINDING
AND DISPOSITION
(Neglect) (Child/Abuse)
(Neglect) (Child/Abuse)
Docket No. [   ]

(assigned judge]

The petition of   under Article 10 of the Family Court Act, sworn to on   , 19   , having been filed in this Court, alleging that the above-named child(ren) (is) (are) (a) (neglected) (abused) child(ren), and that [parent] (is) (are) the parent(s) (person(s) legally responsible for the care) of said child(ren); and

Notice having been duly given to respondent(s) pursuant to section 1036 or 1037 of the Family Court act; and

Respondent(s) and counsel for respondent(s) having appeared before this Court to answer the petition; and

[Omit if inapplicable.] (Respondent(s) having voluntarily, intelligently and knowingly admitted in open court that (s)(he) (they)

;)

[Omit if inapplicable.] (Respondent(s) having denied the allegations of the petition and the matter having duly come on for a fact-finding hearing before this Court); and

The (parent(s)) (person(s) legally responsible for the care) of the above-named child(ren) having been present at the hearing and (having been served with a copy of the petition) (every reasonable effort having been made to effect service of a coy of the petition under section 1036 or 1037 of the Family Court Act); and

The Court, after hearing the proofs and testimony offered in relation to the case, finds on a preponderance of the evidence that respondent(s)

The matter having thereafter duly come on for a dispositional hearing before the Court, and the Court, after having made an examination and inquiry into the facts and circumstances of the case and into the surroundings, conditions, and capacities of the persons involved;

[For use where order provides for placement pursuant to Family Court Act Section 1055. See Family Court Act Section 1052(b). Omit provision if inapplicable.] (and it appearing that continuation in the child's home would be contrary to the best interests of the child and that, where appropriate, reasonable efforts (were) (were not) made to prevent or eliminate the need for removal of the child from (his) (her) home)

[For use where order provides for placement pursuant to Family Court Act Section 1055. See Family Court Act Section 1052(b). Omit provision if inapplicable.] (and it appearing that the removal of the child from (his) (her) home prior to the date of the dispositional hearing was in the child's best interests and that, where appropriate, reasonable efforts (were) (were not) made to enable the child to return to (his) (her) home)

Now therefore, upon findings made in the fact-finding and dispositional hearings herein and upon all proceedings had herein, it is hereby

ADJUDGED that facts sufficient to sustain the petition herein have (not) been established, in that:

and it is hereby

[Omit provision if inapplicable.]

(ADJUDGED that the above-named child(ren) (is) (are) (a) (neglected) (abused) child(ren) as defined in paragraph(s) (i) (ii) (iii) of Section 1012, subdivision (e) of the Family Court Act)

[Omit provision if inapplicable.]

(ORDERED that the petition filed herein be dismissed;) (and it is further)

[Omit provision if inapplicable.]

(ORDERED that the child(ren) be and the same hereby (is) (are) released to the custody of the respondent(s);)

[Omit provisions which are inapplicable.]

(ORDERED that the judgment against the respondent(s) be and the same is hereby suspended for a period of [   ] months upon the following terms and conditions:

[Omit provisions which are inapplicable.]

(ORDERED that the respondent(s) herein be and the same hereby (is) (are) placed under the supervision of [person or agency] for a period of [period] upon (the following terms and conditions:) (the terms and conditions specified in the order of protection entered herein and annexed to this order and made a part thereof;)) (and it is further)

[Omit provisions which are inapplicable.]

(ORDERED that during the period of the aforesaid order of protection, the custody of the child(ren) be and the same hereby is awarded to _____.)

[Omit provisions which are inapplicable.]

(ORDERED that the child(ren) be and the same hereby (is) (are) placed in the custody of _____ for a period of _____ who shall provide for the child(ren) as in the case of a destitute child or as otherwise provided by law;) [See 22 N.Y.C.R.R. Section 205.84.]

[Omit provisions which are inapplicable.]

(ORDERED that in the event that the child absconds from the above-named custodial person or facility, written notice of that fact shall be given within 48 hours to the Clerk of Court by the custodial person or by an authorized representative of the facility, stating the name of the child, the docket number of this procedure, and the date on which the child ran away;) [See 22 N.Y.C.R.R. Section 205.80.]

(ORDERED that the (parent(s)) (person(s) legally responsible for the care) of the child(ren) be and (is) (are) hereby directed to pay to [custodian] during the period of placement of the child(ren) the sum of [amount] for the support of the child(ren);)

(IT IS FURTHER ADJUDGED that the child(ren) (has) (have) been abandoned by the parent(s) (person(s) legally responsible for the care) of the child(ren), and it is therefore

(ORDERED that the child(ren) be and the same hereby (is) (are) discharged to the custody of [custodian], who shall provide for such child(ren) as in the case of a destitute child or as otherwise authorized by law;) (and it is further)

(ORDERED that the (parent(s)) (person(s) legally responsible for the care) of the child(ren) comply with the terms and conditions specified in the order of protection annexed to this order and made a part hereof;) (and it is further)

(ORDERED that [social services official] of [duly authorized agency], undertake diligent efforts to encourage and strengthen the parental relationship, including:

)

[The following provision may be used when an order is made pursuant to Family Court Act Sections 1054 or 1057. See 22 N.Y.C.R.R. Section 205.83.]

(ORDERED that the above-named agency shall furnish a written report to the court on the   day of   19   , and every thereafter;) (and it is further)

(ORDERED

.)

Dated: Enter,

_____

Family Court Judge

_____

*West's McKinney's Forms, vol. 10A, pp. 515–32.

If the child is found to be abused or neglected, the court has the power to remove the child and place the child with the commissioner of social services or in the custody of a suitable person pending a final order of disposition.

Pursuant to paragraph A of Section 1051, the court may enter an order finding that the child is an abused or neglected child without testimony if all of the parties and the law guardian consent to such order.

Sequence of Hearings

Section 1047 of the Family Court provides that upon completion of the fact-finding hearing, and immediately after the required findings are made, the dispositional hearing may commence. In practice, however, the dispositional hearing is usually adjourned for three to six weeks. The judge of the family court will usually request probation or the authorized agency to submit court reports. Section 1047 provides that reports prepared by the probation service or duly authorized association, agency, society, or institution for use by the court at any time for making of an order of disposition shall be deemed confidential information furnished to the court, which the court shall make available for inspection and copying by all counsel.

Since the party in a dispositional hearing is the commissioner of social services and not the voluntary child foster-care agency, the attorney for the foster-care agency, who has the physical custody of the child, may wish to make a motion to intervene either in the dispositional hearing or in any extension of placements.

In a recent dispositional hearing the attorneys for the authorized agency made a motion to intervene in the dispositional phase of a child abuse proceeding, and Judge Bruce Kaplan granted the application to intervene that had been made by the authorized agency and wrote the decision in sidebar 7–8. The names of the parties and identifying information and page two of the decision are omitted purposely to protect the confidentiality of the persons involved.

Disposition on Adjudication

Section 1052 of the Family Court Act provides that at the conclusion of a dispositional hearing the court shall enter one of the following types of order:

1.   Suspend judgment;
2.   Release the child to the custody of his parent or other person legally responsible;
3.   Place the child in accordance with Section 1055, i.e., the Commissioner of Social Services or other suitable person;
4.   Make an order of protection or place the respondent under supervision pursuant to Section 1056 of the Family Court Act.

The court shall state the grounds for any disposition if it does place the child with the commissioner of social services or other local agency. In such cases the court must also determine that continuation in the child's home would be contrary to the best interest of the child and that, where appropriate, reasonable efforts were made prior to the date of the dispositional hearing to prevent or eliminate the need for removal of the child from his/her home and, further, if the child was removed from his/her home prior to the date of such hearing, that such removal was in the child's best interest, and where appropriate, reasonable efforts were made to make it possible for the child to return home.

Sidebar 7-8. Decision Granting Agency's Application to Intervene

FAMILY COURT OF THE STATE OF NEW YORK
COUNTY OF NEW YORK: CITY OF NEW YORK

In the Matter of a Proceeding Under Article 10 of the Family Court Act

Docket No. [   ]
DECISION OF
MOTION

A Child Under the Age of Eighteen Years of Age Alleged to Be Neglected

[child]

[judge]

On [date] [the natural mother] consented to a finding of child abuse based on her actions . . .   her admission was based on the following paragraphs contained in the addendum to a September 30, 1985 child abuse petition:

No proceeding more strongly implicates the Court's parens patriae responsibilities than one whose gravamen is child abuse.

No proceeding more urgently demands that the Court elicit the greatest quantum of relevant information.

After considering the applicable decisional law this Court concludes that its clear mandate requires that [agency] be granted leave to intervene.

In *Matter of T. Children,* 123 A.D. 2d 390 (2nd Dept., 1986), the Appellate Division, while noting that CSS had not proved its case, sent the matter back for a new trial, and directed that CSS present evidence from persons it did not call at the original trial.

In *Dara R.,* 119 A.D. 2d 579 (2nd Dept., 1986) the Court concluded there was evidence that the child was abused but not that respondent was culpable. It ordered a further fact finding at which testimony would be taken from a physician and a psychiatrist who were to be appointed by the court to examine the child.

In *Matter of Gale,* 135 Misc. 2d 225 (F. Ct. NY Co., 1987) Judge Gallet collected the cases in which "Appellate Courts have directed judges in child protective proceedings to call certain witnesses including health and mental health professionals and paraprofessionals."

The teaching of these cases is that in child protective proceedings a court must have access to the greatest quantum of information.

A judge must not be permitted to make his or her determination based on an insufficient, or incomplete presentation. The consequences are too great, and [the child's] interests too vital to allow this to happen. Instead, the court must take the laboring oar to insure that all probative evidence is presented to it.

This matter focuses on the question of whether it is in the child's best interests to have visitation with his mother, and if so, under what circumstances. It necessitates a particularly searching inquiry because . . .

The painstaking examination which the Court intends to conduct will be aided by granting [agency's] application to intervene. It is [agency's] social workers who, for the last several years, have had ongoing responsibility for [the child's] supervision in a foster home licensed by them. It is [agency's] workers who regularly visit the foster home, meet with [the child], his foster parents, and monitor his progress. They are the ones who have the most insight into the impact that [the mother's] request for formalized visitation could have on his best interests.

It is inconceivable that these social workers would not be called as witnesses. Through its ongoing involvement and familiarity with the case [the agency] has a far greater ability to present the testimony of its own employees in a manner that will substantially increase the breadth and depth of probative information that could be elicited from them.

[The child's] best interests require that the greatest quantum of relevant evidence will be made available to the Court in the most effective manner. In order to assure that endeavor the application to intervene is granted.

Notify attorneys.

Dated: Enter,

_____
Family Court Judge

Suspended Judgment

Section 1053 of the Family Court Act provides that Rules of the Court shall define permissible terms and conditions of a suspended judgment. These terms and conditions must relate to the act or admissions of the parent. The maximum duration of any term or condition of a suspended judgment is one year, unless the court finds at the conclusion of that period, upon a hearing, that exceptional circumstances require an extension thereof for an additional year. For the terms and conditions of a suspended judgment see 22 N.Y.C.R.R. 205.83A, as reproduced below:

> Terms and conditions of order in accordance with sections 1053, 1054 and 1057 of the Family Court Act (child protective proceeding). (a) An order suspending judgment entered pursuant to section 1052 of the Family Court Act shall contain at least one of the following terms and conditions that relate to the adjudicated acts or omissions of the respondent, directing the respondent to:
>
> 1. refrain from or eliminate specified acts or conditions found at the fact-finding hearing to constitute or to have caused neglect or abuse;
> 2. provide adequate and proper food, housing, clothing, medical care, and for the other needs of the child;
> 3. provide proper care and supervision to the child and cooperate in obtaining, accepting or allowing medical or psychiatric diagnosis or treatment, alcoholism or drug abuse treatment, counseling or child guidance services for the child;
> 4. take proper steps to insure the child's regular attendance at school; and
> 5. cooperate in obtaining and accepting medical treatment, psychiatric diagnosis and treatment, alcoholism or drug abuse treatment, employment or counseling services, or child guidance, and permit a child protective agency to obtain information from any person or agency from whom the respondent or the child is receiving or was directed to receive treatment or counseling.

Release to Custody of Parent or Other Person Responsible for Care; Supervision or Order of Protection

Section 1054 of the Family Court Act provides that if an order of disposition releases a child to the parent, the court may place the parent or other suitable person to whose custody the child is released under supervision of a child protective agency, or of a social services official or duly authorized agency; or it may issue an order of protection pursuant to Section 1056; or it may do both. The rules of the court define permissible terms and conditions of supervision. Pursuant to Section 1057, an amendment to which became effective July 24, 1989, duration of any period of supervision shall be for the initial period of no more than twelve months, and the court may at the expiration of that period, upon a hearing and for good cause shown, make successive extensions of such supervision of up to one year each. For the terms and conditions of orders pursuant to Sections 1054 and 1057, see 22 N.Y.C.R.R. 205.83B-D, as reproduced below:

> (b) An order pursuant to section 1054 of the Family Court Act placing the person to whose custody the child is released under the supervision of a child protective agency, social services officer or duly authorized agency, or an order pursuant to section 1057 placing the respondent under the supervision of a child protective agency, social services official or authorized agency, shall contain at least one of the following terms and conditions requiring the respondent to:
>
> 1. observe any of the terms and conditions set forth in subdivision (a) of this section;
> 2. cooperate with the supervising agency in remedying specified acts or omissions found at the fact-finding hearing to constitute or to have caused the neglect or abuse;
> 3. meet with the supervising agency alone and with the child when directed to do so by that agency;
> 4. report to the supervising agency when directed to do so by that agency;
> 5. cooperate with the supervising agency in arranging for and allowing visitation in the home or other place;
> 6. notify the supervising agency immediately of any change of residence or employment of the respondent or of the child; or
> 7. do or refrain from doing any other specified act of omission or commission that, in the judgment of the court, is necessary to protect the child from injury or mistreatment and to help safeguard the physical, mental and emotional well-being of the child.
>
> (c) When an order is made pursuant to section 1054 or 1057 of the Family Court Act:
>
> 1. the court shall notify the supervising agency in writing of its designation to act and shall furnish to that agency a copy of the order setting forth the terms and conditions imposed;
> 2. the order shall be accompanied by a written statement informing the respondent that a willful failure to obey the terms and conditions imposed may result in commitment to jail for a term not to exceed six months; and
> 3. the court may, if it concludes that it is necessary for the protection of the child, direct the supervising agency to furnish a written report to the court at stated intervals not to exceed six months, setting forth whether, and to what extent:

(i) there has been any alteration in the respondent's maintenance of the child that is adversely affecting the child's health or well-being;

(ii) there is compliance with the terms and conditions of the order of supervision; and

(iii) the supervising agency has furnished supporting services to the respondent.

(d) A copy of the order, setting forth its duration and the terms and conditions imposed, shall be furnished to the respondent.

Placement

Pursuant to Section 1055 of the Family Court Act, the court may place the child in the custody of a relative or other suitable person, or of the commissioner of social services, or of such other officer, board, or department as may be authorized to receive children as public charges, or a duly authorized association, agency, society or an institution suitable for the placement of a child. The placements under Section 1055 may be for an initial period of twelve months, and the court, in its discretion, may make successive extensions for additional periods of one year each. The petition to extend a placement accompanied by supporting affidavits or reports shall be filed at least sixty days prior to the expiration of the period of placement, except for good cause shown.

No placement shall be extended or continued except upon a hearing held concerning the need for extending or continuing the placement.

Pending final determination of a petition to extend placement, the court, for good cause shown, may enter a temporary order extending the placement for a period not to exceed thirty days. Such temporary order may be renewed upon good cause shown.

In addition to or in lieu of an order of placement or extension or continuation of a placement, the court may order the child protective agency to undertake diligent efforts to encourage and strengthen the parental relationship when it finds such efforts will not be detrimental to the best interest of the child. Such order may include a specific plan of action for such agency including, but not limited to, assisting the parent and obtaining adequate housing, employment, counseling, medical care, or psychiatric treatment.

Further, in addition to or in lieu of an order of extension or continuation of a placement, the court may make an order directing a social services official or other duly authorized agency to initiate a proceeding to legally free the child for adoption if the court finds reasonable cause to believe that grounds exist to initiate a petition pursuant to Section 384 B of the Social Services Law. Upon the failure of the agency to initiate a proceeding to terminate parental rights within ninety days, the court may permit the foster parents or the law guardian to initiate a proceeding to terminate parental rights.

No placement may be made or continued under Section 1055 of the Family Court Act beyond the child's eighteenth birthday without his/her consent and in no event past his/her twenty-first birthday.

At the extension of placement hearing, the court must consider the parent's present ability to care for the child. If the parent is not able to care for the child, the placement will be extended. On the other hand, if the parent is presently able to care for the child, the court must consider the child's best interests. Therefore, the court can find that the parent is presently able to care for the child, but may find that for some reason affecting the child's best interests, placement should be continued. For a case discussing extensions of placements in general and that held that the extension of a child's placement runs from the date of the expiration of the last temporary extension rather than from expiration of the original placement, see In re Riddle v. Rapp [127 Misc. 2d 835, 487 N.Y.S. 2d 477 (Family Court, Queens County, 1985)].

Section 1055 of the Family Court Act was recently amended effective July 24, 1989, to the effect that the court may place the child in the custody of a relative or other suitable person or of the commissioner of social services or of such other officer, board, or department as may be authorized to receive children as public charges, or in a duly authorized association, agency, or society, or in an institution suitable for the placement of a child. Section 1055 A is also new in that the legislature has specifically stated that the court may place the child in the custody of a relative (see next section). The amendment to Section 1055 is consistent with respect to Section 1017 A, which is new and effective July 24, 1989, and focuses upon relatives of the child.

Section 1017 A of the Family Court Act provides that in a court proceeding, where there is an allegation of neglect or abuse and a child is court placed, the court shall direct the commissioner of social services to conduct an immediate investigation to locate relatives of the child and to inform those relatives that there is a proceeding pending in the family court and that they may apply to become foster parents of that child or may seek custody or care of that child.

Once that relative is located, the commissioner must determine whether that person who is related to that child is a suitable person to either become a foster parent or provide free care and custody for the child during the pendency of any orders pursuant to Article 10 of the Family Court Act. A written report must be then given to the court, and the court will determine whether the child should reside with a relative; be remanded to the commissioner of social services; be remanded to the commissioner of social services with a direction that the commissioner place the child with said relative; or if there are no relatives, be placed directly with a specific certified foster home.

It should also be noted that Section 384 A of the Social Services Law has also been amended. Section 384 A now directs the commissioner of social services, before accepting a voluntary commitment, to conduct an immediate investigation to locate relatives of the child and to determine whether the child may appropriately be placed with a suitable person related to the child and whether that person seeks approval as a foster parent or wishes to provide care and custody for the child until the parent or other person responsible for the care of the child is able to resume custody.

As can be seen from these two amendments, the legislature has made it clear that children should not be placed with strangers if relatives are available and are ready, willing, and able to provide care either as certified foster parents or as relatives providing free care and custody.

Status of Children Freed for Adoption; Periodic Court Review

Section 1055 A—new and effective January 1, 1989—was intended to make sure that the foster-care system did not lose sight of those children already freed for adoption either by surrender, pursuant to Section 384 of the Social Services Law or by court order pursuant to Section 384 B of the Social Services Law. Pursuant to Section 1055 A of the Family Court Act, a child in this context means a child under the age of eighteen years for whom an authorized agency is providing foster care. This section requires that a petition be drafted to review the foster-care status and said petition, together with a copy of the placement instruments, must be filed in the family court by the authorized agency charged with the guardianship and custody of said foster child, but may be filed by another authorized agency who is providing the care for the foster child and may be filed by the foster parent in whose home the child presently resides or has resided during such period of twelve months.

The petition must be filed in the family court in the county in which the order committing the custody and guardianship of the child was entered and must set forth the disposition sought and the grounds therefore and must be filed at least sixty days prior to the end of the month, which would constitute the eighteenth month of the period of placement or sixty days prior to the expiration date of any subsequent order of extension granted by the court, pursuant to Section 1055 of Article 10.

However, for a child who has been freed for adoption and not placed in a prospective adoptive home, such petition shall be filed six months after such child has been freed, or for a child who has been freed for adoption and placed in a prospective adoptive home and no petition for adoption has been filed twelve months after placement, such petition shall be filed twelve months after such child has been in placement in such prospective adoptive home, whichever is sooner.

Notice of the hearing and a copy of the petition shall be served upon:

1. the authorized agency having the guardianship and custody of the child;
2. the authorized agency actually providing care for the child;

3. the foster parent in whose home the child resided or resides at or after the expiration of a continuous period of twelve months in foster care, if such foster parent is not the petitioner;

4. the prospective adoptive parent of the child who has been freed for adoption and in whose home such child has been placed and no petition for adoption has been filed within twelve months after such placement; and

5. such other person as the court may, in its discretion, direct.

In reviewing the foster-care status of the child and in determining its order of disposition, the court shall consider, among other things:

1. the appropriateness of the child's service plan;

2. what services have been provided to insure and expedite the adoption of the child;

3. in the case of a child freed for adoption over the age of fourteen, who has withheld his consent to the adoption, examine the report of the law guardian of such child concerning the facts and circumstances with regard to the child's decision to withhold consent and the reasons therefor; and

4. any further efforts that have been or will be made to promote the best interest of the child.

At the conclusion of such hearing the Court shall, upon the proof adduced and in accordance with the best interest of the child, enter an order of disposition:

1. directing that placement of the child in foster care be extended; or

2. directing that such child be placed for adoption in the foster-family home where he/she resides or has resided or with any other person or persons; and

3. directing the provision of services or assistance to the child and the prospective adoptive parent authorized or required to be made available pursuant to the comprehensive annual services program plan then in effect;

4. recommending that the State Department of Social Services conduct a Child Welfare Services Utilizations Review pursuant to Section 398 B of the Social Services Law or recommending that the State Department of Social Services investigate the facts and circumstances concerning the discharge of responsibilities for the care and welfare of such child by a social services district.

The court, in its discretion, may make successive extensions for additional periods for up to one year each.

The court shall possess continuing jurisdiction in proceedings under Section 1055 A.

If a child previously had a law guardian appointed by the Family Court in a proceeding pursuant to Section 384 B of the Social Services Law, the court shall, if practicable, appoint the same law guardian and if not, appoint a different law guardian.

Order of Protection

Section 1056 of the Family Court Act provides that the court may make an order of protection in assistance or as a condition of any order made pursuant to Article 10 of the Family Court Act. The order of protection may set forth reasonable conditions of behavior to be observed for a specified time by a person who is before the court and as a parent or a person legally responsible for the child's care or the spouse of the parent or other person legally responsible for the child's care or both. Such an order may require any such person to:

1. stay away from the home, the other spouse, or the child;
2. permit a parent to visit the child at stated periods;
3. abstain from offensive conduct against the child, or against the other parent, or against any person to whom the custody of the child is awarded;
4. give proper attention to the care of the home;
5. refrain from acts of commission or omission that tend to make the home not a proper place for the child;
6. provide, either directly or by means of medical and health insurance, for expenses incurred for medical care and treatment arising from the incident or incidents forming the basis for the issuance of the order.

Supervision

Family Court Act 1057 allows the judge of the family court to place the respondent under supervision of a child protective agency, a social services official, or a duly authorized agency. Rules of the Court shall define permissible terms and conditions of supervision, and the duration of any period of supervision shall be for an initial period of no more than one year. The court may, at the expiration of that period, upon a hearing and for good cause, make successive extension of supervision for up to one year each. For terms and conditions of an order of supervision, see 22 N.Y.C.R.R. 205.59.

Abandoned Child

Section 1059 of the Family Court Act provides that if the court finds that a child was abandoned by his/her parents, it may make an order so finding and it may discharge the child to the custody of the commissioner of social services, who shall provide for such child as in the case of a destitute child or as otherwise authorized by law. In such a case, the court shall direct the commissioner of social services to institute a proceeding pursuant to Section 384 B of the Social Services Law to legally free such child for adoption. It must be noted, however, that Social Services Law Section 384 B provides that a proceeding to terminate parental rights cannot be initiated until the child has been in foster care for six months.

Staying, Modifying, Setting Aside, or Vacating an Order

Section 1061 of the Family Court Act provides that for good cause shown and after due notice, the court, on its own motion or on the motion of the corporation counsel, county attorney, or district attorney, or on motion of the petitioner, or on motion of the child or on his behalf, or on the motion of the parent, may stay execution, arrest, set aside, modify, or vacate any order issued in the course of a proceeding under Article 10 of the Family Court Act.

This section is utilized at times when the judge's order is no longer practicable. For example, if the court ordered an authorized agency to initiate proceedings to terminate parental rights and it comes to the attention of the authorized agency that the parent had made substantial contacts with the child that would break any abandonment, it would be reasonable to ask the court to vacate that portion of its prior order directing the agency to begin termination proceedings.

Petition to Terminate Placement

The child's parent may petition the court for an order terminating placement. The petition must be verified and must:

1. allege that an application for the child's return to his home was made to the appropriate person in the place in which a child was placed;
2. allege that the application was denied or was not granted within thirty days from the day the application was made; and
3. state the grounds for the petition.

Usually, the grounds for the petition are that the parent is now ready, willing, and able to assume adequate and sufficient care for the child.

Service of Petition; Answer

A copy of the petition to terminate placement shall promptly be served upon the authorized agency having custody of the child, and the authorized agency must file an answer to the petition within five days.

Examination of Petition and Answer; Hearing

The court shall promptly examine the petition and the answer, and if the court concludes that a hearing should be had, it may proceed upon due notice to all concerned to hear the facts and determine whether continued placement serves the purpose of Article 10. If the court concludes that a hearing need not be had, it shall enter an order granting or denying the petition.

Orders on Hearing

Section 1065 of the Family Court Act provides that if the court determines after the hearing that continued placement serves the purpose of Article 10, it shall deny the petition. The court may, on its own motion, reduce the duration of the placement, change the agency, or direct the agency to make such other arrangements for the child's care and welfare as the facts of the case may require. If the court determines after the hearing that continued placement does not serve the purposes of Article 10, it shall discharge the child from the custody of the authorized agency and to the parent or other responsible person.

Successive Petitions

Section 1066 of the Family Court Act provides that if a petition to terminate placement is denied, it may not be renewed for a period of ninety days after denial, unless the order of denial permits renewal at an earlier time.

Discontinuance of Treatment by Agency or Institution

Section 1067 provides that a child placed with an authorized agency shall be returned to the court that entered the order of placement if the agency discontinues or suspends its work or is unwilling to continue to care for the child. The court may also change placement if the authorized agency so fundamentally alters its program that the child can no longer benefit from placement at that agency.

Action on Return from Agency or Institution

Section 1068 of the Family Court Act provides that if a person is returned to the court, the court may make any order that might have been made at the time of the order of placement.

Rules of Court

Section 1069 of the Family Court Act provides that Rules of the Court may authorize an agency with which a child is placed to arrange for the child's care by another person or authorized agency. In the event such arrangement is made, the agency making the arrangements shall, within one week of the making of the arrangement, inform the court of the change and the reason therefor.

Failure to Comply with Terms and Conditions of Suspended Judgment

Section 1071 of the Family Court Act provides the parent may be brought before the court for failing to comply with the terms and conditions of a suspended judgment. If, after the hearing, the court is satisfied by competent proof that the parent failed to comply with any of the terms and conditions of the suspended judgment, the court may revoke the suspension of judgment and enter any order that might have been made at the time judgment was suspended. For a discussion involving the revocation of a suspended judgment, see In re Brenda Y.Y. [69 A.D. 2d 966, 416 N.Y.S. 2d 346].

Failure to Comply with Terms and Conditions of Supervision

If a parent is brought before the court for failure to comply with the terms and conditions of an order of supervision or an order of protection, and if the court, after hearing is satisfied by competent proof that the parent did so willfully and without just cause, it may revoke the order of supervision or order of protection and enter any order that might have been made at the time the order of supervision was made or, it may commit the parent, who willfully and without just cause violated the order, to jail for a term not to exceed six months. For a discussion of this section, see In re Ana Maria Q. [52 A.D. 2d 607, 382 N.Y.S. 2d 107] and In re Ella Mae H. [54 A.D. 2d 774, 387 N.Y.S. 2d 303].

Effect of Running Away from Place of Placement

If a child placed under Section 1055 runs away from the place of placement, the court may, after a hearing, revoke the order of placement and make any order, including an order of placement, that might have been made at the time the original order of placement was made. The court may require that the child be present at such hearing and shall appoint a law guardian to represent him/her.

Release from Responsibility under Order of Placement

Section 1074 of the Family Court Act provides that those responsible for the operation of a place where a child has been placed under Section 1055 may petition the court for leave to return the child to the court and, for good cause shown, be released from responsibility under the order of placement. After a hearing, the court may grant the petition and may make any order, including an order of placement, that might have been made at the time the order of placement was made.

Visitation Rights

Section 1081 of the Family Court Act provides for visitation rights by the noncustodial parent or by the grandparent of a child who has been remanded or placed in foster care by order of the family court or by any order or judgment of the supreme court or by written agreement between the parents. Stated differently, the noncustodial parent or the grandparents may have visitation with a foster child who has been placed either by court order or by the written consent of the custodial parent.

The noncustodial parent or grandparent who is denied these visitation rights may petition the court for enforcement of visitation rights. The necessary allegations of the petition are outlined in the remaining sections of Section 1081 of the Family Court Act.

Approval, Modification, or Denial of Visitation Rights

Upon receipt of the petition requesting visitation rights, the Department of Social Services shall make inquiry of the state's Central Register of Child Abuse and Maltreatment to determine whether the petitioner is the subject of an indicated report of child abuse or maltreatment.

The section further provides that, after a hearing, the court should approve visitation by the petitioner unless it finds upon competent, relevant and material evidence that enforcement of visitation rights described in any order, judgment, or agreement would endanger the child's life or health.

Duration of Orders Affecting Visitation Rights

Any order incorporating an order, judgment, or agreement confirming visitation rights with the child of a noncustodial parent or grandparent into a dispositional order under Article 10 of the Family Court Act shall remain in effect for the length of time the child remains in foster care, unless such order is subsequently modified by the court for good cause shown.

Out-of-Wedlock Children; Paternity

Pursuant to Section 1084 of the Family Court Act, no visitation rights shall be enforceable under Article 10 of the Family Court Act concerning any person claiming to be a parent of an out-of-wedlock child without an adjudication of paternity of such person by a court of competent jurisdiction or without an acknowledgment of the paternity of such person executed pursuant to applicable provisions of law.

8
The Foster Child:
Suspension of Parental Visitation

Perhaps the most serious interruption of the parent-child relationship outside of termination of parental rights is suspension of parental visitation. So serious is the suspension of parental visitation that it should only be accomplished by court order except for emergency situations.

Contrary to popular belief, the great majority of children in foster care are not court-remanded but are voluntarily committed by a parent of the child.

Once a child is placed in foster care, the authorized agency has an obligation to strengthen parental ties with the child. Section 384 B of the Social Services Law mandates that the agency must use diligent efforts to strengthen the relationship between parent and child. Specifically, the agency must:

1. consult with the parent(s) in order to develop a plan to return the child to his/her parent(s);
2. encourage and aid in visitation between parent(s) and child;
3. provide services leading to return of the child to the parent(s); and
4. inform the parent(s) of the child's progress.

If return of the child is the obligation of the agency, then visitation is its primary tool.

Visitation is no longer limited to once each month for two hours. Agencies now are obligated to offer more frequent visitation—once a week and weekend visitation, if indicated.

Since visitation is crucial to building a relationship, its suspension is destructive to that relationship and may lead to the termination of parental rights and adoption.

Guidelines Listed

Parental visitation should not be suspended except for the most compelling reasons. Some examples that require court intervention are:

1. the physical abuse of the child at a visit;
2. the psychological abuse of the child at a visit;
3. a visit by a parent who is intoxicated or "high" on drugs; and
4. a serious detrimental effect on the child after a visit.

Once the caseworker is aware that the visits are detrimental to the child, the case supervisor should be informed and a staffing conference should be scheduled. At the staffing conference, a consensus should be reached among the caseworker, case supervisor, and psychiatrist or psychologist. If possible, visitation should be continued after parental therapy and/or supervised visitation. If, after therapy and supervised visitation, the problem still exists, the agency should seek court-ordered suspension of visitation.

Legal Guidelines for Suspension of Parental Visitation

The authorized voluntary agency cannot unilaterally decide to seek a court order but must seek approval of the commissioner of social services.

The Department of Social Services of the City of New York has promulgated rules relating to termination of parental visitation, known as SSC Procedure No. 43 (revised June 1978). Procedure No. 43 may be outlined as follows:

1. Parental visitation can only be terminated by court order on notice to the parent.
2. Visitation is to continue until the court order is obtained, except in case of immediate danger to the child's life, health, or safety;
3. In cases of immediate danger to the child, visitation may be suspended without court order but only for two calendar weeks;
4. The agency and the parent may agree in writing to suspend visitation.

With respect to voluntary agencies that wish to terminate parental visitation, the agency must:

1. Notify the Office of Placement and Accountability (OPA) on Form W853C, explaining the reasons for suspending visitation and requesting approval.
2. Within five days of receipt of Form W853C, the OPA must respond to the agency, either approving or disapproving the plan.
3. If the agency obtains approval, it must obtain a court order before suspending visitation.

    The following procedure is suggested:

    If the child is court-remanded because of abuse or neglect pursuant to Article 10 of the Family Court Act, then a notice of motion with supporting affidavit may be drafted using the same docket numbers in the abuse or neglect proceeding. If, on the other hand, the child is voluntarily committed, then an order to show cause [see sidebar 8–1] with supporting petition may be used, pursuant to Section 651 of the Family Court Act. The relief requested should be for the suspension of visitation or, in the alternative, for whatever limitations on visitation the court deems to be in the child's best interest. The supporting affidavit [see sidebar 8–2] or petition should stress the adverse effects upon the child that visitation with the mother has had. For example, if after visitation, the child has acted out in a violent manner or has become physically sick, this should be noted. Further, any psychological or psychiatric evaluations indicating effects that such visitation has on the child or setting out an opinion as to future deleterious effects that such visitation would have upon the child should be attached as exhibits.

4.   The agency and parent may agree in writing to suspend visitation and eliminate court intervention.

Sidebar 8–1. Order to Show Cause
to Suspend Parental Visitation

FAMILY COURT OF THE STATE
OF NEW YORK
COUNTY OF NEW YORK

———————————————————x

In the Matter of   ORDER TO SHOW CAUSE

[children]
Dependent children under the age
of 14 years, pursuant to Article 10
of the Family Court Act.

———————————————————x

Upon the annexed papers and the Affidavit of [caseworker], caseworker [date] the   day of   , 19   , and upon all the pleadings and proceedings heretofore, it is hereby

ORDERED, that cause be shown by respondents, [respondents], and [law guardian] Esq., Law Guardian, Legal Aid Society, at a term of this Court, to be held in the Courthouse hereof at 60 Lafayette Street, New York, Part [part] on the ____ day of _____ 19__ at 9:30 o'clock in the forenoon of that date, or as soon thereafter as Counsel can be heard why an Order should not be made suspending the visitation scheduled between the children, [children], or in the alternative, permitting the agency, [agency], to so limit or restrict the visitation schedule in the manner it determines to be in the children's best interests, and for such other and further relief as the Court shall deem just and proper, and it is further,

ORDERED, that there being sufficient evidence set forth in the supporting Affidavit of [caseworker], caseworker, [agency], sworn to the ___ day of _____ , 19__ that all visitation be stayed pending the determination of the motion herein.

It is further,

ORDERED, that service of a copy of this Order to Show Cause and supporting papers and Affidavit upon [law guardian] Esq., Law Guardian for the above named infants, Legal Aid Society, Family Court, New York County, 60 Lafayette Street, New York, New York 10013, and upon [respondents] on or before the ___ day of _____ , 19__ shall be deemed timely and sufficient service.

Dated: _____ , 19   Enter,

_____
Family Court Judge

Sidebar 8–2. Affidavit of Caseworker
for Suspension of Parental Visitation

FAMILY COURT OF THE STATE
OF NEW YORK
COUNTY OF NEW YORK
_____x

In the Matter of   AFFIDAVIT

[children]
Dependent children under the age
of 14 years, pursuant to Article 10
of the Family Court Act.
_____x

        STATE OF NEW YORK)
) ss:
        COUNTY OF [county])

[Caseworker] being duly sworn, deposes and says:

1. I am an Adoption Caseworker employed by [agency], having an office at [address].

2. I am the Adoption Caseworker assigned to the case of the children, [children].

3. I am fully familiar with the infants, and with all the case records in this matter.

4. I make this Affidavit in support of an Order to Show Cause requesting that visitation between the natural mother, [mother] and the above-named infants cease because of the negative psychological effects such visitation has on the children.

5. The putative father of the infants is [putative father].

6. With respect to dates of birth of the children they are as follows: [child] was born on [date]; [child] was born on [date]; [child] was born on [date]. All of the children were Court placed with the Commissioner of Social Services of the City of New York on [date]. The Commissioner of Social Services of the City of New York in turn placed the children with [agency] on the same date.

7. The history of this case shows the visits between the natural mother and the children to be negative. During recent months, the visitation has worsened to the extent that to allow it to continue would be against the best interests of the children.

8. Annexed hereto and made a part hereof and marked as Exhibit "A" is a copy of an "indicated" Office of Confidential Investigations Report dated [date]. The Confidential Investigations Report, which is based on an incident that occurred while the children were in the natural mother's home during a weekend visitation of [date] through [date] is founded based on bruises, sexual abuse and inadequate guardianship in the home.

9. Subsequent to the above incident, unsupervised visitation was suspended. The natural mother, [mother], then was scheduled to attend bi-weekly parent-child visits at the agency offices. The natural mother failed to attend these visits for long periods of time, and when she did attend she threatened the children and damaged any potential for developing a relationship with them. The natural mother, [mother], canceled all visits with her children between October, 1989 and the end of January, 1990. She then canceled all visits during March and April of 1990 claiming that the children needed to be disciplined for lying. During visits held at [location] on [date] and [date] the natural mother called the children liars and told them that she would punish them when they came home. Subsequently on [date], the natural mother left a visit because an agency case aid refused to leave her alone with her children. Thus, the natural mother has done nothing to alleviate the trauma caused to the children as a result of the abuse suffered on [date].

10. The fact that the natural mother does not understand the deleterious effects of the abuse has been made clear in other ways as well. This was exemplified during a caseworker contact on May 15, 1990. During that contact, the natural mother told the caseworker that [name] who is alleged to have conducted the

abuse of the children during the weekend visit, was living at her apartment and that he used her address to open his public assistance case. The natural mother told the caseworker that she would stand behind [name] "all the way" and that she will "punish the children for lying by teaching them what real sex is all about." The natural mother also told the caseworker that she would be putting out a contract on the SSC worker.

11. A letter forwarded to the agency by [attorney] Esq., Assistant District Attorney involved in the criminal proceedings against [name] as a result of the above-described incident, further supports the position that continued visitation between the natural mother and the children would be against the children's best interest. The letter recommends the termination of parent-child visitation and sets out the opinion that the natural mother poses "a present threat to the safety of all four of her children." A copy of the letter is annexed hereto and marked as Exhibit "B".

12. WHEREFORE, the depondent respectfully requests that all visitation between [children] and the natural mother [mother] be suspended on the ground that it would be against the best interest of the children for such visitation to continue, and for such other and further relief as to this Court may be just and proper.

_____

Sworn to before me this day of [date].

_____
Notary Public

Imminent Danger to the Life, Health, or Safety of the Child

When an agency decides that visitation poses an imminent danger to the life, health, or safety of a child in care, it may immediately terminate or limit already-scheduled visitation.

Simultaneously, the agency director shall request approval by telephone from the personnel of the Special Services for Children (SSC) program, carrying planning responsibility to terminate or limit parental visitation. The agency director must submit a written request for approval within twenty-four hours of the phone call. The SSC program personnel must respond in writing within seventy-two hours of receipt of the agency's written request.

If the SSC approves the agency's decision to terminate or limit visitation, the voluntary agency is responsible for obtaining a court order on notice to the parent or guardian, terminating or limiting visitation within ten calendar days of receipt of the SSC's approval of the agency's request. The agency shall notify the SSC in writing within twenty-four hours of the results of the court proceeding.

If, after obtaining SSC approval of the decision to terminate or limit visitation, the agency and the parent or guardian reach agreement on the new terms of visitation, it is not necessary to refer the matter to court. However, parental visits shall not be terminated or limited until a supplement to the placement instrument embodying the new agreement has been duly executed by the parent or guardian.

If the SSC does not approve the agency's request to limit or terminate visitation, visitation shall continue as previously scheduled.

Part III
Freeing the Foster Child for Adoption

9
Foster-Care Review Proceedings

June 20, 1972, was an important day for the foster child in New York state. It was the first day that a 392 foster-care review hearing was held at the Family Court, New York County, Honorable Edith Miller presiding. Prior to the enactment of Section 392 of the Social Services Law, there was no court review of the thousands of children in foster care when they had been voluntarily placed. See In re Denlow [384 N.Y.S. 2d 621 (Family Court, Kings County, 1976)], wherein the court, in a termination of parental rights proceeding, stated that the case would probably never have surfaced from the so-called "limbo" of foster care if it were not for the 392 review of the child's status mandated by law. There was criticism that because of the lack of court review, many children in foster care remained in foster care needlessly and many more should have been adopted, while others should have returned home to their natural parents.

The Petition

Section 392 of the Social Services Law mandates that once a child has been in foster care for a continuous period of eighteen months, the authorized agency charged with the care of the child must file a petition in family court seeking review of the child's status.

The petition must set forth the disposition sought (that is, the return of the child to his/her natural parents, continuing foster care, or initiating proceedings to free the child for adoption), and the grounds or reasons for such disposition. All interested parties—such as the authorized agency, the natural parents, and the foster parents—are given notice by mail of the hearing. The complete text of Section 392 of the Social Services Law may be summarized as follows*:

Where a child under eighteen has remained in foster care for a continuous period of eighteen months, a petition to review the foster care of such child shall be filed in the family court, and such petition shall be filed in the county

---

*See *West's McKinney's Forms*, vol. 52A.

where the child care agency has its principal office or where the child resides. In the City of New York, all 392 proceedings are held in the Family Court, New York County, 60 Lafayette Street, New York. The petition shall set forth the disposition sought and the grounds therefor. Notice of the hearing and a copy of the petition shall be served upon the natural parents and the foster parents. The court must decide the status of the child based upon the child's best interests and enter an order of disposition:

1. directing that foster care of the child continue;
2. directing that the child be returned to his/her parent; or
3. directing that proceedings be instituted to free the child for adoption.

The court has the power to direct that the agency undertake diligent efforts to encourage and strengthen the parent-child relationship when it finds such efforts will not be detrimental to the best interests of the child. Finally, the family court possesses continuing jurisdiction and may rehear the matter whenever it deems necessary, but within at least twenty-four months. See Matter of Sheila G. [61 N.Y.S. 2d 368, 474 N.Y.S. 2d 421], wherein the Court of Appeals wrote:

> Once a child has been voluntarily placed with an authorized child-care agency and is under foster care, the Family Court is vested with continuing jurisdiction over the child until there has been a final disposition of custody.

On the other hand, if the child is returned by the Department of Social Services to the natural parents, the family court loses jurisdiction. See Matter of Lucinda G. [122 Misc. 2d 416, 471 N.Y.S. 2d 736 (1983)]. In Lucinda G., the court wrote:

> The Court holds that the return by the Department to their natural father of the two children constitutes a voluntary termination by the Department of the foster care status of the children, notwithstanding the concurrent filing of a petition to review that foster care status. Under the circumstances, there is no foster care status to review, and the Court is without jurisdiction to entertain a proceeding to continue the children in foster care.

Discovery and Inspection Prior to the Hearing

It has been the practice of the attorney for the natural parents and foster parents to serve upon the attorney for the agency a notice of discovery and inspection that, if not objected to, would permit the attorney to inspect, review, and make notes of the entire case record kept by the agency. The case record would contain among other things:

1. how the child came into care;
2. background material on the natural parents, foster parents, and the child;
3. medical and psychological materials concerning the natural parents, foster parents, and the child;
4. the amount of contact, visitation, and planning by the natural parents; and
5. diligent efforts the agency has undertaken to strengthen the parental ties.

It therefore becomes important for the agency representing the natural or foster parent to review the case record prior to a contested 392 hearing. The leading cases on the scope of disclosure are the trilogy of In re Carla L., Sarah R., and Irene F. and Lisa F. [45 A.D. 2d 375 N.Y.S. 2d 987 (Appellate Division, 1st Dept., 1974)].

In Carla L., the Appellate Division permitted disclosure of the agency case records by the attorney for the natural parents in a 392 foster-care review proceeding and set forth the following procedure to be followed:

1. The attorney for the natural parent should serve a notice of disclosure.
2. The agency should permit such discovery and inspection by the attorney for the natural parent of the agency's records at the agency's office or at the family court and under supervision. See In re Leon R.R. [421 N.Y.S. 2d 863 (1979)] wherein the Court of Appeals held that it was appropriate for an agency attorney to photostat that portion of the record he/she intended to introduce into evidence and that it be served on all other counsel prior to the hearing.
3. As to those records for which the agency seeks protection, the agency must furnish counsel for the natural parents before the hearing with a list of the material to be withheld.
4. The agency must move for a protective order, pursuant to C.P.L.R. 3103, with the contested matters to be viewed by the family court *in camera*.

The procedure for inspection of the agency case record by a foster parent is somewhat more limited. In Irene F. and Lisa F., the Appellate Division held that disclosure by a foster parent may be had:

1. only upon a proper showing of necessity;
2. coupled with *in camera* viewing by the family court, and that
3. initial disclosure by way of stipulation may be had, but only where court approval is obtained.

The court in Irene F. and Lisa F. concluded:

Thus, the family court is of necessity involved *ab initio* with the disclosure process when disclosure is sought by a foster parent . . .

See also In re Louis F., [54 A.D. 2d 104, 387 N.Y.S. 2d 856], affirmed by the Court of Appeals, [42 N.Y.S. 2d 260 (1977)], (foster parent's motion to inspect the agency's records after the court inspected case records *in camera* is denied).

Oral Examination before Trial

In Irene F. and Lisa F., [45 A.D. 2d 375, 357 N.Y.S. 2d 987 (1st Dept., 1974)], the attorney for the foster parents sought to examine the natural father by oral examination. The Appellate Division denied the request stating:

With respect to the part of the foster parent's application seeking to depose the natural father, special circumstances must be shown to warrant such examination. In proceedings such as this where there is a need for expedition in determining what will be the best interests of the affected child, there is no basis, absent a showing of special circumstances, for imposing on a party the burden of attendant risk that extensive pre-trial discovery proceedings will delay the Court's making its determination. On this record, such a showing has not been made by the foster parents.

Photocopying Case Records of the Agency

In Irene F. and Lisa F., [47 A.D. 2d 619, 366 N.Y.S. 2d 423 (1st Dept., 1975)] the court permitted the attorney for the foster parents to photocopy medical, psychiatric, and school reports contained in the case records of an authorized agency.

The 392 hearings are held in family court in counties and cities throughout New York State. In New York City, the hearings are held at 60 Lafayette Street before a family court judge. The hearings are held in New York County, even though the parent may reside in Brooklyn, the agency may have its office in Nassau County, and the child may reside with foster parents in Suffolk County. This is because the child is in the custody of the commissioner of social services, who signs the 392 petition and has his office in New York County.

The calendar usually contains between fifteen and twenty-five cases to be reviewed, and there is usually a morning and afternoon calendar. Depending upon the judge presiding, the hearing can take the form of an informal conference or a full trial. At a 392 review, the parent is entitled to a plenary and evidentiary hearing; see In re Denlow [384 N.Y.S. 2d 621 (Family Court, Kings County, 1976)]. At the initial hearing, the natural parent is informed of the right to have an attorney, and if the parent cannot afford an attorney, one will be appointed free of charge from the 18B Panel. The terminology *18B counsel* refers to Article 18B of the County Law, Section 722,* entitled "Representation of Persons Accused of Crime or Parties before the Family Court." This panel consists of attorneys who have placed their names on a list, from which the Appellate Division of the Supreme Court assigns counsel on a rotating basis for indigent natural parents or foster parents, and law guardians for foster children. See also In re Janice K. [82 Misc. 2d 983, 372 N.Y.S. 2d 381 (Family Court, New York County, 1975)]. The foster parent is also entitled to be represented by an attorney. In a contested matter, the court will appoint a law guardian on behalf of the foster child to protect the child's rights. The law guardian is an attorney and may be assigned from the 18B panel from the Legal Aid Society, or from Lawyers for Children.

If the plan of the agency is one that is agreeable to the natural parent and the foster parent, there is usually no need to have attorneys appointed, and the hearing is usually informal. The court—after hearing the attorney for the agency, the caseworker for the agency, the parent, and the foster parent—will direct that foster care continue with a view toward a return of the child and usually will set the date by which this is to be accomplished. The court, pursuant to Section 392, Subdivision 9, can and usually does direct the agency to undertake diligent efforts to encourage and strengthen the parental relationship when it finds such efforts will not be detrimental to the best interests of the child. Such order may include a specific plan for agency action for the authorized agency, including, without limitation, requirements that the agency assist the parent in obtaining adequate housing, employment, counseling, or medical or psychological treatment.

On the other hand, if the agency is requesting that the court direct the agency to free the child for adoption, the natural parent would be wise to—and usually does—request that an attorney be appointed. The court will then appoint an attorney for the natural parent and an attorney for the child. The matter is adjourned for a month or two, after which time a "long hearing" is scheduled. A "long hearing" is one that is expected to last two hours or longer. Prior to the scheduled hearing, the court may order a mental examination of the natural parents and the child by a psychiatrist or psychologist attached to the Bureau of Mental Hygiene. See Freeman v. Freeman [408 N.Y.S. 2d 994 (Family Court, Rockland County, 1978)].

On the return date of the hearing, the agency, through the testimony of the caseworkers and through its case records, must show that the parent or parents have abandoned the child or failed for a period of more than one year, fol-

---

West's McKinney's Forms, vol. 11.

lowing the date such child came into care of an authorized agency, substantially and continuously or repeatedly to maintain contact with or plan for the future of the child, although physically and financially able to do so, notwithstanding the agency's diligent efforts to encourage and strengthen the parental relationship when such efforts would not be detrimental to the best interests of the child. It would be wise for the caseworker to have prepared a written progress report outlining all basic facts, the status of the case, the agency's recommendations, and the basis for the recommendations. This report will be offered and received in evidence and will permit the judge to ascertain the agency's position and will form part of the record. The written report prepared in advance is usually well developed and may be more reliable than oral testimony in a situation where the court is faced with a long calendar and is short on time. This report should outline all affirmative acts on the part of the agency to strengthen parental ties between parent and child, including but not limited to:

1. encouraging visiting by the parent and, when necessary, bringing the child to the parent for a home visit;

2. aiding the parent to obtain satisfactory housing, employment, or public assistance. See In re Otis A. [390 N.Y.S. 2d 518 (Family Court, Kings County, 1976)], wherein Judge Stanley Gartenstein held the commissioner of social services of the City of New York in contempt of court for failure to comply with an order of the court directing him to obtain adequate housing for the sister of three neglected children who had been placed in her custody. The commissioner would be sentenced to fifteen days in jail if he failed to comply with the order within six weeks;

3. assisting the parent in obtaining medical assistance;

4. counseling the foster parents and enlisting their aid in strengthening the parental ties between the parent and child;

5. counseling the child to accept a parent who may have become an "uncle" or "aunt" figure or even a stranger to the child.

The attorney representing the natural parent will attempt to show the contrary—that is, that the parent did visit and plan for the child, or if the parent did not visit or plan for the child, that the agency did not use its best effort to strengthen the parental ties between the parent and child. In the case of Anthony T. [389 N.Y.S. 2d 86 (Family Court, New York County, 1976)], Judge Louis Otten held that in a 392 Foster Care Review Hearing initiated by the commissioner of social services, the child's father could properly counterclaim for the custody of his child and denied the commissioner's motion to strike the counterclaim.

In some cases, the foster parents will be supportive of the agency's position. However, the foster parents who are not caring for the child at the time of the foster-care review proceeding lack standing to participate. See Matter of

Ida Christina L. [506 N.Y.S. 2d 535, 133 Misc. 2d (1986)]. If the child is old enough, the court will interview the child in chambers with the child's law guardian present. Some judges prefer to have an attorney present when the child is questioned by the court; others permit the attorney to ask questions of the child if the child is old enough.

It is not unusual for the court to have previously ordered the natural parent have a Bureau of Mental Health Service (BMHS) examination by a psychologist or psychiatrist, which report is then reviewed by the court and may be used by the court in its determination. See Freeman v. Freeman [408 N.Y.S. 2d 994 (Family Court, Rockland County, 1978)], wherein the court stated:

> While the Court may not compel a parent in a custody proceeding to undergo therapy or analysis, it has the right to order a parent of the infant to be examined by a psychologist or psychiatrist and to consider such report in arriving at its judgment in the custody proceeding. (Grado v. Grado 3rd Dept. or analysis, 44 A.D. 2d 854, 356 [N.Y.S. 2d 85 (1974)]; Bennett v. Jeffreys [40 N.Y. 2d 543 (1976)].

The court does not usually reserve decision but immediately directs one of the following:

1. that foster care of the child be continued because it would not be in the best interests of the child to be returned home to the parent;

2. in the case of a child who has been committed temporarily to the care of an authorized agency by a parent, guardian, or relative, that the child be returned to such parent, guardian, or relative. See Matter of Rodriquez v. Dumpson [383 N.Y.S. 2d 883 (Appellate Division, 1st Dept., 1976)], wherein the court directed the return to a blind mother custody of her three-year-old son, who had been placed with foster parents shortly after birth. See also In re Jennifer Lynn [405 N.Y.S. 2d 988 (Family Court, Suffolk County, 1978)], wherein Judge Fay dismissed the agency's petition and returned the infant to the natural mother when the agency did not obtain a court order within twenty days from the mother's demand to return the child pursuant to Section 384 A of the Social Services Law; or

3. in the case of a child who has been committed temporarily to the care of an authorized agency by a parent, guardian, or relative, that the agency institute a proceeding to legally free such child for adoption, and that upon a failure by such agency to institute such a proceeding within ninety days after entry of such order, the foster parent or parents in whose home the child resides or the infant's law guardian be permitted to institute such a proceeding. See Matter of Sanjivini [40 N.Y. 2d 1025, 391 N.Y.S. 2d 535 (1977)], wherein the Court of Appeals reversed the Appellate Division and reinstated the family court direction to the agency to initiate proceedings to terminate parental rights. The majority held that the Appellate Division

had to be reversed in view of its reliance on a result and *ratio decidendi,* recently overturned by this court in Matter of Bennett v. Jeffreys [40 N.Y. 2d 543 (1976)].

In a concurring opinion, Judge Cooke wrote that the Appellate Division decision had to be reversed because of its reliance upon the interests of the natural mother rather than on the best interests of the child.

Interestingly, the Court of Appeals stated that the standards enunciated in Matter of Bennett v. Jeffreys [40 N.Y. 2d 543 (1976)], a custody contest between the natural mother and a third person who had physical custody of the child, apply to a permanent neglect proceeding. See also Matter of Richard N. [389 N.Y.S. 2d 525 (Family Court, New York County, 1976)], wherein Judge Louis Otten held that although the petition seeking review of foster-care status did not specifically request termination of parental rights, specific reference in the petition to Section 392 of the Social Services Law was sufficient. The court found that based on the entire record, there was reasonable cause to believe that legal grounds existed to free the child for adoption, and it directed the agency to institute a proceeding to terminate parental rights.

Best Interests of the Child

The disposition of custody of the child is controlled by what is in his or her best interests. See Matter of Jean Yvette E. [59 A.D. 2d 907, 399 N.Y.S. 2d 249 (Appellate Division, 2d Dept., 1977)], wherein the court said that disposition of the custody of the child should be influenced by what is in the best interest of the child where there has been surrender, abandonment, persisting neglect, unfitness, or other like extraordinary circumstances. See also In re L. [77 Misc. 2d 363, 353 N.Y.S. 2d 317], which was modified on other grounds [45 A.D. 2d 375, 357 N.Y.S. 2d 987]. In this case, the court said that *best interests of child* is not merely a descriptive statutory phrase but an expression of that which must be given overriding concern.

Also, as soon as the transfer of custody of a child to the commissioner of social services is approved, the responsibility for caring for the child's best interests vests with the agency: "This obligation is to be discharged without interference by the court unless 18 months have elapsed, and the child is still in foster care." See In re Damon A. [61 N.Y. 2d 77, 471 N.Y.S. 2d 838, 459 N.E. 2d 1275 (1983)].

In Matter of Lisa M. [387 N.Y.S. 2d 46 (Family Court, New York County, 1976)], Judge Stanley Gartenstein held that the court, on its own motion, could substitute the foster parents for the agency in a proceeding pursuant to family court direction in a 392 foster-care review proceeding when the agency failed to prosecute.

If the agency has been directed by court order to initiate proceedings to free the child on the basis that legal grounds do not exist, the agency may make a motion to amend the original order. The court may then recalendar the case and either adhere to its original order or amend the order; or there may be an appeal. In the case of In re Gaskin, Jr., v. Harlem Dowling Children's Services [387 N.Y.S. 2d 586 (Appellate Division, 1st Dept., 1976)], the Appellate Division reversed an order of the Family Court, New York County, that had directed that a proceeding be initiated to terminate parental rights because the family court judge failed to make *findings* in support of the court's determination that the order was in the best interests of the child. Simply to state that the agency has shown a sufficient basis that it should proceed to present the case for termination is not a sufficient finding as required by Section 392 of the Social Services Law.

However, if the agency is directed to free the child for adoption, the agency can free the child by:

1. petition based upon death of a parent or parents;
2. written surrender (pursuant to Section 384 B of the Social Services Law);
3. court order based upon abandonment (pursuant to Section 384 B of the Social Services Law);
4. court order based upon permanent neglect (pursuant to Article 6);
5. court order based upon mental illness or mental retardation of the parent (pursuant to Section 384 B of the Social Services Law); or
6. severe and repeated abuse.

10
Death of the Natural Parent or Parents

C hildren whose parents are deceased are not freed for adoption. The commissioner of social services or the authorized agency having care and supervision of the child must obtain an order committing the guardianship and custody of the child from either the family court or the surrogate's court, pursuant to Section 384 B of the Social Services Law.

In order to obtain a court order granting custody and guardianship, the attorney for the agency must draft a citation or a summons giving notice to the commissioner of social services and to any other interested person as directed by the court.

In a case before the judge of the surrogate's court in Nassau County, the court directed that the citation be served upon the commissioner of social services and the grandparents of the children and upon the foster parents and aunts and uncles.

The citation signed by the clerk of the court is shown in sidebar 10-1.

The Petition

The petition must allege that both parents are deceased and that the agency is seeking an *ex parte* order of commitment thereby freeing the child for adoption. A typical petition is shown in sidebar 10-2.

The Hearing

If the grandparents or other extended family oppose the agency's goal of having the foster parents adopt, the court will hold a hearing. At the hearing the court will inquire into the best interests of the child. See Matter of Daniel D.D. [106 Misc. 2d 370, 431 N.Y.S. 936 (Family Court, New York County, 1980)].

In deciding that two children should remain with their foster parents, the judge of the surrogate's court in Nassau County (file numbers 247, 248), in an unreported case, held:

Sidebar 10-1. Citation to Living Relatives of Children Whose Parents Are Deceased

By the Grace of God, Free and Independent:

TO: [foster parents, grandparents] and the Commissioner of Social Services of the City of New York, the persons interested in the commitment of [children], dependent children under the age of 14 years, to the custody of [agency] and the Commissioner of Social Services of the City of New York, under Section 384-b of the Social Services Law,

SEND GREETINGS:

WHEREAS, [agency], an authorized foster care agency, has applied lately to the Surrogate's Court of the County of [county] for an Order committing the custody and guardianship of the persons of [child] and [child], to said [agency], and the Commissioner of Social Services of the City of New York, pursuant to Section 384-b of the Social Services Law.

THEREFORE, YOU ARE HEREBY CITED to show cause before the Surrogate's Court of the County of [county] at [courthouse and address], on the [day] day of [month, year], at 9:30 o'clock in the forenoon of said day or as soon thereafter as counsel can be heard, why such an Order committing the custody and guardianship of the persons of said dependent children to [agency] and the Commissioner of Social Services of the City of New York, pursuant to Section 384-b of the Social Services Law, with the power of [agency] or the Commissioner of Social Services of the city of New York to place said children for adoption and to consent to their adoption, dispensing with the further notice to or consent of the parents based upon the children being without a living parent.

PLEASE TAKE NOTICE that if said children are adjudged to be without a living parent and, if custody is awarded to said authorized agency, said children may be adopted with the consent of said authorized agency, without further notice to you and without your consent.

In the event of your failure to appear, said failure to appear will result in the termination of all your parental rights to the children.

PLEASE TAKE FURTHER NOTICE that failure to appear shall constitute a denial of an interest in the children, which denial may result in the transfer of commitment of the children's care, custody, guardianship or adoption of the children all without further notice to the parent of the children.

PLEASE TAKE FURTHER NOTICE that you have a right to be represented by an attorney, and if you cannot afford an attorney, the Court will appoint an attorney for you free of charge.

IN WITNESS WHEREOF, we have caused the seal of the Surrogate's Court, Nassau County, at the Nassau County Courthouse, 262 Old Country Road, Mineola, New York in the said County, the [day] of [month], 19   .

_____
Clerk
Surrogate's Court, Nassau County

Attorneys for Petitioner

Sidebar 10-2. Petition of Agency Seeking Order of Commitment of Child of Deceased Parents

SURROGATE'S COURT OF THE STATE OF NEW YORK
COUNTY OF [county]

_____ x

In the Matter of guardianship and custody pursuant to 384-b of the Social Services Law of

[child]   PETITION

A child under the age of 14 years,   Docket No.
to [agency], alleged to be without
a living parent.

_____ x

TO THE SURROGATE'S COURT OF [county] COUNTY:

The undersigned Petitioner, [agency], respectfully shows to the Court as follows:

1. The Petitioner, [agency], is an authorized agency, having an office for the place of business at [agency address].

2. [Child] is a male child under the age of 14 years, born on [child's birthdate] in [location], and the infant presently resides with his foster parents, [foster parents], who wish to adopt the infant. The birth certificate of the infant, [child] is annexed hereto and marked as Exhibit "A."

3. The full name and address of each parent custodian of said child are:

NAME   LAST KNOWN ADDRESS

[natural mother], natural
mother   Deceased

[putative father], putative
father   Deceased

COMMISSIONER OF SOCIAL   220 Church Street
SERVICES CITY OF   New York, New York 10013
NEW YORK

4. [maternal grandfather], the maternal grandfather of the infant herein, has expressed an interest in adopting the child.

5. [paternal uncle and aunt], the paternal uncle and aunt of the infant herein, have expressed an interest in adopting the child.

6. [maternal grandmother], the maternal grandmother of the infant, is a potential party interested in adopting the infant.

7. The name and address of each other interested party who should be afforded notice of this proceeding are:

NAME   LAST KNOWN ADDRESS

[foster parents], foster
parents

[maternal grandfather],
maternal grandfather,

[paternal uncle and aunt],
paternal uncle and aunt

[maternal grandmother],
maternal grandmother

8. Upon information and belief, the mother of the infant, [child], is deceased. Annexed hereto and made a part of hereof and marked as Exhibit "B" is a copy of the Death Certificate of the mother showing that the mother died on [date].

9. Upon information and belief, no guardian of the person of said child has been lawfully appointed on behalf of the infant.

10. It is unknown whether the putative father of the infant herein, [putative father], was married to the natural mother.

11. Upon information and belief, the putative father of the infant herein [putative father], is deceased. Annexed hereto and made a part hereof and marked Exhibit "C" is a copy of the

Death Certificate of the putative father showing he died on [date].

12. The child came into care of the Bureau of Child Welfare of the City of New York on [date], and the child was placed with [agency] on [date].

13. The Petitioner is seeking an ex-parte Order of Commitment from this Court, as the Bureau of Child Welfare of the City of New York has informed [agency] that they will not transfer custody of the infant to [agency] with the power to place for adoption until and unless an Order of Commitment is obtained from a Court of competent jurisdiction on the ground that no one has legal custody of the infant and an Order of Commitment of a Judge is necessary.

14. The best interests of said child will be promoted by commitment of the guardianship and custody of the child to the Commissioner of Social Services of the City of New York and to [agency], an authorized agency, for the reason that the child is without a living parent and is an adoptable child.

15. No previous Petition has been filed for the relief sought herein.

WHEREFORE, your Petitioner, [agency], prays for an Order adjudicating the above-named child, a child whose parents are deceased, and committing the guardianship and custody of said child to the Commissioner of Social Services of the City of New York and to [agency], with the power of the Commissioner of Social Services of the City of New York or [agency] to place for adoption without further notice to or consent of any persons and for such other further relief as may be in the interests of the child.

Dated: [agency]

                                          By _____
                                             Executive Director

STATE OF NEW YORK)
) ss.:
COUNTY OF NASSAU)

[Agency director], being duly sworn, deposes and says that he is the Executive Director of [agency], petitioner herein; that he has read the foregoing Petition and knows the contents thereof; that the same is true to his own knowledge, except as to matters therein stated to be alleged on information and belief, and as to those matters he believes it to be true.

_____
Executive Director

Sworn to before me this
[day] of [month], 19   .

_____
Notary Public

All of the evidence submitted, including the case report, the psychological evaluations, the testimony, and the interview of the children, support an inescapable conclusion that the custody of these children should remain with their foster parents and that their best interests will be served by granting the applications now before the court. On the issue of the grandfather's right to visitation, the court refuses to grant any visitation at this time. However, it does agree that family and a sense of family history is important to everyone. If at some later date, based upon medical and psychological evaluations, these infants are better equipped to resume a relationship with their grandfather, then at that time the court may entertain an application for visitation if an extra-judicial agreement on visitation with the grandfather cannot be reached among the parties.

Settle orders in accordance with the findings made in this decision.

At the conclusion of the hearing the judge will direct that an order of commitment be drafted, served, and filed.

Sidebar 10–3 is a form of order of commitment where both parents are deceased.

Sidebar 10-3. Order of Commitment
of Child of Deceased Parents

At the Surrogate's Court held in and for the [county] at the courthouse, [address] on the [day] of [month], 19 .

PRESENT:
HON. [judge]

Judge of the Surrogate's Court.

_____ x

In the Matter of the Commitment
of Guardianship and Custody of
the Person of

[child]

Pursuant to Section 384-b of
the Social Services Law of the
State of New York, a child
without a living parent, to
[agency]

ORDER COMMITTING
CUSTODY OF DEPENDENT
CHILD TO AUTHORIZED
AGENCY

_____ x

A Petition having been duly presented to be by [agency], verified on the [day] of [month], 19 , praying that the guardianship of the person and custody of [child], the above-named child, be committed to [agency] and the Commissioner of Social Services of the City of New York to place [child] for legal adoption, subject to the customary approval of the Court, and it appearing by said Petition that said child was under the age of fourteen (14) years, having been born on [date] and having been placed with the petitioning agency on [date] and that the child has no living parents as the mother of the infant, [mother], is deceased having died on [date], and the natural father of the infant, [father], is deceased having died on [date], and that [agency] is an institution incorporated under the laws of the State of New York, having its place of business in this State and approved, visited, inspected and supervised by the State Board of Social Welfare of the State of New York, and the Commissioner of Social Services of the City of New York, and the maternal grandfather, [maternal grandfather], having been personally served with a Citation and Petition in this matter and any objections that the maternal grandmother, [maternal grandmother], or the paternal uncle and aunt, [paternal uncle and aunt], may have had to the Petition herein having been resolved pursuant to a Stipulation of Settlement entered on the record, and the petitioner having been represented by [attorney], Esq., [attorney], Esq., of counsel, attorneys for petitioner, [agency], and the maternal grandfather, [maternal grandfather], having been represented by [attorney], attorneys at law, and the infant, [child], having been represented by [attorney], Esq., Guardian ad litem, and the hearing having taken place on [date] and continued on [date], and the Court having made examination and inquiry into the facts and circumstances of the case and into the surroundings, conditions and capacities of the persons involved in this proceeding, and the Court having heard the testimony of caseworkers [caseworkers], and having heard the testimony of the maternal grandmother and the foster mother and the Court having heard the testimony of the maternal grandfather and the Court having considered the views of the infant and the Court having considered the Post-Trial Memorandum of Law and Reply Post-Trial Memorandum of Law submitted on behalf of the petitioner, [agency], and the Court having considered the Post-Trial Memorandum of Law on behalf of respondent, [maternal grandfather], and the Court having considered the Report of Guardian ad litem, [attorney], Esq., and based upon the proofs submitted and the testimony taken and based upon the decision of this Court dated [date], and in accordance with Section 384-b Subd. 4 (a) of the Social Services Law, the application for commitment of the infant to [agency] and the Commissioner of Social Services of the City of New York is granted,

NOW, ON MOTION OF [attorney], attorneys for said petitioner, it is

ADJUDGED, that both parents of the infant, [child], are dead, to wit: [mother and father], and no guardian of the person of said child has been lawfully appointed; and it is

ORDERED, ADJUDGED AND DECREED, that said [child] is a dependent child and a child without a living parent, and it is further

ORDERED, ADJUDGED AND DECREED, that the guardianship of the person and custody of said [child] be committed to [agency] and the Commissioner of Social Services of the City of New York with the right of [agency] or the Commissioner of Social Services of the City of New York to consent to the child's legal adoption subject to the customary approval of the Court to which the Petition for adoption is presented.

Dated: ENTER:

_____

HON. [judge]

Judge, Surrogate's Court

11
The Surrender

Another method of placing a child into foster care is by written surrender, executed by the natural parent or parents. The written surrender not only places a child into foster care but also terminates the parental rights of the natural parent or parents. In a surrender, the natural parent loses the right to custody of the child, and to visit with, speak with, write to, or learn about the child forever, unless the parties agree otherwise.

The surrender that terminates parental rights should not be confused with the voluntary commitment, which is termed "transfer of care and custody of children instrument," as governed by Section 384 A of the Social Services Law. The written surrender that terminates parental rights, thereby freeing the child for adoption, at least with respect to the parent executing the surrender, is governed by Section 383 C of the Social Services Law. See also In re Ruth J. [55 A.D. 2d 52, 389 N.Y.S. 2d 473 (Appellate Division, 3rd Dept., 1976)].

The written surrender provides that the natural parent or parents relinquish legal custody of the child to the commissioner of social services, who in turn executes a transfer of custody, transferring custody of the child to the authorized agency, which in turn consents to the adoption of the child.

Legislative Changes

Prior to October 1, 1989, when a child who was to be surrendered by a parent for adoption was in foster care, the surrender instrument was signed by the parent, acknowledged before a notary public, and witnessed.

The surrender was then recorded in the county clerk's office where it was executed or where the authorized agency had a place of business. The parent had thirty days to revoke the surrender for any reason and could always invoke the aid of the courts to revoke for fraud or duress.

It was felt by the legislature that an amendment was needed to expedite procedures and assure all parties that the procedures were performed lawfully by requiring the surrender to be executed before a family court judge.

Effective October 1, 1989, Section 384 of the Social Services Law of the

State of New York was amended to require that the surrender instrument be executed before a judge of the family court. The twofold purpose of the October 1, 1989, amendment was, first, to insure that when the parent or guardian surrenders a child for adoption, which child is in foster care, the rights of all the parties, especially of the natural parent, are protected by requiring that the surrender instrument be executed before a family court judge. The other purpose was based on a finding by the legislature that there had been delays involving the validity of surrenders of children in foster care.

But the new law simply did not work. It was too restrictive, and the number of surrenders decreased dramatically—between 60 and 80 percent over the previous year.

The legislature's most recent enactment, Section 383 C, was signed by Governor Mario Cuomo on July 16, 1990, and is effective as of January 1, 1991. The main effect of the new law is to eliminate the need to have the parent sign the surrender before a judge of the family court.

Judicial and Extrajudicial Surrenders

Pursuant to Section 383 C, effective January 1, 1991, agencies now have an option to have a judicial surrender—one taken before a judge of the family court or the surrogate's court; or an extrajudicial surrender—one taken out of court, before a notary public and two witnesses. One of these witnesses must be an employee of an authorized agency with special training concerning surrenders, and the other witness must be either a certified social worker or an attorney not employed by or connected with the agency.

Judicial Surrender

Pursuant to Section 383 C(3), the surrender of a child in *foster care* to an authorized agency may be executed before a judge of the family court or a surrogate.

When the surrender is executed, the judge must inform the natural parent that he/she has the right:

1. to be represented by legal counsel;
2. to obtain supportive counsel;
3. to be assigned counsel, free of charge, if qualified; and
4. to be informed of the consequences of signing the surrender—losing the right to custody of the child, to visit with, speak with, write to, or learn about the child forever, unless the parties agree otherwise (an open adoption).

The judge must also inform the parents that the surrender is final and irrevocable immediately upon its execution and acknowledgment.

Extrajudicial Surrender

Where a surrender is not executed and acknowledged before a judge or surrogate, the written surrender must be executed and acknowledged by the parent in the presence of at least two witnesses and before a notary public. At least one witness must be an employee of an authorized agency and have been trained in accordance with the regulations of the Department of Social Services to receive surrenders. At least one of the witnesses must be either a certified social worker or an attorney, and he/she cannot be an employee, volunteer, consultant, or agent of an attorney employed by the authorized agency to which the child is being surrendered.

Court Approval Required. When an extrajudicial surrender is properly executed by the parent, the authorized agency must file an application for the approval of the extrajudicial surrender with the court in which the adoption proceeding is expected to be filed, or if not known, in the family court or the surrogate's court in the county in which the agency has its principal office.

The application must be filed no later than fifteen days after the execution of the surrender, and the application must be accompanied by two affidavits: one from the employee or volunteer of the authorized agency and another from the nonemployee, volunteer, consultant, agent, or attorney before whom the surrender was executed and acknowledged. These affidavits must state the following:

1. the day, time, and place where the surrender was executed and acknowledged:
2. that the parent was provided with a copy of the surrender;
3. that the surrender was read in full to the parent in his/her principal language and that the parent was given an opportunity to ask questions and obtain answers regarding the nature and consequence of the surrender; and
4. that the parent executed and acknowledged the surrender.

A third affidavit must also be supplied by the authorized agency from the employee responsible for providing or arranging supportive counseling. This affidavit must state:

1. when supportive counseling was offered to the parent;
2. whether the parent accepted the offer of supportive counseling; and
3. if accepted, when supportive counseling was provided and the nature of such supportive counseling.

Venue

With respect to which county is the proper venue, there is a choice. The petition to approve the extrajudicial surrender may be filed in the court where it is believed that the adoption will take place or where the agency has its principal place of business.

Parents

No Presumption of Superior Right

Where a child not in foster care has been surrendered, and there is a proceeding to revoke or annul the surrender instrument in the case of a child placed in an adoptive home, the parent who surrendered the child shall have no right to the custody of said child superior to that of the adoptive parents, notwithstanding that the parent who surrendered the child may be fit, competent, and able to maintain, support, and educate the child. The custody of a surrendered child not in foster care shall be awarded solely on the basis of the best interests of the child, and there shall be no presumption that such interests will be promoted by any particular custodial disposition.

Paternity

Married Father

If the natural mother was married at the time when the child was born, the husband, whether he is the father of the child or not, who wishes to relinquish his parental rights, must also execute a surrender.

Putative Father

A putative father or unwed father who wishes to relinquish whatever rights he has to the child and who acknowledges that he is the father of the child, should sign a waiver by father. The waiver signed by the father of the child who had not married the mother must be in writing, signed, witnessed, and acknowledged before a notary public or commissioner of deeds.

Denial of Paternity by Unwed Named Father

From time to time, a mother will name a person as the father of the child, which person does not acknowledge that he is the father. In that case, said person may sign a denial of paternity. The denial of paternity alleges that the person denies that he is the father of the child and waves any notification of future planning for and adoption of the child. Said denial of paternity must be in writing, signed by the person denying paternity, and witnessed and acknowledged by a notary public or commissioner of deeds.

Surrender by Parents in Foster Care

A surrender for adoption executed by a parent who is in foster care shall be executed only before a judge of the family court. The fact that the parent who executes the surrender was a child at the time of the signing does not impair the validity of the surrender. See People Ex re Skolas v. McCarthy [164 N.Y.S. 2d 198 (Superior Court, New York County, 1957)], in which the court held the surrender of a sixteen-year-old valid.

But see Janet G. v. New York Foundling Hospital [403 N.Y.S. 2d 646 (Family Court, New York County, 1978)], in which an eleven-year-old mother's surrender of a child was required to be reaffirmed in a judicial proceeding in which she would have benefit of a guardian *ad litem* when the initial surrender was not taken before a judicial officer, and the mother had neither a fiduciary nor the aid of counsel. See also In re Adoption of Male L. [125 Misc. 2d 787, 407 N.Y.S. 2d 750 (Appellate Division, 3rd Dept., 1978)].

Notification to Parent

Before a judge of the family court or a surrogate approves an extrajudicial surrender, the judge or surrogate shall order notice to be given to the person who executed the surrender, to persons required to be given notice of the proceeding pursuant to Section 384 C of the Social Services Law, and to such other persons as the judge or surrogate may in his/her direction prescribe.

The petition shall set forth the names and last-known addresses of all persons required to be given notice of the proceeding, pursuant to Section 384 C of the Social Services Law.

Mental Capacity

A surrender must be executed by a parent with full understanding of its effect. However, in the case of In re Adoption of E.A.V. [86 Misc. 2d 507 (Surrogate's Court, Bronx County, 1976)], the court held that a surrender by an unwed mother was valid even though her condition had been diagnosed as paranoid schizophrenia. The court so held after reviewing an affidavit submitted by the attorney for the natural mother and the complete hospital record. The court was satisfied that the mother, at the time she executed the surrender, was aware that she had surrendered all rights to her child. The court held:

> In the instant case, it appears that the natural mother had substantiated periods of lucidity in which she completely understood her circumstances. The record reflects a clear understanding of the difficulties of raising her child in view of her condition and marital status and desire to relieve herself of this responsibility while she coped with her other problems.
>
> The Court is satisfied that, at the time of the execution of the Petition, the natural mother represented by counsel, voluntarily surrendered any right to the infant and, accordingly, is not a party to the instant pro-

ceedings (Domestic Relations Law, Section 111 [4]). The Petition for adoption is granted.

Surrender of Children Not in Foster Care

Section 384 of the Social Services Law deals with surrenders of children not in foster care and who are usually surrendered at birth to an authorized agency for the purpose of adoption only. Section 384 of the Social Services Law permits surrenders to be executed in or out of court, except that surrenders by parents who are themselves in foster care must be executed before a judge of the family court.

Regulations

The State Commission of Social Services, after consultation with the chief administrator of the courts, has been directed by this section to promulgate regulations to help insure the impartial selection and independence of the witnesses. Appropriate forms of surrender shall also be drafted and promulgated.

Independent Counsel

Section 262 of the Family Court Act provides that if the surrendering parent is indigent, counsel must be assigned to said parent. Section 262 (4) provides for counsel to an indigent parent having physical or legal custody of the child in any proceeding under Section 384 of the Social Services Law. Further, Section 262 B provides for assignment of counsel to indigent parents where such assignment is mandated by the constitution of the State of New York or of the United States. Independent counsel will assist in the execution of the surrender and will help determine whether the surrender is being executed knowingly and freely. Presumably, the attorney could also counsel the parent to the possibility of receiving emotional and financial assistance in order to retain custody of the child and not sign the surrender.

The Instrument

There are two forms of instrument, one for a judicial surrender, and one for an extrajudicial surrender. Both forms of surrender shall state in plain language, in conspicuous bold print on the first page, that:

1. the parent has the right before signing the surrender to speak to an attorney of his/her own choosing or to any other person he/she may wish to speak to;
2. the parent has the right to have that lawyer or other person present with her/him at the time of the execution of the surrender;
3. the parent has the right to ask the court to appoint an attorney, free of charge, if the parent cannot afford to hire one; and
4. the parent has the right to supportive counseling.

The form of the instrument shall also state that the parent is giving up all right to have custody, visit with, speak with, write to, or learn about the child forever, unless the parties have agreed to different terms (more commonly known as an open adoption).

The form of instrument shall also state that the child will be adopted without the parent's consent, without further notice to the parent, and will be adopted by any person that the agency chooses unless the surrender paper contains the name of the person or persons who will be adopting the child. (This is considered a conditional surrender.)

The form of instrument shall state that the parent cannot be forced to sign the surrender paper and cannot be punished if he/she does not sign the paper and would not be subject to any penalty for refusing to sign the surrender.

Judicial Surrender

A surrender instrument for judicial surrender shall also state in plain language, in conspicuous bold print on the first page, that the surrender becomes final and irrevocable immediately upon execution and acknowledgment, and that the parent cannot bring a case in court to revoke the surrender or to regain custody of the child.

Extrajudical Surrender

An extrajudicial surrender shall also state in plain language, in conspicuous bold print on the first page:

1. the name and address of the court in which the application for approval of the extrajudicial surrender will be filed;
2. that a revocation of the surrender will be effective if it is in writing and postmarked or received by the court named in the surrender within forty-five days of the signing of the surrender; and
3. that a revocation of the surrender more than forty-five days after its signing will not be effective if the child has been placed in an adoptive home, and the surrender shall be final and irrevocable, and the parent cannot revoke the surrender or bring a case in court to revoke the surrender or regain

custody of the child, and that the agency will not notify the parent when the child is placed in an adoptive home and that the parent may lose all right at the end of the forty-five-day period without further notice.

Procedure for Surrender before Family Court Judge

When a parent who has a child in foster care and who has been counseled by a caseworker decides to terminate parental rights and sign a surrender, both the caseworker and the parent who is to sign the surrender should appear in family court at 9:00 A.M.

It is recommended that the caseworker prepare four surrender instruments, completely typed except for the signature of the parent who is to surrender the child. The other two documents that should be completed prior to the appearance in family court are the application to execute written surrender of a child in foster care and the attestation of execution. The former is signed by the parent in the presence of the court, and the latter is signed by the judge after the surrenders have been executed (see sidebars at the end of the chapter for sample related to the surrender procedure).

Filing the Petition and Supporting Documents

When the caseworker arrives in the family court with the parent, the caseworker should immediately go to the petition clerk's office and file the unsigned completed surrenders, the application to execute written surrender of a child in foster care, and the attestation of execution. These papers should be given to the petition clerk at 9:00 A.M. on the day during which the execution is to be made. If time permits, the petition clerk will docket the papers, prepare the file jacket, and complete the other appropriate paperwork and thereafter forward the surrender and other documents to the Assignment Part, which is known as Part A. The family court will give these applications priority.

Some judges have their law assistant review the surrenders, appoint an attorney to represent the mother, and have the parties come back on another day to execute the surrenders. Presently in the Family Court of New York County, the surrenders are submitted to the judge of Part I and two appearances are required. In other counties, the surrenders are submitted to the judge sitting in Part A. Some judges complete the execution of the surrender in one day, while other judges require that the parent sign on another day.

Execution

The parent, when the case is called in Part A, will execute the surrender and the application before the judge. The judge, in turn, will sign the form entitled "attestation of execution," and the clerk of the part will affix the court seal to the attestation. The signed surrender and attestation will then become part of the court file.

While this procedure, as outlined by the deputy chief clerk, indicates that only one surrender will be signed, it is suggested that four surrenders be executed, as the agency will need them for other purposes. First, one must be recorded in the county clerk's office, as required by law. The second one will be needed in any court proceeding to terminate parental rights of the other parent. The third will also be required to be filed with the adoption clerk when the adoption takes place.

The procedure for executing the surrender further provides that if the matter cannot be resolved on that particular day, the judge at Part A will then adjourn the matter to a future date, but that particular judge will keep the matter even if the judge is then assigned to another part. This is considered good procedure and should expedite the matter.

Recording of Surrender

The signature of the parent must be attested to by a judge of the Family Court of the State of New York, and the written surrender is then recorded in the county clerk's office in which the commissioner or agency has an office of the conduct of business. After the surrender is recorded, it is returned to the authorized agency or its attorney. There is a five-dollar fee for recording the surrender.

The court shall enter an order either approving or disapproving the surrender. If the judge or surrogate disapproves the surrender, the surrender shall be deemed a nullity.

The surrender shall be recorded in the office of the county clerk in the county where the surrender is executed, or where the principal office of such authorized agency is located, in a book in which such county clerk shall provide and shall keep under seal.

Fraud, Duress, or Coercion

Nothing contained in this section shall bar actions or proceedings brought on the grounds of fraud, duress, or coercion in the execution or inducement of the surrender.

The amount of stress that must be imposed on a parent who has executed a surrender under Section 384 (5) of the Social Services Law before the court abrogates the surrender appears to be quite high. This is largely a result of the balancing process that takes place between the interests of the people involved as well as the interests of society. See Matter of T.W.C. [(N.Y.L.J.) Dec. 18,

1974, p. 17, col. 6], citing Matter of Surrender of Minor Children [344 Mass. 230, 181 N.E. 2d 836, affd. 48 A.D. 2d 893, 369 N.Y.S. 2d 783, affd. 38 N.Y. 2d 128, 379 N.Y.S. 2d 1, 341 N.E. 2d 526], in which the court stated that:

> Contemplation of the surrender of one's own child is in many, if not all, cases a cause of emotional and mental stress. . . . No statute has said that surrenders are valid only if executed free from emotions, tensions and pressure caused by the situation. No principle of law requires the rule. A balance of the interests of the persons concerned and of society weighs strongly against it.

In Matter of Commissioner of Social Services, Suffolk County, v. Sandra G. [529 N.Y.S. 2d 883 (Appellate Division, 2nd Dept., 1988)], the Appellate Division upheld a Suffolk County Family Court ruling that the natural mother of a child conceived as a result of rape failed to establish fraud, duress, or coercion sufficient to abrogate an otherwise duly executed surrender. The court noted that both the natural mother and her husband had received counseling from a clergyman, a psychiatric social worker, and a caseworker, who explained all of the options available. Further, although the natural mother's husband encouraged her to surrender the child, "that did not render the circumstances coercive nor did his entreaties impair her ability to exercise her free will" [Id at 884]. The court reasoned that "while the natural mother had misgivings about consenting to the adoption, there is no evidence of any fraud, duress or coercion which would vacate her consent" (Id at 884].

Revocation of Surrender

Notification to Court

The agency to which the child is surrendered shall promptly notify the court of any correspondence or communication received from the parent or anyone on the parent's behalf, subsequent to the execution of the surrender and prior to a final order of adoption of the child, if such correspondence or communication could reasonably indicate the parent's wish to revoke the surrender.

Effect of Revocation

If the court disapproves a surrender, or if a parent delivers or mails a revocation of an extrajudicial surrender to the court named in the surrender within forty-five days of the execution of the surrender, such surrender shall be deemed a nullity, and the child shall be returned to the care and custody of the authorized agency.

If a parent delivers or mails a revocation of an extrajudicial surrender to the court named in the surrender more than forty-five days after its execution, and the child has not been placed in an adoptive home, such surrender shall be deemed a nullity, and the child shall be returned to the care and custody of the authorized agency.

Intervention in Proceedings to Set Aside a Surrender

Any person having custody of a child for the purpose of adoption through an authorized agency shall be permitted as a matter of right to intervene in any proceeding commenced to set aside a surrender. Any person having custody for more than twelve months through an authorized agency for the purpose of foster care shall be permitted as a matter of right to intervene in any proceeding commenced to set aside a surrender.

Intervention of Adoptive Parents in Revocation Proceedings

Adoptive parents having custody of a child through an authorized agency have the right, as an interested party, to intervene in any proceeding to set aside a surrender. See the Domestic Relations Law, Section 112 (1).

Adoption

Proceedings

The adoptive parents may commence the adoption proceeding in a court of competent jurisdiction other than the court named in an extrajudicial surrender, provided that such commencement is initiated more than forty-five days after the surrender is executed.

Once an adoption has been finalized, the adoption is unassailable by the parent who executed a surrender. See McGaffin v. Family and Children's Services of Albany [164 N.Y.S. 2d 444 (Superior Court, New York County, 1957)].

Failure to Adopt

In any case in which the authorized agency determines that the person specified in the surrender will not adopt the child, the agency promptly shall notify the parent thereof, unless such notice is expressly waived by a statement written by the parent appended to or included in such instrument.

Recordation in Bound Volume

No child shall be deemed to have been placed in the home of adoptive parents unless the fact of such placement, the date thereof, the date of the agreement pertaining thereto, and the names and addresses of the adoptive parents shall have been recorded in bound volume maintained by the agency for the purposes of recording such information in chronological order.

Sidebar 11-1. Order to Show Cause
(Needed to Obtain Court Approval of Surrender)

FAMILY COURT OF THE STATE OF NEW YORK
COUNTY OF KINGS

———————————————————— x

In the Matter of   ORDER TO SHOW CAUSE
, an Infant for an Application of Judicial Approval of an Extra-Judicial Surrender Pursuant to 383-c of the Social Services Law of the State of New York

———————————————————— x

Upon the Petition verified February   , 1991, the affidavits of Caseworker #1, Caseworker #2, non-employee Certified Caseworker and the Surrender dated, signed and acknowledged on January 30, 1991 and upon the proceedings heretofore had herein, it is hereby

ORDERED, that cause be shown at a term of this Court, to be held in the Courthouse thereof at 283 Adams Street, Brooklyn, New York, Intake Part A on the   of   , 1991 at 9:30 o'clock in the forenoon of that date, or as soon thereafter as Counsel can be heard why an Order should not be made pursuant to Section 383-c of the Social Services Law of the State of New York judicially approving the extra-judicial Surrender signed by   , the father of the infant,   and further relief as the Court shall deem just and proper, and it is further

ORDERED, that service of a copy of this Order to Show Cause, the Petition, the Surrender and supporting papers and Affidavits upon Legal Aid Society, Family Court, Kings Court, 283 Adams Street, Brooklyn, New York,   , the father of the infant, residing at   , the mother of the infant, residing at   , and the Commissioner of Social Services of the City of New York by his attorneys, Victor L. Kovner, Corporation Counsel, by Barry Ensminger, Special Assistant Corporation Counsel, Martin Barron,

Esq., of Counsel, 220 Church Street, New York, New York 10013
by certified mail, return receipt requested, and by ordinary mail,
postmarked on or before the   day of February, 1991 shall be
deemed timely and sufficient service.

Dated: , 1991   ENTER:

_____

J.F.C.

Sidebar 11-2. Petition for Approval of Surrender Instrument, Child in Foster Care

COURT OF THE STATE OF NEW YORK
COUNTY OF [county]

_____ x

In the Matter of the   (Docket) (File) No.
Application Approval of a
Surrender Instrument   PETITION FOR APPROVAL
Concerning   OF SURRENDER
                                    INSTRUMENT (CHILD
                                    IN FOSTER CARE)

Pursuant to Section 383-c of the Social Services Law.

_____ x

TO THE   COURT OF THE COUNTY OF   :
    The undersigned Petitioner respectfully alleges that:

1. Petitioner   is an authorized agency having its office
    and place of business at   in the County of   ,
    State of New York.

2.   , is a (fe)male child under the age of eighteen years,
    born on   , at   , who now resides in the County
    of   , State of New York.

3. The child is now in the custody of the petitioner and resides
    at   .

4. The guardianship of the person and custody of the child have
    been committed to the petitioner by a written instrument of
    surrender, signed by

    *(, mother and   , father of the child).

*(, (mother) (father) of the child,   (father) (mother) being deceased).

*(, (mother) (father) of the child, (father) (mother) having abandoned the child for a period of six months immediately preceding the filing of this petition).

*(mother of such child, who was born out of wedlock and by   , father of such child whose consent is required pursuant to Section 111 of the Domestic Relations Law).

*(, guardian of the person of such child lawfully appointed by (the   Court of   County, State of   ) (   )** (both parents of such child being dead) (said child being out of wedlock and the mother of such child being deceased) with the approval of the (Court) (   )** herewith attached and made a part hereof) in accordance with Section 383-c of the Social Services Law; a copy of the instrument of surrender being attached hereto and made a part hereof.

5. The instrument of surrender was executed and acknowledged before   and   whose affidavits are attached herewith and made a part hereof.

6. The names and last known addresses of the child's parents and all persons required to be given notice of this proceeding are:

Name   Address   Relationship

and there are no persons other than those set forth above entitled to notice pursuant to Section 384-c of the Social Services Law.

7. No previous application has been made for the approval of this instrument of surrender to any court of judge (except   ).

WHEREFORE, petitioner prays that this Court enter an order approving such instrument on such notice to such persons as the Court may in its discretion provide.

_____
Petitioner

*delete if inapplicable.
**insert other appointing officer, if applicable.

VERIFICATION IN PROCEEDING
BY AUTHORIZED AGENCY

STATE OF NEW YORK)
) ss.:

COUNTY OF   )

        , being duly sworn, deposes and says:

     That (s)he is   and is acquainted with the facts and cir-
cumstances of the above-entitled proceeding; that (s)he has read
the foregoing petition and knows the contents thereof; that the
same is true to (his) (her) own knowledge except as to those matters therein stated to be alleged upon information and belief, and
that as to those matters (s)he believes it to be true.

                                                _____
                                                Petitioner

Sworn to before me this
         day of   , 19 .

_____
(Deputy) Clerk of the Court
Notary Public

Sidebar 11–3. Notice of Proceeding for
Approval of Surrender Instrument

COURT OF THE STATE OF NEW YORK
COUNTY OF [county]

_____ x

In the Matter of the Application for Approval of a Surrender Instrument Concerning

Pursuant to Section 384-c of the Social Services Law

_____ x

TO:

     PLEASE TAKE NOTICE that the annexed petition requesting
approval of an instrument of surrender concerning the above-
named child has been presented to the   Court of the

State of New York,   County, and that a hearing on the petition will be held on the   day of   , 19 , at o'clock in the   noon of that day at which time you will have an opportunity to be heard.

PLEASE TAKE FURTHER NOTICE that you have the right to be represented by a lawyer and, if you are the (mother) (father) of the above-named child and the Court finds that you are unable to pay for a lawyer, you have the right to have a lawyer assigned by the Court.

FAILURE TO APPEAR MAY RESULT WITHOUT FURTHER NOTICE IN COURT APPROVAL OF THE TRANSFER OF CUS-TODY AND GUARDIANSHIP OF THE CHILD TO A SOCIAL SER-VICES OFFICIAL FOR THE PURPOSE OF ADOPTION.

Dated:

_____
Attorney(s) for Petitioner
Office and P.O. Address
Telephone Number

Sidebar 11-4. Affidavit in Support of Request in Court Approval of Surrender

FAMILY COURT OF THE STATE OF NEW YORK
COUNTY OF KINGS

_____ x

In the Matter of
        , an Infant
for an Application of Judicial
Approval of an Extra-Judicial
Surrender Pursuant to 383-c of the
Social Services Law of the State of
New York.

CASEWORKER TRAINED
IN TAKING
SURRENDERS

_____ x

STATE OF NEW YORK)
) ss.:
COUNTY OF KINGS   )

Caseworker #1, being duly sworn, deposes and says:

1. I am a certified social worker employed as a supervisor by
    , an authorized agency, having an office at   .

2. The infant,   , born on   is presently in foster
    care under the custody and control of CWA who in turn placed
    the child with   , an authorized agency. The child is
    now in a foster home under the control and supervision of
    [agency]. I have been a social worker employed by [agency]
    for the last eight years and as such I have been involved in
    numerous terminations of parental rights proceedings. I have
    also been assigned to numerous cases where I have worked
    closely with biological parents, and I have worked with them
    using diligent efforts to obtain housing, public assistance,
    counseling, parental training, rehabilitation from drugs and
    alcohol and other services.

3. I have been trained to accept surrenders and have been
    accepting surrenders for the last eight years. Specifically, I
    have been trained by the Director of the Brooklyn office of
    , who has been a social worker for 20 years, and I
    have been trained by [attorney], Esq., the attorney for
    . I have reviewed the statute and I am familiar with
    the taking of surrenders. After being trained by Mr. Carrieri
    and   , and after reviewing Mr. Carrieri's article and the
    new law, 383-c of the Social Services Law, I understood and
    was aware of my responsibility that the surrender instrument
    must be read in full to the parent signing the surrender. On
    January 30, 1991, I was present in the same room at the New
    York office of   located at   , along with
    Caseworker #2, an employee and social worker for
    and   , a certified social worker employed as Director
    of   , the statutory non-employee, and, also present
    was the father of the infant,   .

4. I was present at our office at   when the father of the
    infant,   , had come to the office to sign the extra-
    judicial surrender. It was 1:00 P.M. on January 30, 1991 and I
    had explained the terms of the surrender on this date, and I
    was convinced on January 30, 1991 that he was fully familiar
    with the terms and conditions of the surrender, that he was
    giving up all parental rights to the child, except he had agreed
    with the foster parents that he would have an open adoption
    and would be able to visit the child from time to time as
    agreed on between him and the foster parents. I then ex-

plained the terms of the surrender to   , and then I read the entire surrender instrument out loud in the English language to   and I know that he speaks and understands the English language. At the execution of the surrender on January 30, 1991, I had given   an opportunity to ask questions concerning the surrender and its execution and I and Caseworker #2 were prepared to answer any of his questions, but there were no questions, as Caseworker #2 had had several conferences with him concerning the surrender prior thereto.   acknowledged on January 30, 1991, that he fully understood the terms and conditions of the surrender and he knew he was giving up all parental rights to his child.

          informed me that he was assured by the foster mother that he could visit the child after the adoption from time to time. I am convinced that   understood his rights and the consequences of signing the surrender. Caseworker #2 offered him an attorney on a prior occasion and on January 30, 1991, but he said he did not want an attorney to represent him. Caseworker #2 and I offered him support of counseling services and specifically offered him help in getting appropriate housing for his child,   . I offered him parent training services in order to have his child returned to him, but he refused all services saying that he thought it would be best for the child to be adopted by the foster parent.

5.   I explained to   that the law required that we had to seek approval of this extra-judicial surrender and that the agency was going to file the application for approval of this extra-judicial surrender in the Family Court, Kings County, where this case originated. I also informed him that the surrender may be revoked by him within 45 days of the signing of the surrender, and therefore he had 45 days from January 30, 1991 to revoke the surrender. I informed him that if he wanted to revoke the surrender, the request to revoke the surrender must be in writing and post-marked or received by the court, which in this case is the Family Court, Kings County. I informed him that the surrender may not be revoked after 45 days after signing the surrender, if the child had been placed in an adoptive home. I informed him that if more than 45 days had passed since the signing of the surrender and the child was placed in an adoptive home, then the surrender becomes final and irrevocable and he could not revoke the surrender or commence a court proceeding to revoke the surrender or to regain custody of the child. I further informed that the surrender may still be revoked more than 45 days after the execution if the child had not been placed in an adoptive home

and if he delivered or mailed a revocation, in writing, of this surrender to the court, and in this case the Family Court, Kings County. I further informed him that the surrender would be binding whether or not he appeared in court at a later date. I informed him that the law, 383-c of the Social Services Law required that the agency make an application in the Family Court, Kings County, within 15 days of the signing of the surrender. I made sure that   signed the surrender and requested he sign five copies of the surrender, and he was given a copy of an executed and notarized surrender for his own use and review. I observed the notary notarize the signatures of   ,   , the father, and myself. The notary public asked all of us to identify ourselves and I indentified to the notary public,   , and she notarized the signatures of   and   and me.   was present as the certified social worker who was employed by   and he was a certified social worker who witnessed the execution of the extra-judicial surrender on January 30, 1991 at 1:00 p.m. at the office of   and who was the statutory non-employee witness. Neither   nor   received any compensation for his witnessing the execution of the surrender.

6. I explained the religious faith requirements of Section 373 of the Social Services Law to   and   requested, in writing, that he preferred the child to be in a foster home of the Baptist religion, but with religion as a secondary concern.   signed the designation of religious preference for his child on January 30, 1991 at 1:00 p.m. at the same time and place he signed the surrender. With respect to the terms and conditions of the surrender,   has placed a condition that he be able to visit the child from time to time after the adoption as agreed on between him and the foster parent and he informs me and I do know the foster parent has agreed to permit the father,   , to visit the child after the adoption.

Caseworker #1

Sworn to before me this
      day of February, 1991.

Notary Public

Sidebar 11–5. Order-Approval of Surrender Instrument

At a term of the
Court of the State of New
York, held in and for the
County of   at
New York .

on   .

PRESENT:
Hon. Judge

_____ x

In the Matter of the Application for   (Docket) (File) No.
Approval of a Surrender Instrument
concerning

Pursuant to Section 383-c of the Social
Services Law

_____ x

The petition of   an authorized agency dated the
day of   , 19   , having been filed requesting Court approval of an instrument of surrender executed on the   day of
        , 19   , committing the guardianship of the person and
custody of   , a child under the age of eighteen years to
        , an authorized agency and

Affidavits of two witnesses to the execution of such surrender
instrument having been filed with the petition in accordance with
Section 383-c (4) (b), and   (parents) (guardians) (having
been duly served with notice of this proceeding and having (personally) appeared before this Court with (out) (by) counsel), (failed
to appear); (and a law guardian having been appointed to represent the child) and

The matter having duly come on for a hearing before this
Court, and the Court, after hearing the proof and testimony offered
in relation to the case, being satisfied that the (parent(s)) (guard-
ian(s)) executed such instrument knowingly and voluntarily,

NOW THEREFORE, it is

ORDERED that the petition herein is hereby GRANTED, and
the instrument dated   , executed by   , is hereby
approved; and it is further

ORDERED that the transfer of custody and guardianship to the Petitioner is hereby approved; (and it is further)

*ORDERED that a copy of this Order shall be served (personally) (by certified mail) by the Petitioner upon the (parent(s)) or (guardian(s)) who executed the aforesaid instrument of transfer. Such service shall be made within   days from the date hereof, together with a notice of the terms and conditions, if any, under which the custody and guardianship of such child may be returned to the (parent(s)) (guardian(s)).

Dated: , 19   .

                              ENTER:

                              _____
                              (J.F.C.) (Surrogate)

*Delete inapplicable provisions.

Sidebar 11-6. Judicial Surrender

COURT OF THE STATE OF NEW YORK
COUNTY OF   .

_____ x

In the Matter of the Surrender   Docket No.:
for Adoption of a Child Whose
Name Is

_____ x

I. THE PARENT OF THE CHILD NAMED HEREIN HAS THE RIGHT, BEFORE SIGNING THIS JUDICIAL SURRENDER, TO SPEAK TO A LAWYER OF HIS/HER OWN CHOOSING AND ANY OTHER PERSON HE/SHE WISHES: TO HAVE THAT LAWYER AND ANY OTHER PERSON PRESENT WITH HIM/HER AT THE TIME OF SIGNING THIS JUDICIAL SUR-RENDER; AND HAS THE RIGHT TO ASK THE COURT TO AP-POINT A LAWYER FREE OF CHARGE IF THE PARENT CAN-NOT AFFORD TO HIRE ONE; AND HAS THE RIGHT TO HAVE SUPPORTIVE COUNSELING.

II. THE PARENT IS GIVING UP ALL RIGHTS TO HAVE CUSTODY, VISIT WITH, WRITE TO OR LEARN ABOUT THE

CHILD, FOREVER, UNLESS THE PARTIES HAVE AGREED TO DIFFERENT TERMS PURSUANT TO SOCIAL SERVICES LAW SECTION 383-C(2), AND UNLESS SUCH TERMS ARE WRITTEN IN THIS JUDICIAL SURRENDER, OR IF THE PARENT REGISTERS WITH THE ADOPTION INFORMATION REGISTER, AS SPECIFIED IN PUBLIC HEALTH LAW SECTION 4138-D, THAT THE PARENT MAY BE CONTACTED AT ANY TIME AFTER THE CHILD REACHES THE AGE OF 21 YEARS, BUT ONLY IF BOTH THE PARENT AND THE ADULT CHILD SO CHOOSE.

III. THE CHILD WILL BE ADOPTED WITHOUT THE PARENT'S CONSENT AND WITHOUT FURTHER NOTICE TO THE PARENT AND WILL BE ADOPTED BY ANY PERSON THE AGENCY CHOOSES UNLESS THIS JUDICIAL SURRENDER CONTAINS THE NAME OF THE PERSONS WHO WILL BE ADOPTING THE CHILD.

IV. THE PARENT CANNOT BE FORCED TO SIGN THIS JUDICIAL SURRENDER, AND CANNOT BE PUNISHED IF HE/SHE DOES NOT SIGN THIS JUDICIAL SURRENDER, AND WOULD NOT BE SUBJECT TO ANY PENALTY FOR REFUSING TO SIGN THIS JUDICIAL SURRENDER.

V. THIS JUDICIAL SURRENDER BECOMES FINAL AND IRREVOCABLE IMMEDIATELY UPON EXECUTION AND ACKNOWLEDGMENT, AND THE PARENT CANNOT BRING A CASE IN COURT TO REVOKE THE SURRENDER OR TO REGAIN CUSTODY OF THE CHILD.

I/we understand that _____

_____

_____

(include any other terms and conditions agree upon by all parties)

(I) (we) residing at _____ (mother)(father) (parents) (legal guardian) of _____ do hereby voluntarily surrender guardianship and custody of (my) (our) (daughter) (son) (ward) _____ born on _____ to the Commissioner of Social Services of the City of New York, a duly authorized agency.

Dated: _____   _____
                                   (Father)

                                   _____
                                   (Mother)

STATE OF NEW YORK)
                    : SS.:
COUNTY OF   )

On this   day of   , 19   , before me personally came
         , to me known and known to be the person(s) in who ex-
ecuted the foregoing instrument and duly and severally acknowledged to me that   executed the same.

_____
Notary Public

State of   )
                   : ss.:
County of

On this   day of   19   , before me personally came
         , the person(s) described in and who executed the forego-
ing instrument, and (he) (she) (they) acknowledged that (he) (she)
(they) executed the same. I have informed such person(s) of the
consequences of the act of execution and acknowledgment pursuant to the provisions of Section 383-c of the Social Services Law
including that the parent(s) (is) (are) giving up all rights to have
custody, visit with, speak with, write or learn about the child,
forever, unless the parent(s) and the authorized agency agree to
different terms as specified in this surrender or if the parent and
the adult child register with the adoption information register. I
have informed the parent(s) that the surrender becomes final and
irrevocable immediately upon its execution and acknowledgment.
I have informed (him) (her) (them) of the right to be represented
by legal counsel of (his) (her) (their) own choosing; of the right to
obtain supportive counseling and of any rights to assigned
counsel pursuant to Section 262 of the Family Court Act, Section
407 of the Surrogate's Court Procedure Act, or Section 35 of the
Judiciary Law. I have given (him) (her) (them) a copy of this surrender upon execution thereof.

_____
Judge of the   Court
County of

(Seal of Court to be affixed together
with Court Clerk's certification)

Sidebar 11-7. Extra-Judicial Surrender

THIS CERTIFIES THAT (I) (We),   , residing at   ,
City (Town) of   , County of   , State of   ,
(am) (are) the (natural mother), (natural father) (natural parents)
(legal guardian) of   , born on   , and do hereby
voluntarily surrender the guardianship and custody of my (son)
(daughter) (ward) to   , a duly authorized agency.

(I) (We) understand that (I have) (we have) the right, before
signing the surrender, to speak to a lawyer of (my) (our) own
choosing and any other person (I) (we) wish; that (I) (we) have the
right to have that lawyer and/or any other person present with
(me) (us) at the time of the signing of the surrender; the right to
ask the court to appoint a lawyer free of charge if (I) (we) cannot
afford to hire one; and that (I) (we) have the right to have supporting counseling;

(I) (We) understand that (I am) (we are) giving up all rights to
have custody, visit with, speak with, write to or learn about (my)
(our) child, forever, unless the authorized agency and (I) (we) have
agreed to different terms as written in this surrender, or, if (I) (we)
register(s) with the adoption information register, as specified in
section 4138 D of the Public Health Law, that the (I) (we) may be
contacted at any time after the child reaches the age of 21 years,
but only if both the parent and the adult child so choose;

(I) (We) understand that the child will be adopted without (my)
(our) consent and without further notice to (me) (us), and will be
adopted by any person that the agency chooses, unless the surrender paper contains the name of the person or persons who will
be adopting the child; and

(I) (We) understand that (I) (we) cannot be forced to sign this
surrender paper, and cannot be punished if (I) (we) do not sign this
surrender paper; and will not be subject to any penalty for refusing
to sign the surrender.

The name and address of the court in which the application
for approval of this surrender will be filed is _____

This surrender may be revoked within 45 days of the signing
of the surrender. The revocation of the surrender must be in
writing and postmarked or received by the court named in this
surrender.

This surrender may not be revoked more than 45 days after
the signing of the surrender if the child has been placed in an
adoptive home. If more than 45 days have passed since the signing of the surrender and the child has been placed in an adoptive

home, (I) (we) cannot bring a case in court to revoke the surrender or to regain custody of (my) (our) child.

(I) (We) understand that the authorized agency will not notify (me) (us) when the child is placed in the adoptive home and that (I) (we) may lose all rights at the end of the 45-day period without further notice.

This surrender may be revoked more than 45 days after its signing only if the child has not been placed in an adoptive home and if (I) (we) deliver or mail a revocation of this surrender to the court named in this surrender.

(I) (We) hereby authorize and empower said authorized agency to consent to the adoption of (my) (our) child in (my) (our) place and stead and with the same force and effect as though (I) (we) personally gave consent at the time of the adoption. (I) (We) hereby waive any notice of the adoption or adoption proceedings.

(I) (We) understand that by surrendering (my) (our) child to said authorized agency, (I) (we) relinquish all of (my) (our) parental rights to such child and that the authorized agency is hereby authorized to place (my) (our) child in an adoptive home or to otherwise assume all parental responsibility for such child. (I) (We) expressly pledge not to interfere hereafter with the care or management of (my) (our) child in any way.

(I) (We) understand that _____

(include any other items and conditions
agreed upon by all parties)

_____   _____

Father's Signature   Mother's Signature

_____

IN WITNESS WHEREOF, I have hereunto set my hand and seal this   day of 1990.

Signature of Father _____
In the presence of

IN WITNESS WHEREOF, I have hereunto set my hand and seal this   day of 1990.

Signature of Mother _____
In the presence of

_____   _____

(Witness)   (Witness)

Section A, Acknowledgment of Father   Section A, Acknowledgment of Mother

_____   _____

166

STATE OF NEW YORK)
COUNTY OF   ) SS.
On this   day of   ,
19 , before me personally
came   to me known
and to me to be the person
described in and who
executed the foregoing instrument and duly acknowledged
that (s)he executed the same.

_____ Notary Public

Section B, Acknowledgment
of Witness

On this day   of   ,
1990, before me personally
came   , to me known,
who, being by me duly sworn
did depose and say that (s)he
resides at   ; that (s)he
knows   , and knew
him to be the person
described in, and who ex-
ecuted the foregoing instrument; that (s)he saw the said
         execute said instru-
ment; and that (s)he
thereupon duly subscribed his
(her) name as witness thereto.

_____ Notary Public

STATE OF NEW YORK)
COUNTY OF   ) SS.
On this   day of   ,
19 , before me personally
came   to me known
and to me to be the person
described in and who
executed the foregoing instrument and duly acknowledged
that (s)he executed the same.

_____ Notary Public

Section B, Acknowledgment
of Witness

On this   day of
1990, before me personally
came   , to me known,
who, being by me duly sworn
did depose and say that (s)he
resides at   ; that (s)he
knows,   , and knew
him to be the person
described in, and who ex-
ecuted the foregoing instrument; that (s)he saw the said
         execute said instru-
ment; and that (s)he
thereupon duly subscribed his
(her) name as witness thereto.

_____ Notary Public

**Sidebar 11-8. Consent to Adoption by Named Father,
or Adjudicted Father, or Acknowledged Father**

I, [father], residing at [address], in the County of [county], City
of [city], and State of [state], having (been named) (been ad-

judicated) (acknowledged that I am) the father of [child], born on
            day of   , 19 , to [mother], at [hospital] Hospital,
County of [county], City of [city] and State of [state], with birth certificate no. [number], do hereby declare as follows:

That I have no interest in or plans for this child.

That I believe adoption to be in this infant's best interests and
that I do hereby accordingly consent to (his) (her) placement for
adoption and adoption.

I do hereby further waive any notice of such adoptive placement and/or adoption proceedings and declare it to be my wish
that I not be further contacted at any time in reference to said
child.

Signature

Witnesses:

STATE OF   , COUNTY OF   ss.:

On this   day of   19 , before me personally came
[father], to me known and known to me to be the individual
described in and who executed the foregoing instrument, and
acknowledged that he executed the same.

Notary Public or Commissioner of Deeds

12
Abandonment Proceedings

I n addition to a written surrender, another method to free a child for adoption is to institute a proceeding pursuant to Section 384 B of the Social Services Law based upon the abandonment of the child by the parent.

Section 384 B of the Social Services Law provides in part as follows:

> An order committing the guardianship and custody of a child pursuant to this section shall be granted only upon one or more of the following grounds:
> (a) Both parents of the child are dead, and no guardian of the person of such child has been lawfully appointed; or
> (b) The parent or parents, whose consent to the adoption of the child would otherwise be required in accordance with section one hundred eleven of the domestic relations law, abandoned such child for the period of six months immediately prior to the date on which the petition is filed in the court.

A proceeding based upon the abandonment of the child may be brought either in the family court or in the surrogate's court, as both have concurrent jurisdiction. If the proceeding is brought in the surrogate's court, the surrogate may, on the court's own motion, transfer the proceeding to the family court. See In re V.S. [394 N.Y.S. 2d 128 (Surrogate's Court, New York County)]. A proceeding begun in the family court may also be transferred on the court's own motion to another county, where the proceeding may have originated. See Brooklyn Home for Children v. Miller [122 Misc. 2d 925, 472 N.Y.S. 2d 282 (1984)].

Construction

Because abandonment proceedings were unknown at common law, Section 384 B must be strictly construed. See In re Madeline R. [457 N.Y.S. 2d 714, 117 Misc. 2d 12, 457 (1982)].

Citation and Petition

If the petition for abandonment is brought in the surrogate's court, the agency's attorney drafts a citation and petition (see sidebar 12–1). The petition is signed by the executive director of the agency and is verified by him before a notary public. The petition and citation are filed with the clerk of the court; the citation is signed by the court, and a conformed copy of the citation is returned to the attorney, to be served upon the parent of the child and upon the commissioner of social services at his office at 220 Church Street, New York City.

The citation must be served personally upon the parents of the child at least ten days before the return date specifed and serve the same purpose—that is, to inform the parent that the agency is applying for a court order to have the child's legal custody committed to the agency and to give the agency the power to consent to an adoption without further notice to or consent of the parent. Section 384 B (e) provides that the notice (either a summons in the family court or a citation in the surrogate's court—see sidebar 12–2) inform the respondent that he/she has a right to be represented by an attorney and that if he/she cannot afford an attorney, one will be assigned free of charge.

Sidebar 12–1. Petition to Commit Guardianship and Custody of an Abandoned Child

FAMILY COURT OF THE STATE OF
NEW YORK
COUNTY OF NEW YORK

———————————————— x

In the Matter of

[child],   ,

A dependent child under the age of 14 years, to the custody of [agency], alleged to be an abandoned child pursuant to Section 384-b of the Social Services Law.

PETITION TO COMMIT GUARDIANSHIP AND CUSTODY OF AN ABANDONED CHILD

———————————————— x

TO THE FAMILY COURT OF NEW YORK COUNTY:

Petitioner, [agency], as and for its Petition for the commitment, guardianship and custody of [child], an infant, respectfully alleges upon information and belief:

1. [Agency] is a not-for-profit corporation, organized and existing by virtue of the laws of the State of New York, having an

for the regular conduct of business at [address] and is an authorized agency approved, visited, inspected and supervised by the State Board of Social Welfare.

2. [Child], infant herein, was born on [date], at [location], and a copy of the Birth Certificate of [child] is annexed hereto and marked as Exhibit "A."

3. The Birth Certificate of the infant, [child], lists [mother] as (his/her) mother and lists ([father]) (no one) as the father of the infant herein.

4. According to the case records of [agency], the putative father of the infant, [child], is [father].

5. The infant, [child], was (voluntarily)(court) placed with the Commissioner of Social Services of the City of New York on [date], by [judge] (Family Court, [county] County, under Docket No. N [number]/), and the Commissioner of Social Services of the City of New York in turn placed the infant with [agency] on [date].

6. According to the case records of [agency] the natural mother of the infant, [mother], was not married to the putative father of the infant, [father].

7. The persons entitled to service of process in this proceeding are:

NAME	LAST KNOWN ADDRESS
[natural mother]	[address]
[putative father]	[address]

COMMISSIONER OF SOCIAL
SERVICES
CITY OF NEW YORK   [address]

AS AND FOR A FIRST CAUSE OF ACTION AGAINST THE RESPONDENT NATURAL MOTHER, [mother], IN ABANDONMENT

8. Petitioner repeats and realleges paragraphs "1" through "7" herein.

9. From [date] to the date of filing of the Petition, the infant's natural mother, [mother], did not visit or communicate with the child, did not make any payments towards his support and withheld from the infant her presence, love and care and neglected and refused to perform her legal obligations of care and support of the infant and by reason of the above, the natural mother abandoned the infant.

10. From [date] to the date of the filing of the Petition, the infant's natural mother, [mother], did not contact the child or the

caseworker herein concerning the child's placement or well-being, and the caseworker did not discourage or prevent her from doing so.

11. In light of the failure of [mother] to contact the caseworker herein regarding the child's placement or well-being, and by reason of the fact that the natural mother did not visit or communicate with the child since [date], the natural mother abandoned the infant.

12. Pursuant to Section 384-b of the Social Services Law of the State of New York, the guardianship of the person and custody of the dependent child may be committed to an authorized agency by an Order of the Family Court where it appears that a child has been abandoned by his parents for a period of six (6) months preceding the filing of the Petition.

13. It would be in the best interests of the infant that the respondent natural mother's rights of guardianship and custody be transferred to [agency] and the Commissioner of Social Services of the City of New York so that either [agency] or the Commissioner of Social Services of the City of New York may consent to the infant's adoption in the place and stead of the natural mother, [mother].

14. The infant, [child], born on [date] is presently in a pre-adoptive home which has been evaluated and assessed as a permanent home for the infant, [child], and it is the recommendation of the petitioner, [agency], that the infant be adopted by his present foster parents.

15. The putative father of the infant herein, [father], has evinced an intent to forego his parental rights by reason of his failure to visit or communicate with the infant since placement of the infant with [agency] on [date] to the present time, and the putative father has not been discouraged or prevented from visiting or communicating with the infant.

16. According to the case records of [agency], from [date] to the present time, [father], the putative father of the infant, has not visited or communicated with the child, has not made any payments towards his [her] support, has withheld from the infant his presence, love and care and has neglected and refused to perform his legal obligations of care and support of the infant. By reason of the above, the putative father has abandoned the infant.

17. According to the case records of [agency], from [date] to the present time, the putative father of the infant herein, [father], has not contacted the child or the petitioner herein concerning the child's placement or well-being, and the petitioner has not discouraged or prevented him from doing so.

18. In light of the failure of [father] to contact the petitioner herein regarding the child's placement or well-being, it is petitioner's belief that it would be in the best interests of the infant, [child], to be freed for adoption.

19. By reason of the fact that the putative father, [father], has not visited or communicated with the child since [date], the putative father has abandoned the infant.

20. Pursuant to Section 384-b of the Social Services Law of the State of New York, the guardianship of the person and custody of the dependent child may be committed to an authorized agency by an order of the Family Court where it appears that a child has been abandoned by his[her] parents for a period of six (6) months preceding the filing of the Petition.

WHEREFORE, your petitioner prays that an order by made pursuant to Section 384-b of the Social Services Law of the State of New York adjudicating the above-named child an abandoned child, that the parents be deprived permanently of said child's custody and that the custody and guardianship of [child], and infant, be committed to [agency] and the Commissioner of Social Services of the City of New York with the right of [agency] or the Commissioner of Social Services of the City of New York to place [child] for legal adoption and to consent to his[her] adoption without further notice to or consent of his[her] parents, subject to the customary approval of the court to which the Petitioner for adoption is presented.

Dated: By: _____
                                                            Executive Director, [agency]

STATE OF NEW YORK   )
)ss.:
COUNTY OF NEW YORK)

[Petitioner], being duly sworn, deposes and says that he is the Executive Director of [agency], petitioner herein, that the foregoing Petition is true to his own knowledge, except as to matters therein stated to be alleged upon information and belief, and, as to those matters, he believes it to be true.

_____
Executive Director

Sworn to before me this
day of   , 1991.

_____
Notary Public

Sidebar 12–2. Summons in Abandonment Proceeding

FAMILY COURT OF THE STATE OF
NEW YORK
COUNTY OF NEW YORK

_____ x

In the Matter of   SUMMONS

[child],   Docket Nos.

A dependent child under the age of
14 years, to the custody of [agency],
alleged to be an abandoned child pursuant to Section 384-b of the Social
Services Law.

_____ x

IN THE NAME OF THE PEOPLE OF THE STATE OF NEW YORK

TO: [parents],
    COMMISSIONER OF SOCIAL SERVICES OF THE CITY OF
NEW YORK

    (Number of petitions) (   ) verified petitions having been filed
in this Court alleging that the above-named child in the care of
[agency] the petitioner, is an abandoned child as defined by Section 384-b of the Social Services Law, copies of said petition being
annexed hereto;
    YOUR ARE HEREBY SUMMONED to appear before the Fam-
ily Court at 60 Lafayette Street, New York, New York, Part [part],
           floor, on the   day of   , before the Hon.
[judge] at 9 o'clock in the forenoon of said day to show cause why
the Court should not enter an order depriving you of all the rights
of custody of [child], awarding the custody of said child to the petitioning authorized agency as an abandoned child as provided
by law.
    PLEASE TAKE NOTICE that if said child is adjudged to be an
abandoned child, and, if custody is awarded to said authorized
agency, said child may be adopted with the consent of said authorized agency without further notice to you and without your
consent.
    In the event of your failure to appear, said failure to appear will
result in the termination of all your parental rights to the child.
    PLEASE TAKE FURTHER NOTICE that your failure to appear
shall constitute a denial of an interest in the child, which denial

may result in the transfer or commitment of the child's care, custody, guardianship or adoption of the child, all without further notice to the parents of the child.

　　PLEASE TAKE FURTHER NOTICE that you are entitled to be represented by an attorney, and, if you cannot afford to retain an attorney, one will be appointed to represent you by the Court free of charge to you.

Dated:

By order of the Court

_____
Clerk, Family Court, New York

　　In the surrogate's court, assuming that the parent's whereabouts are known and that the parent is served personally with the citation ten days prior to the return date, the affidavit of personal service annexed to a copy of the citation is filed with the clerk of the surrogate's court two days before the return date.

　　If the petition is brought in family court, the process is similar to that outlined above except that the petition and summons must be personally served on the parent of the child at least twenty days prior to the specified return date. See 384 B (e) of the Social Services Law and Section 611 of the Family Court Act.

　　On the return date, if the parent appears, the matter will be set for trial on a date certain. If the parent cannot afford an attorney, one will be appointed by the court free of charge. In both the surrogate's court and the family court, the attorney will be selected from the 18B panel and compensated at the rate of $25 per hour for office time and $40 per hour for court time. The court will also appoint an attorney as law guardian to protect the rights of the child.

When Parent's Whereabouts Are Unknown

If the parent's whereabouts are not known, then the agency must outline in an affidavit the diligent efforts made to locate the parent. The diligent efforts to locate the parent or parents must be sufficiently thorough to enable the judge to sign an order dispensing with personal service of the citation upon the parent and to authorize service of the citation by publication one time in a local newspaper. The recitation of diligent efforts to locate the missing parent should include at least the following:

1. a check of the local telephone book and a communication to each person with the same name as the missing parent;

2. letters written to the parent at his/her last known address;

3. a visit to the last known address, and inquiries made of the janitor and tenants of the building;

4. a check with the post office;

5. correspondence with relatives of the missing parent;

6. a check with the Board of Elections;

7. a check with the Department of Motor Vehicles;

8. a check with the Department of Welfare;

9. if appropriate, a check with the Department of Corrections, drug rehabilitation centers, alcohol clinics and the like; and

10. a check with the Department of Health for a death certificate.

A typical recitation of diligent efforts included in the petition that all support a court order for service by publication is as follows:

September 25, 1990. Last known address for subject from case is the Ford Hotel, 111 East 132nd Street, New York, New York.
A visit was made to this hotel, and the building is under renovation.

September 27, 1990. Inquiries were made at the Department of Social Services, 238 Church Street, New York, New York, for the subject. The last address they had for her was 1304 West 331st Street, New York, New York. Checked out this address, and it is the Hotel Blanca. Subject was not known there.
In the same area, checked out the Hotel Johnson, 1230 East 431st Street, New York, New York. She was living there a year ago, but no one knew her whereabouts at this time.
Inquired at the Hotel LaMarca, 117 West 432nd Street, New York, New York, for her. They stated that subject has not been there for a long time. They had no knowledge of her whereabouts.
Visited the Tobb Hotel, 489 West 428th Street, New York, New York, and asked for subject. We were informed that she has not lived there for some time and that they had no knowledge of her whereabouts.

October 8, 1990. A search was made of the records at the New York City Correctional Institution for Women, 15-15 Hazen Street, East Elmhurst, New York. Subject was an inmate there from March 25, 1989, to January 28, 1990. She gave her residence as 1318 West 498th Street, New York New York. She listed an uncle, Tom Johns, 15 Redmond Place, New Jersey (no town).

October 28, 1990. A visit was made to 4316 West 195th Street, New York, New York. This is a hotel. The owner said that she wasn't there, but about a year ago, they had a girl named Blanca for a short time.

Checked out the New Jersey towns in the National Zip Code Directory for Redmond Place. Nobody appeared.

October 30, 1990. Visited the 24th Precinct of the New York City Police Department, which covers the Pennington Hotel at 4316 West 495th Street, New York, New York, and learned of two other hotels in their precinct where the subject might be a resident. The Mid Hotel, Broadway and 1st Street, and the Hudson Hotel, Broadway and 44th St., New York, New York. Inquiries were made at both these hotels, and the subject was not known at either place.

November 7, 1990. A search was made of the records at the Drug Abuse Control Commission, Long Island City, New York, for the subject. She was not known to this agency.

Inquiries were made at the New York State Correctional Services, 314 West 40th Street, New York, New York, for the subject. She was not known to this agency.

November 20, 1990. Researched telephone directories from Manhattan, the Bronx, Brooklyn, Queens, and Staten Island, and Nassau, Suffolk and Westchester Counties for the subject. She did not appear.

November 22, 1990. A search of the voter registration records was made at the Board of Elections, 80 Varick Street, New York, New York, for subject. She was not listed as a registered voter.

November 25, 1990. Inquiries were made at the Department of Motor Vehicles, Albany, New York, for the subject as a licensed driver or automobile owner. She did not appear in their records.

December 2, 1990. Case records allege the subject lived at the following addresses: 1. 44 Penn Avenue, Bronx, N.Y. 2. 5064 Penn Avenue, Bronx, N.Y. 3. 10 Penn Concourse, Bronx, N.Y. 4. 140 Laura Avenue, Bronx, N.Y.

Checked the subject out at these addresses and interviewed neighbors and tenants of these buildings. No information was learned as to the present whereabouts of subject. No forwarding address was found for subject.

December 4, 1990. Visits were made to the United States Post Offices, which cover the aforementioned addresses, as follows: 1. Morrisania Station, 444 East 167th Street, Bronx, New York. 2. Soundview Station, 1687 Gleason Avenue, Bronx, New York. 3. Fordham Station, 420 East 189th Street, Bronx, New York.

A thorough search was instituted in their records for a forwarding address for subject. She did not appear in their files.

December 6, 1990. Inquiries were made at 154 LaSalle Street, New York, New York, for the maternal great aunt, Mrs. Odessa, and at 4121 East 80th Street, New York, New York, for the maternal great aunt, Mrs. O'Brien. Neither person was known at their respective addresses.

December 9, 1990. Case records indicated that subject was known to Central Islip State Hospital, Central Islip, New York.

Inquiries were made, and subject was there from June 10, 1989, to May 17, 1990. She was sent to the Alcohol Clinic at Bellevue Hospital, 127th Street and First Avenue, New York, New York. Inquired at this facility, and subject never appeared.

December 10, 1990. A search of the voter registration records was made at the Board of Elections, 345 Adams Street, Brooklyn, New York, for subject. She did not appear in their records as a voter in the Borough of Kings.

December 12, 1990. A search was made of the voter registration records at the Board of Elections, 30 Bay Street, Staten Island, New York. Subject was not listed as registered voter.

December 16, 1990. A search was made of the voter registration records at the Board of Elections, 77-40 Vleight Place, Flushing, New York, for subject. She did not appear as a voter.

December 20, 1990. Inquiries were made at the Shelter Care for Women, 350 Lafayette Street, New York, New York, for subject. Subject was there in April 1990 for assistance, but was rejected.

December 23, 1990. A search was made of the records at Pilgrim State Hospital, Brentwood, New York, for subject. She was not known at this hospital.

December 27, 1990. Inquiries were made at Creedmore State Hospital, Queens Village, New York, for subject. She was not known to this hospital.

Incarcerated Parents

The fact that a parent is incarcerated does not preclude termination of parental rights, absent showing that the parent was prohibited from contacting agency or child. See In re Stella B. [495 N.Y.S. 2d 128, 130 Misc. 2d 148 (1985)] and Matter of Catholic Child Care Society of Diocese of Brooklyn [112 A.D. 2d 1039, 492 N.Y.S. 2d 831 (1985)]. In this proceeding to terminate parental rights based on abandonment, hardship asserted by the objecting parent had to show at minimum that the hardship permeated the parent's life such that contact with the child or agency was not feasible. See also In re Jasmine T. [557 N.Y.S. 2d 669 (Appellate Division, 3rd Dept. 1990)]. See also chapter 19 of this book.

More Than One Child

If more than one child is involved, a petition should be filed for each child. It would be appropriate for the attorney for the agency to submit an order of consolidation for the judge's signature, which permits one citation to be served upon the parent and a consolidated trial. However, some courts, such as the Family Court, New York County, no longer require orders of consolidation in matters involving more than one child.

Definition of Abandonment

Section 384 B, Subdivision 5(a), of the Social Services Law defines *an abandoned child* as follows:

> For the purposes of this section, a child is "abandoned" by his parent if such parent envinces an intent to forgo his or her parental rights and obligations as manifested by his or her failure to visit the child and communicate with the child or agency. In the absence of evidence to the contrary, such ability to visit and communicate shall be presumed.

No Need to Prove Diligent Efforts

In the case of In re Richard H. (St. Christopher's Home) [40 N.Y. 2d 96, 386 N.Y.S. 2d 59 (1976)], the Court of Appeals held that an authorized agency (a foster-care institution) need not allege nor prove that it used diligent efforts to encourage or strengthen the parental relationship when the agency attempts to gain legal custody of a child based upon abandonment of the child by the parents, when bringing such a proceeding pursuant to Section 384 of the Social Services Law. See also In re Malik M. [40 N.Y. 2d 840, 387 N.Y.S. 2d 835 (1976)], wherein the Court of Appeals affirmed the Appellate Division's finding of abandonment and held that the agency was not required to exercise diligent efforts to encourage and strengthen the parental relationship.

In its decision, the court traced the origin of the permanent neglect proceedings pursuant to Section 611 of the Family Court Act and proceedings to free a child based upon abandonment pursuant to Section 384 of the Social Services Law. It held that both sections were intended to serve as separate and distinct means of termination of parental rights with the choice of which proceeding to initiate dependent upon the circumstances of the case.

The court stated that Section 384 (now 384 B) of the Social Services Law and Section 611 of the Family Court Act were intended to offer alternate and independent means of terminating parental rights. The court noted that the burden of proving abandonment has traditionally been a heavy one and should not be made heavier by an additional requirement not present in the statute.

Section 384 B, Subdivision 5b, effective January 1, 1977, codifies the holding of In re Richard H., and states that in making a determination that the parent abandoned the child, the court shall not require a showing of diligent efforts, if any, by an authorized agency to encourage the parental rights.

The holding of that case is found in the last sentence of the decision, where the court stated:

> The degree of neglect should determine the route chosen to free the child, and if any agency can prove abandonment, i.e., prove that the parent failed to visit or support the child for six months without good cause, it is not also required to prove diligent efforts to encourage and strengthen the parental relationship.

In deciding this matter, the court stated that there were currently three routes by which an individual or agency could terminate a parent's rights to a child, thus placing that child in a position whereby the child would be available for adoption.

1. Article 7 of the Domestic Relations Law, specifically Section 3.
2. a guardianship proceeding, pursuant to Section 384 (now 384 B) of the Social Services Law.
3. a permanent neglect proceeding, pursuant to Article 6 of the Family Court Act, specifically Section 611.

What Constitutes Abandonment?

A case that interpreted Sections 384 and 371 of the Social Services Law is In re Jennifer "S" [69 Misc. 2d 951, 333 N.Y.S. 2d 79 (Surrogate's Court, New York County, 1972)]. In the Jennifer "S" case, Surrogate Millard L. Midonick found the child to be an abandoned child and committed the custody and guardianship of the child to an authorized agency, with the authority of said agency to consent to the adoption of the child by a suitable person subject to the customary approval and decree of the surrogate's court and dispensing with the consent of the natural mother.

Surrogate Midonick stated in his findings of fact that:

> I find that during the five and a half years of Jennifer's life, her mother never made any effort to contact or visit Jennifer or the agency in whose custody she had been placed. No presents, cards or other communications were ever sent from mother to child, and no visits were ever made. The only indication that this mother desires the return of her child is her naked statement to that effect. She has never performed any act that would tend to insure the return of Jennifer to her until her recent move to Beacon, although numerous opportunities

for such actions were afforded to her. Instead, while insisting that she wants the child returned, she has placed more obstacles between herself and this child by setting her own conditions for the child's return and taking no action to fulfull this condition. I, therefore, find that Jennifer is an abandoned child within the meaning of Section 371 and 384 of the Social Services Law [Id at 83].

In effect, Surrogate Midonick was stating that actions speak louder than words and that the mere mouthing of an intention would not be sufficient to overcome a course of conduct or lack of conduct.

In the case of In re Ellick [328 N.Y.S. 2d 587 (Family Court, New York County, 1972)], Judge Justine Wise Polier held that a mother who made no contacts with the children for over eighteen months and who had moved without leaving a forwarding address, had abandoned her children, and the custody of the children in that case was committed to an authorized agency with the right to place them for legal adoption.

Good Reason for Failure to Visit or Communicate

The mere proof of failure to visit with the child or communicate with an agency by a natural parent for a period in excess of six months immediately prior to the filing of the petition to terminate parental rights on the basis of abandonment must be accompanied by an inquiry into whether the parent had good reason for failure to visit or communicate. See Matter of Catholic Child Care Society of Diocese of Brooklyn [112 A.D. 2d 1039, 492 N.Y.S. 2d 831 (1985)].

What Constitutes Good Reason for Failure to Visit or Communicate?

The hardship asserted by an objecting parent in an abandonment proceeding as an obstacle to visiting or communicating with the child must be shown at a minimum to permeate the parent's life to such an extent that contact with the child or agency was not feasible. See Matter of Child Care Society of Diocese of Brooklyn [112 A.D. 2d 1039, 492 N.Y.S. 2d 831 (1985)]. The standard that must be met by an objecting parent is therefore quite high. See also Matter of Trudell J.W. [119 A.D. 2d 828, 501 N.Y.S. 2d 453 (1986)], wherein the court held that the natural mother had abandoned the child, in the absence of sufficient evidence adduced by the mother to establish that her failure to contact was the result of circumstances that made it impossible for her to do so.

Further, an unexplained absence of contact for the statutorily required period may be a sufficient predicate for an abandonment finding. See Matter of Vunk [127 Misc. 2d 828, 487 N.Y.S. 2d 490 (Family Court, Suffolk County, 1985)].

Presumptions

In the dispositional hearing, if held, there is no presumption in favor of a parent. See Star Leslie W. [63 N.Y. 2d 136 (1984)].

Excuse of Distance

The courts have not excused the parent who did not visit the child due to distance when such distance was self-imposed and was not "good reason" for lack of visitation. See In re Adoption of "Infant" G. [360 N.Y.S. 2d (Surrogate's Court, New York County, 1974)]. See also Matter of Stephen B. [60 Misc. 2d 662, 393 N.Y.S. 2d 438 (Family Court, New York County, 1969)].

In the case of "Infant G.," Surrogate Midonick held that communting distances did not provide "good reason" for the natural mother's not visiting her child, and the surrogate stated at p. 793 that "not visiting one's child for three years when the only obstacle is commuting distance, does not constitute 'good reason.' "

Parents' Subjective Intent

The courts have also held that mere intention not to abandon is not sufficient to defeat a finding of abandonment. Section 384 B, Subdivision 5b, effective January 1, 1977, codifies the case law and provides that "the subjective intent of the parent whether expressed or otherwise, unsupported by evidence of the foregoing parental acts manifesting such intent, shall not preclude a determination that such parent has abandoned his or her child." See In re Vanessa F. [Misc. 2d 617, 351 N.Y.S. 2d 337 (Surrogate's Court, New York County, 1974)].

Also in Vanessa F., *supra,* the court reasoned that parents who abandon their children are regarded as strangers and that an agency would be ill-advised to hazard the best interests of the child even if no foster home were available for adoption and would be in error to delay a final determination in order to give a mother more time to rehabilitate herself.

Section 384 B (3)(i), effective January 1, 1977, codifies the decision in In re Vanessa and provides:

> In a proceeding instituted by an authorized agency pursuant to the provisions of this section, proof of the likelihood that the child will be placed for adoption shall not be required in determining whether the best interests of the child would be promoted by the commitment of the guardianship and custody of the child to an authorized agency.

Insubstantial Contacts

Insubstantial contacts by a parent with the foster-care agency during the relevant six-month period do not necessarily rebut proof of abandonment. For example, in the case of In re Green v. Woodycrest Children's Services [109 Misc. 2d 1031, 441 N.Y.S. 2d 325 (1981)], the court held that statements made by the natural mother during telephone conversations with the agency—involving threats of violence to either blow up the agency or to kill the caseworker if the children were not returned to her were a spontaneous emotional outburst rather than genuine communication with another person and fell under Subdivision 5 of Section 384 B, which provides that the subjective intent of the parent not supported by additional evidence does not preclude a determination that the parent has abandoned his/her child. In another recent case, Matter of Starr L.B. [130 Misc. 2d 599, 497, N.Y.S. 2d 597 (1985)], the court held that a single communication with a placement agency during the relevant six-month period was not in itself sufficient to rebut proof of abandonment.

Nonjury Hearing

The hearing is held before the surrogate's or family court judge without a jury. See In re Sean B.W. [381 N.Y.S. 2d 656 (Surrogate's Court, Nassau County, 1976)], wherein Surrogate John Bennett held that there is no constitutional right to trial by jury in adoption proceedings.

Judicial Notice

The court may take judicial notice of its own records that relate to the proceedings before it. See In re Denlow [384 N.Y.S. 2d 621 (Family Court, Kings County, 1976)].

Degree of Proof

Before parental rights may be terminated, the proof offered must be "clear and convincing." See In re Rore, Marie M. [94 A.D. 2d 731, 462 N.Y.S. 2d 483 (1983)].

Burden of Proof

The agency has the burden of proof to show that the parent abandoned the child without good reason.

One court has written that it will not sit to accept a kind of fait accompli and apply the rubber stamp of approval policy. See In re Denlow [384 N.Y.S. 2d 621 (Family Court, Kings County, 1976)]. See also Matter of Gross [102 Misc. 2d 1073, 425 N.Y.S. 2d 220), wherein the court held that the "burden of constitutional magnitude is placed on one who would terminate rights of natural parents through adoption."

Agency Records

The agency will usually have several witnesses—the caseworker, the case supervisor, and the foster parents.

The case supervisor should identify the case records and testify that:

1. it is the regular course of the agency's business to keep records;
2. the records in issue were made in the regular course of business;
3. the entries contained in the records were made contemporaneously with the events described therein (see Saffert v. Orphan Asylum Society of the City of Brooklyn [394 N.Y.S. 2d 419 (Appellate Division, 1st Dept., 1977)]), wherein the court, while affirming the family court's determination of permanent neglect, stated that it was error for the family court to admit into evidence the entire case record where portions were not made contemporaneously with the events described therein;
4. the records were kept under the supervision and control of the witness testifying; and
5. the person making the entries had a duty to so record the events in the records.

With this foundation laid, the case records will be accepted into evidence, and the court may consider the case records in deciding the case. When the records are received into evidence, the case supervisor may testify to events recorded in the records, although he/she has no personal knowledge of the events.

The caseworker will testify to actual eyewitness events, including conversations with the parents and observations of the parents themselves and their residence. The caseworker will testify as to lack of contact by the parent with the child. For example, the caseworker will testify that the parents:

1. did not visit the child;
2. did not support the child;
3. did not send the child presents, letters, or cards; and
4. did not contact the agency concerning the child for at least six months prior to filing the petition for abandonment.

Although it is not necessary, the caseworker may also testify that he/she attempted to help the parent be reunited with the child. The caseworker may testify, for example, that he/she encouraged the parent to visit and, if visiting was difficult, that he/she provided money for transportation or even offered to bring the child to the parent's home.

The foster parents will testify to the lack of contact between parent and child, to the present condition of the child, and generally to the care the child is receiving. They will also try to impress upon the court that the child is loved and receiving good care from them. Foster parents who have had continuous care of children for a period in excess of twelve months may move to intervene in abandonment proceedings. See Matter of Stevens [380 N.Y.S. 2d 137 (Appellate Division, 4th Dept., 1976)], and the Social Services Law, Section 383 (3).

On the other hand, the natural parent will testify that:

1. there were visitations, or some contacts such as cards, letters, and telephone calls, or that a relative kept in touch with the child;
2. the parent did not visit because he/she was physically unable to visit;
3. the agency favored the foster parents over the natural parents;
4. the foster parents undermined the parental relationship; and
5. the natural parents were on welfare and could not support the child.

Child's Wishes

In line with the recent trend to accord greater rights to the child, the legislature provided in Section 384 B, Subdivision 3K, of the Social Services Law, that:

> Where the child is over fourteen years of age, the court may, in its discretion, consider the wishes of the child in determining whether the best interests of the child would be promoted by the commitment of the guardianship and custody of the child.

Law Guardian's Recommendations

The courts have held that the recommendations of the law guardian appointed for the child should be considered. See In re Wesley [423 N.Y.S. 2d 482, 72 A.D. 2d 137 (1980)].

The Decision

After the hearing, the court will usually reserve decision and thereafter make a written decision, directing that an order be submitted for signature. See In re Denlow [384 N.Y.S. 2d 621 (Family Court, Kings County, 1976)], where Judge Joseph A. Doran expressed the view that termination-of-parental-rights cases are hardship cases with strong emotional appeal, and that no two cases are factually the same, and that each case must turn on its own particular facts and totality of circumstances: "There are not precedents of real value." If the court sustains the petition, the order of guardianship will give legal custody to the foster-care agency with the power to consent to an adoption without further notice to or consent of the natural parent, subject to the customary approval of the appropriate court—that is, either the surrogate's or family court (see sidebar 12–3).

Sidebar 12–3. Order of Disposition, Adjudication, Findings of Fact, and Conclusions of Law in Abandonment Proceeding

At the Family Court of the State of New York, held in and for the County of New York, 60 Lafayette Street, New York, New York on the   , day of

P R E S E N T:

HON. [judge]

Judge of the Family Court.

_____ x

In the Matter of
[child],
A dependent child under the age of 14 years, to the custody of [agency] an abandoned child, pursuant to Section 384-b of the Social Services Law.

_____ x

ORDER OF DISPOSITION, ADJUDICATION, FINDINGS OF FACT AND CONCLU- SIONS OF LAW

Docket No.

A Petition, pursuant to Section 384-b of the Social Services Law having been filed in this Court by [agency] alleging that [child], an infant, is an abandoned child; and a Summons and Petition having been duly issued and served upon [mother], the natural mother of said infant, and

The matter having duly come on for a fact finding hearing on [date] before the HON. [judge], Judge of the Family Court, [county] County at a Trial Term Part [part] and the said [mother], the natural mother of said infant, having failed to appear thereon and her default having been duly noted by the Court; and the petitioner, [agency], having been represented by [attorney] of counsel; and the child having been represented by [attorney], Law Guardian, Legal Aid Society, by [attorney]; and this Court after hearing the proofs and the testimony offered in relation to the case the Court having found that the allegations of the Petition required by Section 384-b of the Social Services Law are supported by clear and convincing evidence and the Court having heard the testimony of [caseworker], caseworker, [agency], relating to the abandonment of the natural mother and the Court found upon clear and convincing evidence:

[evidence]

2. [child] was born on [date] in Brooklyn, New York.

3. The natural mother of the infant, [child], is [mother].

4. The infant, [child], was Court placed with the Commissioner of Social Services of the City of New York on [date] by the Family Court, [county] County under Docket No. [number] and the Commissioner of Social Services of the City of New York in turn placed the infant with [agency] on [date]. The infant was subsequently discharged to [relative] on [date] and then readmitted to care on [date].

5. The natural mother of the infant, [mother], evinced an intent to forgo her parental rights by reason of her failure to visit or communicate with the infant since March 30, 1989 and the natural mother was not discouraged or prevented from visiting or communicating with the infant.

6. From [date] to the date of the filing of the Petition, the infant's natural mother, [mother], did not visit or communicate with the child, did not make any payments towards his support and withheld from the infant her presence, love and care and neglected and refused to perform her legal obligations of care and support of the infant and by reason of the above, the natural mother abandoned the infant.

7. From [date] to the date of the filing of the Petition, the infant's natural mother, [mother], did not contact the child or the caseworker herein concerning the child's placement or well-being, and the caseworker did not discourage or prevent her from doing so.

8. In light of the failure of [mother] to contact the caseworker herein regarding the child's placement or well-being, and by reason of the fact that the natural mother did not visit or communicate with the child since [date], the natural mother abandoned the infant.

9. Pursuant to Section 384-b of the Social Services Law of the State of New York, the guardianship of the person and custody of the dependent child may be committed to an authorized agency by an Order of the Family Court where it appears that a child has been abandoned by his parents for a period of six (6) months preceding the filing of the Petition.

THEREFORE, with respect to the natural mother, [mother] the allegations of abandonment in the Petition as required by Section

384-b of the Social Services Law are supported by clear and convincing evidence; and

NOW, THEREFORE, it is upon clear and convincing evidence

ADJUDGED, that the allegations of abandonment as to the respondent natural mother, [mother], required by Section 384-b of the Social Services Law are sustained by clear and convincing evidence; and

The matter having come on for a dispositional hearing before the HON. [judge], Family Court, [county] County on [date] at Trial Term Part [part] and the said [mother], the natural mother of the infant herein, having failed to appear thereon and her default having been duly noted by the Court and [agency], the petitioner, was represented by [attorney] of counsel; and the child was represented by [attorney], Law Guardian, Legal Aid Society, by [attorney] and this Court having taken testimony and made examination and inquiry into the facts and circumstances of the persons involved in this proceeding and the Court having heard the testimony of [caseworker], caseworker, [agency] that the natural mother was not a resource for the future of said child and that the foster parents wish to adopt the infant herein and are viable resources for the future of said child and the Court having found upon clear and convincing evidence that:

1. It would be in the best interests of the infant that the respondent natural mother's rights of guardianship and custody be transferred to [agency] and the Commissioner of Social Services of the City of New York so that either [agency] or the Commissioner of Social Services of the City of New York may consent to the infant's adoption in the place and stead of the natural mother, [mother].

2. The infant, [child], born on [date], is presently in a pre-adoptive home which has been evaluated and assessed as a permanent home for the infant, [child], and it is the recommendation of the petitioner, [agency], that the infant be adopted by his present foster parents.

NOW, THEREFORE, upon the dispositional hearing and upon clear and convincing evidence,

IT APPEARING, that the best interests of the infant, [child], require that the respondent natural mother's rights of guardianship and custody of the infant be transferred and committed to the Commissioner of Social Services of the City of New York and [agency], it is

ORDERED, that the best interests of the child require that the custody and guardianship rights of [mother], the natural mother, over said child be terminated; and it is further,

ORDERED, that such rights of the legal custody and guardian-ship of said infant, [child], by the respondent natural mother, [mother], be and the same hereby are transferred and committed to the Commissioner of Social Services of the City of New York and [agency], an authorized agency, and it is further,

ORDERED, that the Commissioner of Social Services of the City of New York or [agency] be and is hereby authorized and empowered to consent to the adoption of said minor child, [child] in the place and stead of the natural mother, [mother], by a suit-able person or persons subject to the customary approval of the Court of competent jurisdiction and that the consent of and notice to the natural mother of [child] to said adoption be and the same hereby are dispensed with and it is further,

ORDERED, that the Law Guardian and the Commissioner of Social Services of the City of New York be notified of all future legal proceedings concerning the infant herein, and it is further,

ORDERED, that all papers and records in this proceeding be filed in the Office of the Clerk of the Family Court of the State of New York, County of New York, in accordance with Section 384-b, Subd. 3 (j) of the Social Services Law, and it is further,

ORDERED, that a certified copy of this Order be filed in the Office of the Clerk, New York County.

Dated:

E N T E R:

_____
[judge]
Family Court, [county] County

The order of commitment should provide that legal custody be placed in both the voluntary agency *and* the commissioner of social services, with the power of either to consent to the adoption of the child. The attorney for the agency will draft the proposed Order of Disposition, Adjudication, Findings of Fact, and Conclusions of Law, with notice of settlement and serve the same upon the attorney for the parent, giving five days' notice with five extra days if the order with notice of settlement is served by mail. After the order is signed by the judge or surrogate, the order with notice of entry is served upon the attorney for the parent and any other attorney, such as law guardian for the child and the attorney for the Department of Social Services, in order to start the time to appeal running. After receipt of the order with notice of entry, the parent has thirty days within which to appeal the order of guardianship to the Appellate Division. If the notice of entry is served by mail, the parent has an extra five days to appeal to the Appellate Division.

13
Permanent Neglect Proceedings

I n addition to a written surrender and abandonment proceedings pursuant to Section 384 B of the Social Services Law, another method to free a child for adoption is to institute a proceeding pursuant to Article 6 of the Family Court Act and Section 384 B of the Social Services Law based upon the permanent neglect of the child by the parent or parents.

In Matter of Carl and Annette N. [398 N.Y.S. 2d 613 (Family Court, Schenectady, 1977)], the respondent parents challenged the permanent neglect statute as unconstitutional on three grounds: (1) for vagueness in violation of the due process clause of the U.S. Constitution; (2) as an infringement of their first amendment rights; and (3) for denying them equal protection of the laws as guaranteed under the Fourteenth Amendment of the U.S. Constitution. The court ruled against the respondents in all three areas. With respect to the due process clause, the court looked to an earlier case to hold that within the meaning of the statute, the requirement "of the parent to substantially plan means not only to formulate but also to accomplish a feasible and realistic plan to restore the child to a permanent, stable home with the parent" [Id at 617]. See also Matter of Steven B. [60 Misc. 2d 662, 303 N.Y.S. 2d 438]; Matter of Orzo [84 Misc. 2d 482, 374 N.Y.S. 2d 554]; and Matter of Orlando F. [40 N.Y. 2d 103, 386 N.Y.S. 2d 64, 351, N.E. 2d 711]. The court found these interpretations to be authoritative constructions of the statute, then held that the statute survived a challenge for vagueness based upon the well-settled principle of constitutional law that an authoritative construction of a state statute by its courts must be considered and is binding in any attack on the statute for vagueness. See Matter of Carl and Annette N. [91 Misc. 2d 738, 398 N.Y.S. 2d, 617].

The court then dealt with the right-to-privacy issue and held against the respondents, noting that the right to privacy is not absolute "but must be balanced against legitimate state interests" [Id at 618].

Finally, the court held that the statute did not violate the equal protection clause of the Fourteenth Amendment, noting that even if the strict scrutiny test were to be applied, the state had a compelling interest in providing permanent and stable placement for foster children. Further, the court found the statute to be narrowly tailored to accomplish the goal and that there was no less restrictive alternative available [Id at 620, 621, 622]. For a detailed discussion of the constitutionality of the permanent neglect statute, see Matter of Carl and Annette N. [398 N.Y.S. 2d 613 (Family Court, Schenectady, 1977)].

Purpose of the Law

Section 611 of the Family Court Act is derived from Chapter 450 of the Laws of 1959, which amended the Children's Court Act.

Governor Rockefeller's memorandum of approval of this law stated the purpose of the law:

> The purpose of these bills is to provide procedures with adequate safeguards to permit the adoption of a permanently neglected child, without the consent of his parents or parent.
>
> Under existing law a great many children are doomed to grow in institutions or foster homes at public expense and are prevented from forming normal, lasting family relationships because minimal contacts between a parent and a child who remains in an institution or foster home act as a bar against a judicial finding that the child has been abandoned. Such a finding is necessary in order to permit the adoption of the child without parental consent and it cannot be made even where the contacts between parent and child are so infrequent and superficial as to be completely meaningless.
>
> These bills act to remedy this situation and at the same time protect the rights of a parent who has a real interest in his or her child, but due to financial or other circumstances is unable to have the care and custody of the child (McKinney's Session Laws of New York, 1959, p. 1749).

Definition of Permanent Neglect

Section 384 B Subdivision 7(a) of the Social Services Law effective January 1, 1977, defines a permanently neglected child as a child who is in the care of an authorized agency and whose parent or custodian has failed for a period of more than one year following the date such child came into the care of an authorized agency substantially and continuously or repeatedly to maintain contact with or plan for the future of the child, although physically and financially able to do so, notwithstanding the agency's diligent efforts to encourage and strengthen the parental relationship when such efforts will not be detrimental to the best interests of the child.

Presumption of Financial and Physical Ability

In the event that the parent defaults, after due notice of a proceeding to determine such permanent neglect, such physical and financial ability of such parent may be presumed by the court.

Insubstantial Contact

Section 384 B, Subdivision 7(b), of the Social Services Law further provides with respect to the effect of infrequent visitation:

> Evidence of insubstantial or infrequent contacts by a parent with his or her child shall not, of itself, be sufficient as a matter of law to preclude a determination that such child is a permanently neglected child. A visit or communication by a parent with the child which is of such character as to overtly demonstrate a lack of affectionate and concerned parenthood shall not be deemed a substantial contact.

Exclusive Jurisdiction

Only the family court has the jurisdiction over a permanent neglect proceeding. The venue is (1) in the county in which the child resides or is domiciled at the time of the filing of the petition; (2) in the county in which the parent of the child resides or is domiciled; or (3) in the county in which the authorized agency has an office for the regular conduct of business. See Section 384 B, Subdivision 3(c), of the Social Services Law, effective January 1, 1977.

The Petition

The proceeding to permanently terminate the parents' custody of a child on the ground of permanent neglect is originated by a verified petition (see sidebar 12–1). The petition must allege:

1. that the child is under eighteen years of age;
2. that the child is in the care of an authorized agency (to permanently terminate a parent's custody, the petition must allege that the child is in the care of an authorized agency, but the legality of the initial placement is irrelevant to a permanent neglect proceeding. See In re Amos H.H. [59 A.D. 2d 795, 398 N.Y.S. 2d 771 (Appellate Division, 3rd Dept., 1977)]);
3. that the agency has made diligent efforts to encourage and strengthen the parental relationship, specifying the efforts made or that such efforts would be detrimental to the best interests of the child, specifying the reasons therefore;
4. that the parent, notwithstanding the agency's efforts, has failed for a period of more than one year following the date such child came into the care of the agency, substantially and continuously or repeatedly to maintain contact with or plan for the future of the child although physically and financially able to do so; and

5. that the best interests of the child require that the custody of the child be committed to an authorized agency or foster family. See Section 614 of the Family Court Act, as amended effective January 1, 1977.

Only an authorized agency, law guardian, or guardian *ad litem* or a foster parent authorized by a court order pursuant to Section 392 or 384 B of the Social Services Law may originate a proceeding for permanent neglect. See Section 615 of the Family Court Act.

Once the petition is filed with the clerk of the family court, the clerk will cause to be issued a summons (see sidebar 12–2). Both the summons and the petition must be served upon the parent, informing the parent that a petition has been filed to permanently terminate the parent's rights to custody of the child and awarding custody of the child to the petitioner on the grounds that the child is permanently neglected and that the agency may consent to an adoption of the child without further notice or consent of the parent. See Section 616 of the Family Court Act.

The summons and petition must be served upon the parent or parents at least twenty days prior to the initial court appearance. If after reasonable effort personal service cannot be made upon the parent or parents, the court may order, on good cause shown, substituted service or service of the summons by publication. See Section 617 of the Family Court Act.

In some family courts, such as those in New York County, the summons is prepared by the attorney for the petitioner, who must see to the service of the summons and petition upon the defendant and also upon the commissioner of social services at 220 Church Street, New York, New York. In the Family Court of Nassau County, the summons is served by a marshal or other court-related person and not the process server chosen by the attorney for the petitioner.

Sidebar 13–1. Petition to Commit Guardianship and Custody of a Neglected Child

FAMILY COURT OF THE STATE OF
NEW YORK
COUNTY OF NEW YORK

——————————————— x

In the Matter of

[child],
A dependent child under the age of 14 years, to the custody of [agency], alleged to be a permanently neglected child pursuant to Section 384-b of the Social Services Law.

PETITION TO COMMIT GUARDIANSHIP AND CUSTODY OF A NEGLECTED CHILD PURSUANT TO SECTION 384-B OF THE SOCIAL SERVICES LAW

——————————————— x

TO THE FAMILY COURT OF [county] COUNTY:

Petitioner, [agency], as and for its Petition for the commitment, guardianship and custody of [child], an infant, respectfully alleges upon information and belief:

1. [Agency] is a not-for-profit corporation, organized and existing by virtue of the laws of the State of New York, having an office for the regular conduct of business at [address], New York, and is an authorized agency approved, visited, inspected and supervised by the State Board of Social Welfare.

2. [Child] was born on [date], at [location], New York, and a copy of the Birth Certificate of [child] is annexed hereto and marked as Exhibit "A."

3. The Birth Certificate of the infant, [child], lists as (his/her) mother, [mother], and lists ([father]) (no one) as the father of the infant herein.

4. The infant, [child], was (court) (voluntarily) placed with the Commissioner of Social Services of the city of New York on [date], by [court] Court, [county] County, Docket No. [number]. The Commissioner of Social Services of the City of New York in turn placed the infant with [agency] on [date].

5. According to the case records of [agency], the putative father of the infant, [child], is negligent.

6. The persons entitled to service of process in this proceeding are:

NAME   LAST KNOWN ADDRESS

_____ [address]
natural mother

COMMISSIONER OF SOCIAL
SERVICES
CITY OF NEW YORK

AS AND FOR A FIRST CAUSE OF ACTION AGAINST THE RESPONDENT NATURAL MOTHER, [mother], IN PERMANENT NEGLECT

7. Petitioner repeats and realleges paragraphs "1" through "6" as if fully set forth herein at length.

*(8. Petitioner has made diligent efforts to encourage and strengthen the parental relationship by visiting with the natural mother and encouraging her to visit and plan for the infant. When this has not been possible, petitioner has made diligent efforts to attempt to locate [mother]. Petitioner realized the obstacles preventing the return of the infant herein in that 1) [mother] lacked an

adequate parent-child relationship with the infant herein, 2) the natural mother required parenting skills training, and 3) the natural mother required housing suitable and adequate for the return of the infant herein. Petitioner, therefore, informed [mother] that in order to overcome these obstacles, she must visit the infant on a regular and consistent basis, maintain adequate and consistent contact with the agency, attend and follow through with parenting skills training sessions and obtain housing suitable and adequate for the return of the infant. The aforesaid goals were designed as a plan for the return of the infant and were outlined and reiterated during visits, telephone communications and written correspondence between [mother] and the caseworker herein. Petitioner informed [mother] that in order to improve the parent-child relationship, she would have to visit the infant on a regular and consistent basis. Petitioner offered a minimum of bi-weekly visitation and made provisions for carfare for [mother] to attend visits. However, [mother] visited the infant on only one (1) occasion since the date of placement of the infant herein, namely [date]. [Mother] failed to appear and to cancel for any good reason almost all of the scheduled visits with the infant herein. Further, on one occasion, namely [date], when the caseworker asked the natural mother if the natural mother would like to visit with the infant, the natural mother, [mother], responded that she would be interested in considering signing a surrender for the child. Subsequent to that date, on [date] when asked whether she wished to visit with the infant, [mother] responded that she did not have the time. Additionally, petitioner informed [mother] that she must maintain adequate and consistent contact with the agency. Petitioner explained to [mother] that this consistent contact would allow her to better plan for the return of the infant and also keep the petitioner apprised of the progress and/or problem areas relating to the planning of [mother] for the return of the infant herein. However, from the date of placement of the infant herein to the present time, [mother], has been evasive and resistant to the efforts of the petitioner in assisting her in planning for the return of the infant. Additionally, petitioner informed [mother] that she must attend and follow through with parenting skills training so that she could come to understand and ameliorate her inability to develop a parent-child relationship with the infant herein. Referrals were made for therapy to the agency staff psychologist on a number of occasions, including [dates]. However, the natural mother attended only one session with the staff psychologist, was resistent to any further referrals and failed to follow through. The natural mother was also referred for family therapy. Again, however, [mother] failed to follow through. Additionally, petitioner informed [mother] that she must obtain housing suitable and adequate for the return of the infant herein and explained to [mother] that her current pattern of living from place to place was inadequate for the return of the infant. [Mother] was offered housing services and an appointment was made with the agency Housing Coordinator on [date]. Subsequently, a housing meeting with the natural mother was held, and an appointment was made with [landlord] for [date]. [Mother] failed to attend the initial appointment, and an additional appointment was scheduled for [date]. While [mother] attended the latter appointment, as of [date] she had failed to produce the appropriate documentation for her housing applications. [Mother] has resisted the efforts of the agency in obtaining suitable and adequate housing, has not obtained needed services in this area elsewhere and continues to require services in the area of housing.)* In general, [mother] has been unresponsive to the efforts of the petitioner in both developing a meaningful relationship between the parent and the child and in assisting her in planning for the return of the infant despite the above-described diligent efforts of the petitioner. Notwithstanding petitioner's efforts, said parent failed for a period of more than one (1) year following the placement and commitment of said child in the care of the petitioner, substantially, continuously and repeatedly, to maintain contact with and plan for the future of the child although physically and financially able to do so.

9. The best interests of said child require that the parent's custody and guardianship of the child be terminated permanently for the reason that the child's mother has not planned for the infant's return. The infant is entitled to permanency and thereby should be freed for adoption.

10. [Putative father], the putative father of the infant herein, is not a person whose consent is necessary to the adoption of this child since he has not maintained substantial and continuous or repeated contact with the child, has not supported the child financially, and has not visited the child monthly or kept regular communication with the child or agency. Furthermore, no notice need be given to him as he does not meet any of the criteria set forth in Section 384-c of the Social Services Law. He has not been adjudicated by a Court in this State to be the father of said child. He has not been adjudicated by a Court in another state or territory of the United States to be the father of said child. He has not timely filed an unrevoked Notice of Intent to claim paternity of the child. He is not recorded on the child's birth certificate as the

child's father. He did not openly live with the child and the child's mother at the time that this proceeding was initiated or at the time said child was placed in the care of [agency] and did not hold himself out to be the child's father. He has not been identified as the child's father by the mother in a written, sworn statement. He was not married to the child's mother within six (6) months subsequent to the birth of the child and prior to the initiation of this proceeding. He has not filed with the Putative Father Registry, an instrument acknowledging paternity of the child pursuant to Section 4-1.2 of the Estates, Powers and Trusts Law. Petitioner seeks a finding that the putative father is not entitled to notice of this proceeding.

WHEREFORE, the petitioner prays that an Order be made directing that a Summons be issued to the respondents, [parents], and the Commissioner of Social Services of the City of New York, to show cause why an Order should not be made by this Court determining that said respondent, [mother], has permanently neglected the infant in committing the custody and guardianship of the infant to [agency] and the Commissioner of Social Services of the City of New York with the right of [agency] or the Commissioner of Social Services of the City of New York to place [child] for legal adoption and to consent to (his/her) adoption without further notice to or consent of (his/her) parent, subject to the customary approval of the court to which the Petition for adoption is presented and directing that all papers and records in this proceeding be sealed and filed in the office of the Clerk of the Family Court, County of New York, and further directing that a certified copy of said order be filed in the office of the County Clerk of the County of New York pursuant to the provisions of the Social Services Law in the State of New York, and for such other and further relief as may be in the interests of the infant herein.

Dated: New York

         , 19   .   [agency]

                              By: _____
                                   Executive Director

STATE OF NEW YORK)
) ss.:
COUNTY OF [county])

[Executive director], being duly sworn, deposes and says that he is the Executive Director of [agency], petitioner herein, that the foregoing Petition is true to his own knowledge, except as to matters therein stated to be alleged upon information and belief, and, as to those matters, he believes it to be true.

_____
Executive Director

Sworn to before me this day of
, 1991.

_____
Notary Public

Sidebar 13–2. Summons in a Permanent Neglect Proceeding

FAMILY COURT OF THE STATE OF
NEW YORK
COUNTY OF [county]
—————————————————— x
In the Matter of   SUMMONS

[child],

A dependent child under the age of 14 years, to the custody of [agency], alleged to be a permanently neglected child, pursuant to Section 384-b of the Social Services Law.
—————————————————— x

IN THE NAME OF THE PEOPLE OF THE STATE OF NEW YORK

TO: [mother] [father]

A verified Petition having been filed in this Court alleging that the above-named child in the care of the petitioner, is a permanently neglected child, as defined by Article 6, Part 1, of the Family Court Act and Section 384-b of the Social Services Law, a copy of said Petition being annexed hereto;

YOU ARE HEREBY SUMMONED to appear before the Family Court at [address] Part [part] on the   , day of   , at 9:00 o'clock in the forenoon of said day to show cause why the Court should not enter an Order depriving you of all the rights of custody of [child] awarding the custody of said child to the petitioning authorized agency as a permanently neglected child as provided by law.

PLEASE TAKE NOTICE that if said child is adjudged to be a permanently neglected child, and if custody is awarded to said authorized agency, said child may be adopted with the consent of said authorized agency, without further notice to the parent of the child.

PLEASE TAKE FURTHER NOTICE that your failure to appear shall constitute a denial of an interest in the child, which denial may result in the transfer or commitment of the child's care, custody, guardianship or adoption of the child, all without further notice to the parent of the child.

PLEASE TAKE FURTHER NOTICE that you are entitled to be represented by an attorney, and if you cannot afford to retain an attorney, one will be appointed to represent you by the Court free of charge to you.

Dated:

By Order of the Court

_____
Clerk, Family Court, [county] County

Court-Appointed Lawyers

On the return date of the summons, if the parent appears at the court without an attorney and cannot afford an attorney, the judge will appoint an attorney for the parent free of charge. The court will appoint a law guardian for the child or children. See In re Orlando [40 N.Y. 2d 103, 386 N.Y.S. 2d 64 (1976)] and Matter of Karl S. [118 A.D. 2d 1002, 500 N.Y.S. 2d 209 (Appellate Division, 3rd Dept., 1986)], wherein the Court of Appeals stated that although no statute now so provides, the family court in a permanent neglect proceeding should appoint a law guardian to represent the child in order to protect and represent the rights and interests of the child so that the child will have the chance to focus on the question of "whether this parent belongs to me." See In re Carmen G.F. [404 N.Y.S. 2d 381 (Appellate Division, 2nd Dept., 1978)]. See also Matter of Tyease J. [373 N.Y.S. 2d 447, 83 Misc. 2d 1044 (Surrogate's Court, New York County, year 1975)]. Also, only the child may waive the right to the representation of his/her counsel, and only when the child possesses the "requisite" knowledge and willingness. See Matter of Karl S. [118 A.D. 2d 1002, 500 N.Y.S. 2d 209, 210 (Appellate Division, 3rd Dept., 1986)]. The court will also set the matter for a fact-finding hearing, and the court must determine whether the allegations that are alleged in the petition are supported by clear and convincing evidence. See Section 622 of the Family Court Act.

Prior to the return date of the fact-finding hearing, the attorney representing the parent would do well to serve a notice of discovery and inspection upon the attorney for the agency to review the case records of the agency prior to the hearing. In this way, the attorney will be prepared to refute, if possible, the agency's allegation that it used diligent efforts to strengthen the parental ties.

Of course, if the attorney for the agency feels that the discovery and inspection will lead to the disclosure of confidential material that should not be disclosed, he/she should make a motion for a protective order limiting the scope of the disclosure of the agency's case records.

The Fact-Finding Hearing

The attorney for the agency will usually call at least two witnesses: the agency case supervisor and the agency caseworker. Usually, the supervisor will not be personally familiar with the everyday occurrences relating to the case.

Whereas the case supervisor may have had little or no contact with the parent or the child, the agency caseworker would have had many contacts with the natural parents and the foster child. Some agencies divide casework responsibilities and designate one caseworker to work with the natural family and another caseworker to work with the foster family and foster child. In that event, the agency attorney will call at least three witnesses: the case supervisor, the natural-father caseworker, and the foster-family and foster-child caseworker.

Although the case supervisor may not be personally familiar with the interaction between the natural parent and the child and the foster parent and the child, the supervisor will most certainly have read the entire case record. After the case record has been put into evidence, the case supervisor may testify from his/her remembrance of the case record by using the case record to refresh his/her recollection, or he/she may read from the case records.

The case records will be placed into evidence after a proper foundation has been laid by asking the case supervisor:

1. if it was the duty and obligation of the agency to make records in its regular course of business;
2. whether these particular records were kept in the regular course of business;
3. whether the records were made contemporaneously with the events described therein;
4. whether the records were kept under the supervision and control of said witness; and
5. whether the person who made the entries had duty to make the entries.

If the answers to these questions are yes, the records will be placed into evidence, and, as stated above, the case supervisor may testify from the records.

The records themselves become evidence, subject, of course, to cross-examination of the witnesses by the attorney for the natural parent and by the law guardian for the child. The case supervisor will testify that the agency used its best efforts and was diligent in attempting to encourage and strengthen the parental ties but that despite the agency's efforts, the parent neglected either to visit or to formulate a plan for the child's return. It should be noted, however, that the entire case records may not be received into evidence by the judge presiding. In Matter of Leon R.R. [48 N.Y. 2d 117, 421 N.Y.S. 2d 863 (1979)], the Court of Appeals reversed a finding of permanent neglect and held that it was an error to admit into evidence the child's entire case file as a business record of the agency where many of the entries consisted of statements, reports, or even rumors made by persons under no business duty to report to the agency.

Diligent Efforts

The caseworker for the natural parent will testify that he/she was assigned to work with the natural parent with the ultimate goal of having the child returned to the parent. The caseworker will outline all the diligent efforts made to encourage and strengthen the parental ties, such as mailing regular visiting notices to the natural parent, making monthly home visits to the parent or more frequent visits if indicated, encouraging the parent to visit the child, and, if the parent does not have sufficient carfare, supplying sufficient sums so that the parent may visit with the child and, if need be, bring the child to the parent's home. The caseworker should be able to testify that he/she assisted in other ways, such as aiding the parent in receiving welfare payments if indicated, assisting the parent in enrolling in a drug program, or Alcoholics Anonymous if the parent has a drinking problem, and where needed, assisting in obtaining employment or larger living quarters.

In Matter of Sheila G. [61 N.Y.S. 2d 368, 474 N.Y.S. 2d 421, 462, N.E. 2d 1139 (1984)], the New York Court of Appeals redefined the form that diligent efforts by the agency must take. The court held that the agency must make "affirmative, repeated and meaningful efforts to assist" a parent to overcome the obstacles preventing the return of the child [Id at 430].

The court also held that "proof by the child care agency that it has satisfied its statutory obligation is a threshold consideration" to any determination of permanent neglect [Id at 430].

Excused from Using Diligent Efforts

If the agency did not use diligent efforts to strengthen and encourage the parental relationship, the caseworker must be prepared to testify that it would have been detrimental to the interests of the child to do so. For example, if the parent abused the child physically in the initial visits, or the child had nightmares after each of those visits, then the agency may be justified in not continuing efforts to strengthen the parental ties. In Matter of Terry D. [385 N.Y.S. 2d 844 (Appellate Division, 3rd Dept., 1976)], the authorized agency was relieved of its duty to strengthen the parental ties where the mother used drugs, did not seek help, was incarcerated, and was involved in crime in which she and another woman "rolled" an elderly man.

The caseworker assigned to the foster family and foster child will testify to the type of care that the child is getting at the foster home, to the physical condition of the child, and to the progress the child has made since being placed with the foster family. Where indicated, the attorney for the agency may call as a witness the agency's psychologist or psychiatrist, or an independent psychologist or psychiatrist who has examined or treated the child. Such psychologist's or psychiatrist's testimony may be needed to fortify the agency's position that it did not encourage or strengthen the parental relationship because it would not have been in the best interests of the child.

Cross-Examination

The attorney for the natural parents will attempt to show on cross-examination that the caseworker did not make diligent efforts to encourage and strengthen the parental relationship, but instead favored the foster parent over the natural parents.

Respondent's Testimony

The parent may testify to the fact that the agency caseworker from inception talked about the natural parent or parents signing a surrender freeing the child for adoption and did little or nothing to aid the natural parent except for possibly sending out monthly notices of visitation, but neither encouraging nor assisting in those visits. The parent may testify that he/she did not plan for the return of the child because he/she was financially unable to do so. There may have been a period when he/she was out of a job and could not find work. Welfare payments perhaps were insufficient or ceased at a particular time.

The natural parent may also testify that he/she could not visit or plan because of some physical problem, such as being in a hospital, being out of town for a good reason, or being pregnant and temporarily not able to plan for the return of the child.

The Ruling

If the agency has proved its case by clear and convincing evidence, and the petition is sustained, then the court will hold a dispositional hearing to determine whether the interests of the child require that the parent's custody be terminated permanently and, if so, what order of disposition should be made. If the petition is dismissed, the court should not return the child without a further dispositional hearing inquiring into the best interests of the child. See In re Jonathan D. [403 N.Y.S. 2d 750 (Appellate Division, 1st Dept., 1978)].

Visitation During Pendency of Hearing

The Appellate Division affirmed an order of the Family Court, Queens County, that authorized and directed weekend visiting between mother and child, supervised by the Bureau of Child Welfare, pending a final determination of the permanent neglect proceedings. See In re Ernestine H. [390 N.Y.S. 2d 148 (Appellate Division, 2nd Dept., 1976)].

Since the Appellate Division held that it was in the discretion of the family court to order visitation pending the determination of a permanent neglect proceeding, the opposite should be true—that is, the court can suspend visitation during the pendency of the trial. In an unreported case, In re M. (St. Christopher's Home), the Family Court, Suffolk County, did suspend visitation between the putative father and his three children during the pendency of a permanent neglect proceeding.

The Dispositional Hearing

Section 623 of the Family Court Act, as amended January 1, 1977, defines a dispositional hearing as a hearing to determine what order of disposition should be made in accordance with the best interests of the child.

The dispositional hearing may commence immediately upon completion of the fact-finding hearing. Further, with the consent of all parties, the court may dispense with the dispositional hearing and make an order of disposition on the basis of competent evidence admitted at the fact-finding hearing. (See section 625 of the Family Court Act, as amended, effective January 1, 1977. However, the court may not on its own motion dispense with a dispositional hearing. To do so is reversible error. See In re Roy Anthony A. [59 A.D. 2d 662, 298 N.Y.S. 2d 277 (Appellate Division, 1st Dept., 1977)]).

Section 625 B of the Family Court Act, as amended, effective January 1, 1977, provides that:

> Reports prepared by the probation services or a duly authorized agency for use by the court prior to the making of an order of disposition shall be deemed confidential information furnished to the court which the court in a proper case may, in its discretion, withhold from or disclose in whole or in part to the law guardian, counsel, party in interest, or other appropriate person. Such reports may not be furnished to the court prior to the completion of a fact finding hearing, but may be used in a dispositional hearing or in the making of an order of disposition without a dispositional hearing pursuant to subdivision (1) of this section.

Adjournment

In re Hanson [379 N.Y.S. 2d 415 (Appellate Division, 1st Dept., 1976)], the court held that where the mother's psychological and probation reports were not available, and her witness was also not available, a postponement was in order, and the family court was in error to conclude the dispositional hearing. It stated that "Due process is required to be observed in child neglect proceedings."

Dispositions

At the conclusion of the dispositional hearing, the court may enter any one of the following dispositions:

1. dismiss the petition;
2. suspend judgment, but not for longer than one year; or
3. permanently terminate custody of the parent and award custody to the authorized agency.

The order of disposition (see sidebar 13-3) must be made solely on the basis of the best interests of the child, and there is no presumption that such interests will be promoted by any particular disposition. See Section 631 of the Family Court Act, as amended, effective January 1, 1977.

Appeal

On appeal, the findings of the family court must be accorded the greatest respect. See In re Judy V. [400 N.Y.S. 2d 916 (Appellate Division, 3rd Dept., 1977)].

Default of Parent

In the case of In re Ycm [388 N.Y.S. 2d 7 (Appellate Division, 1st Dept., 1976)], the Appellate Division held that the family court judge erred in failing to hold a hearing to ascertain whether the mother's nonappearance was inadvertent or willful. See also In re Jaclyn [382 N.Y.S. 2d 569 (Appellate Division, 2nd Dept., 1976)].

Present Law to Apply

If, subsequent to the petition being filed, the law is changed, the trial court should apply the law as it exists at the time of the hearing. On appeal, the reviewing court will decide the case on the basis as it exists at the time of the decision. See Matter of Ray A.M. [376 N.Y.S. 2d 431 (1975)], wherein the Court of Appeals stated: "This Court decides the case on the basis of the law as it exists today."

Sidebar 13–3. Order of Disposition, Adjudication, Findings of Fact, and Conclusions of Law in a Permanent Neglect Proceeding

At the Family Court of the State of New York, held in and for the [county] on the   , day of   .

P R E S E N T:

HON. [judge]

Judge of the Family Court.

_____ x

In the Matter of

[child],

A dependent child under the age of 14 years, to the custody of [agency] an abandoned child, pursuant to Section 384-b of the Social Services Law.

_____ x

ORDER OF DISPOSITION, ADJUDICATION, FINDINGS OF FACT AND CONCLU-SIONS OF LAW

Docket No.

A Petition, pursuant to Section 384-b of the Social Services Law having been filed in this Court by [agency] alleging that [child], an infant, is an abandoned child; and a Summons and Petition having been personally served upon [putative father], the putative father of said infant, and upon [mother], the natural mother of said infant, having been served by publication pursuant to an Order of this Court, and

With respect to the natural mother of the infant, [mother], the matter having duly come on for a fact finding hearing on [date] before the HON. [judge], Judge, Family Court, [county] County at a Trial Term Part 4, and the said [mother], the natural mother of said infant, having failed to appear thereon and her default having been duly noted by the Court; and the petitioner, [agency] having been represented by [attorney], of counsel; and the child having been represented by [attorney], Law Guardian, Legal Aid Society, by [attorney]; and this Court after hearing the proofs and the testimony offered in relation to the case of the Court having found that the allegations of the Petition required by Section 384-b of the Social Services Law are supported by clear and convincing evidence and the Court having heard the testimony of [case-worker] [agency] relating to the neglect of the natural mother and the Court found upon clear and convincing evidence:

1. [Agency] is a not-for-profit corporation, organized and existing by virture of the laws of the State of New York, having an office for the regular conduct of business at [address], New York and is an authorized agency approved, visited, inspected and supervised by the State Board of Social Welfare.

2. [Child] was born on [date] at [hospital] Hospital, at [location].

3. The natural mother of the infant, [child], is [mother].

4. The infant, [child], was Court placed with the Commissioner of Social Services of the City of New York on [date] by the Family Court, [county] County under Docket No. [number] and the Commissioner of Social Services of the City of New York in turn placed the infant with [agency] on [date].

5. The putative father of the infant, [child], is [putative father]. The petitioner did not proceed against [putative father] at this [date] hearing.

6. The natural mother of the infant, [mother], evinced an intent to forgo her parental rights by reason of her failure to visit or communicate with the infant since [date] and the natural mother was not discouraged or prevented from visiting or communicating with the infant.

7. From [date] to the date of the filing of the Petition, the infant's natural mother, [mother], did not visit or communicate with the child, did not make any payments towards her support and withheld from the infant her presence, love and care and neglected and refused to perform her legal obligations of care and support of the infant and by reasons of the above, the natural mother neglected the infant.

8. From [date] to the date of the filing of the Petition, the infant's natural mother, [mother], did not contact the child or the caseworker herein concerning the child's placement or well-being, and the caseworker did not discourage or prevent her from doing so.

9. In light of the failure of [mother] to contact the caseworker herein regarding the child's placement or well-being, and by reason of the fact that the natural mother did not visit or communicate with the child since [date], the natural mother neglected the infant.

10. Pursuant to Section 384-b of the Social Services Law of the State of New York, the guardianship of the person and custody of the dependent child may be committed to an authorized agency by an Order of the Family Court where it appears that a child has been abandoned by her parents for a period of six (6) months preceding the filing of the Petition.

THEREFORE, with respect to the natural mother, [mother], the allegations of neglect in the Petition as required by Section 384-b of the Social Services Law are supported by clear and convincing evidence; and

NOW, THEREFORE, it is upon clear and convincing evidence;

ADJUDGED, that the allegations of neglect as to the respondent natural mother, [mother], required by Section 384-b of the Social Services Law are sustained by clear and convincing evidence; and

The matter having come on for a dispositional hearing before the HON. [judge], Judge, Family Court, [county] County on [date] at a Trial Term Part [part] and the said [mother], the natural mother of said infant, having failed to appear thereon and her default having been duly noted by the Court, and [agency], the petitioner, was represented by its attorneys, [attorneys], and the child was represented by [attorneys] Law Guardian, Legal Aid Society, by [attorney], and this Court having taken testimony and made examination and inquiry into the facts and circumstances of the case and into the surroundings and capacities of the persons involved in this proceeding and the Court having heard the testimony of [supervisor] Supervisor, [agency], that the natural mother was not a resource for the future of said child and that the foster parents wish to adopt the infant herein and are viable resources for the future of said child, and the Court having heard and considered the recommendation of the Law Guardian and the Court having found upon clear and convincing evidence that:

1. It would be in the best interests of the infant that the respondent natural mother's rights of guardianship and custody be transferred to [agency] and the Commissioner of Social Services of the City of New York so that either [agency] or the Commissioner of Social Services of the City of New York may consent to the infant's adoption in the place and stead of the natural mother, [mother].

2. The infant, [child], born on [date], is presently in a pre-adoptive home which has been evaluated and assessed as a permanent home for the infant, that said foster parents wish to adopt the infant, [child], and it is the recommendation of the petitioner, [agency], that the infant be adopted by her present foster parents.

NOW, THEREFORE, upon the dispositional hearing and upon clear and convincing evidence,

IT APPEARING that the best interests of the infant, [child] require that the respondent natural mother's rights of guardianship and custody of the infant be transferred and committed to the Commissioner of Social Services of the City of New York and [agency], it is

ORDERED, that the best interests of the child require that the custody and guardianship rights of [mother], the natural mother, over said child be terminated; and it is further,

ORDERED, that such rights of the legal custody and guardianship of said infant, [child], by the respondent natural mother, [mother], be and the same hereby are transferred and committed to the Commissioner of Social Services of the City of New York and [agency], an authorized agency, and it is further,

ORDERED, that the Commissioner of Social Services of the City of New York or [agency] be and is hereby authorized and empowered to consent to the adoption of said minor child, [child], in the place and stead of the natural mother, [mother], by a suitable person or persons subject to the customary approval of the Court of competent jurisdiction and that the consent of and notice to the natural mother of said minor child, [child] to said adoption be and the same and hereby are dispensed with; and

With respect to the putative father of said infant, [putative father], the matter having duly come on for a fact finding hearing on [date] before the HON. [judge], Judge, Family Court, [county] County at a Trial Term Part [part] and the said [putative father], the putative father of said infant, having appeared thereon with his attorney, [attorney], and the petitioner, [agency] having been represented by [attorney] of counsel; and the child having been represented by [attorney], Law Guardian, Legal Aid Society, by [attorney], and this Court after hearing the proofs and testimony offered in relation to the case the Court having found that the allegations of the Petition required by Section 384-b of the Social Services Law are supported by clear and convincing evidence and the Court having heard the testimony and cross-examination of [supervisor, agency], relating to the neglect of the putative father and, [putative father], the putative father of said infant, having testified on his own behalf, and that the Court found upon clear and convincing evidence:

1. [Agency] is a not-for-profit corporation, organized and existing by virtue of the laws of the State of New York, having an office for the regular conduct of business at [address], and is an authorized agency approved, visited, inspected and supervised by the State Board of Social Welfare.

2. [Child] was born on [date] at [location].

3. The natural mother of the infant, [child], is [mother]. [Mother's] parental rights were terminated on [date] at the aforementioned proceeding.

4. The infant, [child], was Court placed with the Commissioner of Social Services of the City of New York on [date] by the Family Court, [county] County under Docket No. [number] and the Commissioner of Social Services of the City of New York in turn placed the infant with [agency] on [date].

5. The putative father of the infant, [child], is [putative father].

6. The putative father of the infant herein, [putative father], evinced an intent to forgo his parental rights by reason of his failure to visit or communicate with the infant since [date] to the date of the filing of the Petition and the putative father was not discouraged or prevented from visiting or communicating with the infant.

7. From [date] to the date of the filing of the Petition, the infant's putative father, [putative father], did not visit or communicate with the child, did not make any payments towards his/her support and withheld from the infant his presence, love and care and neglected and refused to perform his legal obligations of care and support of the infant and by reason of the above, the putative father abandoned the infant herein.

8. From [date] to the date of the filing of the Petition, the infant's putative father, [putative father], did not contact the child or the caseworker herein concerning the child's placement or well-being, and the caseworker did not discourage or prevent him from doing so.

9. In light of the failure of [putative father] to contact the petitioner herein regarding the child's placement or well-being, and by reason of the fact that the putative father did not visit or communicate with the child since [date], the putative father abandoned the infant.

10. Pursuant to Section 384-b of the Social Services Law of the State of New York, the guardianship of the person and custody of the dependent child may be committed to an authorized agency by an Order of the Family Court where it appears that a child has been abandoned by her parents for a period of six (6) months preceding the filing of the Petition.

THEREFORE, with respect to the putative father, [putative father], the allegations of abandonment in the Petition as required by Section 384-b of the Social Services Law are supported by clear and convincing evidence; and

NOW, THEREFORE, it is upon clear and convincing evidence;

ADJUDGED, that the allegations of abandonment as to the respondent putative father, [putative father], required by Section 384-b of the Social Services Law are sustained by clear and convincing evidence; and

The matter having come on for a dispositional hearing before the HON. [judge], Judge, Family Court, New York County on [date] at a Trial Term Part [part] and the said [putative father], the putative father of said infant, having appeared thereon with his attorney, [attorney], and [agency], the petitioner, was represented by its attorneys, [attorneys], and the child was represented by [attorney], Law Guardian, Legal Aid Society, by [attorney], and this Court having taken testimony and made examination and inquiry into the facts and circumstances of the case and into the surroundings and capacities of the persons involved in this proceeding and the Court having heard the testimony of [caseworker] that the putative father was not a resource for the future of said child and that the foster parents wish to adopt the infant herein and are viable resources for the future of said child, and the Court having heard and considered the recommendation of the Law Guardian and the Court having found upon clear and convincing evidence that:

1. It would be in the best interests of the infant that the respondent putative father's rights of guardianship and custody be transferred to [agency] and the Commissioner of Social Services of the City of New York so that either [agency] or the Commissioner of Social Services of the City of New York may consent to the infant's adoption in the place and stead of the putative father, [natural father].

2. The infant, [child], born on [date], is presently in a pre-adoptive home which has been evaluated and assessed as a permanent home for the infant, that said foster parents wish to adopt the infant, [child], and it is the recommendation of the petitioner, [agency], that the infant be adopted by his/her present foster parents.

NOW, THEREFORE, upon the dispositional hearing and upon clear and convincing evidence,

IT APPEARING that the best interests of the infant, [child], require that the respondent putative father's rights of guardianship and custody of the infant be transferred and committed to the Commissioner of Social Services of the City of New York and [agency] it is

ORDERED, that the best interests of the child require that the custody and guardianship rights of [putative father], the putative father, over said child be terminated; and it is further,

ORDERED, that such rights of the legal custody and guardianship of said infant, [child], by the respondent putative father, [putative father], be and the same hereby are transferred and committed to the Commissioner of Social Services of the City of New York and [agency], an authorized agency, and it is further,

ORDERED, that the Commissioner of Social Services of the City of New York or [agency], Brooklyn, New York be and is hereby authorized and empowered to consent to the adoption of said minor child, [child], in the place and stead of the putative father, [putative father], by a suitable person or persons subject to the customary approval of the Court of competent jurisdiction and that the consent of and notice to the putative father of said minor child, [child], to said adoption be and the same hereby are dispensed with, and it is further,

ORDERED, that the Law Guardian and the Commissioner of Social Services of the City of New York be notified of all future legal proceedings concerning the infant herein, and it is further,

ORDERED, that all papers and records in this proceeding be filed in the Office of the Clerk of the Family Court of the State of New York, County of New York, in accordance with Section 384-b, Subd. 3 (j) of the Social Services Law, and it is further,

ORDERED, that a certified copy of this Order be filed in the Office of the Clerk, [county] County.

Dated:

ENTER:

_____

HON. [judge]
Family Court, New York County

What Constitutes Diligent Efforts?

Section 384 B, Paragraph 4, Subdivision 7(a), of the Social Services Law as amended, effective January 1, 1977, provides that before a child can be declared to be permanently neglected, the agency must prove that it made "diligent efforts to encourage and strengthen the parental relationship."

For the first time, the legislature has attempted to define *diligent efforts.* Section 384 B, Subdivision 7(f), of the Social Services Law, provides:

As used in this subdivision, "diligent efforts" shall mean reasonable attempts by an authorized agency to assist, develop and encourage a meaningful relationship between the parent and child, including but not limited to:

(1) consultation and cooperation with the parents in developing a plan for appropriate services to the child and his family;

(2) making suitable arrangements for the parents to visit the child;

(3) provisions of services and other assistance to the parents so that problems preventing the discharge of the child from care may be resolved or ameliorated; and

(4) informing the parent at appropriate intervals of the child's progress, development and health.

As explained earlier, the burden is on the agency to show, before the termination proceeding, that it made "some attempt" to assist parents with counseling, planning, visitation, the procurement of housing, and employment where that is necessary in order to help them overcome the problems that separate them from their children. See Matter of Jamie M. [63 N.Y. 2d 388, 394–5, 482 N.Y.S. 2d 461, 472 N.E. 2d 311].

What constitutes diligent efforts will depend on the peculiar facts of each individual case. Some guidelines can be gleaned from the cases. In Matter of Sydney [377 N.Y.S. 2d 908 (Family Court, Queens County, 1975)], Judge Shorter dismissed the agency's petition alleging that the mother permanently neglected her child, relying on his finding that the agency had failed to use diligent efforts in working with the mother. He stated that the agency should have explored the maternal grandmother as a resource and should have worked harder with the natural mother, knowing that (1) she had limitations, (2) she was emotionally upset, (3) she had cooperated in the past, and (4) she had expressed a desire to have her child.

In re Antonio G. (408 N.Y.S. 2d 818 (Appellate Division, 2nd Dept., 1978)], the court held that the agency had failed to prove permanent neglect. The Court dismissed the petition in which the agency refused to discharge the child until the mother obtained a larger apartment, but the mother could not get a larger apartment until she received the child. The agency failed to use diligent efforts in enlisting support of other family members to help the mother and would not allow home visits, overnight visits, and unsupervised visits.

It would appear that the degree of diligent effort required of the agency hinges upon the stability of the foster home and on that of the parent.

In Matter of Ray A.M. [48 A.D. 2d 161, 368 N.Y.S. 2d 374 (Appellate Division, 2nd Dept., 1975)], the court indicated that the diligent efforts rule is flexible, depending on the mother's behavior and the future of the child with the foster parents as opposed to the natural parent. The court, in analyzing the degree of diligent effort required, stated:

This is not simply a case where the neglect by the parent may have been matched by the neglect of the agency to attempt the strengthening of the parental relationship (cf. *Matter of Anonymous*, App. Div. 368 N.Y.S. 2d 374 [decided herewith]). It may be that the adoption agency could have tried harder to encourage the natural mother-child relationship in order to satisfy the most searching mind that no more could reasonably be done. However, we must not get lost in an analysis of the niceties of the precise degree of required diligence of effort where the life-style and apparent sociopathology of the mother (joined with her undoubted past neglect) indicate a bleak future indeed for the child). As stated in *Matter of Raymond M.*, Fam. Ct., 81 Misc. 2d 70, 79, 364 N.Y.S. 2d 321, 329, "The welfare of the child is not served if permanent termination is delayed in order to penalize the agency for its failure to make diligent efforts or in order to give the natural parent recompense against the agency in the form of a second chance."

The Court of Appeals in In re Ray A.M., in effect, excused the agency in not using the highest degree of diligent effort because of the attitude of the parent, stating:

Only by sophistic analysis can it be argued that the child care agency failed in its duty to "encourage and strengthen the parental relationship" between this unfortunate child and the troubled and trouble-making mother. The mother exhibited not isolated instances of parental incapacity but a pattern of intransigence, instability, and abusive conduct toward the child which, perforce, must have practically limited the agency in its efforts, if the best interests of the child were to govern the actions of parties and agencies involved (See *Matter of Barbara P.*, 71 Misc. 2d 965, 972, 337 N.Y.S. 2d 203, 210–211; see also *Gordon*, op. cit., 46 St. John's Law Rev. 215, 238–239).

The parent's way of life is germane to the degree of diligent effort required of the agency. In In re Anthony L. CC [48 A.D. 2d 415, 370 N.Y.S. 2d 219 (Appellate Division , 3rd Dept., 1975)], the court stated:

The record is convincing that the mother was more interested in her selfish desires than in the infant and that the agency gave her as much encouragement to enter into a continuing parental relationship as her way of life permitted.

Rejection by the parent of the agency's caseworker will not negate the agency's diligent efforts attempted. In In re Tyease J. [373 N.Y.S. 2d 447 (Surrogate's Court, New York County, 1975)], Surrogate Midonick wrote:

Agency records reveal that substantial efforts were made by petitioner to speak with both natural mother and grandmother about plans for this infant when very young. Respondent-mother testified that her negative reaction to the petitioner's attempts to strengthen the parental ties was a result of the social worker's seemingly unsympathetic attitude. At the hearing, it became evident that, since her early years, respondent has viewed parental figures as unsympathetic to her needs and desires and as imposing upon her unwarranted supervision. Petitioner's social workers became parental figures in the eyes of this natural mother and as such were rejected by her.

In the case of In re Joyce A.R. [383 N.Y.S. 2d 58 (Appellate Division, 2nd Dept., 1976)] the Appellate Division reversed the Family Court and held that the agency met its burden of proof with respect to diligent efforts to encourage and strengthen the parental relationship. The court stated:

> Special arrangements for parental visiting were made and, by respondent's own admission, concrete suggestions for support, so as to the natural mother's custody, were made on numerous occasions. While it is possible that the petitioner could have done more in order to satisfy the most searching mind, we must not become enmeshed in an analysis of the niceties of diligence of effort, where to do so would jeopardize the welfare of the child (See *Matter of A.M.*, 48 A.D. 2d 161, 368 N.Y.S. 2d 374, affd. 27 N.Y. 2d 619, 376 N.Y.S. 2d 431, 339 N.E. 2d 135).

For a discussion of the diligent efforts necessary in the case of a minor mother, see In re Guardianship of Alexander [127 A.D. 517, 512 N.Y.S. 2d 32 (Appellate Division, 1st Dept., 1987)], wherein the Appellate Division in the First Department held that the child care agency had incurred diligent efforts to help a sixteen-year-old natural mother develop a parent-child relationship with her child wherein: (1) the agency was extremely patient with the mother; (2) the agency reviewed plans with the mother; (3) the agency called the natural mother; (4) the agency made extensive referrals for the natural mother; (5) the agency attempted to help the natural mother obtain housing and assistance; and (6) the agency scheduled regular visits, but the mother lacked commitment to plan for herself and the child and failed to follow through with agency efforts [Id at 34–35].

What Constitutes Failure on the Part of the Parent to Substantially and Continuously or Repeatedly Maintain Contact with or Plan for the Future of the Child?

It has been held that the parent's failure to contact or plan is not confined to a one-year-period immediately preceding the filing of the petition, but may be any one-year period prior to the filing of the petition. See In re Joyce Ann R. [371 N.Y.S. 2d 607 (Family Court, Kings County, 1975)]; In re B. [Misc. 2d 662, 303 N.Y.S. 2d (Family Court, New York County, 1969)]; and In re Jones [59 Misc. 2d 69, 297 N.Y.S. 2d (Family Court, New York County, 1969)]. See also In re Satosky [393 N.Y.S. 2d 486 (Family Court, Ulster County, 1976)], wherein the court held that the period of neglect required to trigger the permanent neglect statute need not be the interval immediately prior to the filing of the neglect petition but may embrace earlier periods of time.

The most obvious failure on the part of a parent that could lead to a termination of parental rights is to have no contact with the child for a one-year period. See In re Coddington [376 N.Y.S. 2d 387 (Family Court, Ulster

County, 1975)]. For example, if a parent does not write, call, make payments, or visit the child during a one-year period, the parent would have "abandoned" the child, and this could lead to a complete severance of parental rights.

Prior to the August 9, 1975, amendment of Section 384, Subdivision 6, of the Social Services Law and Section 611 of the Family Court Act, a few insubstantial contacts by the parent were sufficient to prevent the termination of parental rights. See Matter of Susan W. v. Talbot G. [34 N.Y. 2d, 356 N.Y.S. 2d 34 (Court of Appeals of New York, 1974)]. The "flicker of interest" rule in Matter of Susan W. is no longer the law, since the amendments now provide that evidence of insubstantial and infrequent contacts by a parent with his/her child shall not, of itself, be sufficient as a matter of law in the case of Section 384 of the Social Services Law and Section 111 of the Domestic Relations Law, "to preclude a finding that such parent has abandoned such child" and, in the case of Section 611 of the Family Court Act, "to preclude a determination that such child is a permanently neglected child." See Section 384 B(7)(a) of the Social Services Law.

Further, the trend of the recent cases is to give less to the articulated intentions of a parent with respect to be rid of parental rights. See In re Coddington, *supra* and In re Vanessa F. [76 Misc. 2d 617, 351 N.Y.S. 2d 337 (Surrogate's Court, New York County, 1975)].

In In re Coddington, Judge Hugh Elwyn wrote:

> With all due respect to our state's highest court, the trouble with applying the *Matter of Susan W.* rule to cases of alleged permanent parental neglect is that it places the emphasis upon a parent's intent—"a settled purpose to be rid of all parental [rights]," rather than upon the effect of the parent's conduct upon the child with its consequent deprivation of the child's right to concerned, functioning parents. The result of applying the "settled purpose rule" would be, in most cases, as is illustrated here, to enshrine parental rights at the cost of leaving the child forever in limbo wholly at the mercy of the parents' wavering and fluctuating intent. In short, to borrow a phrase from another context, it would leave the child "twisting slowly in the wind." This result ought to be avoided at all costs.
>
> Rather, I am of the opinion that in cases brought by the Commissioner of Social Services for the permanent termination of parental rights under either Section 384 of the Social Services Law or Article 6 of the Family Court Act, the parents' purpose of intent, while not wholly irrelevant, is certainly not controlling.
>
> More complicated is the problem of what constitutes lack of planning on the part of the parent. Some examples would be a parent who refuses professional help with a drug or drinking problem, or a parent who refuses a job, a larger apartment or more adequate housing.

In In re A.M. [37 N.Y. 2d 619, 376 N.Y.S. 2d 431 (1975)], Judge Charles Breitel of the Court of Appeals found that the parent failed substantially and continuously or repeatedly to maintain contact or plan for the future of the child. He stated:

> The mother failed for more than the prescribed period of one year substantially and continuously or repeatedly to maintain contact with her child or to plan for her future. The record is replete with evidence of a pattern of neglect by the mother. Indeed, on this evidentiary issue both the Family Court and the Appellate Division are in substantial agreement. Poignant and telling of her attitude toward her daughter is the mother's statement to the court psychiatrist to the effect that either she would regain custody of the child or she would have nothing further to do with it.

In In re Ray A.M. [48 A.D. 2d 161, 368 N.Y.S. 2d 374 (Appellate Division, 2nd Dept., 1975)], the court granted the agency's petition and, in writing about the parent's failure, stated:

> The record impels the conclusion that the respondent has failed for the entire time since May 29, 1969, "substantially and continuously or repeatedly to maintain contact with or plan for the future of the child" (Family Ct. Act, Section 611). The respondent's behavior during her sporadic contacts with the agency and the child did not serve the purpose of easing and adjusting the child to return to her; they constituted a disruptive and harmful factor to the child's well-being, far beyond that normally to be expected in such a delicate situation.

The Court of Appeals in In re Orlando F. [40 N.Y.S. 2d 103, 386 N.Y.S. 2d 64 (1976)], in reversing the Appellate Division, sustained the agency's petition charging the natural mother with permanent neglect. The court made it clear that the terminology *maintain contact with or plan for* may not be read in the conjunctive, but must be read in the disjunctive and as separate requirements. Hence, while a parent may contact a child weekly, if the parent does not plan for the child the court may terminate parental rights "in the best interests of the child." The court stated that "a finding of a failure to plan, in and of itself, suffices to support a determination of permanent neglect." The court also stated that the parent's "burning desire to have the child returned is insufficient if not accompanied by . . . affirmative steps necessary to insure Orlando would be the rightful beneficiary of an adequate home life if returned to her." These cases holding that intentions alone cannot frustrate a finding of abandonment or permanent neglect were codified by Section 384 B(5)(b), which provides:

> The subjective intent of the parent, whether expressed or otherwise, unsupported by evidence of the foregoing parental acts manifesting such intent, shall not preclude a determination that such parent has abandoned his or her child. In making such determination the court shall not require a showing of diligent efforts, if any, by an authorized agency, to encourage the parent to perform acts specified in paragraph (a) of this subdivision.

The Court of Appeals stated that *substantially plan* means to formulate, and act to accomplish, a feasible and realistic plan. The court, however, refused to define *substantially plan* rigidly and wrote:

> Indeed each factual pattern will undoubtedly reveal peculiarities of its own but the particular facts and totality of circumstances must be scrutinized and weighed carefully in rendering decisions in such delicate human affairs (cf. *Matter of Klug*, 32 A.D. 2d 915).

The case-by-case approach has been amplified in several recent cases. See O. Children v. Doris O. [A.D. 2d 513 N.Y.S. 2d 1531 (1987)], which found it an error to deny termination of parental rights for the agency's failure to provide psychological evaluations and tests of parents, where the agency had made all other diligent efforts in compliance with Social Services Law. See also Matter of Charles R. [A.D. 2d 512, N.Y.S. 2d 469]; Matter of June Y. [A.D. 2d 512, N.Y.S. 2d 469]; Matter of Ann Marie D. [A.D. 2d 512, N.Y.S. 2d 157], which upheld findings of permanent neglect where the parents had failed to follow through with referrals for therapy and parenting training.

When a Parent Can Be Considered Physically and Financially Unable to Substantially and Continuously or Repeatedly Maintain Contact or Plan for the Future of the Child

If a parent fails to visit, maintain contact with, or plan for the future of the child because the parent is incarcerated or hospitalized, the court will not find that the child is permanently neglected based upon the theory that the parent is physically unable to maintain contact with or plan for the child. See Matter of Klug [32 A.D. 2d 915, 302 N.Y.S. 2d 418 (Appellate Division, 1st Dept., 1969)], wherein Judge George Tilzer wrote in a concurring opinion with respect to physical and financial ability:

> The words "although physically and financially able to do so" also require an interpretation in the light of their use in the statute. Physical inability might arise from incarceration of a parent or it might result from hospitalization due to injury or the presence of mental or physical ailments which prevent a mother from exercising her parental obligation. So far as financial ability to care for the child is concerned, the court is well aware of the fact that in this City a mother may obtain support to maintain herself and her child.

Hospitalization because of mental illness is also considered physical inability, but mental illness without hospitalization is not considered physical inability to contact and visit with the child. See Matter of Stephen B. [60 Misc. 2d 662, 303 N.Y.S. 2d 438 (Family Court, New York County, 1969)], where Judge Nanette Dembitz wrote:

It is clear therefore that the omission of such a term as "mentally," "emotionally," or "physically" for the proviso as to a mother's inability to contact her child was deliberate and that "physically able" is to be construed literally to refer to powers of locomotion. Accordingly, during periods when Miss B. was not hospitalized she will be deemed to have been physically able to maintain contact with her child.

Failure to visit because of a drug or alcohol problem is not considered "good reason" or physical inability. For the first time, the legislature provided guidelines relating to the inability to plan for or contact the child. Section 384 B(7)(d) provides:

> For the purposes of this subdivision:
>
> (i) A parent shall not be deemed unable to maintain contact with or plan for the future of the child by reason of such parent's use of drugs or alcohol, except while the parent is actually hospitalized or institutionalized therefore;
>
> (ii) A parent shall be deemed unable to maintain contact with or plan for the future of the child while such parent is actually incarcerated;
>
> (iii) The time during which a parent is actually hospitalized, institutionalized or incarcerated shall not interrupt, but shall not be part of, a period of failure to maintain contact with or plan for the future of the child.

In Vanessa F. [76 Misc. 2d 617, 351 N.Y.S. 2d 337 (Surrogate's Court, New York County, 1974)], Surrogate Midonick wrote:

> It is obviously not "good reason" for parents to fail to visit their child for two years, that they were narcotic addicts at the time when the child was born.

However, it has been suggested that failure to visit because the mother was out of state was "good reason" and excusable where she and her father contacted the agency to claim the child. See In re Anonymous [48 A.D. 2d 696, 368 N.Y.S. 2d 372 (Appellate Division, 2nd Dept. 1975)].

Finally, it has been held that a child was permanently neglected where the mother was a heroin addict and incarcerated and there was no evidence that the mother was physically and financially able to visit and plan. In re Anthony L. [A.D. 2d 415, 370 N.Y.S. 2d (Appellate Division, 3rd Dept., 1975)], the court wrote:

> The troublesome part of the statute as to the present facts is the ability of the parent physically and financially to provide for the child. The record does not establish affirmatively that the mother was physically or financially able to so provide, but that such failure was the direct result of her own transgressions and while the statute speaks affirmatively, the purpose thereof should not be defeated by negative action and considering the facts in this proceeding, the intent and purpose of the statute has been satisfied.

In Matter of Santosky [393 N.Y.S. 2d 486 (Family Court, Ulster County, 1976)], the court refused to find permanent neglect where the parents received full public assistance, including food stamps and Medicare. The court held that such did not mean that the parents were "financially able" to plan the children's future. On the contrary, the court held that the parents' failure to plan was excused by their poverty and stated that "their very eligibility for full public assistance presupposes that they are 'financially unable.'"

See, however, In re Karasz [399 N.Y.S. 2d 758 (Appellate Division, 4th Dept., 1977)], wherein the court affirmed a finding of permanent neglect even though the mother was on welfare, stating she could have arranged for visitations. See also In Re John W. [404 N.Y.S. 2d 717 (Appellate Division, 3rd Dept., 1978)], wherein the court stated that:

> . . . absent evidence that a parent is receiving an inadequate amount of public assistance does not automatically excuse that parent from substantially planning for the future of a child.

When Would It Be Considered Detrimental to the Best Interests of the Child to Make Diligent Efforts to Encourage and Strengthen the Parental Relationship?

An agency has the duty to make diligent efforts to strengthen the parental relationship. Compare, however, Matter of Nicolle R.R. [379 N.Y.S. 2d 204 (Appellate Division, 3rd Dept., 1976)], wherein the court stated:

> Moreover, even assuming that the local agency failed to make the required effort, the evidence is overwhelming that the best interests of the child would be served by the termination of appellant's right to custody, and, therefore, said termination should not be delayed merely to punish the local agency for its alleged dereliction of duty (cf. *Matter of M. [Sugarman]*, 48 A.D. 2d 161, 368 N.Y.S 2d 374).

There comes a time when for the good of the child such efforts must stop: for example, the parent is on hard drugs, is contantly drunk, is physically abusive to the child, or leaves a young child alone at night.

The agency would likewise be excused from diligent efforts when the parent has an emotional disturbance or sociopathology. See In re Denlow [384 N.Y.S. 2d 621 (Family Court, Kings County, 1976)], wherein Judge Joseph A. Doran gave examples of when it may be detrimental to the moral and temporal welfare of the child or the agency to use diligent efforts to strengthen the parental ties:

1. alcohol addiction;
2. drug usage;
3. mental illness.

See also Family Court Act, Sections 611, 614, and 622.

In these cases, the agency should devote its energy to the future of the child with a view to an adoption and permanency. See In re Ray A.M. [48 A.D. 2d 161, 368 N.Y.S. 2d 374 (Appellate Division, 2nd Dept., 1975)].

Evidence of Diligent Efforts by Agency Not Required When Parent Fails for Period of Six Months to Keep Agency Apprised of His/Her Location

Pursuant to Section 384 B(e) of the Social Services Law, "evidence of diligent efforts by an agency to encourage and strengthen the parental relationship shall not be required when the parent has failed for a period of six months to keep the agency apprised of his/her location." However, practitioners should note that this is a fairly narrow exception and will not excuse the agency from its diligent efforts obligation after the respondent parent's whereabouts become known to the agency. See Matter of Guardianship of Antoinette Francis G. [135 Misc. 2d 1034, 517 N.Y.S. 2d 680 (Family Court, New York County, 1987)]. (Section 384 B(e) held not to excuse diligent efforts by the agency subsequent to the period that a parent had failed to keep the agency apprised of her location where thirteen months elapsed from the time the agency learned of the parent's whereabouts).

Problem of Separating Siblings

Where possible, it is important to keep siblings together. See Obey v. Degling [37 N.Y. 2d 768, 375 N.Y.S. 2d 91 (1975)], wherein the Court of Appeals stated:

> Young brothers and sisters need each other's strengths and association in their everyday and often common experiences, and to separate them unnecessarily is likely to be traumatic and harmful. The importance of rearing brothers and sisters together, and thereby nourishing their familial bonds, is also strengthened by the likelihood that the parents will pass away before their children.

Keeping siblings together should be one of the goals in any type of proceeding whether it is a *habeas corpus,* neglect proceeding, 382 foster-care review proceeding, or any other proceeding involving the custody of children. See Ebert v. Ebert [38 N.Y. 2d 699, 382 N.Y.S. 2d (1976)], wherein the Court of Appeals modified the Appellate Division's order and directed that the two oldest children be awarded to their mother, who had custody of the youngest child, so that the children could stay together. The court stated:

Furthermore, the separation of siblings, where, as here, the custodial parent in whose care all three had been entrusted, is fit and willing and able to function as such, is to be frowned upon. Close familial relationships are much to be encouraged.

See, however, In the Matter of Proceeding for the Custody and/or visitation of minors under Article 6 of the Family Court Act [383 N.Y.S. 2d 928 (Family Court, Rockland County, 1975)], wherein the court recognized that it is beneficial for the siblings to be reared together but, because of the factual situation, separated siblings, stating:

> However, because of the particular needs of these children and a severe rivalry between Martin and Christopher, it will be most harmful to all of the children if they were united and forced to live in the same home.

With respect to the wishes of the children, the court further stated:

> When siblings are separated by a court, it has frequently been determined that, in the best interests of children of sufficient age and understanding, their expressed wishes are not to be disregarded. Pact, supra *People ex rel. Repetti*, 50 A.D. 2d 913, 377 N.Y.S. 2d 571; *Ebert v. Ebert*, 38 N.Y. 2d 700, 382 N.Y.S. 2d 472, 346 N.E. 2d 240.

Language or Cultural Barrier between Caseworker and Parent

In Matter of "Male" Chiang, *N.Y. Law Journal*, June 30, 1977, Col. 2, Judge Shirley Wohl, Family Court, New York County dismissed permanent neglect and abandonment petitions against the natural mother, who was born in China, and criticized the authorized agency. The court ordered the return of the child after a consolidated hearing which included a 392 social services foster-care review hearing, even though the child was living with the foster family for seven years. The court pointed out that the agency did not meet its obligation to the natural mother by not engaging in effective and appropriate casework. The court noted that the infant, although Chinese, was placed with a family consisting of a Puerto Rican woman and an Italian husband who had two natural children and numerous foster children from time to time. The court stated:

> This case history is mainly one of failure on the part of the social work staff at the agency to comprehend and empathize with this woman's problems. The young and inexperienced Caucasian worker apparently had no frame of reference within which to understand this highly educated and sensitive Chinese woman attempting to adjust to an alien world. The problems were exacerbated when the Chinese child was placed so inappropriately.

Psychiatric Assistance

The family court has at its disposal the aid of probation officers' psychiatric and psychological reports. Psychiatric reports are especially utilized by the family court judge at the dispositional stage of permanent neglect proceedings. However, the Court of Appeals cautioned in Bennett v. Jeffreys [40 N.Y. 2d 543, 387 N.Y.S. 2d 821 (1976)]:

> In custody matters, parties and courts may be very dependent on the auxiliary services of psychiatrists, psychologists, and trained social workers. This is good. But, it may be an evil when the dependence is too obsequious or routine or the experts too casual. Particularly important is this caution where one or both parties may not have the means to retain their own experts and where publicly compensated experts or experts compensated by only one side have uncurbed leave to express opinions which may be subjective or are not narrowly controlled by the underlying facts.

In-Camera Interview

Many times the judge will interview the child in chambers, and this is permissible. See In Re Bernelle [59 A.D. 2d 764, 398 N.Y.S. 2d 714 (Appellate Division, 2nd Dept., 1977)], wherein, in neglect proceedings, the court wrote:

> . . . the in-chambers interview of the child conducted by the Court was permissible to ascertain what was in his best interests.

14
Mental Illness

Besides a written surrender; abandonment proceedings, pursuant to Section 384 B of the Social Services Law; permanent neglect proceedings, pursuant to Article 6 of the Family Court Act and Section 384 B of the Social Services Law; and abandonment proceedings pursuant to Section 111 of the Domestic Relations Law, another method to free a child for adoption is based upon mental illness pursuant to Section 384 B (4)(c). This section provides that:

> The parent or parents, whose consent to the adoption of the child would otherwise be required in accordance with Section 111 of the Domestic Relations Law, are presently and for the foreseeable future, unable, by reason of mental illness or mental retardation, to provide proper and adequate care for a child who has been in the care of an authorized agency for the period of one year immediately prior to the initiation of the proceeding under this section.

Mental illness is defined by Section 384 B (6)(a) of the Social Services Law as:

> An affiliation with a mental disease or mental condition which is manifested by a disorder or disturbance in behavior, feeling, thinking or judgment to such an extent that if such child were placed in or returned to the custody of the parent, the child would be in danger of becoming a neglected child as defined in the Family Court Act.

In mental illness cases, the parent must be personally served with a summons and petition. If the parent is in a state institution the director of the institution must be served with six copies of the summons and petition.

Section 384 B (6)(e) provides that the judge must take the testimony of a psychiatrist, in the case of a parent alleged to be mentally ill. Such a psychiatrist shall be appointed by the court, and in the Family Court of the City of New York, the psychiatrist is employed by the Bureau of Mental Health Services.

Sidebar 14–1. Summons in a Case of Mental Illness

FAMILY COURT OF THE STATE OF NEW YORK
COUNTY OF NEW YORK

——————————————————— x

In the Matter of [child]   SUMMONS

A dependent child under the age of 14 years, to
the custody of [agency] alleged to be the child of
a mentally ill parent, pursuant to Section 384-b of
the Social Services Law.

——————————————————— x

In the Name of the People of the State of New York

TO: [mother, father], COMMISSIONER OF SOCIAL SERVICES OF
THE CITY OF NEW YORK

A verified Petition having been filed in this Court alleging that
the above-named child in the care of [agency], the petitioner, is the
child of a mentally ill parent as defined by Article 6, Part 1 of the
Family Court Act and Section 384-b of the Social Services Law, a
copy of said Petition being annexed hereto;

YOU ARE HEREBY SUMMONED to appear before the Family
Court at 60 Lafayette Street, New York, New York, Part [part] on
[date] at 9:00 o'clock in the forenoon of said day to show cause
why the Court should not enter an Order depriving you of all the
rights of custody of [child] awarding the custody of said child to
the petitioning authorized agency as the child of a mentally ill
parent as provided by law.

PLEASE TAKE NOTICE that if said child is adjudged to be the
child of a mentally ill parent, and if custody is awarded to said
authorized agency, said child may be adopted with the consent of
said authorized agency, without further notice to the parent of the
child.

PLEASE TAKE FURTHER NOTICE that failure to appear shall
constitute a denial of an interest in the child, which denial may
result in the transfer or commitment of the child's care, custody,
guardianship or adoption of the child, all without further notice to
the parent of the child.

PLEASE TAKE FURTHER NOTICE that you are entitled to be
represented by an attorney, and if you cannot afford to retain

an attorney, one will be appointed to represent you by the Court free of charge to you.

Dated: By Order of the Court

_____
Clerk, Family Court, [county] County

Sidebar 14–2. Petition in a Case of Mental Illness

FAMILY COURT OF THE STATE OF NEW YORK
[county]

_____ x

In the Matter of [child]	PETITION PURSUANT TO
	SECTION 384-B OF THE
A dependent child under the age	SOCIAL SERVICES LAW
14 years, to the custody of	
[agency], alleged to be the child of	
a mentally ill parent pursuant to	
Section 384-b of the Social Ser-	
vices Law.	

_____ x

TO THE FAMILY COURT OF [county] COUNTY:

Petitioner, [agency] as and for its Petition for the commitment, guardianship and custody of [child], an infant, respectfully alleges upon information and belief:

1. [Agency] is a not-for-profit corporation, organized and existing by virtue of the laws of the State of New York, having an office for the regular conduct of business at [address] and is an authorized agency approved, visited, inspected and supervised by the State Board of Social Welfare.

2. [Child] was born on [date] at [location] and a copy of the birth certificate of the infant is annexed hereto and marked as Exhibit "A."

3. The birth certificate of the infant, [child], lists as her mother

[mother] and lists father [father] as the father of the infant herein

4. The infant, [child], was voluntarily placed with the Commissioner of Social Services of the City of New York on [date] by the presumed natural father of the infant. The Commissioner of Social Services of the City of New York in turn placed the infant with [agency] on [date].

5. According to the case records of [agency], [mother], the natural mother of the infant, was not married to [father], the putative father of the infant.

6. The presumed natural father of the infant, [putative father], had indicated that he signed a surrender terminating his parental rights to the infant. A copy of the surrender is annexed hereto as Exhibit "B."

7. The persons entitled to service of process in this proceeding are:

NAME	LAST KNOWN ADDRESS
[mother]	[address]
COMMISSIONER OF SOCIAL SERVICES CITY OF NEW YORK	220 Church Street New York, New York 10013

AS AND FOR A FIRST CAUSE OF ACTION AGAINST THE RESPONDENT NATURAL MOTHER, [mother], IN MENTAL ILLNESS

8. Petitioner repeats and realleges paragraphs "1" through "7" as if fully set forth herein at length.

9. Upon information and belief, [mother], the natural mother of the infant herein, is mentally ill as defined by Section 384-b of the Social Services Law of the State of New York.

10. [Mother], the natural mother of the infant herein, has a long and extensive psychiatric history based upon an unstable emotional condition. [Mother] is currently hospitalized at [hospital] where she has been since [date]. Prior to that time, she was hospitalized at [hospital], where she was admitted on [date] with a history of unpredictable bizarre behavior. In a psychiatric evaluation conducted by [doctor] of [hospital] and dated [date], [mother] was diagnosed on Axis I as an undifferentiated chronic schizophrenic with acute exacerbation [295–94], alcohol and cannabis abuse episodic, and mild men-

tal retardation. Along Axis II she was diagnosed as atypical or mixed personality disorder. [Mother]'s condition was continued to be such that if the child were returned to her, the child would be in danger of becoming a neglected child. In a prognosis prepared by [doctor] on [date] the doctor indicates that "At present, the patient denies hearing voices but continues to get easily irritable, suspicious, hostile and paranoid. Her insight and judgment remain grossly impaired. Patient tends to neglect her personal hygiene and needs reminders with supervision regarding her ADL. Patient needs continued care in a well-structured supervised environment with a great deal of support to function in current level. Considering patient's level of functioning at present and in the past six months, her current prognosis can be stated as follows: Because of patient's fluctuating mental status and behavior she is likely to be in need of continued psychiatric hospitalization with in-patient care at current level which is likely to stabilize her and improve her behavior." Copies of the psychiatric assessment prepared by [doctor] and dated [date] along with a copy of the prognosis report dated [date] are annexed hereto and marked as Exhibits "C" and "D."

11. By reason of the mental illness of [mother], the natural mother of the infant herein, said infant would be in danger of becoming a neglected child as defined in the Family Court Act, if said child was placed in or returned to the custody of said respondent [mother]. The respondent [mother] did not in the past and it is believed cannot in the future provide adequate care, shelter or clothing for the infant and because of her mental illness cannot take care of herself and it is believed cannot take care of her child.

12. Based upon the mental illness of the respondent [mother] and her inability to care for the infant in the near future, the best interests of said child would be promoted by the commitment of the guardianship and custody of the child to [agency], an authorized agency, in order that the child may have permanency and be nurtured in a family atmosphere.

WHEREFORE, the petitioner prays that an Order be made directing that a Summons be issued to the respondent, [mother] and the Commissioner of Social Services of the City of New York, to show cause why an Order should not be made by this Court determining that said respondent, [mother], is mentally ill within the meaning of Section 384-b of the Social Services Law of the State of New York, and committing the custody and guardianship of the infant herein to [agency] and the Commissioner of Social Services of the City of New York with the right of [agency], the Commissioner of Social Services of the City of New York to place the infant herein for legal adoption without further notice to or consent of her natural mother, subject to the customary approval of the Court, to which the Petiton for adoption is presented.

Dated: [agency]

By _____

Executive Director

STATE OF NEW YORK)
)ss.:
COUNTY OF NASSAU)

[Petitioner], being duly sworn, deposes and says that he is the Executive Director of [agency], petitioner herein, that the foregoing Petition is true to his own knowledge, except as to matters therein stated to be alleged upon information and belief, and as to those matters, he believes it to be true.

_____

Executive Director

Sworn to before me this
day of , 1989.

_____

Notary Public

Section 384 (7) of the Social Services Law, the predecessor of Section 384 B (6), has been held to be constitutional. See In re Helen H. [374 N.Y.S. 2d 693 (Appellate Division, 2nd Dept., 1975)].

In In re Bradley U. [389 N.Y.S. 2d 431 (Appellate Division, 3rd Dept., 1976)], the court held that the evidence warranted termination of the natural mother's parental rights on the ground that she was unable to care for the child by reason of mental illness. The court wrote:

The evident purpose of the proceeding was to facilitate the adoption of Bradley "U" by the foster parent with whom he had been continuously residing (cf. *Matter of Berman*, [Beckey A.H.], 49 A.D. 2d 327, 374 N.Y.S. 2d 693, mot. for lv. to app. den. 38 N.Y. 2d 708, 382 N.Y.S. 2d, 345 N.E. 2d 604). We agree that clear and convincing proof of appellant's mental illness was adduced at the hearing.

In the case of Joan R. [403 N.Y.S. 2d (Appellate Division, 3rd Dept., 1978)], the Court of Appeals affirmed the family court's order terminating parental rights, thus freeing the child for adoption based upon mental illness of the parent. It stated:

> The orders appealed from should be affirmed. Expert testimony at the trial by Dr. Clifford, a psychiatrist, establishes clear and convincing evidence that appellant suffers from mental illness, i.e. schizophrenia chronic undifferentiated type, and that, as a result of said illness, she is unable now and will likely remain unable in the future to properly care for a child. Under these circumstances, the record amply justifies the finding that David "R" was a neglected child within the definition of that term contained in Section 1012 (subd. [f]) of the Family Court Act (cf. *Matter of Millar,* 40 A.D. 2d 637, 336 N.Y.S. 2d 144, affd. 35 N.Y. 2d 767, 362 N.Y.S. 2d 149, 320 N.E. 2d 865) and also the termination of parental custody rights concerning Cheryl "R."

Right to Attorney at Mental Examination

The Court of Appeals in the case of In re Alexander L. [60 N.Y. 2d 329, 469 N.Y.S. 2d 626, 457 N.E. 2d 731 (1983)] has held that the respondent parent who was to be evaluated by the court-appointed psychiatrist had the right to have his/her attorney present during the evaluation as a matter of right. The Court of Appeals cited Section 262 A (4) of the Family Court Act, which provision provides the parent with the right to have the parent's counsel present from the time that the respondent parent appears in the termination of parental rights proceeding. The Court of Appeals, however, did not provide that the agency's attorney or the law guardian representing the child have a similar right, and the lower courts have not extended such right to the agency's attorney or the infant's attorney—that is, the law guardian.

It is, therefore, important for the attorney for the respondent parent to make certain that the order obtained by the agency attorney provides that when the parent is examined by the court-appointed psychiatrist, the respondent's attorney be permitted as an observer to the examination.

Counsel for all parties must also remember that it is not the mental illness per se that establishes the statutory ground for termination of parental rights, but said conditions plus the inability to provide adequate care to the infant. This judgment is a legal one that must be supported by expert testimony, including social work history and evaluation. See Matter of Richard M [110 Misc. 2d 1031, 443 N.Y.S. 2d 291 (Family Court, New York County, 1981)]. Attorneys representing parents who are alleged to be mentally ill should not always accept the opinion of the court-appointed psychiatrist or psychologist if the finding is one of mental illness.

Section 384 B does not mandate a dispositional hearing once there has been a finding at the fact-finding hearing of mental illness. Some judges of the family court do hold dispositional hearings and some do not. The disparity brings uncertainty to the proceeding, and it is recommended that the legislature amend Section 384 B to mandate a dispositional hearing following a positive finding of mental illness after the fact-finding hearing. Since the majority of the judges of the family court do direct a dispositional hearing in mental illness proceedings the legislature should make such dispositional hearing mandatory.

No Need for Diligent Efforts

In a proceeding to terminate parental rights based upon mental illness, it is not necessary for the agency to prove diligent efforts to strengthen parental relationship or show that such efforts would have been detrimental to the children. See In re Everett S. [403 N.Y.S. 2d 802 (Appellate Divison, 3rd Dept., 1978)].

Present Mental State

The petition must allege and the agency must prove that the parent presently suffers from some mental illness (see sidebar 14–3). See In re Kevin R. [49 N.Y.S. 2d 875, 112 A.D. 2d 462 (3rd Dept., 1985)].

Prior History of Parent

It is important for the agency to prove that the parent's mental illness is of some duration and is chronic. One psychiatrist defined *chronicity* as the duration of the illness for at least two years. See In re L. Children [499 N.Y.S. 2d 587, 131 Misc. 2d 81 (Family Court, Kings County, 1986)], wherein Judge George L. Jurow, in dismissing the petition, wrote:

> Ordinarily, the inference of future incapacity is drawn from a combination of factors, including an extensive prior history of incapacity; the severity of present incapacity; and the failure of remedial efforts to make any difference in adaptive functioning.

Future Mental State

In order to terminate the parental rights of a parent over an infant, the agency must plead in the petition and prove by competent medical testimony at the hearing that the parent cannot care for the infant for the foreseeable future. See In re Susan F. [106 A.D. 2d 282, 482 N.Y.S. 2d 488 (Appellate Division, 1st Dept., 1984)].

Sidebar 14-3. Order of Disposition, Adjudication, Findings of Fact, and Conclusions of Law in a Case of Mental Illness

At the Family Court of the State of New York, held in and for the County of New York, 60 Lafayette Street, New York, New York on the   day of   , 19   .

PRESENT:

HON. [judge]
Judge of the Family Court

_____ x

In the Matter of

[child] A dependent child under the age of 14 years, to the custody of [agency], the child of a mentally ill parent, pursuant to Section 384-b of the Social Services Law.	ORDER OF DISPOSITION ADJUDICATION, FINDINGS OF FACT AND CONCLUSIONS Docket No.

_____ x

A Petition, pursuant to Article 6, Part 1 of the Family Court Act and Section 384-b of the Social Services Law having been filed in this Court by [agency], an authorized agency, alleging that [child] is the child of a mentally ill parent; and a Summons and Petition having been duly issued and served upon [mother], the natural mother of said child; and

The matter having duly come on for a fact-finding hearing on [date] before the HON. [judge] at Trial Term Foster Care Review Part, and the said [mother], the natural mother of said infant, having appeared thereon and having been represented by her attorney, [attorney]; and the petitioner [agency], having been represented by [attorney], of counsel; and the child having been represented by [attorney], Law Guardian, Legal Aid Society, by [attorney]; and this Court, after hearing the proofs and testimony offered in relation to the case, having found that the allegations in the Petition required by Section 384-b of the Social Services Law are supported by clear and convincing evidence, and the Court having heard testimony of [doctor], Psychiatrist, with the Bureau of Mental Health Services at Family Court, [county] County relating to the mental illness of the natural mother, and the Court found upon clear and convincing evidence:

1. [Agency] is a not-for-profit corporation, organized and existing by virtue of the laws of the State of New York, having an office for the regular conduct of business at [address] and is an authorized agency approved, visited, inspected and supervised by the State Board of Social Welfare.

2. [Child] was born on [date] at [location].

3. The natural mother of the infant [mother] and the father of the infant is [putative father].

4. The infant [child] was voluntarily committed to the Commissioner of Social Services of the City of New York by the presumed natural father on [date] and the Commissioner of Social Services of the City of New York in turn placed the infant with [agency] on [date].

5. [Mother], the natural mother of the infant herein, was not married to [putative father], the presumed father of the infant herein.

6. [Agency] is not proceeding against [putative father], the presumed natural father of the infant herein in this action.

7. The respondent, [mother], is mentally ill as defined by Section 384-b of the Social Services Law.

8. [Mother], the natural mother of the infant herein, has a long and extensive psychiatric history based upon an unstable emotional condition. [Mother] is currently hospitalized at [hospital], where she has been since [date]. Prior to that time, she was hospitalized at [hospital], where she was admitted on [date] with a history of unpredictable bizarre behavior. In a psychiatric evaluation conducted by [doctor] of [hospital] and dated [date], [mother] was diagnosed on Axis I as an undifferentiated chronic schizophrenic with acute exacerbation (295–94), alcohol and cannabis abuse episodic, and mild mental retardation. Along Axis II, she was diagnosed as atypical or mixed personality disorder. [Mother]'s condition is such that if the child was returned to her, the child would be in danger of becoming a neglected child. In a prognosis prepared by [doctor] on [date] the doctor indicated that "At present, the patient denies hearing voices but continues to get easily irritable, suspicious, hostile and paranoid. Her insight and judgment remain grossly impaired. Patient tends to neglect her personal

hygiene and needs reminders with supervision regarding her ADL. Patient needs continued care in a well-structured supervised environment with a great deal of support to function in current level. Considering patient's level of functioning at present and in the past six months, her current prognosis can be stated as follows: Because of patient's fluctuating mental status and behavior she is likely to be in need of continued psychiatric hospitalization with in-patient care at current level which is likely to stabilize her and improve her behavior."

9. By reason of the mental illness of [mother], the natural mother of the infant herein, said infant is in danger of becoming a neglected child as defined in the Family Court Act, if said child was placed in or returned to the custody of [mother]. Mother did not in the past and cannot in the future provide adequate care, shelter or clothing for the infant and because of her mental illness cannot take care of herself and cannot take care of her child.

THEREFORE, with respect to the natural mother [mother], the allegations of the Petition herein required by paragraph 6(a) of Section 384-b of the Social Services Law are supported by clear and convincing evidence in that she has an affliction with a mental disease or mental condition which is manifested by a disorder or disturbance in behavior, feeling, thinking or judgment to such an extent that if such child were placed in or returned to the custody of the parent, the child would be in danger of becoming a neglected child as defined in the Family Court Act;

NOW, THEREFORE, it is upon clear and convincing evidence

ADJUDGED, that the allegations as to the respondent natural mother, [mother] required by paragraph 6(a) of Section 384-b of the Social Services Law are sustained by clear and convincing evidence; and

The matter having come on for a dispositional hearing before the HON. [judge], Judge, Family Court, [county] County on [date] at Trial Term Foster Care Review Part, and the said [mother], the natural mother of said infant, having appeared thereon and having been represented by her attorney, [attorney]; and [agency], the petitioner, was represented by its attorneys, [attorneys], of counsel; and the child was represented by [attorney], Law Guardian, Legal Aid Society, by [attorney]; and this Court having taken testimony and made examination and inquiry into the facts and circumstances of the case and into the surroundings and capacities of the persons involved in this proceeding and the Court having heard the testimony of [caseworker], caseworker, [agency], that the natural mother was not a resource for the future of said child and that the foster parents wish to adopt the infant herein and are viable resources for the future of said child, and the Court having heard and considered the recommendation of the Law Guardian and the Court having found upon clear and convincing evidence that:

1. It would be in the best interests of the infant that the respondent natural mother's rights of guardianship and custody be transferred to [agency] and the Commissioner of Social Services of the City of New York so that either [agency] or the Commissioner of Social Services of the City of New York may consent to the infant's adoption in the place and stead of the natural mother, [mother].
2. The infant, [child] born on [date], is presently in a pre-adoptive home which has been evaluated and assessed as a permanent home for the infant, that said foster parents wish to adopt the infant, [child], and it is the recommendation of the petitioner, [agency], that the infant be adopted by her present foster parents.

NOW, THEREFORE, upon the dispositional hearing and upon clear and convincing evidence,

IT APPEARING that the best interests of the infant, [child], require that the respondent natural mother's rights of guardianship and custody of the infant be transferred and committed to the Commissioner of Social Services of the City of New York and [agency], it is

ORDERED, that the best interests of said child require that the custody and guardianship of [mother], the natural mother, over said child be terminated; and it is further,

ORDERED, that such rights of the legal custody and guardianship of said infant, [child], by the said respondent natural mother, [mother], be and the same hereby are transferred and committed to the Commissioner of Social Services of the City of New York and [agency], an authorized agency, and it is further,

ORDERED, that the Commissioner of Social Services of the City of New York or [agency] be and is hereby authorized and empowered to consent to the adoption of said minor child, [child], in the place and stead of the natural mother, [mother], by a suitable person or persons subject to the customary approval of the Court of competent jurisdiction and that the consent of and notice to the parents of said minor child, [child], to said adoption be and the same hereby are dispensed with, and it is further,

ORDERED, that [agency] facilitate one final visit between [mother] and the child herein prior to any cessation of visitation, and it is further,

ORDERED, that the Law Guardian and the Commissioner of Social Services of the City of New York be notified of all future legal proceedings concerning the infant herein, and it is further,

ORDERED, that all papers and records in this proceeding be filed in the Office of the Clerk of the Family Court of the State of New York, County of [county], in accordance with Section 384-b, Subd. 3 (j) of the Social Services Law, and it is further,

ORDERED, that a certified copy of this Order be filed in the Office of the Clerk, [county] County.

Dated: ENTER:

_____
HON. [judge]
Family Court, [county]

A recent case that clearly sets out each of the above described factors is Matter of Andrew Jermaine R. [525 N.Y.S. 2d 664 (Appellate Division, 2nd Dept., 1988)]. In reaching its holding with respect to the natural mother, the court looked at six factors: (1) psychotic acts of violence on the command of hallucinative voices; (2) lack of basic living skills; (3) lack of family support; (4) impaired judgment in insight; (5) continuing symptoms of mental illness; and (6) discontinuing medication and follow-up therapy whenever released from in-patient hospital status. The court then noted the two additional factors of testimony by the social worker and documentary evidence in the form of agency records and the mother's hospital records before reaching its finding that the natural mother was unable to care properly and adequately for her child because of mental illness and "that this illness will continue for the foreseeable future" [Id at 665].

Order of Disposition

If the court sustains the petition the attorney for the agency must draft, serve, and file on order of disposition. When the order is signed by the judge the child is freed for adoption.

15
Mental Retardation

Mental retardation is defined by Section 384 B (b)(c)(b) of the Social Services Law as

> Sub-average intellectual functioning which originates during the developmental period and is associated with the impairment of adaptive behavior to such an extent that if such child were placed in or returned to the custody of the parent, the child would be in danger of becoming a neglected child as defined in the Family Court Act.

The mental retardation proceeding is initiated by serving the parent with a copy of a summons and petition (see sidebars 15-1 and 15-2). In a mental illness case, the judge must appoint a psychiatrist to evaluate, make a diagnosis, and testify with respect to the mental capacity of the mentally ill parent. With respect to proving a case based upon mental retardation, the judge must appoint not only a psychiatrist but a certified psychologist as well. The attorney for the agency who submitted the petition alleging that the parent is mentally retarded must also submit a proposed order, to be signed by the judge, directing the Bureau of Mental Health Services to appoint both a psychiatrist and a psychologist to interview, evaluate, and make a diagnosis as to the mental capacity of the parent. The attorney for the respondent parent under recent cases has the right to be present at the evaluation, and the judges have required that a provision permitting the attorney for the respondent to be present be contained in the order.

Once a judge signs the order directing that a psychiatrist and psychologist evaluate the parent, said order is served upon the Bureau of Mental Health Services, which facility then contacts the parent and the parent's attorney to be present at the scheduled interview. The interview with the psychiatrist will take approximately one hour. It is incumbent upon the attorney for the agency to subpoena any relevant medical records that would shed light upon the mental capacity of the parent. The psychiatrist will basically interview and observe the parent and make a diagnosis based upon many histories, the observation, and the interview and conversation of the parent.

Sidebar 15–1. Summons in a Case of Mental Retardation

FAMILY COURT OF THE STATE OF NEW YORK
[county]

_____ x

In the Matter of

[child]   SUMMONS
A dependent child under the age of 14 years, to
the custody of [agency], alleged to be the child
of a mentally retarded parent pursuant to Section
384-b of the Social Services Law.

_____ x

IN THE NAME OF THE PEOPLE OF THE STATE OF NEW YORK

TO: [mother]
    COMMISSIONER OF SOCIAL SERVICES OF THE CITY OF
    NEW YORK

A verified Petition having been filed in this Court alleging that the above-named child in the care of [agency], the petitioner, is the child of a mentally retarded parent as defined by Section 384-b of the Social Services Law, copies of said Petition being annexed hereto;

YOU ARE HEREBY SUMMONED to appear before the Family Court at 60 Lafayette Street, New York, New York, Part   , on the   day of   , 19   , before the Hon. [judge] at 9 o'clock in the forenoon of said day to show cause why the Court should not enter an order depriving you of all the rights of custody of [child], awarding the custody of said child to the petitioning authorized agency as the child of a mentally retarded parent as provided by law.

PLEASE TAKE NOTICE that if said child is adjudged to be the child of a mentally retarded parent, and, if custody is awarded to said authorized agency, said child may be adopted with the consent of said authorized agency without further notice to you and without your consent.

In the event of your failure to appear, said failure to appear will result in the termination of all your parental rights to the child.

PLEASE TAKE FURTHER NOTICE that your failure to appear shall constitute a denial of an interest in the child, which denial may result in the transfer of commitment of the child's care, custody, guardianship or adoption of the child, all without further notice to the parents of the child.

PLEASE TAKE FURTHER NOTICE that you are entitled to be represented by an attorney, and, if you cannot afford to retain an attorney, one will be appointed to represent you by the Court free of charge to you.

Dated: By Order of the Court

_____
Clerk, Family Court, New York

Sidebar 15–2. Petition in a Case of Mental Retardation

FAMILY COURT OF THE STATE OF NEW YORK
COUNTY OF [county]

_____ x

In the Matter of

[child]
A dependent child under the age of 14 years, to the custody of [agency], alleged to be the child of a mentally retarded parent pursuant to Section 384-b of the Social Services Law.

PETITION PURSUANT TO SECTION 384-B OF THE SOCIAL SERVICES LAW
Docket No.

_____ x

TO THE FAMILY COURT OF [county] COUNTY:

Petitioner, [agency], as and for its Petition for the commitment, guardianship and custody of [child], an infant, respectfully alleges upon information and belief:

1. [Agency] is a not-for-profit corporation, organized and existing by virtue of the laws of the State of New York, having an office for the regular conduct of business at [address], and is an authorized agency approved, visited, inspected and supervised by the State Board of Social Welfare.
2. [Child] was born on [date] at [name, town, state of hospital],

and a copy of the Birth Certificate of [child] is annexed hereto and marked as Exhibit "A."

3. The Birth Certificate of the infant, [child], lists as her mother, [mother], and lists no one as the father of the infant herein.

4. The infant, [child] was [court][voluntarily] placed with the Commissioner of Social Services of the City of New York on [date of placement] by Family Court, [county, docket number]. The Commissioner of Social Services of the City of New York in turn placed the infant with [agency] on [date of agency placement].

5. According to the case records of [agency], the putative father of the infant herein is unknown and unidentified.

6. The persons entitled to service of process in this proceeding are:

NAME	LAST KNOWN ADDRESS
[mother] natural mother	(street address) (town, state, zip code)
COMMISSIONER OF SOCIAL SERVICES CITY OF NEW YORK	220 Church Street New York, New York 10013

AS AND FOR A FIRST CAUSE OF ACTION AGAINST THE RESPONDENT NATURAL MOTHER, [mother], IN MENTAL RETARDATION

7. Petitioner repeats and realleges paragraphs "1" through "6" as if fully set forth herein at length.

8. Upon information and belief, the natural mother of the infant [mother], is mentally retarded as defined in Section 384-b of the Social Services Law in that she has been repeatedly diagnosed as a person afflicted with mental retardation. Annexed hereto and marked as Exhibits "B," "C," "D," "E," and "F" are reports exhibiting that the natural mother has tested at an I.Q. of approximately 65 and that she is within the mentally retarded range.

9. As the annexed reports show, by reason of said mental retardation of the natural mother, [mother], the infant herein would be in danger of becoming a neglected child as defined in the Family Court Act if said child was placed in or returned to the custody of said respondent, [mother], in that she has in the past neglected the infant herein and that in light of the fact that [mother] has been diagnosed mentally retarded, meaning that she has a sub-average intellectual function which originated during the developmental period of said [mother],

and said retardation impairs [mother's] ability to properly care for the infant herein, it is believed that [mother] cannot in the future provide adequate care, shelter or clothing for the child because of her mental retardation and cannot adequately take care of herself or the child.

10. Based upon [mother]'s mental retardation and her inability to take care of the infant in the near future, the best interests of said child will be promoted by commitment of the guardianship and custody of the child to [agency], an authorized agency, in order that the child may have permanency and be nurtured in a family atmosphere.

11. The natural mother, [mother], is unable to provide proper and adequate supervision and guidance for said child in the foreseeable future due to her aforesaid mental retardation, and said child would be in danger of being neglected as she has been neglected in the past, and said [mother] is unable to provide for said child's physical and emotional needs in the future.

WHEREFORE, the petitioner prays that an order be made pursuant to Section 384-b of the Social Services Law of the State of New York adjudicating the above-named child, the child of a mentally retarded parent, that the child's natural mother be deprived permanently of said child's custody and that the custody and guardianship of [child], an infant, be committed to [agency] and the Commissioner of Social Services of the City of New York with the right of [agency] or the Commissioner of Social Services of the City of New York to place [child] for legal adoption and to consent to her legal adoption without further notice to or consent of her natural mother subject to the customary approval of the court to which the Petition for adoption is presented.

Dated: [Agency]

By: _____

On the other hand, the psychologist who will also interview the parent, perhaps for an hour or two, will make his/her findings based upon testing. It is the psychologist who will testify as to the intelligent quotient of the parent based upon a number of tests. The attorneys for the agency, the child, and the parent should obtain copies of the reports and evaluations of the psychiatrist and the psychologist well before the actual hearing in order to prepare a proper examination and cross-examination of the medical witnesses.

It would also be appropriate for the attorney of the respondent parent to request the court to provide monies in order for the parent to obtain independent medical experts whose views may contrast with those of the court-appointed psychiatrist and psychologist. If the attorney for the agency refuses the reports and it is clear from the psychiatrist and the psychologist that the parent is not so mentally retarded that he/she cannot take care of the child presently and for the foreseeable future, the attorney for the agency, instead of wasting the time of the court, will withdraw the petition, unless there are other causes of action pending.

The Hearing

The hearing takes place before a judge of the family court without a jury, and the testimony of the caseworker is basically limited. In any mental retardation case, the caseworker basically will have to testify to the names of the parties involved; when the child was born; how the child came into foster care; what were the facts and circumstances surrounding the child coming into foster care; that the child is presently in foster care; and any unusual behavior of the parent as observed by the caseworker. Mental retardation and mental illness cases are basically won or lost upon the testimony of the medical witnesses. In a mental retardation case, the psychiatrist and the psychologist must testify that the respondent is mentally retarded and that the mental retardation is of such a nature that the parent cannot care for the infant presently or for the foreseeable future, and that if the child were returned to the parent, the child would be in danger of becoming a neglected child as defined by Article 10 of the Family Court Act.

The Best Interests Test

In re Strasberg [400 N.Y.S. 2d 1013 (Family Court, Rockland County, 1977)], the court held that the best interests test is applicable to a proceeding to free the infant for adoption based upon mental retardation of the parent, pursuant to Section 384 B (4)(c). In Strasberg, the respondent was found to be a borderline retarded person, and the court held that the infant should not be held in limbo for an indefinite period of time for the purpose of training the mother in the area of child care, without any guarantee of success, and that if the infant were placed in the mother's custody, the infant would be in danger of becoming neglected.

The Court Can Order Second Mental Examination of Parent

In Catholic Child Care Society of Diocese of Brooklyn vs. Evelyn F. [128 Misc. 2d 1023, 492 N.Y.S. 2d 338 (Family Court, Kings County, 1985)], it was held that a court may order a second mental examination of a parent in order to move forward with proceedings to terminate parental rights based on grounds of mental disability.

The Constitutionality of the Mental Illness and Mental Retardation Sections of 384 B

The New York Court of Appeals has upheld the constitutionality of Section 384 B (4) on due process and equal protection grounds. See In re Guardianship and Custody of Neireida S. [57 N.Y. 2d 636, 454 N.Y.S. 2d 61]. In Neireida, the court reasoned that:

> The statutes provide significant procedural safeguards for the natural parent's rights and authorize the termination of parental rights only when specific and definite criteria are met and when necessary in the best interest of the child [Id at 62].

Failure to Provide a Dispositional Hearing Does Not Violate Equal Protection

In the case of In re Sylvia M. [82 A.D. 2d 217, 443 N.Y.S. 2d 214 (Appellate Division, 1st Dept., 1981)], the court held that failure to provide a dispositional hearing in a mental illness situation does not violate equal protection. In reaching its conclusion, the court noted that:

> [in a mental illness] situation, the impossibility of the child's return to the natural family is already decided once a finding of such mental illness is made, and a separate dispositional hearing is not required [Id at 224].

Court Order

If the court sustains the petition, the attorney for the agency must draft, serve, and file an Order of Disposition, Adjudication, Findings of Fact, and Conclusion of Law (see sidebar 15-3).

Sidebar 15-3. Order of Disposition, Adjudication, Findings of Fact, and Conclusions of Law in a Case of Mental Retardation

At the Family Court of the State of New York, held in and for the County of New York, 60 Lafayette Street, New York, New York, on the   day of   , 19   .

PRESENT:

HON. [judge]

_____ x

In the Matter of

[child]
A dependent child under the age
of 14 years, to the custody of
[agency], the child of a mentally
retarded parent pursuant to
Section 384-b of the Social
Services Law.

ORDER OF DISPOSITION,
ADJUDICATION,
FINDINGS OF FACT AND
CONCLUSIONS OF LAW

Docket No.

_____ x

A Petition pursuant to Section 384-b of the Social Services Law having been filed in this Court by [agency], an authorized agency, alleging that [child] is the child of a mentally retarded parent; and a Summons and Petition having been duly issued and served upon [mother], the natural mother of said infant; and

The matter having duly come on for a fact-finding hearing on , 19   , before [justice] at Trial Term Part [part]; and the said [mother], the natural mother of the infant, having appeared thereon and having been represented by her attorney, [attorney]; and the guardian *ad litem* for the natural mother [attorney], having been appointed by the Court on [date], and having thereafter appeared thereon; and the petitioner, [agency], having been represented by [attorney]; and the child having been represented by [attorney], Law Guardian; and this Court, after hearing the proofs and testimony offered in relation to the case, having found that the allegations required by Section 384-b of the Social Services Law are supported by clear and convincing evidence; and the Court having heard testimony of [caseworker] relating to the mental retardation of the natural mother; and the Court found upon clear and convincing evidence:

1. [Agency] is a not-for-profit corporation, organized and existing by virtue of the laws of the State of New York, having an office for the regular conduct of business at [street address, town, state], and is an authorized agency approved, visited, inspected and supervised by the State Board of Social Welfare.

2. [Child] was born on [date of birth] at [name, town, state of hospital].

3. The natural mother of the infant, [child], is [mother], and the putative father is unknown and unidentified.

4. The infant, [child], was [court] [voluntarily] committed to the Commissioner of Social Services of the City of New York on [date of placement] by Family Court [county, docket number]. The Commissioner of Social Services of the City of New York in turn placed the infant with [agency] on [date of agency placement].

5. The natural mother of the infant herein, [mother], is mentally retarded as defined in Section 384-b of the Social Services Law. Psychological evaluations performed indicate that [mother] is afflicted with mental retardation to the extent that the infant herein would be in danger of becoming a neglected child as defined in the Family Court Act if said infant was placed in or returned to the custody of said respondent, [mother].

6. A psychological evaluation conducted by [psychiatrist] on [date of evaluation], indicates that the natural mother, [mother], exhibited functioning at the mentally deficient level with a prorated WAIS-R IQ of 62 and was diagnosed on Axis I at 317.1 Mental Retardation and Axis II at 301.89 Inadequate Personality Disorder. This diagnosis was then born out by later psychological and psychiatric evaluations, including those of [doctors]. Further, the testimony of [doctor] supports the conclusion that the natural mother is mentally retarded, as that term is defined in Section 384-b of the Social Services Law.

7. By reason of said mental retardation of [mother], the natural mother of the infant, [child], the infant would be in danger of becoming a neglected child as defined in the Family Court Act if said child was placed in or returned to the custody of said respondent, [mother], in light of the fact that [mother] has been diagnosed as mentally retarded, having subaverage intellectual functioning which originated during the development period and which is associated with impairment and

adaptive behavior, and because it is believed that said mental retardation of [mother] exists to the extent that if the child, [child], was returned to [mother], the child would be in danger of becoming a neglected child as defined in the Family Court Act.

8. The natural mother, [mother], is unable to provide proper and adequate supervision and guidance for said child in the foreseeable future due to her aforesaid mental retardation, and said child would be in danger of being neglected, and [mother] is unable to provide for the child's physical and emotional needs.

THEREFORE, with respect to the natural mother, [mother], the allegations of the Petition herein required by Paragraph 6(b) of Section 384-b of the Social Services Law are supported by clear and convincing evidence in that she has subaverage intellectual functioning which originated during the developmental period and is associated with impairment and adaptive behavior to such an extent that if such child was placed in or returned to the custody of the parent, the child would be danger of becoming a neglected child as defined in the Family Court Act; and

NOW, THEREFORE, it is upon clear and convincing evidence

ADJUDGED that the allegations as to the respondent natural mother, [mother], required by Paragraph 6(b) Section 384-b of the Social Services Law are sustained by clear and convincing evidence; and it is further

The matter having come on for a dispositional hearing before [justice] of the Family Court, New York County, on [date] at Part [part]; and the said [mother], natural mother of said infant, having failed to appear thereon, and her default having been duly noted by the Court; and [agency], petitioner, was represented by its attorneys, [attorneys]; and the infant was represented by [attorney], Law Guardian; and this Court having taken testimony and made examination and inquiry into the facts and circumstances of the case and into the surroundings and capacities of the persons involved in this proceeding; and the Court having heard the testimony of caseworker, [name], employed by [agency], that [mother] is not a resource to the future of the child based upon her mental retardation, that the infant herein currently resides in an excellent foster home and that the foster mother wishes to adopt the infant; and the Court having heard and considered the recommendation of the Law Guardian;

ORDERED that the best interests of the child require that the custody and guardianship rights of [mother], the natural mother, over said child be terminated; and it is further

ORDERED that the rights of legal custody and guardianship of the infant, [child], by the said respondent natural mother, [mother], be and the same hereby are transferred and committed to the Commissioner of Social Services of the City of New York and [agency], an authorized agency; and it is further

ORDERED that the Commissioner of Social Services of the City of New York or [agency] be and is hereby authorized and empowered to consent to the adoption of said minor child, [child], in the place and stead of the natural mother, [mother], by a suitable person or persons subject to the customary approval of the Court of competent jurisdiction, and that the consent of and notice to the natural mother of said minor child, [child], to said adoption be and the same hereby are dispensed with; and it is further

ORDERED that the Law Guardian and Commissioner of Social Services of the City of New York be notified of any further litigation concerning the infant herein; and it is further

ORDERED that all papers and records in this proceeding by filed in the office of the Clerk of the Family Court of the State of New York, County of New York, in accordance with Section 384-b, Subd. 3(j), of the Social Services Law; and it is further

ORDERED that a certified copy of this order by filed in the office of the New York County Clerk.

Dated: ENTER:

_____
Family Court Judge

16
Severe or Repeated Abuse

In addition to freeing a child for adoption based upon a surrender, abandonment, permanent neglect, mental illness, or mental retardation, a child may also be freed pursuant to Section 384 B of the Social Services Law, where the agency proves by clear and convincing evidence that the child was severely or repeatedly abused by his/her parent. The authorized agency must attempt to rehabilitate the parent, but if after one year the parent cannot or will not be rehabilitated, the agency may bring a proceeding pursuant to Section 384 B of the Social Services Law to terminate the parental rights on the basis that the infant was severely or repeatedly abused. As in permanent neglect cases, in abuse cases the agency must show diligent efforts to encourage and strengthen the parental relationship, unless such efforts would be detrimental to the best interests of the child.

Section 384 B of the Social Services Law, Subparagraph 4(e) provides that an order committing the guardianship and custody of a child may be granted if:

> The parent or parents, whose consent to the adoption of the child would otherwise be required in accordance with Section 111 of the Domestic Relations Law, severely or repeatedly abused such child, and the child has been in the care of an authorized agency for the period of one year immediately prior to the initiation of the proceeding under this Section.

Severe Abuse

Paragraph 8 of Section 384 B of the Social Services Law defines the term *severely abused* as follows:

> For the purposes of this section a child is "severely abused" by his parent if (i) the child has been found to be an abused child as a result of reckless or intentional acts of the parent committed under circumstances evincing a depraved indifference to human life, which result in serious physical injury to the child as defined in Subdivision 10 of Section 10.00 of the Penal Law, and (ii) the agency has made diligent efforts to encourage and

strengthen the parental relationship, including efforts to rehabilitate the respondent, when such efforts will not be detrimental to the best interests of the child and such efforts have been unsuccessful and are unlikely to be successful in the foreseeable future.

Serious physical injury is defined by Subdivision 10 of Section 10 of the Penal Law as "physical injury which creates a substantial risk of death or which causes death or serious and protracted disfigurement, protracted impairment of health or protracted loss or impairment of the function of any bodily organ."

Repeated Abuse

Section 384 B, Subparagraph 8(b), provides that a finding of repeated abuse may be made under two conditions. One is that the child has been found abused under Paragraph (i) of the Family Court Act, Section 1012, Subparagraph E. Paragraph (i) refers to a parent or other person legally responsible for a child's care who "inflicts or allows to be inflicted upon such child physical injury by other than accidental means which causes or creates a substantial risk of death, or serious or protracted disfigurement, or protracted impairment of physical or emotional health, or protracted loss or impairment of the function of any bodily organ."

Subparagraph 8 (b) of Section 384 B also allows for a finding of repeated abuse if the child was found abused under the Family Court Act, Section 1012, Subparagraph (e) (iii). However, there are two additional requirements if a finding is to be made based upon a prior finding of abuse under Subparagraph (e) (iii). First, the respondent parent must have committed, or knowingly allowed to be committed, a felony sex offense against the child, as defined under one of the following Penal Law sections:

130.25, Rape in the third degree;

130.30, Rape in the second degree;

130.35, Rape in the first degree;

130.40, Sodomy in the third degree;

130.45, Sodomy in the second degree;

130.50, Sodomy in the first degree;

130.65, Sexual abuse in the first degree;

130.70, Aggravated sexual abuse.

Second, the child involved in the termination proceeding, or another child who was the legal responsibility of the parent, must have been previously found to be an abused child under Paragraph (i) or (iii) of the Family Court Act, Section 1012. Additionally, the prior finding must have been made within five years of the initiation of the termination proceeding, and if the prior finding of abuse was under the Family Court Act, Section 1012 (e) (iii), it must have been within one of the Penal Law categories listed above.

Finally, like a finding of severe abuse, a finding of repeated abuse requires that "the agency has made diligent efforts to encourage and strengthen the parental relationship, including efforts to rehabilitate the respondent, when such efforts will not be detrimental to the best interests of the child, and such efforts have been unsuccessful and are likely to remain unsuccessful in the foreseeable future." See Social Services Law 384 B (8)(b).

If the court finds at a fact-finding hearing by clear and convincing evidence that the child was severely abused or repeatedly abused, the court shall hold a dispositional hearing. At the dispositional hearing the court may enter an order freeing the child for adoption if the court finds it to be in the best interests of the child to do so.

This section is rarely used because of the complicated procedural requirements. The new law became effective in October 1981 and amends Article 10 of the Family Court Act and Section 384 B of the Social Services Law.

Special Warrant and Summons Requirements Upon Initial Allegations of Abuse

When there is an initial allegation of abuse against the parent in family court, the warrant and summons to be served upon the parent must contain a statement, clearly marked on its face that the initial abuse proceedings could lead to a proceeding to terminate parental rights and to commit guardianship and custody of the child to an authorized agency, thereby freeing the child for adoption (sidebar 16-1). See Family Court Act, Sections 1036 and 1037.

Only the family court has jurisdiction over these proceedings, and if the family court does find after the fact-finding hearing that the allegations of the initial abuse are sustained, the court may, after the dispositional hearing, place the infant with the commissioner of social services for a period of twelve months.

Sidebar 16–1. Petition in Commitment of Guardianship and Custody Where Child Is (Severely) (Repeatedly) Abused

FAMILY COURT OF THE STATE OF NEW YORK
COUNTY OF ......

In the Matter of the Commitment of Guardianship   PETITION
and Custody pursuant to § 384-b of the Social
Services Law of .....   Docket No.
A Child under the Age of Eighteen Years, alleged
to be a (Severely)(Repeatedly) Abused Child

TO THE FAMILY COURT

The undersigned Petitioner respectfully alleges that:

1. Petitioner(s) .... (is)(are) (an authorized agency) (foster parent(s)) having (its office and place of business) (his)(her)(their) (residence) at .... in the County of ...., State of New York.

2. .... is a (fe)male child under the age of eighteen years born on .... at .... who now resides at .... in the County of ...., State of New York.

3. The full name and address of each parent and custodian of the child is:

   (Name)   (Last-known address)

4. The name and address of each other interested party who should be afforded notice of this proceeding is:

   (Name)   (Last-known address)

   and there are no persons other than those set forth entitled to notice of this proceeding.

5. The child has been in the care of (an) authorized agency(y)(ies) for a period of more than one year immediately prior to the initiation of this proceeding as follows:

   (name of agency)   (date)

6. (Upon information and belief) (T)(t)he authorized agenc(y)(ies)

(has)(have)(not) made diligent efforts to encourage and strengthen the parental relationship (because such efforts would be detrimental to the best interests of the child) in that

(Specify the efforts made or the reasons such efforts would be detrimental to the best interest of the child.)

and such efforts have been unsuccessful and are unlikely to be successful in the foreseeable future in that ....

7. (Upon information and belief) (T)(t)he respondent(s), (father)(mother) (has)(have) severely abused the above-named child, in that:

....)

8. (Upon information and belief) (T)(t)he respondent(s), (father)(mother) (has)(have) repeatedly abused the above-named child, in that:

....)

9. The best interests of the child will be promoted by commitment of the guardianship and custody of the child to ...., (an authorized agency) (foster parent(s)) for the following reasons:

(If appropriate, include facts regarding a non-respondent parent.)

10. No previous application has been made to any court or judge for the relief sought herein (except ....)

WHEREFORE, your Petitioner prays for an order determining that the above-named child is a (severely) (and) (repeatedly) abused child, and committing the guardianship and custody of the child to .... (an authorized agency) (foster parent(s)), and for such other and further relief as in the best interests of the child may be granted.

Dated: ...., 19....

_____

(Agency) (Foster Parent(s))

(by) _____
Name

_____
Title

VERIFICATION

STATE OF NEW YORK
COUNTY OF ....   ss.:

Sidebar 16–2. Order of Disposition in Commitment of Guardianship and Custody Where Child Is (Severely) (Repeatedly) Abused

At the term of the Family Court of the State of New York, held in and for the County of ...., at ...., New York, on ...., 19...

PRESENT:
  Hon. ...., Judge

In the Matter of Commitment of Guardianship
and Custody pursuant to Section §
384-b of the Social Services Law of ....   Docket No.

                                                    ORDER OF
A Child under the Age of Eighteen Years,   DISPOSITION
alleged to be a (Severely)(Repeatedly) Abused
Child

A Petition under Section 384-b of the Social Services Law, dated the .... day of .... 19...., having been filed in this Court alleging that .... is a (severely)(and)(repeatedly) abused child; and summons having been issued and duly served upon and notice having been duly given to all proper parties hereto, and

The matter having duly come on for a fact-finding hearing and .... (parent(s)) (custodian(s)) (having appeared) (having failed to appear) thereon, the Court, after hearing the proofs and the testimony offered in relation to the case, finds that the allegations that the (mother)(father)(custodian(s)) of the child (has)(have) (severely) (and) (repeatedly) abused the child are supported by clear and convincing proof, and further finds that

....;
and

The matter having duly come on for a dispositional hearing and the (parent(s)) (custodian(s)) (having appeared) (having failed to appear) thereon, the Court, having made examination and inquiry into the facts and circumstances of the case and into the surroundings, conditions and capacities of the persons involved in this proceeding, finds upon clear and convincing evidence that the best interests of the child require the disposition hereinafter made;

NOW THEREFORE, it is

ORDERED AND ADJUDGED that .... is a (severely)(and) (repeatedly) abused child as defined by Section 384-b of the Social Services Law; and it is

*ORDERED that the guardianship and custody rights of .... the parent(s) are transferred to .... (an authorized agency)(foster parent(s)) and such guardianship and custody of the child are committed to the (authorized agency) (foster parent(s)) (upon the following terms and conditions:) .... ;

**ORDERED that the Family Court shall retain jurisdiction over the parties and child in accordance with Social Services Law, Section 384-b;

*ORDERED that ...., an authorized agency, is authorized and empowered to consent to the adoption of the child subject to the order of a Court of competent jurisdiction to which a petition for adoption is submitted (without the consent of or further notice to .... the .... of the child).

***ORDERED that judgment is suspended upon the following conditions: .... ; and it is

ORDERED that a certified copy of this Order be filed in the office of the Clerk of .... County, pursuant to Section 384-b of the Social Services Law of the State of New York; and it is further

ORDERED ....

Dated: ...., 19....

Part IV
The Parties in Foster-Care Custody Proceedings

17
The Rights of the Natural Parents

The natural parents, by statute, common law, and the moral law, have a superior right to the custody and bringing up of their child. The [Social Services Law, Section 384B, provides that a child's best interest, all things being equal, would be best served if the child is nurtured by the natural parent] The law requires that the caseworker use all diligent efforts to help reunite the child with the natural parent. In order to do this, once a child is in foster care, the social worker must be keen enough to ascertain all of the problems faced by the parent that are barriers to the return of the child. The social worker, after reviewing the case dictation and the intake notes, and after discussing the matter with the prior caseworkers, the supervisor, and the parents themselves, will determine what problems must be faced. The usual problems faced by natural parents whose children are in foster care are drug abuse, alcohol abuse, lack of appropriate housing, emotional or psychological problems, or living with an abusive husband or wife. Once the caseworker ascertains what the problems are, it is the duty of the caseworker to try to either solve or ameliorate these problems. The caseworker must be involved in active casework and must make actual referrals, including transporting the parent to initial conferences with Alcoholics Anonymous or a drug rehabilitation center.

It is not enough to point out the problems to the parent and suggest that the parent find appropriate facilities to deal with those problems. It is important for the caseworker to use diligent efforts and to document those diligent efforts in the case dictation and progress notes. If the parent does not respond to the outreach and diligent efforts of the caseworker, the law requires that the child receive permanency. The caseworker is now gathering information in order for the agency attorney to draft a petition to terminate parental rights upon grounds of abandonment, permanent neglect, mental illness, or mental retardation.

The rights of the natural parents of a child have been the subject of much litigation since foster-care review hearings were initiated in June 1972 (Section 392 of the Social Services Law). Prior to family court review hearings, children were more apt to stay in foster-care, whereas today, the family court, after the foster-care review hearing, many times directs the authorized agency either to initiate proceedings to free the children for adoption or to return the children to the natural parents.

The commissioner of social services of the City of New York has attempted to educate natural parents so that they will not be placed in a position in which the parent-child relationship will be permanently severed through lack of information. To that end, the commissioner has distributed "The Parent's Handbook—A Guide for Parents of Children in Foster Care" to all parents of children in foster care. The handbook discusses: (1) the ways that the child comes into foster care, (2) working with the caseworker, (3) planning for the child's future, (4) parental rights and responsibilities, (5) parents' rights to a fair hearing, (6) how to obtain a lawyer, and (7) court actions relating to the child, such as:

1. 358A proceedings;
2. 392 foster-care review hearings;
3. extension of court placement hearings;
4. abandonment proceedings; and
5. permanent neglect proceedings.

Traditionally, the courts of New York have protected the rights of natural parents. See Matter of Susan W. v. Talbot G. [34 N.Y. 2d, 356 N.Y.S.2d 34 (1974)], wherein the Court of Appeals cited numerous precedents where the courts have "jealously guarded" the relationship between minor children and their natural parents.

As pointed out by the Court of Appeals in the Susan W. case:

1. Thus, abandonment can be made out only from "a settled purpose to be rid of all parental rights" (*Matter of Maxwell*, 4 N.Y.2d 429, 433, 176 N.Y.S.2d 281, 283, 151 N.E.2d 848, 850; see, also, *Spence-Chapin Adoption Serv. v. Polk*, 29 N.Y.2d 196, 324 N.Y.S.2d 937, 27 N.E.2d 431; *People ex rel. Scarpetta v. Spence-Chapin Adoption Serv.* 28 N.Y.2d 185, 321 N.Y.S.2d 65, 269 N.E.2d 787, cert. den. 404 U.S. 805, 92 S.Ct. 54, 30 L.Ed.2d 38; *People ex rel. Anonymous v. Anonymous*, 10 N.Y.2d 332, 222 N.Y.S.2d 945, 179 N.E.2d 200; *Matter of Bistany, supra*).

2. As in those unwed mother cases where this Court found abandonment to have been established, there must be a complete "repudiation of [parent]hood and an abandonment of [parental] rights and responsibilities," (*People ex rel. Anonymous v. Anonymous, supra*, p. 336, 222 N.Y.S.2d p. 947, 179 N.E.2d p. 201; *Matter of Maxwell, supra*).

3. Even where the flame of parental interests is reduced to a flicker, the courts may not properly intervene to dissolve the percentage. The relationship between minor children and their natural parents is jealously guarded (*Matter of Livingstone*, 151 App. Div. 1, 7, 135 N.Y.S. 328, 332; *Matter of Anonymous*, 178 Misc. 142, 146, 33 N.Y.S.2d 793, 798; *Caruso v. Caruso*, 175 Misc. 290, 392, 23 N.Y.S.2d 239, 241).

Two of the most-often-used methods of terminating parental rights and freeing children for adoption are: abandonment, pursuant to Section 384 B of the Social Services Law; and permanent neglect, pursuant to Section 611 of the Family Court Act and Section 384 B of the Social Services Law. A strict interpretation of Section 384 B of the Social Services Law and Section 611 of the Family Court Act would make it extremely difficult for the agency to terminate parental rights.

The Court of Appeals, the highest court in the State of New York, however, decided two cases within weeks of each other. One dealt with abandonment, pursuant to Section 384 of the Social Services Law, and the other dealt with permanent neglect, pursuant to Section 611 of the Family Court Act. Both of these cases have made it easier for the authorized agency to terminate parental rights, freeing the child for adoption and with the natural effect of lessening parental rights.

In the case of In re Roberta H. [40 N.Y. 2d 96, 386 N.Y.S. 2d 59 (1976)], the Court of Appeals, in reversing the Appellate Division, Second Department, held that the authorized agency need not show diligent efforts on its part to strengthen the parental ties between parent and child. See also In re Malik M. [40 N.Y. 2d 840, 387 N.Y.S. 2d 385 (1976)], wherein the Court of Appeals held that the agency was not required to exercise diligent efforts to encourage and strengthen the parental relationship in an abandonment proceeding and that the finding of abandonment was supported by sufficient evidence "even if one considers in favor of the mother the disadvantages and misfortunes under which she functioned and which undoubtedly contributed to the abandonment."

Before the Court of Appeals eliminated the agency's duty to attempt to strengthen the parental relationship, the lower court cases had made it a condition precedent to the termination of parental rights. See Matter of Anonymous (St. Christopher's Home) [48 A.D. 2d 696, 368 N.Y.S. 2d 372]; Matter of Vanessa F [76 Misc. 2d 617, 351 N.Y.S. 2d 337]; Matter of Jennifer S. [69 Misc. 2d 942, 330 N.Y.S. 2d 872; 333 N.Y.S.2d 79]; and Matter of Ellick [69 Misc. 175, 328 N.Y.S.2d 587]. The Court of Appeals held that if an agency can prove abandonment in accordance with Section 384—that is, by showing the parents' failure to visit or support the child for six months without good reason—it need not also establish its diligent efforts to encourage and strengthen the parental relationship as required by Article 6 of the family court. The court stated:

> While the burden of proving abandonment has traditionally been a heavy one, it is not to be made heavier by an additional requirement not present in the statute. The degree of neglect should determine the route chosen to free the child and, if an agency can prove abandonment, i.e., prove that the parent failed to visit or support the child for six months without good reason, it is not also required to prove diligent efforts to encourage and strengthen the parental relationship.

Since the Court of Appeals' decision in In re Roberta H., it has been easier to terminate parental rights in an action initiated pursuant to Section 384 of the Social Services Law based upon alleged abandonment of a child by the parent. See Section 384 (5)(b), which eliminates the need by an agency to use diligent efforts to encourage parental ties.

What the case of Roberta H. has done with respect to abandonment, In re Orlando F. has done with respect to permanent neglect pursuant to Section 611 of the Family Court Act.

In In re Orlando F. [40 N.Y. 2d 103, 386 N.Y.S. 2d 64 (1976)], the Court of Appeals in effect reversed both the Family Court, New York County, and the Appellate Division, First Department, and held that the agency as a matter of law proved that the parent permanently neglected the child, as defined by Section 611 of the Family Court Act. In so deciding, however, the Court made it clear that even though a parent maintains frequent contact with the child, parental ties can be terminated where the parent has no plan for the return of the child.

The Court of Appeals stated that the family court and the Appellate Division had been incorrect in interpreting the phrase *maintained contact with or planned for* as comprising only one requirement—that is, it was read in the conjunctive rather than in the distinctive—and the court concluded that a finding of the failure to plan in and of itself suffices to support a determination of permanent neglect, even though there has been frequent contact. Further, it appears that the Court of Appeals lessened the degree of importance attached to the intention of the parent, at least with respect to permanent neglect proceedings, when it stated:

> To be sure, the mother has evinced a "burning desire" to regain custody of the child, but it is undisputed that in the three years preceding this litigation she has failed to take the affirmative steps necessary to insure that Orlando would be the rightful beneficiary of any adequate home life if returned to her.

Based upon the Court of Appeals' cases in In re Roberta H. and Orlando F., it should now be easier for an authorized agency to terminate parental rights based upon abandonment and permanent neglect. It naturally follows that the rights of the natural parents have been weakened.

Natural Parent v. Natural Parent

In a custody contest between natural parents, there is no *prima facie* right to custody for either parent. See Domestic Relations Law, Sections 70 and 240. Change of custody should not be decreed lightly. Where there has been a judicial determination of custody in one parent, custody should not be changed except upon a showing that the custodial parent is unfit or less fit to serve as a proper custodian. See Meirowitz v. Meirowitz [96 A.D. 2d 1030, 466 N.U.S. 2d 434 (Appellate Division, 2nd Dept., 1983)]; In re Robert C. [376 N.Y.S. 2d 951 (Appellate Division, 3rd Dept.).

In a custody proceeding between natural parents, the court is concerned with the best interests and welfare of the child. See Domestic Relations Law, Sections 70 and 240. See also McIntosh v. McIntosh [87 A.D. 2d 968, 451 N.Y.S. 2d 200 (Appellate Division, 3rd Dept., 1982)]; Obey v. Degling [37 N.Y. 2d 91 (1976)].

Joint Custody

The prevailing view of the New York courts toward joint custody has most clearly been defined in Braiman v. Braiman [44 N.Y. 2d 584, 407 N.Y.S. 2d 449, 378 N.E. 2d 1019 (1978)]. In this case the Court of Appeals held that:

> It is understandable . . . that joint custody is encouraged primarily as a voluntary alternative for relative stable, amicable parents behaving in mature, civilized fashion. . . . As a court-ordered arrangement imposed upon already embattled and embittered parents, accusing one another of serious vices and wrongs, it can only enhance familial chaos. . . . In the rare case, joint custody may approximate the former family relationships more closely than other custodial arrangements. It may not, however, be indiscriminately substituted for an award of sole custody. Divorce dissolves the family as well as the marriage. [Id at 451–452]

See also Dodd v. Dodd [403 N.Y.S. 2d 401 (Superior Court, New York County, 1978)], wherein the court refused to decree joint custody, although it noted that joint custody was an appealing concept and defined it as "giving both parents legal responsibility for the child's care and alternating companionship."

Natural Mother v. Putative Father

While there is no presumption or prima facie right to custody of the child between married parents, the rule appears to be otherwise when the custody "battle" is between the mother and the putative father. In the case of Barry W. v. Barbara K. [389 N.Y.S. 2d 624 (Superior Court, Appellate Division, 2nd Dept., 1976)], the court granted custody of two children to the putative father, stating that while prima facie the mother of an illegitimate child is entitled to custody, the best interests of the child are of paramount importance. See, however, Boatwright v. Otero [398 N.Y.S. 2d 391 (Family Court, Onondaga

County)], wherein the court stated that there is no *prima facie* right to custody in either parent regardless of whether the father was married to the mother, and that the best-interests-of-the-child test is applicable. The court awarded the children to the putative father as against the mother.

Natural Parent v. Custodial Parent

While recent decisions have given foster and adoptive parents more rights, the courts have refused to terminate parental rights where the parents have not abandoned or neglected the child. See Matter of Bennett v. Jeffreys [40 N.Y. 2d 543, 387 N.Y.S. 2d 821, 956, N.E. 2d 277], wherein the court held that "[absent] surrender, abandonment, persisting neglect, unfitness or other like extraordinary circumstances . . . [the] State may not deprive a parent of the custody of a child."

The view of the courts in New York is exemplified by Matter of Dixon v. Lascaris [53 N.Y. 2d 204, 440 N.Y.S. 2d 884, 423 N.E. 2d 361 (1981)], wherein the Court of Appeals held that the year-long separation between a father and his children, during which time the father had contacted his children on only one or two occasions and had attempted both formally and informally to obtain custody, did not reach the level of an actual abandonment and did not constitute the extraordinary circumstance, as the term was used in Bennett v. Jeffries. The court went on to note that "quite bluntly, a child is not a piece of property over whom title may be acquired by adverse possession" [Id at 887].

Natural Parents v. Grandparents

Custody

In a custody proceeding between a natural parent and a grandparent, it is no longer automatic that the parent will gain custody. As the Court of Appeals stated in Gomez v. Lozado [40 N.Y. 2d 839, 387 N.Y.S. 2d 834]:

> The Appellate Court seems to have accorded a parental primacy which, as developed in the *Bennett* case (*supra*) is not as absolute as argued by the father.

In Raysor v. Gabbey [395 N.Y.S. 2d 290], the Appellate Division reversed the family court's order that had awarded custody of the infant to the maternal grandmother instead of the natural father with a direction that a prompt decision be made upon appropriate social investigations, interviews, and reports and upon the existing record.

The Appellate Division has stated the new rule of law relating the rights of natural parents as follows:

> This presumption in favor of the natural parent has subsequently been modified by the Court of Appeals to the extent that the rule is now stated that a natural parent has a superior right to the care or custody of his child and this right may not be dissolved "absent surrender, abandonment, persisting neglect, unfitness or other like *extraordinary circumstances* [emphasis added]. If any of such extraordinary circumstances are present, the disposition of custody is influenced or controlled by what is in the best interests of the child" (*Bennett v. Jeffries*, 40 N.Y.2d 543, 544, 387 N.Y.S.2d 821, 823, 356 N.E.2d 277, 280; see also, *Matter of Gomez v. Lozado*, 40 N.Y.2d 839, 387 N.Y.S.2d 834, 356 N.E.2d 287).

Visitation

Grandparents who are denied visitation with their grandchildren may petition the Supreme Court in a *habeas corpus* proceeding, pursuant to Section 72 of the Domestic Relations Law. A hearing must be held to ascertain whether grandparent visitation would be in the best interests of the infant. See In re Norah G. [398 N.Y.S. 2d 743 (Appellate Division, 2nd Dept., 1977)]. Whether grandparents receive visitation rights is a matter of the court's discretion. See LoPresti v. LoPresti [40 N.Y. 2d 522, 387 N.Y.S. 2d 412, 355 N.E. 372 (1976), on remand 54 A.D. 2d 582, 387 N.Y.S. 2d 153]. In the case of Vacula v. Blume [384 N.Y.S. 2d 208 (Appellate Division, 2nd Dept., 1976)] the Appellate Division reversed the order of the Supreme Court, sustained the writ, and ordered visitation, stating:

> "Animosity between the mother of the children and their grandparents is not a proper basis for the denial of visitation privileges to the grandparents; nor is it a proper yardstick by which to measure the best interests of the children" (*Lo Presti v. Lo Presti*, 51 A.D.2d 578, 378 N.Y.S.2d 487). "Visits with a grandparent are often a precious part of a child's experience and there are benefits which devolve upon the grandchild from the relationship with his grandparents which he cannot derive from any other relationship. Neither the Legislature nor this Court is blind to human truths which grandparents and grandchildren have always known" (*Mimkon v. Ford*, 66 N.J. 426, 437, 332 A.2d 199, 204).

See also Lachow v. Barasch [394 N.Y.S. 2d 284 (Appellate Division, 2nd Dept., 1977)], wherein the Appellate Division remanded the proceedings to the family court, stating that the family court had abused its discretion in denying the grandparent's petition for visitation based upon the ground of animosity between the grandparent and the father of the child. The court stated:

We remand the proceeding to the Family Court to take testimony and make a determination under the standards set forth in Section 72 of the Domestic Relations Law, as interpreted in *LoPresti v. LoPresti*, 40 N.Y.2d 522, 387 N.Y.S.2d 412, 355 N.E.2d 372.

See also Tarulli v. D'Amico [400 N.Y.S. 2d 15 (Appellate Division, 2nd Dept., 1977)], wherein the Appellate Division affirmed the family court's decision to allow visitation between grandparents and children but modified the provisions that conditioned the visits based upon the wishes of the children, none of whom were over age ten. The court held that to subject the children to making such a choice was against their best interests.

Grandparents v. Adoptive Parents

The court denied the grandparents' *habeas corpus* proceeding requesting visitation of a grandchild who was placed with an adoptive home. It stated that the research had not disclosed any cases dealing with the issue of whether adoption of the child by unrelated third parties would bar assertion of visitation by grandparents. See In re Wilder [403 N.Y.S. 2d 454 (Superior Court, New York County, 1978)].

However, the grandparents' *habeas corpus* petition to custody of the child will be dismissed where the natural mother has signed a surrender. See In re Marian P.P. [377 N.Y.S. 2d, 306 (Appellate Division, 3rd Dept., 1975)], wherein the court stated:

A change in custody which is permitted after the surrender for adoption operates only in favor of the natural parent as it is grounded on the presumption that the best interests of the child will be promoted thereby.

Death of a Natural Parent

Upon the death of one parent, the other automatically becomes, in the absence of special circumstances, the custodian and/or guardian of the child. See In re Tamara I. [399 N.Y.S. 2d 98 (Family Court, Kings County, 1977)]. In this case, the court denied an *ex parte* application by the maternal grandmother for guardianship after the death of the child's mother.

Lawless Self-Help

The Court of Appeals has discouraged one parent from unlawfully taking possession of an infant from another jurisdiction and coming to New York and petitioning the court for custody. In In re Nehra [401 N.Y.S. 2d 168 (1977)], the court held that the father was entitled to custody of the children where he was a fit parent, had custody based upon a Michigan decree and since the mother had obtained custody of the children by lawless self-help.

Full Faith and Credit

In custody proceedings, decrees of sister states are not entitled to full faith and credit. See Obey v. Delging [37 N.Y. 2d 768, 275 N.Y.S. 2d 91 (1975)]. However, a court can, within its discretion, accord the decree of such a sister state's recognition. See Matter of Lang v. Lang [9 A.D. 2d 401, 193 N.Y.S. 2d 763 affd. 7 N.Y. 2d 1029, 200 N.Y.S. 2d 71]. However, before relying on custody decree of another state, the court should determine whether there was a full and plenary hearing in the sister state on the issue of the best interests of the child. See Levine v. Tommasi [389 N.Y.S. 2d 114 (Appellate Division, 2nd Dept., 1975)].

Stipulation of the Parties

The stipulation of the parties relating to the custody of the child is not binding on the court. In Levine v. Tommasi [389 N.Y. 2d 114 (Appellate Division, 2nd Dept., 1976)], the court wrote:

> The best interests of the infant must come before the parent's stipulation (See *Matter of Araujo v. Araujo*, 38 A.D. 2d 537, 327 N.Y.S. 2d 217). We are, of course, concerned solely with the best interests and the welfare of the child . . .

However, although an agreement between the parties is not binding on the court, the court may give weight to the priority the agreement expresses. See Eschbach v. Eschbach [56 N.Y.2 d 167, 451 N.Y.S. 2d 658, 436 N.E.2d 1260 (1982)].

18
The Rights of Putative Fathers

The rights of unwed biological fathers, or putative fathers, were first recognized in the case of Stanley v. Illinois [1972, 405 U.S. 645, 92 S.Ct. 1208, 31 L.Ed. 2d 551]. In the Stanley case, the Supreme Court of the United States held that an unwed father who had a relationship with his children had a right to participate in a hearing regarding the best interests of the children prior to having his parental rights terminated.

The Stanley ruling, however, was not interpreted as giving the unwed father a veto to an adoption where the biological mother had consented to the adoption. In the case of In re Adoption of Malpica-Orsini [1975, 36 N.Y. 2d 568, 370 N.Y.S. 2d 511, 331 N.E. 2d 486], the New York Court of Appeals held that an unwed father's consent to an adoption was not needed, and he was merely permitted to participate in a best-interests hearing. All this has now changed. The Supreme Court of the United States gave the unwed father rights akin to those of the biological mother in the case of Caban v. Mohammed [1979, 441 U.S. 380, 99 S.Ct. 1760, 60 L.Ed. 2d 297]. In that case, the Supreme Court of the United States declared Section 111 of the New York Domestic Relations Law unconstitutional, holding that the sex-based distinction of Section 111 violates the equal protection clause of the Fourteenth Amendment of the U.S. Constitution.

Section 111 of the Domestic Relations Law of the State of New York provided that the consent of the following persons was required for an adoption:

1. The adoptive child, if over fourteen years of age, unless the judge or surrogate in his/her discretion dispensed with such consent;
2. The parents or surviving parent, whether adult or infant, of a child born in-wedlock;
3. The mother, whether adult or infant, of a child born out-of-wedlock;
4. Any person or authorized agency having lawful custody of the adoptive child.

In short, Section 111 of the Domestic Relations Law provided that consent to an adoption by an unwed biological mother was required, but not that of an unwed biological father.

In Caban, *supra*, Adbiel Caban and Maria Mohammed lived together for five years, from September 1968 to the end of 1973, but they had never married. They had two children while they were living together: David Caban, born July 16, 1969, and Denise Caban, born March 12, 1971. Adbiel Caban was named on each child's birth certificate, lived with the children as their father for several years, and contributed to their support. However, in December 1973, Maria Mohammed left Adbiel Caban and took the children with her and married Kazim Mohammed on January 30, 1974. For the next nine months, Adbiel Caban saw his children once a week, when they visited their maternal grandmother, who lived in the same apartment house as Adbiel Caban.

In September 1974, the maternal grandmother took the children to Puerto Rico. Adbiel Caban communicated with his children through his parents, who also resided there. In November 1975, Caban went to Puerto Rico, and the maternal grandmother surrendered the children to him for a couple of days, with the understanding that he would return them. However, he brought the children with him to New York. Maria Mohammed, through court proceedings, obtained custody of the children with visitation privileges to Adbiel Caban. Thereafter, Maria and Kazim Mohammed applied to the surrogate's court to adopt the two children. Adbiel Caban was cited, and although his consent was not needed, he was permitted to participate in a best-interests-test hearing. The surrogate granted the Mohammeds' petition to adopt the children, thereby terminating Caban's parental rights.

In his decision, the surrogate noted that the unwed biological father's consent to the adoption was not a legal necessity, and that he was entitled only to an opportunity to be heard in opposition to the proposed stepfather's adoption. The Appellate Division and the Court of Appeals affirmed.

In Caban, *supra*, Mr. Justice Powell delivered the opinion of the Court, in which Mr. Justice Brennan, Mr. Justice White, Mr. Justice Marshall, and Mr. Justice Blackmun joined. Dissenting opinions were filed by Mr. Justice Steward and Mr. Justice Stevens, in which Mr. Justice Burger and Mr. Justice Rehnquist joined. The Supreme Court reversed the New York Court of Appeals' decision [43 N.Y. 2d 708, 401 N.Y.S. 2d 208, 372 N.Ed. 2d 42] and held Section 111 of the Domestic Relations Law unconstitutional, in that Section 111 treated unmarried parents differently according to their sex. In summarizing their opinion, the majority wrote:

In sum, we believe that Section 111 is another example of "overbroad generalizations" in gender-based classifications. See *Califano v. Goldfarb*, 430 U.S. 199, 211 (1977), *Stanton v. Stanton*, 421 U.S. 7, 14–15 (1975). The effect of New York's classification is to discriminate against unwed fathers even when their identity is known and they have manifested a significant paternal interest in the child. The facts of this case illustrate the harshness of classifying unwed fathers as being invariably less qualified and entitled than mothers to exercise a concerned judgment as to the fate of their children. Section 111 both excludes some loving fathers from full participation in the decision whether their children will be adopted and, at the same time, enables some alienated mothers arbitrarily to cut off the paternal rights of fathers. We conclude that this undifferentiated distinction between unwed mothers and unwed fathers, applicable in all circumstances where adoption of a child of theirs is at issue, does not bear a substantial relationship to the state's asserted interests.

Section 384 C of the Social Services Law was passed by the legislature of the State of New York as an attempt to meet the unconstitutionality of sex-based discrimination pointed out in the Caban case. Section 384 C provided that the following class of unwed fathers were to receive notice of proceedings to terminate parental rights.

Persons entitled to notice, pursuant to Subdivision 1 of Section 384 C, shall include:

A. Any person adjudicated by a Court in this state to be the father of the child;

B. Any person adjudicated by a Court of another state or territory of the United States to be the father of the child, when a certified copy of the Court Order has been filed with the putative father registry, pursuant to Section 372-C of the Social Services Law;

C. Any person who has timely filed an unrevoked notice of intent to claim paternity of the child, pursuant to Section 372 of the Social Services Law;

D. Any person who is recorded on the child's Birth Certificate as the child's father;

E. Any person who is openly living with the child and the child's mother at the time the proceeding is initiated or at the time the child was placed in the care of an authorized agency, and who is holding himself out to be the child's father;

F. Any person who has been identified as the child's father by the mother in a written, sworn statement;

G. Any person who is married to the child's mother within six months subsequent to the birth of the child and prior to the execution of a surrender instrument or the initiation of a proceeding pursuant to Section 384-B; and

H. Any person who has filed with the putative father registry an instrument acknowledging paternity of the child, pursuant to Section 4-1.2 of the estates, powers and trusts law.

Section 384 C, Paragraph 3, provides that these unwed fathers may appear and present evidence only in the dispositional hearing.

While Section 384 C provides that the sole purpose of notice thereunder shall be to enable the person served—that is, the putative father—to present to the court evidence relative to the best interests of the child in the dispositional hearing only, the practice (and it would appear to be the better practice) is to serve the putative father in the same manner as the natural mother, and also to serve the summons and petition upon the putative father prior to the fact-finding hearing in order to enable him to participate fully in such hearing as long as he meets the criteria of a person entitled to notice as provided in Subdivision 2 of Section 384 C. For example, if the putative father is identified as the child's father in a written, sworn statement and if he lived with the mother and the child before the child was placed in foster care, he should be served with a summons and petition and given an opportunity to participate in the fact-finding hearing. This practice would avoid questions concerning the order of commitment, since the putative father's rights would be adjudicated fully in the fact-finding and dispositional hearings.

19
The Rights of Incarcerated Natural Parents

Prior to the enactment of Chapter 911 of the Laws of New York (1983) effective January 1, 1984, the consent of an incarcerated parent was unnecessary for the adoption of an infant. At that time, Domestic Relations Law, Section 111 (2)(d), provided that the consent of a parent was unnecessary in the case of a person deprived of civil rights, pursuant to the Civil Rights Law. Civil Rights Law, Section 79, deemed a person serving an indeterminate term with a maximum of life imprisonment to have lost all civil rights. Domestic Relations Law, Section 111 (2)(d), was held not to violate the due process clause of the Fourteenth Amendment of the U.S. Constitution because "nothing in the due process clause prohibits the termination of parental rights when a parent is unable or unwilling to care for the child and the adoption is in the child's best interest." See, for example, In re Eric J.B. [92 A.D. 2d 917, 460 N.Y.S. 2d (Appellate Division, 2nd Dept., 1983)].

However, Domestic Relations Law, Section 111 (2)(d), was in potential conflict with Social Services Law 384 B (7)(d) (iii), as it then existed. The Social Services Law deemed incarcerated parents were unable to maintain contact with their children and thus precluded termination of parental rights.

As of January 1, 1984, Chapter 911 of the Laws of 1983 amended and aligned the Domestic Relations Law and the Social Services Law, Section 384 B. The provision in Domestic Relations Law, Section 111 (2)(d), allowing the adoption of an infant without parental consent, was removed. Further, Section 384 B of the Social Services Law was amended to indicate the conditions that must exist before a finding of abandonment or permanent neglect would be made against an incarcerated parent. See Section 384 B of the Social Services Law, Subdivisions 2 and 7.

Incarcerated Parents and Abandonment

An incarcerated parent is obliged to fulfill the requirements of Social Services Law, Section 384 B, concerning visitation and communication with the child or agency. Thus, an incarcerated parent who has failed to visit or communicate with the child or the agency for at least six months prior to the date of the filing of the petition to terminate parental rights will be deemed to have abandoned the child. Proceedings based on abandonment by incarcerated parents are thus fairly clear-cut. See, for example, In re Stella B. [130 Misc. 2d 148, 495 N.Y.S. 2d 128 (Family Court, Onondaga County, 1985)], wherein the court held that a finding of abandonment was not precluded by the fact that the parent was illiterate, without a showing that an incarcerated parent was unable to communicate with the child or the agency. See also In re Thomas G., Jr. [564 N.Y.S. 2d 32 (Apellate Division, 1st Dept. 1990)].

Chapter 911 and its Effect on Permanent Neglect

Chapter 911 did away with what could be termed "no fault" termination by requiring that the parental rights of an incarcerated parent could be terminated only upon clear and convincing evidence that the parent had permanently neglected the infant. The agency is thus required to exercise diligent efforts to assist the parent and child to develop a meaningful relationship. Additionally, the incarcerated parent is obligated to comply with the planning and contact requirements of Social Services Law, Section 384 B.

Diligent Efforts

The general program that an agency must follow in order to be deemed to have exercised diligent efforts in working with parents was discussed in chapter 12, but there are some additional requirements with respect to incarcerated parents. Pursuant to Section 384 B (7)(f)(5), an agency must make suitable arrangements for an incarcerated parent to be visited by a child within a correctional facility, if such visitation is in the best interests of the child. The arrangements for the visitation should at least include the following:

1. The agency should provide transportation for the child to the correctional facility; and
2. The agency should provide or suggest social or rehabilitative services to resolve or correct problems other than the incarceration itself that impair the parent's ability to maintain contact with the child.

The factors an agency should look to in determining whether parent-child visitation is in the best interests of the child will vary depending upon how the child came into foster care. For example, if a child was placed because of a parent's incarceration, the agency should look to the parent's intent or ability to maintain a parent-child relationship and then establish a permanency planning goal and visitation plan. If, on the other hand, a child was already in placement when the parent was incarcerated, the agency should consider: (1) the permanency planning goal already in place; (2) the length of time the parent is to be incarcerated; (3) the parent-child relationship prior to the parent's incarceration; (4) the child's age and desire to visit; and (5) the nature of the parent's crime and the circumstances surrounding it.

If the parent has been placed in an out-of-state correctional facility, the agency is required to arrange parent-child visitation only if "reasonably feasible." See Social Services Law, Section 384 B (f)(2).

When Diligent Efforts Are Excused

Social Services Law, Section 384 B, provides for three situations in which diligent efforts are not required of the agency. Diligent efforts are not required if (1) the parent has failed for six months to keep the agency apprised of his/her location; (2) the parent has failed on more than one occasion while incarcerated to cooperate with the agency to plan for the child's future or to plan or arrange visits with the child; or (3) such efforts would be detrimental to the best interests of the child. The second and third situations are particularly applicable to incarcerated parents.

Planning

In the view of most lower courts, the practical effect of Chapter 911 was to disallow a finding of permanent neglect against an incarcerated parent based on a failure to plan. The courts reasoned that while Chapter 911 required incarcerated parents to comport with the planning and contact requirements of Social Services Law, Section 384 B, given the position of an incarcerated parent, it was extremely difficult to prove a failure to plan for the child.

However, in a recent case, In re Delores B. [533 N.Y.S. 2d 706 (Appellate Division, 1st Dept., 1988)], the Appellate Division held that a parent who was incarcerated for twenty-five years to life and who had offered a plan for his child that amounted to leaving the child in foster care until adulthood, had failed to realistically plan within the meaning of Section 384 B of the Social Services Law and had permanently neglected his child. The court reasoned that an "incarcerated parent's obligation is now the same as that of any other parent . . . if incarceration rendered a parent unable to plan for his or her child, then every incarcerated parent would have an automatic excuse for failing to meet his or her statutory obligation" [Id at 710]. The court also stressed the legislative intent of Section 384 B, that "children grow up in a normal family setting in a permanent home" [Id at 710].

In a strong dissent, Judge Carro argued that the majority opinion failed to adequately take into account the position of the incarcerated parent. Judge Carro argued that such consideration was necessary for two reasons. First, he asserted, the statute itself allows for a finding of permanent neglect based upon a failure to plan only when the parent is "physically and financially able to do so." See Social Services Law 384 B (7)(a). Judge Carro then noted that the legislative findings accompanying the addition of Chapter 911 specifically include the statement that "such ground of permanent neglect should recognize the special circumstances and need for assistance of an incarcerated parent to substantially and continually or repeatedly maintain contact with or plan for the future of his or her child" [Id at 713], citing the Legislative Findings and Declaration for 1983 Amendment, Subparagraph (iii).

Production of Prisoners in Court

If an incarcerated parent wishes to contest the action brought against him or her, it is the obligation of the attorneys involved, specifically the attorney for the parent and the attorney for the agency, to have the parent produced in court. This is accomplished by drafting an order to produce, which must be signed by the judge presiding over the proceeding (sidebar 19–1). Depending

---

Sidebar 19–1. Order to Produce the Incarcerated Parent in Court

FAMILY COURT OF THE STATE OF NEW YORK
COUNTY OF NEW YORK

_____ x

In the Matter of

[child's name],
A dependent child under the age of 14   Docket No.
years, to the custody of [agency],
alleged to be an abandoned child
pursuant to Section 384-b of the
Social Services Law.

_____ x

WHEREAS, [parent], the above-named respondent, is at present confined at [name and address of correctional facility], Inmate No. 000000000, under the supervision and control of the Department of Corrections;

WHEREAS, her attendance will be necessary as a respondent in the Family Court of the State of New York at 60 Lafayette Street, New York, New York, on the   day of   , 19   , in the above-captioned termination of parental rights proceeding; it is hereby

ORDERED that the warden of the institute or whomsoever shall have the supervision and control of [parent] shall deliver and produce said [parent] directly, in civilian clothes, to Part   of the Courthouse on the   day of   , 19   , at 9 a.m. of that day at the Courthouse located at 60 Lafayette Street, County of New York; and it is further

ORDERED that the warden of said correctional facility shall return [parent] to the institution on the same day of   , 19   .

ENTER:

_____

Family Court Judge

upon the county and court where the case is being heard, the order to produce will then be served either on the appropriate Sheriff's office or on the correctional facility to secure the production of the parent at the trial. For example, to produce a prisoner at Surrogate's Court, Nassau County, it is necessary to serve the Sheriff of Nassau County with the original and three certified copies of the order to produce. The sheriff will then deliver one certified copy to the appropriate correctional facility and produce the prisoner on the given date. In comparison, in Family Court, New York County, the signed order is served on the correctional facility where the prisoner is incarcerated. The correctional facility will then produce the prisoner on the given date.

20
The Rights of Foster Parents

Definition

A *foster parent* is any person with whom a child, in the care, custody, or guardianship of an authorized agency, is placed for temporary or long-term care.

Remuneration

Foster parents receive approximately $400 (1991 figure) each month per child plus an allowance for clothing and medical expenses.

Rights of Foster Parents to Review Removal

There is no question but that foster parents have obtained more rights in recent years. For example, previously, if an agency placed a child with foster parents, then decided to remove the child and place him/her in another foster home, the foster parent had to comply unless they invoked the jurisdiction of the supreme court and initiated a *habeas corpus* proceeding seeking court approval to retain physical custody of the child. The foster parents had the burden of proving that the agency abused its discretion in reaching the decision to remove the child from them. In short, the foster parents had no protection with respect to the removal of the foster child except to obtain a court order after serving and filing a writ of *habeas corpus* and a full court trial. See People ex rel. Marchese v. New York Foundling Hospital [Misc. 2d 234, 278 N.Y.S. 2d 512].

Of course, if the agency sought to regain custody of the child and could not do so by peaceful means, then the agency had to bring a *habeas corpus* proceeding in the supreme court. See In re Jewish Child Care Association of N.Y. [6 A.D. 2d 174, N.Y.S. 2d 335, 698 (2nd Dept., 1958)].

In reality, however, agencies sometimes simply had their caseworker pick up the child after school and return the child to the agency. This placed the foster parents in a vulnerable position. Some foster parents could not afford an attorney, and that was the end of it. Those who could afford an attorney found themselves in court litigation in which the law imposed upon them the burden to prove that the agency had abused its discretion—the "superior right of the authorized agency" theory. See In re Jewish Child Care Association of N.Y. [6 A.D. 2d 698, 174 N.Y.S. 2d 335, affirmed 5 N.Y. 2d 222, 183 N.Y.S. 2d 65].

Today, except for an emergency situation (such as physical abuse or neglect), an agency can no longer physically remove a foster child or initiate a *habeas corpus* proceeding seeking a court order removing the child from the foster home.

If an agency wishes to remove a foster child and place the child in another foster home, it must give the foster parents written notice of its intention to remove the child from the foster home, if the child has been placed with the commissioner of social services of the City of New York.

If the foster parents do not object to the removal of the child, they should be asked to sign a waiver of their rights to a hearing.

If the foster parents object to the removal of the child, they have the right to an agency conference and an independent review.

If the foster parents request an agency conference, it must be held within five days of the request. The purpose of the agency conference is to review the basis for the decision to remove the child. The foster parents and agency staff are the only people present.

The conference shall be conducted in accordance with casework principles and concepts that give the foster parents full opportunity to express their opposition to the removal of the child. A complete summary of the agency conference must be entered into the case records. If the agency abides by its decision to remove the child, the foster parents are entitled to an independent review.

The Independent Review

The independent review must be requested within ten days of the original notice of removal, and the review itself must be held within ten days of the request.

The independent review supervisor shall notify the commissioner of social services, the agency, and the foster parents of the time and place of the review hearing. The foster parents may be represented by counsel.

The independent review is conducted by the independent review officer (an employee of the Department of Social Services), in accordance with the concepts of due process in that:

1. The review shall be heard before an official on a supervisory level of the Department of Social Services who had no involvement with the decision to remove the child.

2. The foster parents may be represented by counsel and have the right to present witnesses and other evidence on their behalf.
3. The agency may be represented by counsel and may present testimony and evidence in support of its decision to remove the child.
4. The witnesses may be cross-examined.
5. The testimony must be either tape-recorded or a stenographic record must be kept and made available to the parties upon payment therefor.
6. The reviewer shall render a written decision:
   (a) within five days after the completion of the hearing,
   (b) setting forth the reasons and basis for the decision,
   (c) advising the foster parents to a state fair hearing if the decision is to remove the child.
7. The decision shall be mailed to the foster parents and their counsel and is binding only upon the agency.

If the decision is to remove the child, the child shall not be removed for at least three days. This three-day grace period will give the foster parents' attorney time to obtain a court order staying the decision to remove the child.

The foster parents may then request a state fair hearing.

The State Fair Hearing

Pursuant to Section 400 of the Social Services Law, the foster parents may appeal to the State Department of Social Services. Upon receipt of the appeal, the department shall review the case and shall give the foster parents an opportunity to a fair hearing thereon and, render its decision within thirty days. The decision is binding upon the agency, but it is not binding upon the foster parents in that the foster parents may review the decision by way of an Article 78 proceeding in the supreme court, or the foster parents may initiate an independent *habeas corpus* proceeding in the supreme court, which is the exclusive remedy of the foster parents. See In re Leonora M. v. Krauskopf [104 A.D. 2d 755, 480 N.Y.S. 2d 479 (1st. Dept., 1984)].

The Article 78 Proceeding

An Article 78 proceeding refers to Article 78 of the Civil Practice Laws and Rules. It permits the foster parents to serve and file a notice of petition and a petition invoking the jurisdiction of the supreme court whereby the court reviews the transcript of the administrative hearing and determines whether there is substantial evidence to sustain the administrative decision. See Gill v. Smith [382 N.Y.S. 2d 626 (Supreme Court, New York County, 1974)], wherein the court dismissed an Article 78 petition, stating "there was adequate and rational basis for the conclusions of the Department of Social Services."

The Habeas Corpus and/or Custody Proceedings

Foster parents' attorneys often seek an order to show cause with a stay, preventing the agency from removing the child. The proceeding is initiated by serving an order to show cause or a writ of *habeas corpus* and a petition upon the agency.

In the past, the courts permitted such a proceeding. See In re Mundie v. Nassau County Department of Social Services [387 N.Y.S. 2d 767 (Superior Court, Nassau County, 1976)]. However, more recent court decisions have clearly stated that neither a *habeas corpus* nor a custody action will be permitted to review the removal of a child from a foster home. See In re Leonora M. v. Krauskopf [104 A.D. 2d 75, 480 N.Y.S. 2d 479 (1st Dept., (1984)]; Ninesling v. Nassau County Department of Social Services [46 N.Y. 2d 382, 413 N.Y.S. 2d 626, 386 N.E. 2d 235 (1978)]. It has become well-settled law that an Article 78 proceeding is the exclusive procedure for a judicial review. The family court does not have jurisdiction to entertain an Article 78 proceeding. See In re Leonora M. v. Krauskopf, *supra*, and Ninesling v. Nassau County Department of Social Services, *supra*.

The Appellate Division, Second Department, spoke on this point in Katie B. v. Miriam H. [116 A.D. 2d 545, 497 N.Y.S. 2d 399 (2nd Dept., 1986)]. In Katie B., the foster parents brought a proceeding to determine custody of a minor child in the Family Court, Queens County. The family court entered an order dismissing the petition, and the foster parents appealed. The Appellate Division, Second Department, held that, *inter alia*, foster parents lack standing to initiate a custody proceeding. The Second Department stated that:

> We agree with the Family Court that petitioners, the foster parents, do not have standing to initiate a custody proceeding. Social Services Section 383(3) provides only that, "[f]oster parents who have had continuous care of a child for more than eighteen months . . . shall be permitted . . . to *intervene* in any proceeding involving . . . custody" [emphasis supplied]. Under that section, foster parents are also granted the rights to apply for adoption *if* the child involved is eligible. The Legislature determines the rights between the foster parent and child (see *Smith v. Organization of Foster Families*, 431 U.S. 816, 846, 97 S. Ct., 2094, 53 L. Ed.2d 14).

In a more recent case, Minella v. Amhrien [516 N.Y.S. 2d 494 (Appellate Division, 2nd Dept., 1987)], the Second Department held that:

> While foster parents who have had continuous care of an infant through an authorized agency for more than twelve months have the right to inter-

vene in any proceeding involving the custody of that infant (Social Services Law, Section [3]), they lack standing to initiate a custody proceeding (*Katie B. v. Miriam H.*, 116 A.D. 2d 545, 497 N.Y.S. 2d 399). . . . This is consistent with the well-settled principle that foster parents are essentially contract-service providers (see *Harris v. State of New York*, 117 A.D. 2d 298, 302, 502 N.Y.S. 2d 760) . . . Nor did the Family Court err in dismissing the application for *habeas corpus* relief. The petitioner's avowed purpose in bringing the writ was to regain custody of the infant. The procedure governing *habeas corpus* proceedings in Family Court is governed by the CPLR [citations omitted] absence any indication that the infant was in any way restrained in her liberty (CPLR 7002 [a]) or that "acceptable reasons of practicability or a necessity" required the petitioner to employ a *habeas corpus* proceeding [citation omitted], the determination of the Family Court is sustained.

The Appellate Division, First Department, in In re Leonara M. v. Krauskopf [104 Appellate Division 2d 755, 480 N.Y.S. 2d 479 (1st Dept., 1984)], and the Second Department in Katie B. v. Miriam H. [116 Appellate Division 2d 545, 497 N.Y.S. 2d 399 (2nd Dept., 1986)] and Minella v. Amhrein [516 N.Y.S. 2d 494 (Appellate Division 2nd Dept., (1987)] have clearly held that neither a *habeas corpus* nor a custody action will lie to review the removal of the child from a foster home. See also the Court of Appeals' pronouncement on this point, that upon the exhaustion of administrative remedies, the sole remedy for judicial review by foster parents is through an Article 78 proceeding as set forth in Nineśling v. Nassau County Department of Social Services [46 N.Y. 2d 382, 413 N.Y.S. 2d 626, 386 N.E. 2d 235 (1978)].

Since Nineśling was decided, foster parents have sought virtually every conceivable way to either stay the removal of the child from their home pending administrative review or to circumvent the administrative procedures entirely by seeking court review of the agency's decision to remove the child. At every turn, the foster parents have been denied in these attempts.

As set forth above, neither a *habeas corpus* nor a custody proceeding will lie to review the removal of a child from a foster home. See Minella v. Amhrein [131 A.D. 2d 578, 516 N.Y.S. 2d 494 (1987)]. See also In re Santos [(Family Court, Kings County, 1988) (Docket No. V6752/88, unreported)]. Judge Leah Ruth Marks recognized that she was compelled to deny the petitioner's custody petititions in the case of Florine Smith v. Aponte, et al. [(Family Court, New York County, 1987) (Docket No. V7928-31/87, unreported)]. Judge Marks held that:

The motion to dismiss these custody petitions is granted for all four children.

The law is clear that this Court has no jurisdiction to decide a custody case brought by a foster parent for custody of her foster children.

Other attempts to avoid the pronouncements of the Court of Appeals in Ninesling have met with similar results. A foster parent cannot bring a writ of *habeas corpus*, pursuant to Family Court Act, Section 651B, to say a removal. See Byers v. Kirby [67 A.D. 2d 727, 412 N.Y.S. 2d 661 (2nd Dept., 1979)]. Foster parents may not seek to reverse the removal of a child by court intervention (other than an Article 78 proceeding to review an adverse fair hearing decision). Foster parents may not use a Social Services Law, Section 392, proceeding to seek review of a decision to remove a child. See In re Kim W. [58 N.Y.S. 811, 459 N.Y.S. 2d 262 (1983)], reversing In re Walker [87 A.D. 2d 435, 452 N.Y.S. 2d 419 (1st Dept., 1982)].

Thus, the court decisions have been clear that the only court action that will lie to review a removal is an Article 78 proceeding after the exhaustion of administrative remedies by the foster parents and an adverse decision at a state fair hearing, pursuant to Social Services Law, Section 400. Neither a custody proceeding, a *habeas corpus* proceeding, nor a 392 proceeding will lie to review removal of a child from a foster parent by the agency.

Exhaustion of Administrative Remedies

Foster parents must exhaust their administrative remedies prior to seeking court review.

Social Services Law, Section 400, provides for the removal of children by the social services official, and also explicitly provides for appeal of such action by a fair hearing procedure, which in turn is judicially reviewable by an Article 78 proceeding. See In re Leonora M. v. Krauskopf [104 A.D. 2d 755, 480 N.Y.S. 2d 479 (1st Dept., 1984)]. It is well-settled law that an Article 78 proceeding is the exclusive procedure for a judicial review, and that the family court does not have jurisdiction to entertain an Article 78 proceeding. Neither a *habeas corpus* proceeding nor a custody action will lie to review the removal of a child from a foster home. See In re Leonora M. v. Krauskopf, *supra;* Ninesling v. Nassau County Department of Social Services [46 N.Y. 2d 382, 413 N.Y.S. 2d 626, 386 N.E. 2d 235 (1978)].

In Matter of Kim W. [58 N.Y. 2d 811, 459 N.Y.S. 2d 262, 445 N.E. 2d 644], the Court of Appeals reversed Matter of Walker [87 A.D. 2d 435, 452 N.Y.S. 2d 419 (1st Dept., 1982)] for the reasons stated by Mr. Justice Markewich in his dissent in the Appellate Division. In that dissent, Mr. Justice Markewich expressly held that an Article 78 proceeding, after the completion of the fair hearing, was the exclusive remedy available to foster parents, and that the court—in this case, the family court—had no power to order a fair hearing or to stay removal of the child pending such a fair hearing. See also Parker

v. Louise Wise Services and Commissioner of H.R.A. [(Superior Court, Richmond County, April 25, 1986) (Index No. SP8163/86, unreported decision, Sullivan, J.)].

Therefore, any court action taken by foster parents must be dismissed if the foster parents have failed to exhaust their administrative remedies. The exclusive remedy for a judicial review after a fair hearing is an Article 78 proceeding. See Byers v. Kirby [67 A.D. 2d 727, 412 N.Y.S. 2d 661 (Appellate Division, 2nd Dept., 1979)]. See also Matter of Walker [87 A.D. 2d 435 (Appellate Division, 1st Dept., 1982)], reversed *sub nom*, and Matter of Kim W. [58 N.Y. 2d 811 (1983)].

Foster Parent v. Natural Parent

Many times natural parents temporarily place a child with an agency. The child is then placed in a foster home. Later, the agency may come to feel that the natural parent is ready to assume custody of the child. But for whatever reason, foster parents sometimes refuse to return the children to the natural parents. In Wallace v. Lhotan [380 N.Y.S. 2d 250 (Appellate Division, 2nd Dept., 1976)], the court held that in a contest between a parent and a nonparent for the custody of a child, the parent's rights are paramount, absent a showing of unfitness or abandonment.

Other principles of law stated by the court in the Wallace case are:

1. the foster parents must make a serious attempt to encourage, not discourage, the improvement of relations between children in their charge and the natural mother who is trying to reestablish the bonds of family love.
2. the child's expression of desire to stay with the foster parents will not be binding on the court, and if the natural parent is a fit parent, the natural parent will regain custody.

The foster parent's obligation was spelled out in Matter of Spence-Chapin Adoption Services v. Polk [29 N.Y. 2d 196, 324 N.Y.S.2d 937], wherein the court stated:

To the ordinary fears in placing a child in foster care should not be added the concern that the better the foster care custodians, the greater the risk that they will assert, out of love and affection grown too deep, an inchoate right to adopt. The temporary parent substitute must keep his proper distance at all costs to himself.

See, however, Application of Kimberly P. [375 N.Y.S. 2d 791 (Family Court, Rensselaer County, 1975)], wherein the court held that a natural parent who had temporarily surrendered her child would not regain custody of the child, stating that the child's psychological well-being was more important to his welfare than his physical or material welfare. The court further stated:

> In a case such as this, the presumption that the parent's rights to custody as against non-parents is overcome by finding the parent not fit to have such custody, and the best interest of the child remains in her current foster home placement.

See also Robertson v. Robertson [388 N.Y.S. 2d 576 (Appellate Division, 4th Dept., 1976)], wherein the court stated that the rule to be applied now in custody cases involving a contest between a natural parent and a nonparent was restated by the Court of Appeals in Matter of Bennett v. Jeffreys [40 N.Y. 2d 543, 387 N.Y.S. 2d 821]. If extraordinary circumstances exist, then the test to be applied is the best interests of the child.

The court stated:

> If the court finds that extraordinary circumstances exist, then it may weigh the child's preferences, the desirability of keeping her with her siblings (*Matter of Ebert v. Ebert*, 38 N.Y.2d 700, 382 N.Y.S.2d 472, 346 N.E.2d 240), and the living conditions of the parties to determine what disposition of the case accords with the best interests of the child.

Foster Parents' Rights of Custody with Respect to Foster Children

The rights of foster parents arise mainly from statutory grants.

It is eminently clear from the New York statutes and the cases discussed herein that foster parents are entitled only to very limited rights with respect to the custody of foster children. See Application of Mavis M. [110 Misc. 2d 297, 441 N.Y.S. 2d 950 (Family Court, Kings County, 1981)].

The Court of Appeals rejected a claim to extend the rights of foster parents in the case of Ninesling v. Nassau County Department of Social Services [46 N.Y. 2d 382, 413, N.Y.S. 2d 626, 386 N.E. 2d 235 (1978)]. In Ninesling, the Supreme Court, Nassau County, upheld a determination of the Department of Social Services denying the application of foster parents to adopt a child placed in their care. The foster parents appealed. The Supreme Court, Appellate Division, affirmed, and the foster parents appealed by permission. The Court of Appeals held that, *inter alia*, foster parents could not be permitted to frustrate the adoptive plan devised by the child's legal custodian—and thereby seriously jeopardize the continued utilization of the foster-care program—by seeking to adopt the child themselves when notified, less than four months after they gained custody, of the intention of the department, as the child's legal custodian, to remove the child for permanent placement with prospective adoptive parents.

As stated in Ninesling:

> Prior to addressing the merits, we comment briefly upon the procedural posture in which this case comes before us. Pursuant to the statutory scheme created by the Legislature (Social Services Law, Section 400), a foster parent aggrieved by the determination of the Social Services Department to remove a child from a foster home may request an internal review of the determination within the Department in the form of a "fair hearing." Upon the exhaustion of this administrative remedy, an aggrieved foster parent may seek judicial review of the agency's determination in the Supreme Court through the vehicle of an Article 78 proceeding [citations omitted]. The administrative and judicial review afforded an aggrieved foster parent under this statutory scheme, although dormant until the removal of a child from a foster home by the Department of Social Services, provides a sufficient forum for the consideration of the interests of foster children and parents to satisfy the demand of due process. (See *Smith v. Organization of Foster Families*, 431 U.S. 816, 847–856, 97 S. Ct., 2094, 53 L.Et. 2d 14.)

The foster parents in Ninesling appeared, from all the testimony elicited at the hearings, to be of fine character, and they undoubtedly were sincere in their offer of love for the child. The agency, charged with the legal custody of the child, was equally zealous in its concern for the child. It maintained that the child should be placed in an adoptive home that it had selected for the child after detailed investigation, rather than remaining for purposes of adoption in the foster home, which, although it had been investigated by the agency prior to the temporary placement for foster care, was investigated solely for that limited purpose without consideration of its future suitability as an adoptive home.

The Court of Appeals went on to state:

> In balancing the parties' competing contentions, both of which are premised upon the best interest of the child, we believe the nature and function of foster care as a program, children who have not as yet been surrendered for adoption are placed by a state welfare commission or a recognized social agency with foster parents for "board of care." (See Goldstein, Freud and Solnit, *Beyond the Best Interests of the Child* [1973], pp. 23–26.) The foster parent–child relationship is a temporary relationship intended to provide the child with the benefits of a family setting, as an alternative to institutionalized care. (See Katz, *Legal Aspects of Foster Care*, 5 Fam. L.Q.283, 285.) As in the present case, foster parents generally enter into this compensatory arrangement with the express understanding that the placement is temporary, rather than permanent as in the case of adoption, and that the legal custodian, here respondent, retains the right to remove the child upon notice at any time.

The court also stated, taking into consideration the future viability of the foster-care program in determining the merits of the appeal, that the court did not abdicate its duty as *parens patriae* to determine custody based upon the best interests of the child. However, the court stated, a finding that the interests of a foster child would best be served by giving custody to foster parents requires more than a mere showing that the foster parents would provide a loving, adoptive home for the child. What must be demonstrated was stated as follows:

> [F]oster parents who seek to retain custody of a child, thereby frustrating the adoption plan devised by the Department of Social Services or an adoption agency, the body charged with legal custody of a surrendered child, must demonstrate not only that they would make suitable adoptive parents, but rather than they would provide a better adoptive home than that planned by the department or agency. In other words, to succeed, foster parents must bear the burden of showing a detrimental impact upon the child resulting from his or her removal from their foster care. (See *State Dept. of Public Assisstance v. Pettrey*, 141 W. Va., 719, 92 S.E.2d 917; see, also *Drummond v. Fulton County Dept. of Family and Children's Services* 237 Ga. 449, 228 S.E. 838, cert. den. 432 U.S. 905, 97 S. Ct. 2949, 53 L.Ed2d 1007.)
>
> As a practical matter, foster parents seeking to retain custody of a child will not, as a general rule, be capable of satisfying this burden. It must be noted that in a case such as the present, we are not reviewing an adoption proceeding in which the qualifications of prospective adoptive parents are at issue. As a result, foster parents who seek to retain custody of a foster child have no medium in which to demonstrate that they would provide a better adoptive home than the, as yet undetermined parents whom the Department of Social Services or an adoptive agency would eventually select to adopt the foster child.

The role of the foster parents and their concomitant rights were expressed as follows:

> In sum, the function served by foster parents plays a vital role in custodial child care. That role is, however, by express agreement a limited and temporary one, the qualifications for which differ markedly from those deemed necessary for permanent placement. To permit foster parents to frustrate the adoptive plan devised by a child's legal custodian, here the Department of Social Services, would seriously jeopardize the continued utilization of the State foster care program. Apart from the detrimental impact which reluctance of foster parents to part with children in their care would have on the foster care program, it would appear virtually impossible, as a practical matter, for foster parents in a proceeding to retain custody of a child to demonstrate that a foster child's best interest dictates that he or she remain in their care, inasmuch as the adoptive plan formulated by the child's legal custodian remains as yet unrealized due solely to the resistance of the foster parents.

The U.S. Supreme Court exhaustively discussed the foster-care system and the nature of the rights of foster parents in Smith v. Organization of Foster Families [431 U.S. 816, 97 S. Ct. 2094, 53 L.Ed. 2d 14 (1977)]. The Supreme Court stated that with respect to the care and custody of foster children, foster parents are not entitled to the same degree of constitutional protection as biological parents are afforded with respect to their natural children. The Court stated that

> where, as here, the claimed interest derived from a knowingly assumed contractual relation with the State, it is appropriate to ascertain from state law the expectations and entitlement of the parties. In this case, the limited recognition accorded to the foster family by the New York statutes and the contracts executed by the foster parents argue against any but the most limited constitutional "liberty" in the foster family.

The Supreme Court reasoned that the foster parents' status as foster parents was significantly different from the status of natural parents, even though foster parents can develop strong emotional ties with their foster children. The status of foster parents is grounded in a "knowingly assumed contractual relationship with the State," whereas the status of natural parents is based upon "intrinsic human rights." See Smith v. Organization of Foster Families, *supra* [at 845, 97 S. Ct. 2110].

The distinctive feature of foster care, as noted by the Supreme Court, is that the child is in a family for a planned period of time that is to be either temporary or extended. It observed that New York views foster care as a temporary transitional situation leading to, *inter alia*, adoption and the establishment of a new permanent home. The court spoke with approval of the lower court ruling that foster parents do not have a justified expectation that their status as foster parents will be continued. Therefore, upon this basis, the Supreme Court concluded that foster parents are entitled to only the most limited rights as set forth in New York State Law [*supra* at 847, 97 S. Ct. at 2110].

Mr. Justice Stewart, in a concurring opinion that was joined in by two other justices, set forth the foster parents' situation as follows:

> The foster parent–foster child relationship involved in this litagation is, of course, wholly a creation of the State. New York law defines the circumstances under which a child may be placed in foster care, prescribes the obligations of the foster parents and provides for the removal of the child from the foster home "in [the] discretion" of the agency with custody of the child. N.Y. Soc. Serv. Law, Section 383 (2). (McKinney 1976). The agency compensates the foster parents and reserves in its contracts the authority to decide as it sees fit whether and when a child shall be returned to his natural family or placed elsewhere. See Part 1A of the court opinion, ante [97 S.Ct.] at 2099–2102. Were it not for the system

of foster care that the State maintains the relationship for which constitutional protection is asserted would not even exist. 431 U.S. at 856, 97 S. Ct. at 2116.

The Court of Appeals subsequently decided the case of O'Rourke v. Kirby [54 N.Y. 2d 8, 444 N.Y.S. 2d 566, N.E. 2d 85 (1981)], wherein the foster mother appealed from an order of the Supreme Court, Appellate Division, that had affirmed a judgment of the Supreme Court, Suffolk County, dismissing a petition to compel a local agency to approve her application to adopt her foster child and that confirmed a determination of a state agency affirming a determination of a local agency to remove the child from the foster mother's home. The Court of Appeals held that the denial of consent to adopt by the local agency was not arbitrary and capricious, and that the state agency's decision to remove the child was not unsupported by substantial evidence. The Court stated that the appropriate standard is the usual Article 78 standard of review, and that a *de novo* judicial review of the "best interests of the child" is not required.

In O'Rourke, the Court of Appeals stated that:

> Although the agency recognized that Stephanie would suffer some amount of trauma by her removal, it also determined that the trauma would be of short duration and eased by supportive services. Thus, it appears that the agency, having due regard for appellant's entitlement to a preference and first consideration, considered appellant not to be a suitable adoptive parent, much less a better adoptive parent than other potential adoptive resources. We cannot say, on this record, that the local agency failed in its responsibility to act in Stephanie's best interests or in its duty to accord appellant a preference and first consideration.

While the court noted that at all times the foster mother had given the child love, warmth, and considerate care, and that her desire to adopt the child was obviously sincere, the legal qualifications required by the courts of prospective adoptive parents differ from those required of foster parents, the latter committing themselves only to temporary care of the child.

Therefore, foster parents received a setback when the Court of Appeals decided the case of Ninesling, *supra*. The Court of Appeals refused to extend the rights of foster parents, and Ninesling and its progeny are the present state of the law regarding the rights of foster parents to custody of their foster children.

Stay of Removal

The Court of Appeals in Ninesling v. Nassau County Department of Social Services [46 N.Y. 2d 382, 413 N.Y.S. 2d 626] stated that the issuance of a stay "runs counter to the scheme adopted by the legislature."

As stated in Matter of Parker v. Louise Wise Services (Supreme Court, Richmond County, unreported decision), decided by Justice Sullivan on April 25, 1986:

> In *Ninesling,* the foster parents, in a situation similar to that in which the petitioners herein find themselves, instituted the habeas corpus proceeding for the purpose of obtaining a stay preventing the removal of the foster child from their home. Special Term granted this stay pending the "Fair Hearing."
>
> The Court of Appeals held in effect that the statutory scheme created by the Legislature for the review of actions by an agency or a local Social Services official is the executive remedy available. Judge Jason at 46 N.Y. 2d 386–387 specifically stated:
>
>> The availability of habeas corpus *as a form of injunctive relief,* to forestall the removal of a child from the foster home until after a "Fair Hearing" and Judicial review of the agency's determination runs counter to the scheme adopted by the Legislature. [emphasis added].
>>
>> If there were any questions that this Court is without power to enjoin the respondents pending the completion of the "Fair Hearing," it was removed by the case of *Matter of Walker,* 87 A.D. 2d 435 (1st Dept. 1982) reversed sub nom *Matter of Kim W.,* 58 N.Y. 2d 811 (1983). In that case, the Court of Appeals reversed the First Department for the reasons stated by Justice Markewich in his dissent in the Appellate Division. In that dissent, Justice Markowich expressly held that an Article 78 proceeding after the completion of the "Fair Hearing" was the exclusive remedy available to foster parents and the Court had no power to order a "Fair Hearing" or stay removal of the child pending such a "Fair Hearing."

Therefore, a "fair hearing" is a postremoval hearing, and a stay "runs counter to the scheme adopted by the Legislature." See Ninesling, *supra,* Matter of Kim W. [58 N.Y. 2d 811 (1983)]; and Matter of Parker v. Louise Wise Services, *supra.*

21

The Role of the Law Guardian in Termination-of-Parental-Rights Proceedings and Foster-Care Review Hearings

I t is difficult to conceive of more important proceedings than termination-of-parental-rights proceedings and foster-care review hearings. No other proceedings affect the life of a little child as much. Abandonment and permanent neglect proceedings are commenced for the express purpose of terminating parental rights and thereby freeing the foster child for adoption. Foster-care review hearings are held at least every twenty-four months, and the judge of the family court presiding can and often does direct the authorized agency to commence proceedings to free the child for adoption. The agency has a choice of commencing either an abandonment proceeding or a permanent neglect proceeding, pursuant to Section 384 B of the Social Services Law, which became effective January 1, 1977. Whichever proceeding is involved, the authorized agency will be represented by counsel; the natural parents will have an attorney; and if their interests are adverse, each natural parent will have his or her own attorney. The foster parents will also be represented by counsel, and the commissioner of social services will have his legal representative present in either the corporation counsel or county attorney.

But who will represent the child? Until recently, in permanent neglect and abandonment proceedings, sometimes the child was represented by an attorney—the law guardian—and sometimes he/she wasn't.

Not until 1976 did the Court of Appeals mandate legal representation of the foster child in permanent neglect proceedings. In the case of In re Orlando F. [40 N.Y. 2d 103, 386, N.Y.S. 2d 64 (1976)], the Court of Appeals stated:

> This issue aside, we turn to another important fact, the appointment of a Law Guardian. Here, a Law Guardian was, in fact, appointed but permitted to withdraw at the commencement of the hearing. This, too, without even a replacement, was an abuse of discretion. Our courts have

been sensitive to the expanding rights of children, including the right to be heard (See, e.g., *Matter of Ceclia R.*, 36 N.Y. 2d 317; see also, *Matter of Michael C.*, 50 A. D. 2d 757) and, only recently, the importance of having the child represented by a Law Guardian was emphasized "[s]ince the child cannot obviously speak for herself" (*Matter of Ray A.M.*, 37 N.Y. 2d 819, *supra* at p.624). The usual situation in a permanent neglect proceeding pits the natural parent, with his or her own special interest at stake, against an agency who seeks termination of parental rights so that the child might ultimately be adopted. These parties may well believe that the "best interest" of the child will be served by a "legal victory" on their part. . . .

Consequently, although no statute currently so provides, we hold that, in the absence of the most extraordinary of circumstances, at the moment difficult to conceptualize, the Family Court should direct the appointment of a Law Guardian in permanent neglect cases to protect and represent the rights and interests of the child in controversy.

Legal representation has also been recognized in an abandonment proceeding. In In re Anonymous (St. Christopher's Home) [No. 362 dated September 14, 1976, Surrogate's Court, Nassau County], upon motion by the counsel for the agency, the surrogate appointed a law guardian to protect the interests of the infant in an abandonment proceeding commenced by the agency. The court stated:

> In this abandonment proceeding the petitioning agency requests the appointment of a Guardian ad litem to represent and protect the interest of the infant, relying upon the Court of Appeals holding in *Matter of Orlando F.*, (40 N.Y. 2d 103), where the importance of appointing a Guardian ad litem for a child in a neglect proceeding pursuant to Article 6 of the Family Court Act was emphasized in order to insure that the interests of the child not be overshadowed by the legal stratagems of the natural parent and the guardianship agency in their contest for the custody of the child.
>
> In order to insure the primacy of the child's interest in this contest between his natural mother and the custodial agency, the court is compelled to apply the holding in the *Orlando F.* decision to this abandonment proceeding and direct the immediate appointment of a Guardian ad litem for the infant.

While the trend is to expand legal representation to the child, no law guardian is appointed to protect the rights of the child in a *habeas corpus* proceeding in the supreme court. It is the opinion of this writer that as soon as this issue of legal representation reaches the appellate courts, such representation in *habeas corpus* proceedings will be mandated. There is no logical reason to deny legal representation to a child in a *habeas corpus* proceeding since the basic issue— custody of the child—is present in abandonment, permanent neglect, and *habeas corpus* proceedings.

The Law Guardian

Once appointed, the law guardian has a choice of:

1. taking a passive role, being present at the hearing, asking a few questions on cross-examination, then taking no position at the end of the hearing; or
2. taking an active, affirmative role.

The time should long be gone where the law guardian merely attends the hearing and "plays it by the seat of his pants."

The law guardian must protect the interests of the child and speak for the child because so many times the child cannot speak for himself or herself. For a case discussing the role of the law guardian, see In re Apel [409 N.Y.S. 2d 928 (Family Court, Ulster County, 1978)], wherein it was suggested that the law guardian should initially be neutral, forming an opinion only after some testimony unfolds. The court stated that the law guardian serves in a quasi-judicial capacity and should aid the court in a proper decision.

Preparation for the Hearing

By law, the authorized agency must keep detailed case records concerning the child and the natural and foster parents. These case records contain information relating to the frequency of contact between natural parents and child, the psychological and medical history of the natural parents and the child, and the plan, if any, of the natural parents to have the child returned home. There will also be information relating to the foster parents and whether they are suitable adoptive parents and whether they wish to adopt.

The law guardian should contact the attorney for the agency and request an opportunity to review the entire case records. The case records may be reviewed either at the agency's attorney's office, the courthouse, or at the agency itself. The law guardian should also request photocopies of pertinent parts of the case records.

If these requests are denied, the cases indicate that a notice of discovery and inspection should be served upon the attorney for the agency. If the notice of discovery and inspection is found objectionable, the attorney for the agency must then make a motion for a protective order. While there does not appear to be any appellate court decision on this point, the trilogy of In re Carla L., Sarah R., and Irene F. and Lisa F. [45 A.D. 2d 375, 357 N.Y.S. 2d 987 (Appellate Division, 1st Dept., 1974)] should be persuasive in allowing the law guardian to review and photocopy the agency case records, as the child's rights should be equal to those of the natural parents and at least those of the foster parents.

In Carla L., the Appellate Division permitted disclosure of the agency case records by the attorney for the natural parents in a 392 foster-care review proceeding and set forth the following procedure to be followed:

1. The attorney for the natural parent should serve a notice of disclosure.

2. The agency should permit such discovery and inspection by the attorney for the natural parent of the agency's records at the agency's office or at the family court and under supervision.

3. As to those records to which the agency seeks protections, the agency must furnish counsel for the natural parents with a list stating generally the nature of the materials withheld. If counsel cannot agree with regard to the materials withheld, then

4. The agency shall move for a protective order pursuant to C.P.L.R. 3103 with the contested matters to be viewed by the family court *in camera.*

The procedure for inspection by a foster parent of the case records kept by the agency is somewhat more limited. In Irene F. and Lisa F., the Appellate Division held that disclosure by a foster parent may be had:

1. only upon a proper showing of necessity,

2. coupled with *in camera* viewing by the family court, and

3. initial disclosure by way of stipulation may be had, but only where court approval is obtained.

The court in Irene F. and Lisa F. concluded: "Thus, the Family Court is of necessity involved *ab initio* with the disclosure if sought by a foster parent." This distinction appears to be unnecessary and involves an already overburdened court in pretrial discovery. Legislative action is needed to codify the scope, extent, and procedures for pretrial disclosure.

It is the writer's opinion that the attorney for the natural parents, and the law guardian, should have the same rights with respect to reviewing and photocopying the case records. If the "best interests of the child" is the pivotal issue in a custody proceeding, then the law guardian should be permitted total and free access to the agency case records, unless a portion of the records are confidential or otherwise privileged and are determined to be so by the court pursuant to a motion for protective order made by the attorney for the agency.

In short, the law guardian should be fully familiar with the agency's records in order to actively and intelligently participate in the hearing, in order to aid the court in arriving at a decision that will be in the best interests of the child.

The Interview with the Child

The a law guardian should interview the foster child in person especially if the child is articulate and can express his/her preference. The law guardian,

guardian, however, should not simply mouth the wishes of the child, but he/she should weigh all facts and circumstances in arriving at a recommendation of the court. It is suggested that the law guardian contact the attorney for the agency who will request the caseworker to bring the child or children to the office of the law guardian. In one case, the law guardian insisted upon visiting the children in the foster home to observe firsthand the living conditions of the children. It would also be advisable for the law guardian to speak to the attorneys for all parties to ascertain their positions.

The Hearing

Whether the hearing is a 392 foster-care review, an abandonment hearing, or a permanent neglect proceeding, the law guardian should actively participate and cross-examine the witnesses in order to make an intelligent recommendation and also as an aid to the court. There should be a plenary and full hearing. A stipulation of facts agreed to by the attorneys for the parties excluding the law guardian will not be sufficient as to a fact-finding hearing, and the court will schedule a new hearing. See In re Amy S. [390 N.Y.S. 2d 530 (Family Court, Westchester County, 1976)].

If the child is old enough to be interviewed, the law guardian should strongly recommend that the judge speak with the child. The interview should be on the record. See Ehlrich v. Ressner [391 N.Y.S. 2d 152 (Appellate Division, 2nd Dept. 1977)]. Section 384 B of the Social Services Law specifically provides that where the child is over fourteen years of age, the court may, in its discretion, consider the wishes of the child in determining whether the best interests of the child would be promoted by freeing the child for adoption.

At the conclusion of the hearing, the law guardian should be prepared to give his recommendation to the court. The recommendation could include a motion by the law guardian for additional fact finding. In one case the motion was granted the court requesting counsel to employ the necessary effort for the "painstaking fact finding" required to determine the issues of abandonment. See In re Amy S. [390 N.Y.S. 2d, 530 (Family Court, Westchester County, 1976)].

In In re Jonathan D., the Appellate Division criticized the family court judge for refusing to permit the law guardian to submit his report. The court stated in this permanent neglect proceeding: "Essential to any determination as to the child's best interest is a consideration of the Law Guardian's Report."

In summary, if the law guardian reviews the case records, interviews the child, and takes an active role at the hearing, the foster child will at last have a voice in his/her own future.

22

The Role of the Social Worker in Foster-Care Proceedings

S ocial workers must not only perform the work for which they have been trained—that is, social work—but must also be familiar with the many and variable court proceedings involving foster children.

Court Report

In foster-care proceedings, the caseworker should appear in court with at least a two-page written court report outlining the following:

1. The name of the child and the date of birth of the child;
2. The name of the natural parents of the child and their address;
3. The names of the foster parents;
4. When and how the child came into foster care, outlining the facts and circumstances connected with the placement;
5. An outline of the presenting problems faced by the natural parent that caused the child to be placed in foster care;
6. The existing problems of the natural parent;
7. The diligent efforts the caseworker used to help ameliorate those problems;
8. A description of the relationship between the natural parents and the child, including the degree of bonding, visitation, and ability to resume care;
9. A background of the foster parents and whether they wish to adopt, if appropriate;
10. A detailed description of the child, including any medical, psychological, or emotional problems. If old enough, the school history of the child and how the child has been assimilated into the foster home and into the community;
11. If there are any medical or psychological problems, a description of these problems and exhibits of any evaluations; and

12. A recommendation as to what is in the best interests of the child—that is, either continued foster care with a view to returning the child to a natural or to a relative, or adoption and the basis for that opinion.

These court reports serve a number of purposes. They provide a review of the facts for the caseworker and a ready and detailed source of information to the judge so that the judge may make an informed finding and determination in a short period of time without sacrificing thoroughness for quickness. The judges are very happy to see thorough reports, as they can then focus on any issues that need to be explored. These reports should be given to the law guardian, who may be either an attorney associated with Lawyers for Children of the Legal Aid Society, or a court-appointed special advocate, commonly known as CASA. Because there are so many 392 review hearings and because many of them are uncontested, the social worker will more times than not appear without an attorney. This is all the more reason that a court report should be in writing and presented to the law guardian, the corporation counsel, the court, and the attorney for the natural parents. All the parties are represented, and if the parent cannot afford an attorney, one is provided free of charge from the 18(B) panel. Although a social worker representing a voluntary agency may not have an agency attorney present, Child Welfare Administration (CWA) has an attorney at all the 392 proceedings from the office of corporation counsel. He/she in effect is representing CWA and indirectly the agency. It is, therefore, important for the social worker to convince the attorney representing CWA that the social worker's position is correct and to urge him/her to put forth that position to the court. Many times the social worker will not see the attorney for CWA until minutes before the case is called, or for the first time in court. If the social worker hands the CWA attorney a two-page court report, he/she can review the report and present the social worker's position to the court with little fear that that position will be misunderstood. Almost universally, the court will accept the report as an exhibit and place it in the court file.

The caseworker must aid the attorney for the agency in drafting a petition to terminate parental rights, especially a petition alleging permanent neglect. The form in sidebar 22–1, completed by the caseworker, will prove valuable to the attorney and will serve as a good preparation for the hearing.

Court Action Form

The caseworker will be involved in many different types of court proceedings, including but not limited to:

1. 358 A hearings
2. 392 proceedings
3. Child abuse proceedings

Sidebar 22–1. Information Sheet
for Termination Proceedings

Please complete one information sheet for each child. In the event we are dealing with siblings or with children of a common parent or parents, and the information for the children is the same as that for the first child, simply write "same." Do not leave any blanks to any questions. If a question is not applicable to the instant case, indicate by "n/a."

1. The name of the infant as it appears on the birth certificate:

   _____

2. Date of birth of the infant:

   _____

3. The name and location of the hospital at which the infant was born (if not born in hospital, indicate the address at which the infant was born):

   _____

4. The name of the natural mother as it appears on the birth certificate of the infant plus all a/k/a's of the mother:

   _____

5. Current address of the natural mother (if current address is unknown, give the last known address of the natural mother, indicating such by l/k/a):

   _____

6. Can the natural mother be served personally?

   _____

7. Is a diligent search for the natural mother required?

   _____

8. If a diligent search is required, was one requested, and on what date?

   _____

9. Name of the father of the infant, as it appears on the birth certificate (if the name of the father does not appear on the birth certificate, the name of the father as the case records indicate), and all a/k/a's of the father:

   _____

10. The current address of the father (if the current address is unknown, the last known address of the father, indicating such by l/k/a):

_____

11. Is a diligent search required for the father of the infant?

_____

12. If a diligent search is required, was one requested and on what date?

_____

13. Were the mother and father married? When?

_____

14. If the mother and father were not married: a. Was the father named on the birth certificate? b. Did the father ever support or live with the mother and child? c. Did the father ever sign a paternity statement? d. Was the father ever named by the mother in a sworn statement as the father? e. Was the alleged father ever adjudged as the father by the court? f. Did the father ever acknowledge paternity and file a notice in the central registry in Albany?

a. _____

b. _____

c. _____

d. _____

e. _____

f. _____

15. The date on which the child was placed with the Bureau of Child Welfare:

_____

16. The date on which the child was placed with the agency (if the dates of #15 and #16 are different, briefly explain):

_____

17. Was the child voluntarily committed?

_____

18. If the child was voluntarily committed, the date on which the commitment was made:

_____

19. The name of the person who committed the infant and the relation of that person to the infant, if any relation exists:

_____

20. Was the infant court-placed?

_____

   a. If the infant was court-placed, the date of placement, the name of the court (indicating the county of the court), and the docket number of the court proceeding:

_____

   b. Was there a finding of abuse? (If so, indicate by the mother, the father, or both.)

_____

   c. Was there a finding of neglect? (If so, indicate by the mother, the father, or both.)

_____

   d. Briefly detail the circumstances surrounding the placement:

_____

21. If the parents' rights to the child are sought to be terminated on the grounds of permanent neglect,

   a. Indicate if it is permanent neglect by the mother, the father, or both:

_____

   b. List in detail in the space provided on this information sheet the diligent efforts used by the agency with the mother, the father, or both depending on the circumstances of the case (actually outline the diligent efforts; do not state "refer to . . .")[a]

_____

   c. List the diligent efforts used by the caserworker to solve or ameliorate the problems. For example: actually taking the mother to welfare or to counseling, making phone calls, arranging visitation, etc. Outline in detail what was done using dates, places, etc.

---

[a]N.B. It is not sufficient to refer to dictation and chronology. Please list in detail the problems faced by the parent that were the barriers to discharge of the child to the parent. For example, some problem areas center on finances, housing, drug or alcohol addiction, living with an abusive paramour, etc.

Also give the response: for example, the caseworker offered to drive the mother to welfare, but mother refused the offer. Or mother went to counseling but quit after second session, etc. Use the first sheet for problems, second sheet for diligent efforts, and third sheet for parents' response.

Problems

Diligent Efforts

Parents' Response

22. If the parents' rights are sought to be terminated on the ground of abandonment,

_____

    a.   Indicate whether the mother, the father, or both has abandoned the infant:

_____

    b.   List the last three visits with the infant by the mother, the father, or both, depending upon the circumstances in the present case, including dates, places, and who requested the visit:

_____

    c.   Indicate the last communication the mother, the father, or both had with the petitioning agency, and the circumstances related thereto:

_____

    d.   List the last communication that the mother, the father, or both had with the infant, and state the circumstances related thereto:

_____

23. Is the infant presently in a foster home?

_____

24. In what county do the foster parents reside?

_____

25. Does the child wish to be adopted?

_____

26. Do the foster parents wish to adopt the infant?

_____

27. Attach to the information sheet a copy of:

    a.   The child's birth certificate (if not yet a part of the case records, request a copy from the Bureau of Vital Statistics);

    b.   The latest W853 and W853 C;

    c.   The chronology;

    d.   The death certificate, if applicable;

    e.   A copy of the diligent search request, if necessary.

28. The caseworkers' names and home office:

_____

a. For the natural family:

_____

b. For the infant and the foster family:

_____

29. The date this form was completed.

_____

4. Extension-of-placement proceedings
5. Termination-of-parental-rights proceedings, including
    a. abandonment
    b. permanent neglect
    c. mental illness
    d. mental retardation
    e. severe or repeated abuse.

Many times caseworkers are asked to go to court without an attorney on extension-of-placement proceedings and 392 proceedings. Many times directives and court orders are made by the court that the caseworker must relay to the supervisor in order for the agency to appropriately abide by the court directives and orders. In order to avoid misunderstanding and improper communication of the court directives to superiors for agency action, the court action form (see sidebar 22–2) will be very useful in providing necessary information to other caseworkers and supervisors in order to understand the court directives and properly abide by the same. This court action form is the one prepared by this writer for the agencies that he represents. The court action form should be completed during the court proceeding or immediately thereafter. It is suggested that the court action form be given to the supervisor to make sure that the court directives, if any, are followed; that the adjourned date, if any, is noted in the diary; and that a caseworker is assigned to appear at the next court date.

Testimony by the Caseworker

Because of frequent turnovers in the foster-care field, the caseworker who testifies in the hearing may not have complete personal knowledge of all of the facts that have been recorded in the case records. It is important, however,

Sidebar 22-2. Court Action Form

This form should be attached to the legal section of the case record. Another copy of the form should be given to your supervisor immediately following the court appearance.

Case Name: _____

Case Number (if known): _____

Type of Proceeding (check one):

_____ Neglect _____ Abuse _____ Extension/Placement

_____ 392 _____ TPR _____ Custody _____ Other (please

specify) _____

Date of Court Appearance: _____

Court Name: _____

Docket Number: _____

Presiding Judge: _____

Attorneys Appearing:

_____

_____

_____

_____

_____

Social Workers Appearing:

_____

_____

_____

1. As a result of this court proceeding, is/are there any action(s) to be undertaken by _____ ? _____ Yes _____ No

2. If yes, please explain what action(s) must be taken.

   (e.g., judge ordered termination of parental rights within ninety days; judge ordered homemaker to be provided for natural mother; judge ordered visitation to be increased to twice monthly rather than once a month; judge ordered that natural mother receive carfare for visits; judge ordered psychological evaluations; judge ordered trial discharge; judge ordered that a relative be evaluated as resource):

_____

_____

_____

_____

_____

_____

_____

_____

_____

_____

_____

Adjourned Date: _____

Copy Received:

_____

Case Supervisor

---

to have the case records of the infant or infants admitted into evidence so that the case records themselves will be an exhibit and will be evidence of the facts contained therein. See Leon R.R. [421 N.Y.S. 2d 863].

Once the records are in evidence, the caseworker can testify from said records concerning events that he/she did not observe or that occurred prior to his/her employment at the agency.

The case supervisor should identify the case records and testify that:

1. It is the regular course of the agency's business to keep records;
2. The records of the infant who is the subject matter of the proceeding were made in the regular course of business;

3. The person making the entries had a duty to report;

4. The entries contained in the records were made contemporaneously with the events described therein; and

5. The records were kept under the supervision and control of the witnesses testifying.

With this foundation laid, the relevant case records will be accepted into evidence, and the court may consider the case records in deciding the case.

As stated above, once the records are introduced into evidence, the caseworker may testify to events recorded in the records, even though the caseworker had no personal knowledge of such events.

It is, of course, preferable for the caseworker to have personal contact with the natural parents, the foster parents, and the infant. The caseworker should know the case records thoroughly and be prepared to testify and have knowledge of the following:

1. The manner in which the child came into foster care:
   a. by voluntary placement;
   b. by abuse or neglect and court remanded;
   c. by juvenile delinquency;
   d. by need for supervision.

2. The date the child came into foster care, and the date he/she was placed with the particular agency, and the date he/she was placed in a particular foster home.

3. The names and background of the natural parents.

4. The efforts made by the caseworker to work with the natural parents and to help reunite the natural parents and the child. The caseworker should be prepared to enumerate the specific diligent efforts utilized by caseworkers, such as
   a. encouraging visitation between parents and child;
   b. facilitating visition between parent and child by supplying either transportation or carfare or, if necessary, by transporting the child to the parents' home;
   c. helping the parents with either a physical or psychological problem by referring the parents to the appropriate facility;
   d. helping the parents with an alcohol or drug problem;
   e. helping the parents locate more appropriate housing;
   f. helping the parents with welfare or Social Security.

5. All visits made by the natural parents and whether the visitations were meaningful; observations made at the visitations.

6. Whether the caseworker helped the natural parents formulate a plan to have the child returned to the parents and, if so, what the plan was and what efforts were made by the parents to effectuate the plan.

7. Details concerning the foster parents, such as:

    a. housing facilities;

    b. the ages and occupations of the foster family;

    c. any observations of interactions between the foster parents and the child;

    d. whether the foster parents are considered a resource to adopt the child;

    e. whether the foster parents wish to adopt the child;

    f. whether the foster child wishes to be adopted by the foster parents.

8. With respect to the child, the caseworker must be prepared to show:

    a. the birth date of the child;

    b. when the child was put into placement;

    c. if the child has any physical or mental problems;

    d. whether the child had any siblings;

    e. the progress made by the child in school and in the foster home;

    f. the wishes of the child.

If the caseworker has a working knowledge of the above facts, he/she should make a convincing witness and certainly will be an aid to the court. As stated above, once the case records are in evidence, the caseworker may refer to them for specific factual items—no caseworker is expected to know all that is contained in the records without referring to them.

Finally and perhaps most important, the caseworker should listen to the questions asked by the attorney, whether on direct examination or cross-examination. Many times a caseworker, not fully understanding a question, will go off on a tangent. This may prove embarrassing when the judge must interrupt the testimony and remind the witness to "please answer the question." If the question is listened to carefully and a distinct, clear answer is given, the caseworker will have done his/her job. If the attorney wishes further information, the attorney will ask further questions. If a question is not clear, the caseworker should not attempt to answer the question, which may be ambiguous, but should simply state that the question is not clear and request of the judge that the attorney who asked the question rephrase the question.

Part V
The Adoption

23
The Adoption

Once a child has been freed for adoption, whether by (1) written surrender; (2) court order based upon abandonment, pursuant to Section 384 B the Social Services Law; (3) court order based upon permanent neglect, pursuant to Article 6 of the Family Court Act and Section 384 B of the Social Services Law; (4) court order based upon abandonment, pursuant to Section 111 of the Domestic Relations Law; (5) court order based upon severe and repeated abuse, pursuant to Section 384 B of the Social Services Law; or (6) court order based on the parent's mental illness or mental retardation, pursuant to Section 384 B of the Social Services Law, the child may be adopted either in the family court or the surrogate's court, pursuant to Section 111 of the Domestic Relations Law.

Definition

Adoption is the legal proceeding whereby an adult person takes another adult or minor person into the relation of child and thereby acquires the rights and incurs the responsibilities of parent with respect to said adult or minor (Section 110 of the Domestic Relations Law). The primary purpose of adoption is to promote the welfare of the child. See In re Adoption of E.W.C. [389 N.Y.S. 2d 743 (Surrogate's Court, Nassau County, 1976)].

Adoption was unknown at common law and exists in New York only by virtue of statute (Section 110 of the Domestic Relations Law). Because adoption is statutory and in derogation of the common law, the statutes relating to adoption must be strictly construed. Matter of Paul P. [63 N.Y.S. 2d 233, 481 N.Y.S. 2d 652, 471 N.E. 2d 424 (1985)] and Adams v. Nadel [124 N.Y.S. 2d 427 (Superior Court, Kings County, 1953)].

An adult unmarried person may adopt, and adult married persons may adopt, but a married person cannot adopt unless his or her spouse joins in the adoption. The person adopted may be a stranger or blood relative. See Stevens v. Halstead [181 A.D. 198, 168 N.Y.S. 142 (Appellate Division, 2nd Dept., 1917)].

Independent Adoption

If the adoptive parents live in New York State, the adoption takes place in the county where the adoptive parents reside. However, in Matter of Adoption of E.W.C. [389 N.Y.S. 2d 743 (Surrogate's Court, Nassau County, 1976)], Surrogate Bennett held that in the light of the purposes to be served by the adoption statute, the term *reside* must be held to refer merely by venue and not to jurisdiction.

Foster-Care Agency Adoption

In an agency adoption, the adoption takes place in the county where the adoptive parents reside.

If the adoptive parents reside outside of New York State, then the adoption takes place either in the family court or the surrogate's court where the agency has its principal office (see Section 113 of the Domestic Relations Law). No one from the agency need appear at the adoption hearing, and the judge can, and almost always does, accept the agency's verified report as the report of investigation required by Section 112 of the Domestic Relations Law. In making the order of adoption, the judge, or surrogate when practicable, must give custody only to persons of the same religious faith as that of the adoptive child (see Section 113 of the Domestic Relations Law). In actual practice, the court pays little attention to religious matching.

Preference to Adopt

Foster parents by law (Section 384 (3) of the Social Services Law) who have been foster parents of the child for twelve months have first preference to adopt the child. The child may be adopted either by a married couple or by a single parent.

Who May Adopt?

An unmarried adult person or an adult husband and his adult wife together may adopt another person. Thus, a married person may not adopt another person unless the spouse joins in the adoption. However, an adult husband or an adult wife may adopt the child of the other spouse, whether born in or out of wedlock (see Section 110 of the Domestic Relations Law).

Legally Separated

A married person may adopt alone if that married person is legally separated by court order or by separation agreement.

There is no provision that the adoptive parents be residents of New York (see Section 113 of the Domestic Relations Law). However, in a private adoption proceeding where the adoptive parents reside in New Jersey with the adoptive child, the court dismissed the petition for lack of jurisdiction. See In re Adoption of Danielle [387 N.Y.S. 2d 48 (Surrogate's Court, Putnam County, 1976)]. See also In re Adoption of E.W.C. [89 Misc. 2d 64, 389 N.Y.S. 2d 743], wherein the court held that to satisfy the traditional requirements of jurisdiction to create the status of adoption, the adoption must be decreed either by the state of the child's domicile or by that of the adoptive parents.

The person adopted may be a minor or an adult and may be a stranger or a blood relative. See Section 110 of the Domestic Relations Law, and Stevens v. Halstead [181 A.D. 198, 168 N.Y.S. 142 (Appellate Division, 2nd Dept., 1917)].

Special Considerations Relating to Consents in Private Placement Adoptions

Under Section 115 B of the Domestic Relations Law, a duly executed and acknowledged consent to a private placement adoption must state that no action or proceeding may be maintained by the consenting parent for the custody of the child to be adopted. There are two forms of consent: judicial consent and extrajudicial consent.

Judicial Consent

With respect to judicial consent, consent to a private placement adoption can be executed or acknowledged before any judge or surrogate in the State of New York having jurisdiction over adoption proceedings. In such instances, the consent will state that it is irrevocable upon such execution or acknowledgment. Further, at the time the parent appears before the judge or surrogate to execute or acknowledge a consent to adoption, the judge or surrogate must inform the parent of the consequences of the act, including informing the parent that he/she has the following rights:

1. the right to be represented by legal counsel of the parent's choosing;
2. the right to obtain supportive counseling; and
3. any rights the parent may have pursuant to Section 262 of the Family Court Act, Section 407 of the surrogate's court Procedure Act, and Section 35 of the Judiciary Law.

Each of these provisions pertain to the assignment of counsel. Further, the judge or surrogate must give the parent a copy of the consent upon its execution.

Extrajudicial Consent

With respect to extrajudicial consents, whenever a consent is not executed or acknowledged before a judge or surrogate, the consent will become irrevocable forty-five days after the execution of the consent unless written notice of revocation is received by the court in which the adoption proceeding is to be commenced within that forty-five-day period.

If a parent does provide written notice of revocation, a best interests hearing will be held to determine which party should be granted custody of the child. See Domestic Relations Law Section 115 B, Subparagraph 6d. See also Dennis T.V., Joseph C. [1981, 82 A.D. 2d 125, 441 N.Y.S. 2d 476]; appeal granted [54 N.Y. 2d 1024, 446 N.Y.S. 2d 1027, 430 N.E. 2d 1322]; appeal denied [55 N.Y. 2d 792, 447 N.Y.S. 2d 250, 431, N.E. 2d 976]; appeal denied [55 N.Y. 2d 603, 447, N.Y.S. 2d 1026, 431 N.E. 2d, 977]; motion dismissed [55 N.Y. 2d 857, 447 N.Y.S. 2d 709, 432, N.E. 2d 602].

The Hearing

The case of In re Donald B.B. [405 N.Y.S. 2d 812 (Appellate Division, 3rd Dept., 1978)] was remanded for a rehearing because the family court had improperly divided the hearing in two parts—the first to determine if the surrender should be annulled, and the second to take testimony with respect to custody if the surrender was annulled. The Appellate Division stated that:

> deferment of evidence concerning custody until after a determination on the annulment of the surrenders was improper. Since a determination had to be made as to the best interests of the children and the fitness of the petitioner to maintain and support the children notwithstanding the surrenders, petitioner should have been allowed an adequate opportunity to address these issues.

The law and procedures regarding adoptions are ever changing. The practitioner should always check with the adoption clerk of the appropriate court to ascertain if the court has any special rules, procedures, and forms. Different courts require different or additional documentation. As a matter of fact, different judges in the same court have different requirements.

24
The Adoption Proceeding

O nce a child is freed for adoption, the agency will contact the foster parents and inform them that they may proceed legally to adopt the child or children by the appropriate court. The foster parents are requested to contact their attorney, who in turn is requested to contact the agency.

If the foster parents do not have an attorney, either one or several attorneys will be recommended by the agency to the foster parents. The usual fee for an agency adoption is $350 to $500.

The agency's adoption staff or the agency's attorney will forward the following papers to the court:

1. a written surrender, or if there was no written surrender, a certified copy of the court order committing custody to the agency;
2. the child's birth certificate;
3. the verified investigative report; and
4. the medical records of the child, which are annexed to the verified schedule.

The attorney for the foster parents will prepare the following:

1. the petition signed and verified by the adoptive parents;
2. the agreement and consent to adoption signed by the adoptive parents and the executive director of the agency, and the signatures must be acknowledged by a Notary Public;
3. the attorney's affidavit;
4. the new birth certificate; and
5. the foster parents' affidavit. The foster parents must supply their marriage certificate.

Documents to be filed vary from court to court. For example, in Nassau County, the surrogate's court requires that the child's full medical records be given to the adoptive parents as well as an affidavit filed by the agency stating that the medical records were received by the adoptive parents; the adoptive parents must so acknowledge. Other courts are satisfied if the medical records are filed with the court, and they do not require proof of service of medical records upon the adoptive parents.

In Suffolk County the medical records are annexed to the verified schedule and are not given to the adoptive parents. However, Suffolk County Surrogate's Court requires that a doctor's certificate be filed certifying that the adoptive parents and the child were examined, and the doctor's findings must be noted thereon. Nassau County does not require such a doctor's certificate, relying instead on the agency's medical staff.

As stated, while the documents that must be filed vary, the following are the usual documents to be filed, whether by mail or in person with the adoption clerk:

1. certificate of birth (new)
2. certificate of birth (old)
3. affidavit of attorney
4. order of adoption
5. petition for adoption
6. notification of order of adoption
7. investigative report
8. agreement of adoption
9. verified schedule annexed to petition
10. affidavits regarding medical history, with medicals annexed thereto
11. order committing custody and guardianship
12. certificate of marriage of adoptive parents
13. certificates of birth of adoptive parents
14. attorney's affidavit of conduct
15. doctor's certificate of health, certifying the health of all parties
16. fingerprints of adoptive parents
17. abuse clearance form for adoptive parents and their household members

If the papers are all in order, the clerk will notify the attorney for the adoptive parents of the hearing date, which date will vary.

The Hearing

The courts usually set aside one morning every week for adoption, and the court will calendar between five and fifteen adoptions that morning.

The adoption hearing takes place in the judge's chambers and is usually informal, with the judge asking the adoptive parents and the attorney to swear to the truth of the statements contained in the petition and affidavits. The child must be present, along with the adoptive parents and their attorney, but no one need appear from the agency. After the judge is satisfied that the adoption will be in the best interests of the child, the judge signs the adoption order.

One or two days thereafter, the adoption clerk, for a nominal fee, forwards certificates of adoption to the attorney for the adoptive parents and forwards a certified copy of the order of adoption to the attorney for the agency. Within four to six weeks, the attorney for the adoptive parents will receive the new birth certificate showing the adoptive parents as the parents of the child. The adoption file is sealed and may not be opened except by court order for good cause shown.

Subsidized Adoptions

The number of adoptions has risen greatly since 1972. One reason for this increase is the financial aid given to adoptive parents after the adoption of a child. This is called subsidized adoptions (see Section 398 of the Social Services Law).

Philosophy of Subsidized Adoptions

The intent of subsidized adoptions is to insure permanent homes for children who would otherwise remain in foster care until they were adults.

Amount and Duration of Subsidy Payments

The amount of monthly payments and the length of time the subsidy is granted are left to the discretion of the social services commissioner and will vary.

Agency's Recommendations

A voluntary agency that has a child in foster care and that wishes to recommend to the local Department of Social Services adoption by the foster parents, with subsidy, may do so. The Department of Social Services may accept such recommendation, which should include the amount of subsidy to be provided in the first year.

Annual Reevaluation of Subsidy

After the adoption, the family is like any other family and is independent of the agency, except for annual evaluations of the need for continued subsidy.

Effect of Adoption

Natural Parents

The adoption divests the natural parents of all rights and obligations to the child, including the obligation to support the child (see Domestic Relations Law, Section 117 [1]; see also Smith v. Jones [43 Misc. 2d 350; 250 N.Y.S. 2d 955 (Family Court, Kings County, 1964)]. This change, which divests the natural parents of all rights and duties, is in no way affected by the death of the adoptive parents. See Anonymous v. Anonymous [15 Misc. 2d 1048, 183 N.Y.S. 2d 955 (Children's Court, Saratoga County, 1959)].

Adoptive Parents

After the adoption, the adoptive parents are the true parents of the child, having all the rights and duties of natural parents. See Domestic Relations Law, Section 117 (1); Levine v. Rado [54 Misc. 2d 843, 283 N.Y.S. 2d 483 (Supreme Court, Nassau County, 1967)]. See also In Re of the adoption of Robet Paul P. [63 N.Y. 2d 233, 481 N.Y.S. 2d 652, 471 N.E. 2d 424]; Doe v. Roe [37 A.D. 2d 433, 326 N.Y.S. 2d 421 (1971)].

The Child

Adoption creates the status of parent and child, and the child acquires all the rights and duties of the legal relation of parent and child (see Section 115 of the Domestic Relations Law).

Inheritance

The legal effect of adoption is to give the adopted child the same legal relation to the adoptive parent as a natural child (see Section 117 of the Domestic Relations Law).

25

The Open Adoption: Parental Visitation after Adoption

The court has the power under the Domestic Relations Law, Section 111, not only to grant an adoption but to grant the natural parents visitation rights even after the adoption, if it is considered in the best interests of the child. This is referred to as an *open adoption*.

The need for open adoptions has grown since 1972 for several reasons. First, foster-care review hearings pursuant to Section 392 of the Social Services Law have resulted in more children being freed for adoption and more children being adopted. Moreover, permanent neglect proceedings may result in the termination of the parental rights of parents who maintained contact with their child but did not plan for the return of the child; therefore, children are being adopted by foster parents who know and, in some cases, have a relationship with the natural parents.

The Surrogate's Court, Nassau County, has recently approved several adoptions in which the natural parents received visitation rights with the consent of the adoptive parents (sidebar 25-1). In each case, abandonment proceedings had been brought, and the natural parents appeared. Conferences were held, and it was clear that it was in the best interests of the child to be adopted. But since there was a relationship between natural parent and child, visitation privileges were given to the natural parents—four visits per year. However, the commissioner of social services of the City of New York will not consent to open adoptions, so the decree terminating parental rights is unconditional and the agreement of visitation is between the natural and adoptive parents only. If the agreement is breached, the court retains jurisdiction and, after a hearing, could enforce the visitation rights of the natural parents if they are found to be in the best interests of the child.

In each case, it was the consensus of all parties, including the court and the law guardian for the child, that it would be in the best interests of the child to have the permanency of an adoptive home and the right to a continued relationship with his or her natural parents. See, for example, In re Raana Beth N. [78 Misc. 2d 105, 355 N.Y.S. 2d 956 (Surrogate's Court, New York County, 1974)]. In this case, surrogate Millard L. Midonick found the father had

Sidebar 25–1. Open Adoption Agreement

Open Adoption Agreement between the adoptive parent(s), (name or names), and the natural parent(s), (name or names), WITNESSETH this   day of   , 19   .

WHEREAS, the natural parent(s), (name or names), residing at   has/have agreed to sign a surrender, surrendering all parental rights to the infant, (name), born on the   day of   , 19   ; and

WHEREAS, (adoptive mother) (and) (adoptive father), residing at   , wish to adopt the infant, (name), and

WHEREAS, the parties have agreed to signing the Surrender and this Open Adoption Agreement simultanously; and

WHEREAS, the parties to this agreement believe it is in the best interest of the child to be adopted but at the same time to have contact and visitation with the natural parent(s).

THEREFORE, IT IS HEREBY STIPULATED AND AGREED that:

1. The infant, born on   , 19   , will be adopted by (adoptive mother) (and) (adoptive father).

2. VISITS PER YEAR:

3. LOCATION OF VISITS:

4. LIMITATIONS ON VISITATIONS:

5. LENGTH OF VISITS:

6. MANNER OF SCHEDULING VISITS:

7. It is the intention to have the adoption take place at the Family Court,   County, and the parties agree that the Family Court,   County, shall have jurisdiction with respect to any disagreement over the visitation arrangements but that the parties understand that this agreement while it survives the adoption, in no way can affect the adoption, and the adoption shall be final as to all parties. In the event that there is a dispute or conflict over the visitation rights, either party may petition the Family Court,   County, where the adoption took place, or any other court of competent jurisdiction that has jurisdiction over custody matters.

8. When the infant reaches the age of fourteen (14) years, any visitation must be with the child's consent.

9. The parties agree that this agreement contains all of the material elements of the agreement, and this agreement cannot be changed except in writing and signed by both parties.

10. The parties agree that it is important that the child develop in a normal atmosphere and that any and all conflicts should be at a minimum and resolved, if possible, without court intervention and that all aspects of this agreement should be viewed in light of what is in the best interest of the child.

_____
Natural Parent

_____
Adoptive Parent

STATE OF NEW YORK)
)ss.:
COUNTY OF   )

On this   day of   , 19 , before me personally came _____(and) _____
   (Adoptive Parent)
to me known to be the individual(s) who signed the foregoing Open Adoption Agreement, and duly acknowledged to me that he/she has signed the same.

_____
Notary Public

STATE OF NEW YORK)
)ss.:
COUNTY OF   )

On this   day of   , 19 , before me personally came _____ (and) _____
   (Natural Parent)
to me known to be the individual(s) who signed the foregoing Open Adoption Agreement, and duly acknowledged to me that he/she has signed the same.

_____
Notary Public

STATE OF NEW YORK)
)ss.:
COUNTY OF   )

On this   day of   , 19 , before me personally
came _____(and) _____
(Adoptive Parent)

to me known to be the individual(s) who signed the foregoing
Open Adoption Agreement, and duly acknowledged to me that
he/she has signed the same.

_____
Notary Public

---

abandoned the child and approved the adoption by the mother and her new husband. Because all parties were in agreement, the court provided for visitation privileges in the decree, stating:

> While it may be unprecedented for an order of visitation to be incorporated with an Order of Adoption, this is an extraordinary case, and there is some precedent for such action by a court of equitable jurisdiction. Thus, in *Matter of McDevitt*, 176 App. Div. 418, 162 N.Y.S. 1032, affirmed on other grounds 221 N.Y. 598, 117 N.E. 1076, the Appellate Division in a dictum stated at page 423, 162 N.Y.S. at page 1035: "The Supreme Court has ample power at law and in equity to promote the welfare of the child, notwithstanding a legal adoption." [citations omitted] The power to permit and to regulate visitation on the part of the mother is, of course, included.

But in Catala v. Catala [57 A.D. 2d 823, 395 N.Y.S. 2d 453 (Appellate Division, 1st Dept., 1977)], Judge Phillip B. Thurston sustained a petition for permanent neglect, committing custody to the commissioner of social services and New York Foundling Hospital, an authorized agency, with the power to consent to adoption without the consent of the parent. In affirming the court's finding, the Appellate Division wrote:

> The disposition made (Sections 631, 634 F.C.A.) is amply justified by the evidence. Nor did the court abuse discretion in declining to hear evidence in favor of so-called open adoption in which the biological parent, though deprived of legal rights, would still maintain contact with the child. Such a relationship could not but confuse the child and result in harm rather than good. The child's interests are, of course, paramount.

Finally, in In re Abraham L. [53 A.D. 2d 669, 385 N.Y.S. 2d 103 (Appellate Division, 2nd Dept., 1976)], the Appellate Division recognized the surrogate court's power to decree visitation after adoption, but only after a plenary hearing and based upon the best interests of the child. The court wrote:

Turning to the question of visitation, we hold that, given the Surrogate's broad equitable powers (See SCPA 209, subds. 9, 10), it is within his jurisdiction to enter an order of visitation in this proceeding (See *Matter of Raana Beth N.*, 78 Misc.2d 105, 110–111, 355 N.Y.S.2d 956, 961–962). However, the Surrogate is bound by the rule that "[t]he issue of visitation, like that of custody, may not be determined on the basis of recriminatory and controverted affidavits, but only after a full and plenary hearing" (*Kresnicka v. Kresnicka*, 48 A.D.2d 929, 369 N.Y.S.2d 522, emphasis applied).

Since the abandonment and visitation issues in this proceeding are closely related, we are of the view that the latter issue should not be determined until after the trial has been held. This case should be promptly tried.

Open Adoption and Siblings

Courts have also entered orders of adoption that include a directive that the adoptive child have continued contact with his/her siblings. See, for example, In re Adoption of Anthony [113 Misc. 2d 26, 448 N.Y.S. 2d 377 (Family Court, Bronx County, 1982)]. In this decision, the court included a directive for sibling visitation in the order of adoption where the twelve-year-old adoptive child (1) knew the facts surrounding his adoption; and (2) had visited and maintained a relationship with his siblings over the years and wished to continue this relationship. Moreover, the adoptive parents' and child's birth siblings knew each other. Therefore, the court decided, contact and visitation with the birth siblings was necessary to promote the adoptive child's best interests. See also In re Patricia Ann W. [89 Misc. 2d 368, 392 N.Y.S.2d (Family Court, Kings County, 1977)].

Conclusion

If the best interests of the child are paramount, it is submitted that visitation with a natural parent after adoption should not automatically be discounted. The following should be considered:

1. If there is a relationship between parent and child, visitation after adoption should be explored and, if beneficial, implemented with the consent of all parties, including the child.

2. The court should not force visitation after adoption without the consent of the adoptive parents and the child.

3. If visitation is provided, the court should retain jurisdiction and modify or vacate visitation where appropriate.

   If an adopted child maintains some contact with his/her natural parents, future psychological trauma could be eliminated.

26
The Adopted Child: Visitation by Grandparents

A newly developing area of the law of domestic relations and adoptions is that relating to visitation of children by grandparents after the children are adopted. Section 72 of the Domestic Relations Law provides:

Where either or both of the parents of a minor child residing within this state is or are deceased, or where circumstances show that conditions exist which equity would see fit to intervene, a grandparent or the grandparents of such child may apply to the Supreme Court for a Writ of Habeas Corpus to have such child brought before such court; on the return thereof, the court, by order, after due notice to the parent or any other person or party having the care, custody and control of such child, to be given in such manner as the court shall prescribe, may make such directions as the best interests of the child may require for visitation rights for such grandparent or grandparents in respect to such child.

This section has as its underlying design the establishment of a procedural vehicle through which grandparents might assert their desire to visit with their grandchildren. See LoPresti v. LoPresti [40 N.Y. 2d 522, 387 N.Y.S. 2d 412 (1976), on remand 54 A.D. 2d 582, 387 N.Y.S. 2d 153 (Appellate Division, 2nd Dept., 1976)].

Scope of Section 72

It was earlier the case that upon adoption, the legal relationship existing between grandparent and grandchild was terminated by the order of adoption and that the grandparent had no legal right to insist upon continued visitation with the child against the adoptive parents' wishes. Therefore, a subsequent order of adoption superseded a judgment in a *habeas corpus* proceeding, pursuant to Domestic Relations Law, Section 72, granting visitation privileges to a grandparent. See State ex rel. Herman v. Lebovits [66 Misc. 2d 830, 322 N.Y.S. 2d 123 (Superior Court, New York County, 1971)]; People ex rel.

Levine v. Rado [54 Misc. 2d 843, 283 N.Y.S. 2d 483 (Superior Court, Nassau County, 1967)]. These decisions were based on public policy considerations; namely, any construction of Section 72 authorizing paternal or maternal grandparents to seek visitation privileges from adoptive parents would serve as a strong deterrent to adoption. In Herman v. Lebovits, *supra,* Judge Mary J. Mangan dismissed the grandparents' petition and wrote:

> Upon adoption, the infant Michael Lebovits was completely assimilated into a new family unit, which the petitioner herein is not part of. The legal relationship formerly existing between petitioner and the child was terminated by the order of adoption, and the petitioner has no legal right to insist upon continued visitation with the child against the wishes of the child's adoptive mother and natural father. It would be against the public policy of this state to hold otherwise.
>
> Accordingly, upon re-evaluation of the appropriate statutory and case law, the Court concludes that the right of visitation afforded a grandparent by Domestic Relations Law, Section 72 does not survive the subsequent adoption of the child.

In Rado, *supra,* Justice William R. Brennan, Jr., wrote:

> If Section 72 were construed so as to authorize paternal or maternal grandparents to seek custodial or visitation privileges from adoptive parents (many, if not most of whom bear no blood relationship whatsoever to the adoptive child), such a construction would work as a strong deterrent from adoption. No such construction is indicated.
>
> It may well be that the respondents, Mr. and Mr. Rado, may feel that it might be in the best interests of the child to maintain some contact with his maternal grandmother through periods of visitation, and this Court would urge that they give serious consideration to such a course. As adoptive parents, however, it is exclusively within their own good judgment. The writ is dismissed.

However, this thinking had changed and a new approach emerged in Scranton v. Hutter [40 A.D. 2d 296, 339 N.Y.S. 2d 708 (Appellate Division, 4th Dept., 1973)]. Therein, the father of the children had married his second wife, who legally adopted the two children. From the time of his second marriage, the father and his second wife refused to allow the maternal grandparents to visit with their grandchildren, whereupon the maternal grandparents petitioned the court, seeking visitation rights in respect to the two infants, pursuant to Section 72 of the Domestic Relations Law. Special term disregarded the previous decisions of Lebovits and Rado, *supra,* by refusing to dismiss the *habeas corpus* proceeding. The petitioners maintained that those decisions, which held that an order of adoption superseded any right that grandparents had under Section 72 of the Domestic Relations Law, were harsh. The Appellate Division, Fourth Department, agreed. The court then reviewed the sparse legislative history of Section 72 in New York, of a similar statute in California, and a decision that construed it, namely, Roquemore v. Roquemore [275 Cal. App. 912, 80 Cal. Rptr. 432 (Appellate Division, 2nd Dist., 1969)].

Justice Moule, writing for the unanimous court, held, as did the court in the Roquemore case, that an adoption does not preclude the natural grandparents from applying for a writ of *habeas corpus* to obtain visitation rights, pursuant to Section 72 of the Domestic Relations Law. Specifically, Judge Moule wrote:

> Section 72 provides for the relief sought after notice to any parent having custody of the grandchild. This implies that a situation such as it is here presented was intended to be covered and it is not subject to an automatic limitation by an adoption order. If we were to read into the statute such a limitation, its purpose and effect would be vitiated in all cases where the surviving parent remarried and the stepparent adopted the child. We believe that if it were the intent of the legislation to exempt such cases from its remedial effects, it would have so provided.

However, the granting of visitation must be in the best interests of the child or children, and a hearing should be held to ascertain whether grandparent visitation would be in the best interests of the child.

Therefore, the Scranton case sets forth the controlling rule that adoption does not totally extinguish the familial relationship. See also Barko v. Dept. of Social Services of the County of Suffolk [N.Y.L.J. July 6, 1978, p. 14, col. 5 (Superior Court, Suffolk County, 1978)].

The Discretion of Court and the Best Interests of the Child

The court has discretion in deciding whether to grant visitation, pursuant to Domestic Relations Law, Section 72. The paramount consideration in the determination is what is required in the best interests of the child or children. LoPresti v. LoPresti [40 N.Y. 2d 522, 387 N.Y.S. 2d 412, 355 N.E. 2d 372 (1976) on remand 54 A.D.. 2d 582, 387 N.Y.S. 2d 153 (Appellate Division, 2nd Dept., 1976)]; Apker v. Malchak [112 A.D. 2d 518, 490 N.Y.S. 2d 923 (Appellate Division 1985)]; Johansen v. Hanphear [95 A.D. 2d 973, 464 N.Y.S. 2d 301 (Appellate Division 2d Dept., 1985)]; Geri v. Fanto [79 Misc. 2d 947, 361 N.Y.S. 2d 984 (Family Court, Kings County, 1974)]; Scranton v. Hutter [40 A.D. 2d 296, 339 N.Y.S. 2d 708 (Appellate Division, 4th Dept., 1973)].

The court must also be guided by the humanitarian purpose of the statute in arriving at an evaluation of how the best interests of the child will be affected. As stated in Matter of Ehrlich v. Ressner [55 A.D. 2d 953, 391 N.Y.S. 2d 152, 153 (Appellate Division, 2nd Dept., 1977)]:

The humanistic concern evinced by the Legislature in enacting this section is an implicit recognition that "[v]isits with a grandparent are often a precious part of a child's experience and there are benefits which devolve upon the grandchild . . . which he cannot derive from any other relationship" (See *Mimkon v. Ford*, 66 N.J. 426, 437, 332 A.D.2d 199, 204; *Matter of Vacula v. Blume*, 53 A.D.2d 633, 384 N.Y.S.2d 208; cf. *Matter of N.*, 78 Misc.2d 105, 109, 355 N.Y.S.2d 956). While control over visitation rests within the sound discretion of the Court (See *LoPresti v. LoPresti, supra; Matter of Boscia v. Sellazzo*, 42 A.D.2d 781, 364 N.Y.S.2d 343), it must be guided by the humanitarian purpose of the statute and by an independent evaluation of the best interests of the children affected (cf. *Matter of Sugameri v. Fortunato*, 55 A.D.2d 936, 391 N.Y.S.2d 12 [2d Dept., dec. Jan. 24, 1977]).

Each case must turn on its own facts as to what is in the child's best interests. See LoPresti, *supra*. Justice Blyn in People ex rel. Wilder v. Spence-Chapin [403 N.Y.S. 2d 454 (Superior Court, New York County, 1978)] stated at p. 455 that "[i]t is clear that the intention of the statute is to provide a means to preserve a beneficial relationship between a grandchild and grandparent consistent with that child's best interests." In Wilder, the infant was born with narcotic withdrawal symptoms. As a result of a neglect petition, physical custody of the infant was given to the commissioner of social services of the City of New York, who thereafter transferred custody to Spence-Chapin. Immediately thereafter, the child was placed with a foster family, where she has remained ever since. Subsequently, the legal custody of the child was awarded to the respondent, Spence-Chapin, pursuant to the Social Services Law, Section 384 B (on abandonment). The child having been freed for adoption, the foster parents notified Spence-Chapin of their desire to adopt. The petitioner, who was the child's maternal grandmother, had never seen the child and had not even known of her existence until the latter part of 1977, almost two and a half years after the birth of the child. The petitioner was caring for the child's sister and had access to other siblings, but Justice Blyn, in his decision, did not find this to be persuasive. Although the separation of siblings is unfortunate, the facts of this case were such as to dictate that separation in favor of her forthcoming adoption. Furthermore, the petitioner did not come within the purview of the statute's intention to preserve and foster a beneficial relationship between grandchild and grandparent because there was no relationship here. The petitioner had never seen the child. While the petition for visitation was dismissed, Justice Blyn reasoned that:

While the petitioner's standing to commence this proceeding may not be obviated by the imminent adoption proceeding or, for that matter, an Order of Adoption (*Matter of Scranton v. Hutter*, 40 A.D.2d 296, 339 N.Y.S.2d 947, 361 N.Y.S.2d 984), it is overwhelmingly clear to this court on the basis of the facts presented that the best interest of this child would not be served by permitting visitation by the petitioner. The authorities holding that the adoption of a child would not preclude the assertion of visitation rights by the grandparents, appear to be in accord with the Court of Appeals' opinion in *LoPresti, supra*. In both *Scranton* and *Geri*, however, the adoption involved was by the new spouse of a natural parent of the child. Research has not disclosed any authority dealing with the question of whether the adoption of the child by unrelated third parties would bar the assertion of visitation rights by grandparents. The statute offers no guidance and a reading of *LoPresti, supra*, indicates that each case must turn on its own facts.

In Geri v. Fanto, *supra*, Judge—now Dean—Glasser held that the acrimonious relationship between the parties necessitated, in the best interests of the child, a denial of the application of the paternal grandparents to enforce visitation rights with their grandchildren. The children resided with their mother, who subsequently married the man who adopted the children. Judge Glasser went on to suggest that the legislature seriously consider repealing Domestic Relations Law, Section 72, because "if affection and regard remain between members of the family, there is no need to invoke Section 72. That statute would be called into play only in a case such as this, where the relationship between grandparents and parents is a hostile one. . . . Sentimental reasons might prompt continued contact between children and grandparents but, I believe ties of nature would prove are more effective in restoring kindly family relations than coercive measures that must follow judicial intervention" [Id at 989].

The court in Geri relied heavily on Noll v. Noll [277 A.D. 286, 289–289, 98 N.Y.S. 2d 938, 940–941 (Appellate Division, 4th Dept., 1950)], which antedated Domestic Relations Law, Section 72, but which Judge Glasser found to have incisive and compelling reasoning. In Noll, the paternal grandparents sought visitation with their grandchild, who was residing with his widowed mother. The court went on to say:

> It follows, therefore, that here, where the mother is the proper, natural and legal custodian of the child, unwilling to have visitation by the petitioner, and the welfare, contentment, peace of mind and happiness of the child do not make it essential to have continued contact with the grandparents, that the court cannot interfere simply to better the moral and temporal welfare of the child against an unoffending parent, even if such a result would be accomplished. In this case, we do not believe it would be accomplished, even if the court had the power to order it.

However, visitation is not per se against the best interests of the child when there is animosity between the parties. See Hayton v. Foster [95 A.D. 2d 77, 466 N.Y.S. 2d 723 aff'd. 61 N.Y. 2d 747, 472 N.Y.S. 2d 916, 460 N.E. 2d 1351]. In reversing an order of the Supreme Court, Nassau County, which had dismissed a *habeas corpus* proceeding brought to determine the visitation rights of grandparents, the Appellate Division, Second Department, in Vacula v. Blume [53 A.D. 2d 633, 384 N.Y.S. 2d 208 (Appellate Division, 2nd Dept., 1976)] stated in part:

> Animosity between the mother of children and their grandparents is not a proper basis for the denial of visitation privileges to the grandparents, nor is it a proper yardstick by which to measure the best interests of the children (*LoPresti v. LoPresti*, 51 A.D.2d 578, 378 N.Y.S.2d 487).

See also Lachow v. Barasch [57 A.D. 2d 896, 394, N.Y.S. 2d 284 (Appellate Division, 2nd Dept., 1977)], where the Appellate Court remanded the proceedings to the Family Court stating that the Family Court abused its discretion in denying the grandparent's petition for visitation based upon the ground of animosity between the grandparent and father of the child. The court stated:

> We remand the proceeding to the Family Court to take testimony and made a determination under the standards set forth in Section 72 of the Domestic Relations Law, as interpreted in *LoPresti v. LoPresti*, 40 N.Y.2d 522, 387 N.Y.S.2d 412, 355 N.E.2d 372.

However, when the animosity between grandparents and parents is so great as to threaten the security of the grandchildren's relationship with their parents, visitation may be denied.

In a recently reported case, MGM v. RM and RF [N.Y.L.J. p. 19 col. 2 (Family Court, New York County, 8/16/88)], the maternal grandmother brought a petition, pursuant to Section 72 of the Domestic Relations Law, for visitation with her two grandchildren, ages three and six. The court based its decision to deny the petition on four factors:

First, the court noted the extremely acrimonious nature of the relationship between the maternal grandmother and the natural parents. The maternal grandmother had been diagnosed as suffering from a mental illness. Further, she was described by an expert psychiatric witness who had evaluated her as "fundamentally hostile, paranoid, and grandiose whose judgment was grossly impaired in regard to entering personal relationships." The psychiatrist also described the behavior of the maternal grandmother toward the natural parents in the two years prior to the trial as "increasingly aggressive, harassing and at times, assaultive."

Second, the court looked to the effect the behavior of the maternal grandmother would have upon the grandchildren. In doing so, the court again relied upon the testimony of the psychiatric expert, who concluded that:

> Visitation should be prohibited because of the petitioner's markedly impaired overall judgment which made her unable to relate in any sensi-

tive ways to the children's general welfare or psychological needs . . . and [the psychiatrist] also recommended against a more limited form of supervised visitation: the doctor pointed out that the petitioner's inability to control her verbally aggressive behavior and her labile mood changes be frightening or at least disturbing to these relatively young children.

Third, the court looked at the fact that the maternal grandmother had no long-standing relationship with the grandchildren that would otherwise be disrupted.

Fourth, the court considered the opinion of the older child as to whether or not he wanted to visit with his maternal grandmother.

As the court summarized:

Under the facts and circumstances of the instant case, the petitioner has not met her burden of demonstrating that it would be in the children's best interests to have visitation with her. This is not the typical situation envisioned by the legislature in which visits with the grandparent are ". . . often a precious part of the child's experience and there are benefits which devolve upon the grandchild . . . which he cannot derive from any other relationship" (*Matter of Ehrlick v. Ressner,* 55 A.D.2d 953; *Mimkon v. Ford.* 66 N.J. 426, 437).

Rather, the petitioner has sought a vehicle in which to vent her anger on her daughter, the most effective vehicle at this point constituting her grandchildren. The court is aware of the fact that human motivation is also mixed and complex in that conflict in and of itself between a grandparent and a grandchild's own parent[s] does not and should not rule out visitation under the circumstances where the conflict is sufficiently confined to the adult level without intruding upon the grandparent-grandchild relationship. (See *LoPresti v. LoPresti,* 40 N.Y.2d 522; *Matter of Vacula v. Blume,* 53 A.D.2d 633; *Matter of Johansen v. Lampitear,* 95 A.D.2d 973.) But under circumstances where, as in the instant proceeding, the level of animosity between the grandparent and the grandparent's own child has reached a level that can only be characterized as venomous and exacerbated by chronic and open displays of aggressive behavior, to allow visitation with relatively young children would threaten the security of the grandchildren's own relationship with their parents and would serve the ignoble purpose of providing a conduit for the continued expressions of vindicative rage without affording substantial offsetting benefits for the grandchildren.

Even in the cases where the petitioner is not unfit as a visiting grandparent, and the court so finds, the writ of *habeas corpus* may still be dismissed because the best interests of the child so dictate. In Barko v. Dept. of Social Services of the County of Suffolk [N.Y.L.J. July 6, 1978, p. 14, col. 5 (Superior Court, Suffolk County, 1978)], the maternal grandmother of four children brought a writ of *habeas corpus* for visitation privileges pursuant to Domestic Relations

Law, Section 72. The father surrendered three of the children. The fourth child was under the jurisdiction of St. Christopher's Home, where the petitioner was allowed visitation, and the writ was withdrawn as to this child. Unlike the petitioner in People ex rel. Wilder v. Spence-Chapin, *supra*, the petitioner here had a relationship with her grandchildren in that they, along with her deceased daughter and son-in-law, lived with her from late summer or fall of 1972 until February 19, 1976. During this period of time, she baby-sat for the children, washed and dressed them, and knew them from birth. The petitioner's daughter moved out on February 19, 1976, two years after her son-in-law left. The daughter moved back on August 5, 1976, without the children, having left them with the respondent, and this greatly upset the petitioner. Subsequently, the petitioner's daughter died in a motorcycle accident on July 20, 1977.

The adoptive parents testified that they felt sorry for the petitioner,

> but they opposed any visitation by the petitioner, feeling that they would have "strings" attached to the adoption, might need permission to leave the state, that the children would not benefit from such visits, that now the children have "new grandparents" and that there is no necessity for reminding the children of the past when looking for a happy future. (col. 5, para. 4)

Justice Thom, after examining the factors and attempting to balance the equities, noted that the issue was not what was in the best interest of the grandmother, but what was in the best interests of the children. He then stated that although the petitioner was not an unfit grandmother, the interest of the children would best be served by denying the petitioner's application for visitation because "to continue a relationship between petitioner and the children in this case would hinder the adoptive relationship" (col. 6, para. 2). See also Apker v. Malchak [112 A.D. 2d 518, 490, N.Y.S. 2d 940 (Appellate Division, 2d Dept., 1985)].

Today, in New York the application of Domestic Relations Law, Section 72, is unsettled. Opinions range from Judge Glasser's in Geri v. Fanto, *supra*, that:

> Sentimental reasons might prompt continued contact between children and grandparents, but I believe ties of nature would prove far more effective in restoring kindly family relations than coercive measures that must follow judicial intervention. I would suggest that the Legislature give serious consideration to the advisability of repealing D.R.L. Sec. 72.

to the opinion of Vacula v. Blume, *supra*, that:

> Visits with a grandparent are often a precious part of a child's experience, and there are benefits which devolve upon the grandchild from the relationship with his grandparents which he cannot derive from any other relationship.

Neither the Legislature nor this Court is blind to human truths which grandparents and grandchildren have always known (*Mimkon v. Ford*, 66 N.J. 426 437, 332 A.2d 199, 204).

It has been difficult for the courts to fashion a clear set of rules and precedent for the application of Section 72. This is understandable in this difficult and emotional area, since the courts must consider and balance many factors such as:

1. the child's need for the benefits that devolve from the blood relationship of grandchild-grandparent, and the need to become entrenched in a happy, forward-looking relationship with the adoptive parents;
2. the adoptive parents feeling that there should be no "strings" attached to the adoption;
3. the grandparents' need to foster their relationship with their grandchildren, assuming that the court finds there is a relationship to foster;
4. the legislature's humanitarian purposes in passing the statute.

Conclusion

The paramount concern of the court in making its final decision as to grandparent visitation must be the "best interests" of the child.

The child's rights and wishes can be best considered if he/she is represented by counsel, and if the judge interviews the child as to his/her preferences. No petition for grandparental visitation should be dismissed without a hearing where the petition alleges that a relationship existed between grandparent and child. Prior to the hearing, a law guardian should be appointed to represent the interests of the child, and if the child is articulate (whether six or sixteen), his/her wishes should be considered and best interests controlling. While each case must be decided upon its own facts, a number of factors should be considered:

1. the relationship between the grandparent and the child;
2. the age of the child and the child's wishes;
3. the benefit to the child by continuing a relationship with the child's grandparents;
4. the recommendation of the law guardian;
5. the contention and wishes of the adoptive parents;
6. the extent to which visitation with grandparents could interfere with the new relationship of the child and adoptive parents; and
7. where indicated, recommendations of professionals, such as social workers, psychiatrists, and psychologists.

27
Sealed Adoption Records: Present State of New York Law

I n recent times, many Americans have tried to find out their origins, or "roots." This awareness of origins has presented problems for a certain class of individuals—namely, persons who have been adopted—adoptees. In New York, the adoptee seeking his/her origins is confronted with Domestic Relations Law, Section 114, which relates to the sealing of adoption records. It provided in part that:

> No person, including the attorney for the adoptive parent, shall disclose the surname of the child directly or indirectly to the adoptive parents except upon order of the court. No person shall be allowed access to such sealed records and order and any index thereof except upon an order of a judge or surrogate of the court in which the order was made or of a justice of the supreme court. No order for disclosure or access and inspection on good cause shown and on due notice to the adoptive parents and to such additional persons as the court may direct.

The keynote of this section is confidentiality, which, if violated, may result in contempt of court.

Constitutionality

The sealing requirements of Domestic Relations Law, Section 114, have been held to be constitutional. See Alma Soc. Inc. v. Mellon [C.A.N.Y., 601 F. 2d 1225 cert. denied 100 S.Ct., 531, 444 U.S. 995, 62 L.Ed. 2d 426]. Here, the court held that the requirements did not violate the equal protection clause of the Fourteenth Amendment of the U.S. Constitution. In Application of Romany [108 Misc. 2d 99, 438 N.Y.S. 2d 967], the court held that the requirements did not violate federal constitutional rights against cruel and unusual punishment and to equal protection of the law, nor did they claim constitutional rights to human identity and social and psychological well-being.

Classifications of Good Cause

The Domestic Relations Law states that "good cause" must be shown before an order for disclosure or access is granted. In reviewing the case law, "good cause," can be classified into three categories: criminal, psychological, and medical.

Criminal

In earlier years, it was the law that although adoption records were filed in the office of a public official—that is, the county clerk—they did not constitute public records. Therefore, a grand jury had to show just cause before demanding the production of all records of all adoptions approved during the preceding year for the purpose of examining them in a proceeding before it. See People v. Doe [183 N.Y.S. 2d 307 (Erie County Court, 1955)]. 49 N.Y. Jur., *Records and Recording Acts*, Section 26].

However, the Domestic Relations Law, Section 114, has since been ruled inapplicable to grand jury subpoenas. See Matter of Grand Jury Subpoenas Duces Tecum [58 A.D. 2d 1, 395 N.Y.S. 2d 645 (Appellate Division, 1st Dept., 1977)], where the Appellate Division of the first Department held that a "Grand jury is not a 'person' within the contemplation of Domestic Relations Law, Section 114" [Id at 648]. The court considered four factors in reaching its conclusion: (1) the broad investigatory power of the grand jury; (2) the lack of any express limit on that power in the Domestic Relations Law, Section 114; (3) the legislative purposes behind the enactment of the Domestic Relations Law, Section 114, of the Social Services Law, Sections 374 B and 389 (2), and of the secrecy of grand jury proceedings; and (4) the paramount importance of ensuring the integrity of the adoptive process [Id at 648].

Psychological

The Courts have held that where the adopted person can substantiate psychological trauma, access to adoption records will be granted. In the case of In re Hayden [106 Misc. 2d 849, 435 N.Y.S. 2d 541 (Superior Court, Albany, 1981)] the Court held that the application to unseal the adoption records must contain, in affidavit form, allegations that substantiate that psychological necessity requires the unsealing of the adoption record for the health and well-being of the petitioning adoptive child, and further stated that the psychological needs must arise above mere desire or curiosity. For another case standing for the proposition that good cause to unsealed records may be established by showing psychological trauma see In re Wilson [153 A.D. 2d 748, 544 N.Y.S. 2d 886 (Appellate Divivision, 2nd Dept., 1989)].

Medical Information as Good Cause and
Limitation of Inquiry

In Chattman v. Bennett [393 N.Y.S. 2d 768 (Appellate Division, 2nd Dept., 1977)], the adult adoptee appealed from the Surrogate's Court, Nassau County, the denial of her application for permission to review and inspect sealed adoption records. The petitioner, a married woman, wanted to start her own family, but she was concerned that some genetic or hereditary factor in her background might possibly adversely affect her children. The Appellate Division, Second Department, modified the order of the Surrogate's Court, Nassau County, and held:

> Her concern or preoccupation with the possibility of some genetic or hereditary factor in her background which might foretell a problem for any issue she might bear constitutes "good cause" to allow her access to any medical reports or related matter contained in the records of her adoption. Medical information of this or any other nature concerning the adoptee should be freely disclosed (see Section 114 of the Domestic Relations Law with respect to the furnishing of the child's medical history to the adoptive parent). We, therefore, direct the Surrogate to make available to petitioner, from the file pertaining to her adoption, her medical records and those of her natural parents, as well as any other material therein relating to possible genetic or hereditary conditions while deleting therefrom any nonpertinent information, including the names of the natural parents.

As this quotation exemplifies, even when the courts have found good cause for allowing an adoptee access to sealed records, the courts have been selective as to which portions of the records the petitioner may inspect.

This policy was clearly demonstrated in Estate of Maxtone-Graham [393 N.Y.S. 2d 835 (Surrogate's Court, New York County, 1975)], in which an application was made by an adoptee, an adult in her thirties, for permission to inspect sealed adoption records pursuant to Section 114 of the Domestic Relations Law. The natural mother appeared in court and consented to the relief requested by the petitioner, who then contended that she was entitled to free access to all of the records of the respondent agencies connected with her adoption. The respondent agencies agreed to turn over all records in their possession. However, they contended that the names and addresses of the foster parents with whom the petitioner resided should be stricken from those records. The petitioner's psychiatrist submitted an affidavit stating that all such records would be necessary for her treatment.

Because of the natural mother's consent, the court decided that copies of all records relating to her should be turned over to the petitioner, and to this the respondents agreed. However, following a hearing, the court decided that good cause had not been established relative to the request for information concerning the names and addresses of the foster parents. An official of one of the respondent agencies testified that it is difficult to recruit foster parents, and the assurance of confidentiality of all personal information better permitted the agency to assist the foster parents in caring for the child. The court reasoned:

> To permit discovery of the names and addresses of the foster parents, after all these years, will serve no purpose with regard to the petitioner and might tend to disrupt the relationship between child care agencies and foster parents with the ultimate harm falling upon the many infants subjected to their care. Copies of all remaining records of the respondent agencies regarding petitioner are to be made available to petitioner's psychiatrist without the names of the foster parents. [Id at 827]

Thus, even when the petitioner has the consent of the natural parent to gain access to and inspect the records, this is not dispositive. The court may still decide that no purpose would be served by permitting access to certain portions of the record and may thus order deletions accordingly.

A Potential Fourth Category of Good Cause— Religious Identity Crisis

A religious identity crisis may rise to the level of good cause sufficient to allow viewing adoption records. See Alma Soc. Inc. v. Mellon [C.A.N.Y. 1979, 601 F.2d 1255, cert. denied 444 U.S. 995, 100 S. Ct. 531, 62 L.Ed 426], in which the court stated "Upon an appropriate showing of psychological trauma, medical need, or of a religious identity crisis, though it might be doubted upon a showing of fear of unconscious incest, New York courts would appear required to grant permission to release all or part of sealed adoption records" [Id at 476].

The Mere Desire to Learn the Identity of Parents or about Ancestry Does Not Constitute Good Cause

The desire to learn the identity of one's parents or to learn about one's ancestry, alone, does not constitute good cause with respect to Domestic Relations Law, Section 114. See Matter of Linda F.M. [52 N.Y. 2d 236, 437 N.Y.S. 2d 283, 418 N.E. 2d 302].

C.P.L.R. Section 3101A (4) Is Inapplicable

The mere fact that sealed adoption records could possibly assist a respondent in his/her defense in a court proceeding does not prima facie qualify as a special circumstance, thereby allowing him/her discovery pursuant to C.P.L.R., Section 3101A (4).

In Application of Minicozzi [51 Misc. 2d 595, 273 N.Y.S. 2d 632 (1966)], the court stated that all of the adoption papers would remain sealed and inaccessible unless good cause were shown to permit access and inspection. The petitioner, Minicozzi, applied to gain access to certain sealed records of the surrogate's court and of the Department of Public Welfare. Minicozzi was the respondent in a paternity proceeding, and it was his belief that those records might contain information vital to his defense. He moved, pursuant to C.P.L.R., Section 3101A (4), to obtain disclosure of material and necessary evidence for his defense by reason of special circumstances. In denying the motions, the court stated:

> We can agree that the records sought to be examined *could conceivably* ("may") assist his defense. On the other hand, it is not so clear that the statutory limitations of access to records can be ignored on grounds that the inaccessibility is a sort of *prima facie* special circumstance. To urge that the announced legislative policy nevertheless permits disclosure [C.P.L.R., Section 3101 A (4)] is to simultaneously demonstrate the futility of that policy. Legislative privacy, or even secrecy, based upon sound considerations of public policy, is ample justification for non-access. Any relaxation of the status of these records as beyond public or even semiprivate perusal requires something more than a judicial activity.

This decision is yet another demonstration of the reluctance of the courts to disrupt the statutory policy of confidentiality on which Section 114 of the Domestic Relations Law is based.

Natural Parents as Parties

In any proceeding brought by an adoptee to examine the adoption records, the court must balance the interests of the adoptee, the adoptive parents, and the natural parents.

Presumably, the adoptive parents fear the adoptee will discover his biological parents and somehow think less of them and sever the psychological bonds of parent and child. However, the adoptee grows up and as an adult may have an overriding interest in finding himself by becoming aware of his biological parents.

The natural parents also presumably wish anonymity and to protect their identity. The usual example given is that of an unwed teenager who places her baby for adoption and then later marries and starts a new family without informing anyone of her illegitimate child. The natural mother may have an interest in keeping the adoption records sealed, while the child may have an interest in finding out what the records contain. While it is difficult to balance these equities, Surrogate Louis D. Laurino, in the case of Application of Anonymous [390 N.Y.S. 2d 779 (Surrogate's Court, Queens County, 1976)] seems to have struck that balance. See, however, In re Linda F.M. [401 N.Y.S. 2d 960 (Surrogate's Court, Bronx County, 1978)], in which the court refused to appoint a guardian *ad litem* for the natural parents or to require notice to the natural parents, especially where the parents would be difficult to locate. If the parents were locatable, the procedure outlined by Surrogate Laurino in In re Anonymous may have been followed. Surrogate Betram R. Gelfand, in deciding the case on its merits—Linda F.M. [409 N.Y.S. 2d 638 (Surrogate's Court, Bronx County, 1978)]—denied the adoptee's application to examine adoption records and analyzed the existing cases on unsealing adoption records. Surrogate Gelfand held the statute that required the adoption records be sealed did not deprive the adoptee of equal protection.

An adoptee had instituted an application to permit access to sealed records of his own adoption. Surrogate Laurino held that the natural parents of the petitioner—an adult adoptive person—were necessary parties to the proceeding, but since the very issue to be litigated involved continued anonymity of parents so as to preclude them from being identified during the pendency of the proceeding, traditional methods of service on the parents were inadequate. The surrogate designated an attorney to act as guardian *ad litem* for natural parents as incapacitated persons:

> Section 311, S.C.P.A., however, provides that the court has the power to designate a person to be served with process on behalf of a "person under disability" when it appears to the court's satisfaction to be "in the interest of such person" under disability. Included within the definition of "person under disability" is an "incapacitated person" (S.C.P.A. 103 [37]), which that statute defines as including "any person who for any cause is incapable adequately to protect his rights" (S.C.P.A. 103 [24]). Surely the natural parents, whose identity is secret and cannot presently come forward to protect their rights, fit the statutory definition of "incapacitated person." [Id at 782]

Furthermore, the person who has been designated pursuant to S.C.P.A., Section 331, has the powers and duties of a guardian *ad litem*, "and as such is not merely an agent to accept service of process but, as a part of his duties, will be expected to determine the present whereabouts of the natural parents, counsel them as to their rights and, in general, represent and protect their interests."

What is the rationale behind this need for confidentiality? Surrogate Laurino, in Application of Anonymous, *supra*, suggested that confidentiality and the sealing of records:

1. facilitates and encourages investigation necessary to adoption planning since personal facts embarrassing to involved parties are not disclosed;

2. prevents natural parents from locating the child and then interfering with his/her new life with adoptive parents;

3. protects illegitimate children from stigmatization associated with illegitimacy;

4. assures the natural mother "who has given birth to a child born out of wedlock and finds that she cannot properly take care of the child, that instead of secreting the child or placing it with persons haphazardly, if she wishes to permit suitable, desirous and qualified persons to adopt the infant, her indiscretion will not be divulged" People v. Doe [138 N.Y.S. 2d 307, 309 (Erie County Court, 1955)].

Thus, confidentiality assures all parties involved in an adoption that the records will remain sealed and secret unless good cause can be shown at some future time. The obvious difficulty with this theory is that the adoptee was *not* a party to the agreement of adoption. The adoption agreement in a private adoption is between the natural and the adoptive parents or, in an agency adoption, between the agency and the adoptive parents. The adoptee becomes a party for the first time when he/she initiates a proceeding to examine the sealed adoption records.

Conclusion

Since adoption is entirely statutory and in derogation of the common law, Domestic Relations Law, Section 114, as well as other adoption statutes, must be strictly construed. See In re Adoption of Pyung B. [83 Misc. 2d 794, 371 N.Y.S. 2d 993 (1975)]. However, decisions such as Application of Anonymous, *supra;* Matter of the Grand Jury, Morgenthau v. Weeks and Shultz, *supra;* and Chattman v. Bennett, *supra,* may be indications that the courts are becoming more liberal in interpreting the statutory policy of confidentiality and secrecy in connection with petitioners' gaining access to sealed adoption records.

Other recent decisions in the foster-care field, such as In re St. Christopher's Home [40 N.Y. 2d 96, 386 N.Y.S. 2d 59 (1976)]; Bennett v. Jeffreys [387 N.Y. 2d 821, 40 N.Y.S. 2d 543 (1976)]; and In re Orsini [36 N.Y. 2d 568, 370 N.Y. 2d 511 (1975)], have made it easier to free the foster child for adoption and have shifted the emphasis from the superior right of the natural parents to the best interests of the foster child.

It is submitted that the "good cause" test in Section 114 of the Domestic Relations Law should be defined and a procedure devised to enable the adult adoptee to gain access to the sealed adoption records on a need-to-know basis.

The following procedure is suggested:

1. When an adult adoptee desires to obtain information contained in the adoption records, the court that made the order of adoption should be involved

ab initio, and there should be an *in camera* examination of the adoption records.

2. The information requested should be made with specificity and granted based upon a need-to-know basis; that is, the following should be made available:

    a. psychological and medical records of the adoptee and natural parents;

    b. whether the adoptee was orphaned;

    c. whether the adoptee was abandoned or surrendered;

    d. the religion of the natural parents; and

    e. whether the adoptee, if Christian, was baptized.

3. If the adoptee is satisfied, that would be the end of the matter. If the adoptee is not satisfied or is denied specific data, such as the names of the natural parents, the next procedure would be to make a formal written application to the court with supporting affidavit(s) substantiating "good cause" as defined by the legislature. A proposed definition of "good cause" may read: "Evidence that the adoptee has a need to know the information requested for a reasonable purpose without which the psychological or physical well-being of the adoptee will be detrimentally affected."

28
Abrogation of Adoption

With respect to abrogation, it specifically provides that:

> In like manner, as a court of general jurisdiction exercises such powers, a judge or Surrogate of a court in which the Order of Adoption was made may open, vacate or set aside such Order of Adoption for fraud, newly discovered evidence or other sufficient cause.

Section 114 of the Domestic Relations Law provides the grounds for abrogating the adoption, which are:

1. fraud,
2. newly discovered evidence,
3. other sufficient cause: see In re Adoption of Emanuel T. [81 Misc. 2d 535, 365 N.Y.S. 2d 709, 714 (Family Court, New York County, 1975)],
4. jurisdictional defect.

The leading case dealing with abrogation of adoption is In re Nicky [364, N.Y.S. 2d 970 (Surrogate's Court, Kings County, 1975)], in which Surrogate Nathaniel R. Sobel held that the natural parents were not entitled to abrogate an order of adoption. The natural parents alleged that they had not understood that they were consenting to the adoption of their child. The natural parents, however, did not allege misrepresentation, fraud, or coercion by the agency with respect to signing the surrender. Surrogate Sobel in granting summary judgment in favor of the agency stated that:

> In the absence of overreaching or knowledge of such by the respondent, Commissioner of agency, no legal basis for the abrogation of the Order of Adoption is stated.

In the more recent, unreported case, In re Edward M.G. [Surrogate's Court, Nassau County, 1987)], the surrogate's court granted a motion to vacate an adoption on the basis of fraud and newly discovered evidence, pursuant to Section 114 of the Domestic Relations Law. In Edward M.G., a single-parent adoption had been granted. The petitioner was a homosexual male living with his lover in the home where the child had been placed. These facts were not known to the court until a custody petition was brought in the family court. Without reaching the question of a homosexual adoption, the court held that the petitioner's homosexuality and the structure of the home in which the adoptive child would live were relevant facts that had not been revealed to the court, in violation of Section 114 of the Domestic Relations Law.

However, an out-and-out misrepresentation is not required to warrant granting of a motion to open, vacate, and/or set aside an adoption order due to fraud. Matters of evasion, withholding information from the court, failure to disclose in an open and fair manner certain material facts in relation to the history of the controversy and the prior conduct of the parties, and the previous custody of the child would be sufficient to warrant the granting of the motion. See Adoption of Lord [28 A.D. 2d 1203, 288 N.Y.S. 2d 25 (1967)]. See also In re Anonymous [390 N.Y.S. 2d 433 (Appellate Division, 2nd Dept., 1977)], wherein the court denied the natural parents' motion to vacate the consent to adoption. The court held that where the parent signed a consent to adoption which became irrevocable after commencement of adoption proceeding, they were not entitled to notice that the adoption proceeding had been commenced.

In the Matter of the Adoption of E.W.C. [389 N.Y.S. 2d 743, 749 (Surrogate's Court, Nassau County, 1976)], a natural mother filed a petition to revoke the consent to adoption and for the return of the custody of the child. She sought a dismissal of the adoption proceeding on the grounds that, *inter alia*, the consent to adoption had been induced by fraud, duress, and coercion—that is, she was depressed and fearful that she would not be able to properly care for the child in a strange city without friends or relatives. She further alleged that the housekeeper closely supervised her; that the attorney demanded $8,000 from her for the return of the child; that her husband threatened to leave her to return to his native country, Iran; that the adoptive father promised to permit her to see the child every year; and that all of her living and transportation expenses were being paid by the adoptive parents. Surrogate John D. Bennett, in finding no merit to these allegations, stated:

> While the record undoubtedly establishes that the mother was "unhappy" and had misgivings about consenting to the adoption, there is no evidence of any fraud, duress or coercion which would vitiate the irrevocable consent (*Adoption of T.W.C.*, [Anon.], 38 N.Y 2d 128, 379 N.Y.S. 2d 1, 341 N.E. 2d 526, affd. 48 A.D. 2d 893, 369, N.Y.S. 2d 783 affd. N.Y.L.J. 12/18/74, p. 17 [Bennett, S.].

Furthermore, even if the natural mother's contentions that the New York attorney cooperated with the Florida attorney to illegally place out the child for compensation were correct, the court was of the opinion "that the adoption itself should not be refused because of a possible violation of a law which calls for a criminal sanction."

29
Appeals

I t is important to the respondent parent that the parent be given full and explicit details on the parent's right to appeal any adverse order or judgment of the family court.

It is incumbent upon the attorney to be aware of what orders are appealable, what orders are appealable as a matter of right, and what orders are appealable at the discretion of the Appellate Division.

After an adverse order or judgment, the attorney should orally inform the respondent parent of the right to appeal and then follow that advice by a written letter explaining in detail the respondent parent's right to appeal. It is then the obligation of the attorney representing the parent in a family court, if the parent wishes to appeal, to make a motion to the appropriate Appellate Division to have appellate counsel appointed to the indigent respondent parent. If an appropriate affidavit of finances is attached, the Appellate Division, in all likelihood, will grant the motion and appoint either different counsel to perfect the appeal or appoint the same counsel, if counsel so requests. The following is an outline of the procedure to appeal orders and judgments from the family court.

Appeals for Appellate Division

Pursuant to Section 1111 of the Family Court Act, an appeal may be taken to the Appellate Division of the Supreme Court of the judicial department in which the family court whose order is appealed from is located. Due to the fact that the interlocutory as well as the final family court order involves child custody, some practitioners attempt to use the writ of *habeas corpus* as a means of challenging a court decision. However, it has been held that *habeas corpus* is not intended, and cannot be used, as a means of appeal from an order of the family court. See People ex rel. McKay v. Barbaro [63 Misc. 2d 138, 310 N.Y.S. 2d 690 (Superior Court, Nassau County, 1970); cf. CPLR 7002 (a) (1980)].

Appealable Orders

Pursuant to Section 1112 of the Family Court Act, an appeal may be taken as a matter of right from any order of disposition. Other than an appeal from the intermediate or final order or decision in a case involving abuse, which may be taken as a right and is given preference, all other appeals may be taken in the discretion of the appropriate Appellate Division. Section 1112 further provides that in any proceeding pursuant to Article 10 of the Family Court Act where the family court issues an order that will result in a return of a child previously remanded or placed by the family court in the custody of someone other than the respondent, such order shall be stayed until 5:00 P.M. of the next business day after the day on which such order is issued, unless such stay is waived by all parties to the proceeding by a written stipulation or upon the record in the family court.

It has been held that no appeal lies as of right from a nondispositional order of the family court in a permanent neglect proceeding brought pursuant to the Social Services Law. See Matter of Shaun C.A. [110 A.D. 2d 697, 488 N.Y.S. 2d 17 (Appellate Division, 2nd Dept., 1985)], appeal denied [65 N.Y. 2d 605, 493 N.Y.S. 2d 1027, 482 N.E. 2d 1230 (1985)].

Time of Appeal

Pursuant to Section 1113 of the Family Court Act, an appeal must be taken no later than thirty days after the entry and service of any order from which the appeal is taken.

Effect of Appeal; Stay

Section 1114 of the Family Court Act provides that the timely filing of a notice of appeal does not stay the order from which the appeal is taken. A judge of the Appellate Division to which an appeal is taken may stay execution of an order from which the appeal is taken on such conditions, if any, as may be appropriate.

Notice of Appeal

Section 1115 of the Family Court Act provides that an appeal shall be taken by filing the original notice of appeal (see sidebar 29–1) and preargument statement (see sidebar 29–2) with the clerk of the family court in which the order was made and from which the appeal is taken, upon the corporation counsel of the City of New York, if the family court involved is in a county within

Sidebar 29-1. Notice of Appeal

FAMILY COURT OF THE STATE OF NEW YORK
COUNTY OF NEW YORK

—————————————————— x

In the Matter of

[child]

NOTICE OF APPEAL
Docket No.
[county]
Family Court

A dependent child under the age of 14
years, to the custody of   , the child
of mentally ill parents, and a permanently
neglected and an abandoned child pursuant to Section 384-b of the Social Services Law.

[respondent]

—————————————————— x

    PLEASE TAKE NOTICE that Respondent,   , hereby ap-
peals to the Appellate Division: First Department from the Orders
of the Family Court, New York County, Honorable   , Judge
of the Family Court entered   (fact-finding) and (disposition)
and from each and every part of said orders.

Dated: Yours, etc.

To:

Sidebar 29-2. Preargument Statement

FAMILY COURT OF THE STATE OF NEW YORK
COUNTY OF [county]

—————————————————— x

In the Matter of

PREARGUMENT
STATEMENT

356

[child]

Docket No.
[county]
Family Court

A dependent child under the age of 14
years, to the custody of   ,
the child of mentally ill parents, and
a permanently neglected and an abandoned
child pursuant to Section 384-b of the
Social Services Law.

[mother]

[putative father]

[respondent]

_____ x

1. There hs been no changes in parties.
    Petitioner -
    Respondent - [mother], Natural Mother
    Respondent - [putative father], Putative Father

2. The Attorney for each party is as follows:

3. This is an appeal from a final order of disposition entered by
    the clerk of the Family Court on the   day of   ,
    [disposition] and   , [fact-finding], Honorable [judge],
    Judge of the Family Court.

4. There are no related actions, proceedings or appeals pending
    in this order or any other jurisdiction.

5. The nature of the proceeding is for a transfer of custody and
    guardianship to the petitioner of the child, [child], to the peti-
    tioning childcare agency for the purposes of adoption, through
    the termination of parental rights based upon the alleged
    mental illness and permanent neglect by the natural mother,
    [mother], and the abandonment by the putative father,
    [putative father].

6. It is respectfully submitted that the Court below terminated
    the parental rights of the Respondent - mother, [mother], in
    error of law and fact because the petitioning agency failed to
    prove with clear and convincing evidence their own diligent
    efforts and further failed to prove that the mother failed to
    maintain substantial contact or failed to plan for the return of
    her child from foster care. The decision was against the great
    weight of the evidence. In the fact-finding and dispositional

hearings below other errors of law and fact were committed which a review of the record of these proceedings will reveal requires reversal of the orders finding permanently neglect and termination of parental rights.

Dated: Yours, etc.

---

the City of New York, upon the county attorney of the county in which the family court is located if not within the City of New York, and upon the appellee.

Printed Case and Brief Not Required

Section 1 116 of the Family Court Act provides that in appeals under Article 11 of the Family Court Act, a printed case on appeal or a printed brief shall not be required. This section dispensing with the requirement that the record on appeal be printed does not excuse compliance with the rule requiring transcription of the record. See Baiko v. Baiko [141 A.D. 2d 635, 530 N.Y.S. 2d 7 (Appellate Division, 2nd Dept., 1988)].

Costs

Section 1117 of the Family Court Act provides, when costs and disbursements on an appeal in a proceeding instituted by a social service official are awarded to the respondent, there shall be a county charge and be paid by the county.

Applicability of the Civil Practice Act and the Rules of Civil Procedure

Section 1118 of the Family Court Act provides that the provisions of the Civil Practice Act and the Rules of Civil Procedure (now covered by C.P.L.R.) apply, where appropriate, to appeals under Article 11.

Counsel or Law Guardian on Appeal

Section 1120 of the Family Court Act provides that if either party in the appeal is indigent, then the Appellate Division shall appoint counsel free of charge.

Section 1120 further provides that the law guardian in the family court shall continue to represent the child on the appeal.

Appellate Divison Rules Regarding Appeals from Family Court

The Appellate Division, First Department, pursuant to Rules of Court, Section 600.6, allows an appeal from the family court to be prosecuted in accordance with any of the procedures specified in Section 600.5 of said rules. Furthermore, any party to such an appeal may elect to file eight reproduced copies of the brief and appendix, if any, with proof of service of one copy, in lieu of a printed or otherwise reproduced brief and appendix as required by Section 600.10 of said rules. The appeal may also be perfected upon the original record, with the transcript of the hearing, if any, to be ordered by the appellant and filed with the clerk of the family court, and eight reproduced copies of the brief. The statement required by C.P.L.R. 5531 shall be prefixed to the record, and an additional copy of the statement shall be filed with the clerk of the Appellate Division, First Department.

The Rules of Court of the Appellate Division, Second Department (Section 670.10), state in pertinent part:

1. that pursuant to the statute (Family Court Act, Sections 1016, 1018), appeals from the Family Court of the State of New York may be prosecuted without printing

    a. upon a record consisting of the original papers, the typewritten transcript of the stenographic minutes (if any) of the trial or hearing, and the statement in duplicate required by C.P.L.R. 5531;

    b. upon typewritten briefs;

    c. in accordance with these rules insofar as they may be otherwise applicable; and

    d. where appropriate, in accordance with the provisions of the C.P.L.R.

2. that the typewritten transcript shall either be stipulated as correct by the parties or their attorneys, or settled and certified by the trial judge, as provided in C.P.L.R. 5525 and 5532, or there must be compliance with Section 699.10 of the rules of this court.

3. that at the time the notice of appeal is filed, appellant shall also file with the clerk of the family court the statement in duplicate required by C.P.L.R. 5531. Within twenty days thereafter, such clerk or the appellant shall cause said record and statement to be filed with the clerk of the Appellant Division, Second Department.

4. that thereafter, the appeal may be brought on for argument by the filing in service of a note of issue (see sidebar 29-3) and briefs in the same manner as any other cause.

The Appellate Division, Third Department, provides in Rules of Court, Section 800.13, that an appeal from the family court shall be prosecuted by the appendix method authorized by Section 800.4 B of the rules upon a single copy of the record prepared in accordance with Section 800.5 and upon seven copies of a brief and appendix in compliance with Section 800.8 B. Application for assignment of counsel and for permission to proceed as a poor person shall be made to the Appellate Division, Third Department, pursuant to Section 1120 of the Family Court Act.

In Appellate Division, Fourth Department, Rules of Court, Section 1000.5 Estates that under an appeal taken pursuant to Article 11 of the Family Court Act, the appellant shall, unless otherwise ordered, within the time limit specified by the Fourth Department rules, file one original record, stipulated or settled pursuant to Paragraph E (3) of the Fourth Department rules, and eight clearly legible copies of a brief containing the statement required by C.P.L.R. 5531, and shall, unless otherwise ordered, serve one copy of the brief upon the attorney for the adverse party. Respondent shall file eight copies of a brief within the time specified in the Fourth Department rules and shall serve one copy thereof upon attorneys for the adverse party. Applications to the Appellate Division, Fourth Department, seeking assignment of counsel pursuant to the Family Court Act shall contain an affidavit from the applicant disclosing income and assets, a copy of the notice of appeal, and a copy of the order being appealed. A copy of the application shall be served upon each adverse party and upon the county attorney. Rules of Court, Section 1105 F, governs an appellant or petitioner in a civil matter seeking poor person's status. Such motion shall be made on notice to the county attorney pursuant to C.P.L.R. 1101 and, if the relief is granted, the appeal or proceeding may be perfected on one original, stipulated or settled record and eight copies of a brief reproduced pursuant to C.P.L.R. 5529, and a respondent may submit eight copies of a brief. In the court's discretion, the appellant, petitioner, or respondent may be given permission to file less than the required number of records and briefs even though said appellant, petitioner, or respondent is not seeking poor person's status pursuant to C.P.L.R. 1101 and 1102.

The practitioner is cautioned to review the most recent, updated version of the Rules of Court, as said rules are amended from time to time.

Sidebar 29–3. Note of Issue

SUPREME COURT OF THE STATE OF NEW YORK
APPELLATE DIVISION: FIRST DEPARTMENT

——————————————————— x

In the Matter of   NOTE OF ISSUE
[child]
a dependent child under the age   Docket No.
of 14 years, alleged to be an
abandoned child pursuant to Section
384-b of the Social Service Law,
to the custody of

Petitioner—Respondent,

Respondent—Appellant.

——————————————————— x

1. The Term noticed for is [term].
2. The Docket number in the court below is B [number]. (A related docket is B [number], respondent-appellant, [mother], natural mother.)
3. The procceding was commenced in Family Court, [county].
4. This is an appeal from the Orders of the Family Court, [county], Honorable [judge], Judge of the Family Court, entered on [date], [terminating all parental rights.]
5. The nature of the appeal is for reversal of the Order of adjudication and finding of abandonment, and for reversal of the Order of Disposition, terminating all parental rights.
6. The Notice of Appeal was served on [date].
7. The Record on Appeal was filed on [date]. (Minutes were filed on [date]).
8. The names, addresses and telephone numbers of each attorney are as follows:

Dated: Yours, etc.

Index

About the Author

Joseph R. Carrieri is a practicing attorney specializing in the field of foster care. He is the general counsel to St. Christopher-Ottilie and Little Flower Children's Services, two of the largest agencies in New York State.

Mr. Carrieri graduated from Fordham College and received the J.D. from Fordham Law School, where he served on the *Law Review*. He has written the commentaries to *McKinney's Social Services Statutes* and has chaired five foster-care seminars given by the Practising Law Institute. Mr Carrieri has published twenty-five lead articles in the *New York Law Journal* on the topic of foster care and adoptions.